# The Bitter End

## The Final Battles on the Eastern Front in World War II

Antonio J. Muñoz

**STACKPOLE BOOKS**
*Essex, Connecticut*

**STACKPOLE BOOKS**
An imprint of The Globe Pequot Publishing Group, Inc.
64 South Main Street
Essex, CT 06426
www.GlobePequot.com

Copyright © 2026 by Antonio J. Muñoz

*All rights reserved.* No part of this book may be reproduced in any form or by any electronic or mechanical means, including information storage and retrieval systems, without written permission from the publisher, except by a reviewer who may quote passages in a review.

British Library Cataloguing in Publication Information Available

**Library of Congress Cataloging-in-Publication Data available**

ISBN 978-0-8117-7771-1 (cloth)
ISBN 978-0-8117-7795-7 (electronic)

*To the seventy-five million people who died
as a result of World War II*

# CONTENTS

| | |
|---|---|
| Author's Note | vii |
| Preface | ix |
| Chapter 1: Breakthrough: Operation Bagration | 1 |
| Chapter 2: The Lviv-Stanislav-Sandomierz Offensive, 13 July–29 August 1944 | 17 |
| Chapter 3: The Baltic States | 28 |
| Chapter 4: Finland Leaves the War | 50 |
| Chapter 5: Romania | 59 |
| Chapter 6: The Red Army in the Balkans | 68 |
| Chapter 7: Into Central Europe | 76 |
| Chapter 8: Budapest and Vienna | 85 |
| Chapter 9: Bratislava and Prague | 97 |
| Chapter 10: *Die Schlacht um Kurland*, 1944–1945 | 107 |
| Chapter 11: *Festungen*: Breakwaters in the East | 129 |
| Chapter 12: Berlin: The Race to the Capital | 147 |
| Chapter 13: Berlin: The Last Battle | 166 |
| Appendix I: Major German and Soviet Armored Vehicles From 1943–1945 | 189 |

Appendix II: Estimate of Casualties Taken by the *Ostheer*, 1941–1945    197

Appendix III: Order of Battle for 11. *SS Panzerarmee*, 10 February 1945    199

Appendix IV: Order of Battle for Army Group Vistula, 1 March 1945    201

Appendix V: Order of Battle for Army Group Vistula, 12 April 1945    205

Bibliography    221

Notes    229

Unit Index    249

Name Index    271

# AUTHOR'S NOTE

> All the sinners of my people shall die by the sword
> —Amos 9:10

Those of us who study World War II and, in particular, the Eastern Front, are quite familiar with the events and progress of the war. The last year of the war specifically is the most interesting for me. For the Germans, it was also the most chaotic period of the Russo-German conflict. It was a time when things began to really fall apart for the Reich. By June 1944, it was clear that Germany was going to lose the war. Any sane leader who found himself in the same situation as Germany in the summer of 1944 would have sued for peace while the Allies were still outside German territory. This was the sentiment of those German civilians and officers who attempted to assassinate Adolf Hitler on 20 July 1944. If the attempt had proven successful, the end of World War II would have been dramatically different. It's not because the Allies would have offered anything better than unconditional surrender but instead that millions of people who needn't have died could have been spared. For Hitler, of course, lives, even German lives, didn't matter. Before he took his own life on 30 April 1945, Adolf Hitler commented that if Germany lost the war, then the German people had proven unworthy and were not fit to live. That was the measure of the man.

That statement alone describes Hitler's indifference to human suffering and shows him to be a person who had narcissistic, megalomaniacal, and psychopathic traits. No one, except the most fanatical follower, wants to be the last person to die for a lost cause. Death in such a situation has no meaning or worth. Yet, that is exactly what happened during that last year of the war to millions of Germans. They died for nothing. Between 6 June 1944 and 8 May 1945, the Germans suffered close to 1,800,000 casualties on the Eastern Front. On the Western Front, the figure for German losses for the same time period was around 1,300,000. That is just over three million men who could have avoided being killed, wounded, or taken prisoner if the war had ended in the summer of 1944. This amount does not even take into account German civilian losses and Allied losses for the same period. During my research for this book, I have discovered that the months between June and August 1944 proved especially disastrous for the German *Ostheer* (Eastern Army). The downfall of German resistance in the East began in earnest with Operation Bagration, the Soviet offensive launched against Army Group Center in the summer of 1944. It was then that the *Ostheer* began to unravel.

The last year of the war in the East proved to be a catastrophe for Germany and the Third Reich. The German soldier fought on because Hitler willed it. The end of the *Ostheer* came when it fought its last battle in April 1945, along the Oder River, defending the German capital. By then only a skeleton of veterans had survived the almost three-and-a-half-year struggle that was the Russo-German War. The rest of the army was now composed of rear-area echelon forces, including sailors and airmen pressed into infantry service, elderly *Volkssturm*, or children from the *Hitler Jugend*. What had been a war of conquest, when Germany invaded the USSR in 1941, had long since turned into a war for the very survival of Germany and her people. When the Red Army entered German territory, its men exacted revenge on the German civilian population for the many horrors which the Third Reich had perpetrated in the USSR. It appears that by early 1945 the war in the East had finally come full circle. The Germans were now the recipients of what they had been dishing out for years. This work covers the story of that last year of the Russo-German War, and the unraveling of the once-mighty *Ostheer*, as it began to fall apart from repeated Soviet blows. It is also a description of the final death throes of the Third Reich during the last year of the war.

Antonio J. Muñoz
5 November 2024

# PREFACE

This work is the culmination of about five years of research on the last year of the Russo-German War. I believe that this study is important because the last year of the war in the East is the least-known and the least understood period of World War II. It is a time when German military records begin to get scarce for various reasons. It is a time when conflicting records also begin to appear because of the military unraveling of the *Ostheer* and the chaos caused by military collapse. All of this worked to muddy the waters of historical truth, leaving us with the fog of chaos and doubt about the last year of the war in the East. This fact alone is sufficient cause, I believe, further study needs to be done in order to better understand the chaotic period of history that was the last year the Russo-German War.

My research spanned two continents and four different archives. These included the U.S. National Archives in College Park, Maryland, the *Bundesarchiv Militärarchiv* in Frieberg, the *Bundesarchiv* in Koblenz, and the *Bundesarchiv* in Berlin. The *Bundesarchiv Militärarchiv*, as the name implies, holds all of the military records that are stored from previous German wars, like operational records, personnel files, and actual military documents. It is in the city of Frieberg, in the Black Forest region of southwestern Germany. The city of Koblenz is located in the Rhineland-Palatinate state. It lies at the confluence of two major rivers: the Rhine and the Moselle. The *Bundesarchiv* in Koblenz is where one would find the vast collection of German photographs, film, sound recording, posters, etc. on the history of Germany. These materials cover a wide range of historical periods, including the Weimar Republic, Nazi Germany, the German Democratic Republic (GDR), and postwar Germany.

The *Bundesarchiv* in Berlin is what used to be the US-run 'Berlin Document Center' (BDC). The BDC was originally established by the Allies after World War II to house documents related to Nazi Germany and its officials, including Nazi Party personnel files and SS files. Since 1994 it has been administered by the German government. However, it is still located in the same building in Lichterfelde, an area that is part of the Steglitz-Zehlendorf district of the city. A secondary building is located in the Köpenick district of Berlin, but the principal storage place for documents is the one located in Lichterfelde. The *Bundesarchiv* building in Lichterfelde and most of its surrounding city block was actually the site where Adolf Hitler's bodyguard regiment, the *SS Leibstandarte 'Adolf Hitler,'* was billeted during the Third Reich era.

It is from these various archives that I drew my information while preparing this book. For those researchers who are unable to travel because of any physical and/or financial reason, there is a vast array of microfilm that you can purchase from the U.S. National Archives online. You will find detailed guides to these microfilms rolls also provided online by the National Archives, so that the historian/researcher can easily target specific rolls based on the topic in question. For many years now, the *Bundesarchiv* has been making an effort to upload documents online, dealing with the two world wars. These can now actually be accessed and downloaded for free online. In addition, no longer does one need to actually travel to Koblenz to select pictures from the *Bundesarchiv*. A researcher can now choose photographs online from the vast German collection, select the pictures, and purchase the rights to use them—all without having to leave the comfort of your home.

The study that I have compiled in the last five years is a concise, yet surprisingly detailed, history of the last year of the war on the Eastern Front. I have written a book that expresses the hardships and difficulties of the last year of the war for the *Ostheer* (Hitler's Eastern Army). I have employed over sixty-six battle maps—many actual German *Kriegsgliederung* maps from the war—to present as accurate a description as I could, of the battles and campaigns that took place along the entire breadth of the Eastern Front during that final, agonizing year. I have covered the period beginning in the spring/summer of 1944, all the way to the fall of Berlin and the end of the war on 8 May 1945. The story of the difficult German withdrawal from Russia and the Russian military's advance into Europe is told from the perspective of the leaders themselves. I believe that I have been able to convey to the reader the difficulty, the agony, and the desperation of this, the last year of the war in the East.

The story begins with chapter 1 describing the Soviet 1944 summer offensive, Operation Bagration. Chapter 2 recounts the Lviv-Stanislav-Sandomierz offensive, while chapter 3 tells of the German withdrawal from Leningrad and the capture of the Baltic States by the Red Army in the late summer and fall of 1944. Chapter 4 is dedicated to the war in Finland and the German withdrawal from Lapland. Chapter 5 covers the invasion of the Balkans through Romania by the Red Army and its implications. Chapter 6 covers operations of the Red Army in the Balkans. Chapter 7 deals with the Red Army advance into central Europe. Chapter 8 details the Red Army advance and capture of Budapest and Vienna. Chapter 9 does the same for Soviet operations which eventually liberated Bratislava and Prague. Chapter 10 tells the story of Army Group Courland and the six major offensives the Soviets launched against it. Chapter 11 is about the so-called 'festungen' ('fortresses') which Hitler declared, for cities that became surrounded. I describe the numerous sieges during that last year of the war in places like Budapest, Posen (Poznan), Memel, Königsberg, Danzig, Breslau, and others. Chapter 12 is titled 'Berlin: The Race to the Capital' and describes the January 1945 Red Army offensive which led Soviet forces into East Prussia, Pomerania, and Silesia, as well as the advance to the Oder River—the last natural barrier separating the Red Army from its final goal: Berlin. Finally, chapter 13 is titled 'Berlin: The Last Battle' and describes the battle for Berlin itself and the end of the war.

Throughout the narration, I believe that I have been able to give the reader a good description of the local military situation facing the German and Russian command. I have also tried to describe the grand strategic implications of German and Russian military doctrine during this last year of the war. I believe that I have been able to explain the final military decisions made by the Germans, such as Hitler's 'Stand Fast' order, his decision to not evacuate Army Group North from Courland, Latvia, the decision to launch the Lake Balaton counteroffensive in Hungary in March 1945, and many others. The book is designed so even the most knowledgeable historian or military enthusiast of World War II or of the Eastern Front will find new perspectives and insights into this, the last year of the conflict between Nazi Germany and the Soviet Union. For the reader who has no knowledge whatsoever of the war in the East, the book is written in a way that he/she can digest and (this is very important) can understand. The course of the last year of the war in the East is easily presented in encapsulated chapters. The evidence presented throughout the study also supports the hypothesis that the *Ostheer* began to unravel as an effective fighting force beginning in the summer of 1944.

## Chapter 1

# BREAKTHROUGH: OPERATION BAGRATION

### THE PREPARATIONS

Lieutenant Popov believed that he had done his job well. His men had worked for weeks in the heat of one of the hottest Belarusian summers on record. During the weeks of labor, several of his men had actually fainted from heatstroke, but the job had been completed on time. As he walked toward the tent where Captain Mikhaylov, his company commander was located, he went over in his mind what he needed to report. Mikhaylov's First Company belonged to the 415th Sapper Battalion. This engineer battalion was a part of the 246th Rifle Division, which was currently under 18th Rifle Corps, 65th Army. The date was 21 June 1944, and the time was a little after five in the afternoon. Upon entering the tent, the platoon commander snapped at attention and said: "Lieutenant Popov, commander of second platoon, reporting as ordered, comrade commander."

"Good Popov," replied Captain Mikhaylov in a relaxed and familiar manner, "tell me, have you finished building the roads through the forest?"

"Yes, comrade commander," was Popov's quick reply. Then he added, "My men, together with Lieutenant Volkov's platoon have built eight corduroy roads."

The corduroy roads were one of the surprises that the Red Army had in store for the Germans. Employing thousands of logs, these temporary roads could hold the weight of most Soviet armored vehicles. They had been employed by both the Germans and Russians, primarily in swampy or marshy regions of the battlefront. Now they would facilitate the employment of armored forces crossing the marshy, forested region around Bobruisk. Once the offensive began, the Russian tanks would appear from a seemingly impossible location, disconcerting the Germans and causing panic. Popov's division was one of several earmarked for the breakthrough effort near Bobruisk, where the enemy *18. Panzergrenadier-Division* had been identified as the main reserve for Hitler's *4. Armee*. His men had been working diligently to prepare numerous corduroy roads that would allow the 91st and 121st Tank Brigades quick passage through the thick, swampy woods just south and west of Bobruisk. A screen of engineers and riflemen had kept the krauts at a distance, in order to prevent the discovery of the roads.

Locally, the plan for the projected attack on 22 June 1944 was to employ an immense artillery and air barrage, followed by a massed attack of armor and infantry just south of Bobruisk, and to link up with our forces attacking from the east. The two pincers would surround the town and thus encircle a substantial German force. In this way, the right wing of *4. Armee* would be overwhelmed and the German front pierced. In addition, the engineers of the 415th Sapper Battalion would build several pontoon bridges across the Berezina River, to allow the infantry to cross before the Germans had time to mount a defense behind it. The pontoon bridging equipment had only just arrived, but the men had begun allocating them at the designated crossing points along the Berezina River.

General Konstantin Rokossovsky, the commander of the 1st Belarusian Front, was intent on destroying the left and the right flank of *Heeresgruppe Mitte* (Army Group Center). He believed that the right and left flanks of the German line needed to be pierced if the Red Army was to achieve the complete annihilation of the entire army group. He had argued with Joseph Stalin during the planning phase for Operation Bagration that there should be two breakthroughs in the German lines. Stalin, however, contended that two breakthroughs were unnecessary, and there should only be a single attack vector. Three times Stalin had chided Rokossovsky, and three times the commander of the 1st Belarusian Front had the nerve to stand up to the Soviet dictator. After the third time Rokossovsky insisted on a two-pronged assault, Stalin stopped his conversation and walked up to the field marshal, placing his right hand on the epaulet of Rokossovsky's left shoulder. To everyone's surprise, instead of ripping off his marshal's epaulet, Stalin simply said: "Rokossovsky, your confidence speaks for your sound judgement." The veteran commander of the battles for Smolensk, Moscow, Stalingrad, and Kursk had won the argument.

All along the Belarusian countryside, Red Army officers like Marshal Rokossovsky and Lieutenant Popov had been hard at work preparing for the offensive. While the commanders were formulating the attack on military maps, the lower ranks were laying out hundreds of miles of telephone cable, establishing ammunition dumps immediately behind the front lines, reinforcing existing bridges to allow tanks passage, doing daily photographic air reconnaissance missions over the region, sighting artillery guns to known German positions, performing long-range ground reconnaissance, and coordinating with partisan forces. Once the offensive began, the Belarusian partisans were to destroy the enemy rail line at hundreds of places in order to prevent the arrival of German reinforcements and to also prevent the rapid withdrawal of *Heeresgruppe Mitte*. The planned day of attack was 22 June 1944. Joseph Stalin had selected the date as a way to mock the German invasion of the Soviet Union on 22 June 1941.

Now, three years later, the Red Army was poised to capture the rest of the German-controlled territory that belonged to the USSR. These preparations however, had not gone unnoticed by *Fremde Heere Ost* (Foreign Armies East)—the military intelligence organization of the *Oberkommando des Heeres* (OKH), or (German) Army High Command. *Fremde Heere Ost* was headed by General Reinhard Gehlen. In Gehlen's headquarters, reports kept being received regarding the arrival of more divisions immediately behind the Red Army lines facing Army Group Center. There was also above-normal activity just behind the Soviet frontline positions, although some of that was defensive in nature. German air reconnaissance had spotted dozens of newly created Russian military depots close to the front lines. Many captured Russian prisoners were pointing to a coming offensive, although no one knew when.

It didn't take a military genius to come to the conclusion that something was afoot. All of this activity indicated that the Red Army was planning a major offensive. The problem that Gehlen had was that he did not yet know where the main thrust of this future Soviet offensive would land and with what purpose. Gehlen had not contemplated that the Red Army was now aiming to punch two major holes in the German defense lines, with the ambitious intent of eventually surrounding the entire army group. Another issue facing the *Ostheer,* which Gehlen and many other officers fretted about, was the total lack of available reinforcements.[1] Gehlen kept insisting that in order to block the coming Red Army offensive, the *OKW*—the *Oberkommando der Wehrmacht* (Armed Forces High Command)—needed to send a sizable force to act as a strategic reserve in the East.[2]

That possibility, however, was negated when the western Allies landed 160,000 men in Normandy in early June 1944. Now almost every available formation that wasn't committed was being diverted to France. Elsewhere, the Italian campaign and the war in Yugoslavia and Greece was drawing additional German forces. By the summer of 1944, the Germans had nearly half a million men chasing Tito and his Yugoslav partisan army. In Greece, a combined Italian and German army group had likewise been tied down in occupation duty and anti-partisan operations. Poland was restive, and it seemed that the Polish guerrillas were becoming more active, thus drawing further German troops. Europe, in general, began to smolder and burn. As a result, German occupation forces all across Europe, including Scandinavia, were stretched to their limit. The *Wehrmacht* in the summer of 1944 found itself in an impossible situation.[3] This was particularly true of the *Ostheer.* The *Ostheer* even had been forced to recruit non-German volunteers from all over the USSR in order to fill in the empty ranks left behind by those Germans who had been killed or wounded in almost three years of bloody warfare. By 1944 on the Eastern Front, one out of every five men wearing the uniform of the *Feldheer* (field army) was an eastern volunteer.

Many high-ranking officers within the German military had known, as early as January 1942, that Hitler's declaration of war against the United States on 11 December 1941 was a grand-strategic mistake which would have monumental political and military consequences. As 1941 turned into 1942, the German nation, which then contained only eighty million people, was now basically fighting the entire world. It was madness. Two and a half years later, the military and political consequences of that ill-advised decision made by the German dictator were coming home to roost. In the summer of 1944, the Third Reich was being crushed by a military vise that was slowly snuffing the life out of Nazi Germany. While it is true that the Russians defeated the Germans employing basically their own tanks, built in Russian factories, the Red Army infantry, which was about to ground Army Group Center into the ground and cause 400,000 casualties (from 22 June and 19 August 1944), would do so with the aid of half a million Ford trucks. Russian troops would enter eastern and central Europe riding in American-built lorries. The American and British lend-lease program was having its effect. The industrial might of both the United States and the Soviet Union had long overshadowed Germany's war production.

Beginning in 1943, the Allies began to pound German factories and other facilities vital to the war effort from the air. By the middle of 1944, many of these German factories had been turned into rubble or forced into underground facilities. And still, the German arms industry persisted as best it could. And further still, Hitler chose to ignore the fact that Nazi Germany was now being progressively ground down, in what all but the most fanatical or ignorant knew was a losing struggle. Millions of Germans at home and on the front lines continued to suffer and reap the whirlwind for Hitler's crimes.[4] Another long and agonizing year remained for the German nation to experience and suffer through before Hitler's war would come to an end.

For the 1944 summer offensive against Army Group Center, the STAVKA, the Soviet Supreme High Command, planned to employ a total of three fronts (1st, 2nd, and 3rd Belarusian Front), plus parts of one (1st Baltic Front).[5] These four fronts included a total of nineteen Russian armies comprising 5,818 tanks and assault guns, 32,718 artillery pieces, Katyusha rockets, and mortars. The Red Air Force would employ almost 8,000 aircraft. The *Luftwaffe* presence over Army Group Center was overwhelmed in the first two days of the assault. Facing this huge Russian ground force were about 486,000 German troops that formed *Heeresgruppe Mitte*.

Army Group Center had perhaps 700 armored vehicles, but that figure included tanks, assault guns, and armored halftracks. The real tank and assault gun strength was somewhere around 450 to 500. The Red Army had close to 6,000 tanks and assault guns for Operation Bagration. This means that when the battle began on 22 June 1944, for every German panzer, there were twelve Red Army tanks and assault guns. Statistically speaking, it was unlikely that even the most accomplished German tank commander could destroy twelve Russian armored vehicles without his tank getting destroyed in the process as well. Even if we factor in the destruction of Russian tanks by infantry, anti-tank, and Stuka and indirect fire, the ratio only goes down to ten to one. Thus, from the start of the offensive, the odds of surviving the battle for German tank crews was extremely low.

The fact is that during the battle the Russians would come to overwhelm the German defenders in an operational war of maneuver that even the gifted tank expert, Colonel-General Heinz Guderian, would come to praise. Three years to the day when the Nazi blitzkrieg had crossed the Soviet border and conquered most of European Russia, the Soviets were now about to give the Germans a large gulping taste of their own medicine. To millions of Russians who had suffered terribly during the war, payback was certainly a form of consolation. It could not replace their destroyed homes or loved ones who had been killed in the war, but at least now the Nazis were receiving what they had been dishing out for three long years. That this was extremely important for Stalin to show is reflected by the fact that even before the battle ended, Stalin ordered that German POWs be marched through Red Square for all Muscovites to see. This occurred in July 1944, when approximately 57,000 German prisoners, freshly captured, were made to march past the Kremlin to Stalin's nodding approval.

## THE CONCEPT OF *FESTE PLÄTZE*

Beginning in the second half of 1943, as the Germans began to go almost completely on the defensive, Adolf Hitler introduced a new tactic that he believed would help prevent further loss of conquered territory. This new strategy called for major road and rail hubs, usually in towns and cities, to be defended stubbornly by the *Wehrmacht* during any retreat because of their operational importance as transportation and supply hubs. These towns and cities, even if surrounded, were to be defended to the last man and were not to be abandoned. This order was to be obeyed even in the event of a major enemy offensive, or even if holding the town or city would result in the Red Army encircling the defending German forces. Hitler's experiences in World War I were definitely the breeding ground for this illogical defensive tactic. What the Führer had failed to take into account was that armies moved significantly faster during World War II, and therefore, a major city or town stuck deep behind the enemy's line no longer offered the kind of problems and disruptions that would have occurred during World War I.

The concept was officially introduced in March 1944 and was termed by Hitler as '*Feste Plätze*' (Fixed Places). However, this strategy, which seemed like a throwback to tactics from World War I, actually proved detrimental and was shown to be ultimately unsuccessful. The strategy resulted in greater losses and a disruption of what normally should have been orderly withdrawals. This policy of defense was a recipe for disaster, as the Red Army pincers struck deep behind the German lines. By ordering German divisions to hold on to these towns and cities, Hitler facilitated the encirclement and systematic destruction of a large number of forces under the *Ostheer* simply because they were forbidden from withdrawing.

6   *The Bitter End*

During Operation Bagration, the towns and cities that Hitler had designated as *Feste Plätze* were: Vitebsk, Orsha, Mogilev, Baranówichi, Minsk, Bobruisk, Slutsk, and Vilnius. These towns and cities turned out to be the graveyard of many German divisions.

## THE BREAKTHROUGH

To say that *Heeresgruppe Mitte* was prepared for the Soviet summer offensive of 1944 would be to lie. On paper, it appeared that there were sufficient forces available if the enemy should attack, but in reality, the condition of these divisions varied greatly. Most were worn out from years of heavy fighting. On paper, *Heeresgruppe Mitte* was organized and was composed of the following armies, corps, and divisions as of 15 June 1944:

> *Heeresgruppe Mitte:*
> (directly under army group control): *390. Feldausbildungs-Division.*
> OKH Reserve: *Panzergrenadier-Division Feldherrnhalle.*[6]
> *z.b.V. (zur besondere Verwendung*—for special use): *14. Infanterie-Division, 707. Infanterie-Division.*
> *Wehrmacht Befehlshaber Weissruthenien:*
> *221. Sicherungs-Division, 391. Sicherungs-Division.*
> *4. Armee:*
> *z.b.V. (zur besondere Verwendung): 286. Sicherungs-Division.*
> *XII. Armeekorps: 57. Infanterie-Division* (bulk), *267. Infanterie-Division, 18. Panzergrenadier-Division.*
> *XXXIX. Panzerkorps: 12. Infanterie-Division, 31. Infanterie-Division, 110. Infanterie-Division, 337. Infanterie-Division.*
> *XXVII. Armeekorps: 57. Infanterie-Division* (parts), *78. Sturm-Division, 25. Panzergrenadier-Division, 260. Infanterie-Division.*
> *9. Armee:*
> *LV Armeekorps: 102. Infanterie-Division, 292. Infanterie-Division.*
> *XLI Panzerkorps: 35. Infanterie-Division, 36. Infanterie-Division (motorisiert), 129. Infanterie-Division* (bulk).
> *XXXV Armeekorps: 6. Infanterie-Division, 45. Infanterie-Division, 129. Infanterie-Division* (parts), *134. Infanterie-Division, 296. Infanterie-Division, 383. Infanterie-Division.*
> *3. Panzerarmee:*
> (directly under army control): *schwere Panzerjäger-Abteilung 519*[7]
> *z.b.V. (zur besondere Verwendung): 201. Sicherungs-Division, 95. Infanterie-Division.*
> *VI. Armeekorps: 197. Infanterie-Division, 256. Infanterie-Division, 299. Infanterie-Division.*

LIII. *Armeekorps*: *4. Feld-Division (L), 6. Feld-Division (L), 206. Infanterie-Division, 246. Infanterie-Division.*

IX. *Armeekorps*: *Korpsabteilung D* (created from a battle group of *56. Infanterie-Division* and a battle group from *262. Infanterie-Division*), *252. Infanterie-Division.*

2. *Armee*:

z.b.V. *(zur besondere Verwendung)*: 5th Hungarian Reserve Division, 23rd Hungarian Reserve Division, 1st Hungarian Cavalry Division, *4. Kavallerie-Brigade.*[8]

VIII. *Armeekorps*: 12th Hungarian Reserve Division, *211. Infanterie-Division, 5. Jäger-Division.*

XX. *Armeekorps*: *Korpsabteilung E*,[9] *3. Kavallerie-Brigade.*[10]

XXIII. *Armeekorps*: *Brigade Stab z.b.V. 17 (Jäger-Bataillon 8* and *Jäger-Bataillon 13), 203. Sicherungs-Division, 7. Infanterie-Division.*

When the time came in the early morning hours of 22 June 1944 for the Red Army to launch its offensive, Soviet artillery let loose a horrific and sustained barrage that shook the very ground. For the offensive, the Soviets had been able to concentrate approximately 250 barrels (artillery, Katyusha rockets, and mortars) per kilometer of front line in both breakthrough points. The battle began with the employment of numerous squadrons of Petlyakov Pe-8 heavy bombers carpet

**Figure 1.** A Red Army anti-tank unit, supported by tanks and infantry, quickly fords a river during the summer of 1944. The Soviet summer offensive against Army Group Center in 1944 was the start of the collapse of German resistance on the Eastern Front. It is when the *Ostheer* began to unravel. MINSK STATE ARCHIVE.

**Figure 2.** Soviet tanks and infantry charge through a field, summer 1944. After the destruction of Army Group Center, the Red Army turned its attention to defeating the *Ostheer* in other sectors of the Eastern Front. MINSK STATE ARCHIVE.

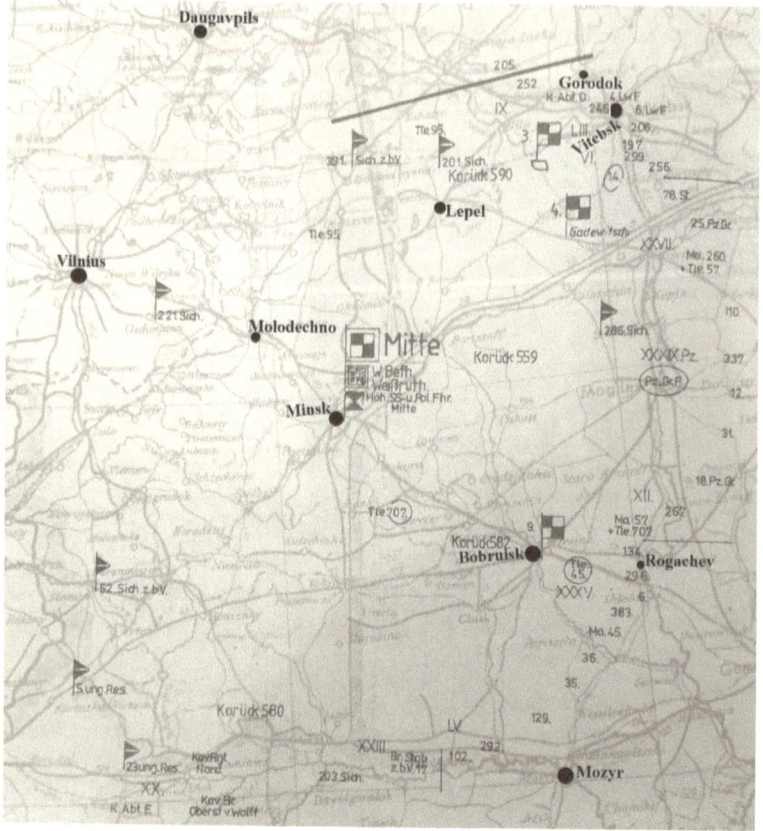

**Figure 3.** Location of Army Group Center forces in mid-June 1944.

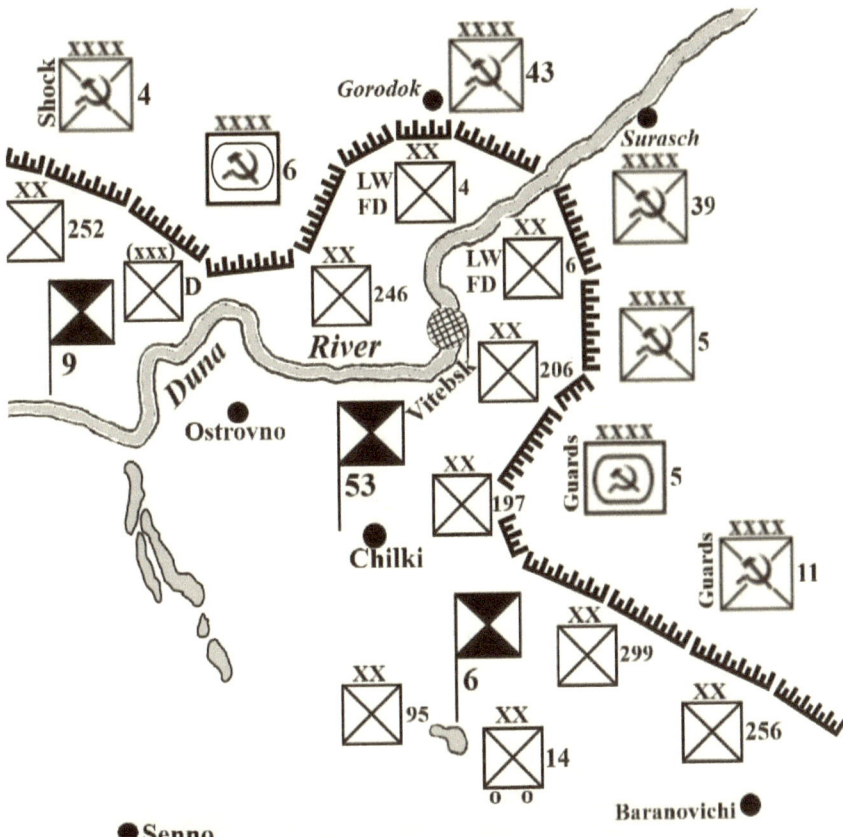

**Figure 4.** The northernmost right wing of the Russian 1944 summer offensive would involve Red Army forces from the 1st Baltic Front, working in tandem with units from the 3rd Belarusian Front.

bombing the immediate rear of the German front earmarked for the breakthrough. This was augmented by a savage artillery barrage that lasted over an hour. Thereafter the shelling stopped and wave upon wave of massed infantry and tanks rushed forward, with most of the Red Army troops yelling the customary 'hurrah!'

Most of the German recipients of this brutal assault simply folded. Everywhere, the German front line cracked, and soon, entire field positions that had protected German troops for months lay shattered and overrun. Survivors of the barrage would later comment that as hot as the Belarusian summer was, it felt like the artillery barrage had actually raised the temperature by several degrees. Those who weren't killed outright from the artillery bombardment stumbled out of their destroyed fortifications and positions, only to be shot down by the first wave of Red Army troops and armored vehicles. Many Germans attempted to surrender, but about half were shot on sight. Surrendering safely all depended on which Red

Army troops one encountered. If you were a lucky *Landser*, you were roughed up, robbed, and beaten, but you were eventually sent to the rear as a prisoner of war.[11] If you were unlucky, you would be shot while trying to surrender. In some instances, a captured German soldier, especially if he was an SS man, could expect to be executed immediately or, worse still, tortured briefly before being killed.

In the northernmost region of the battlefront, the 6th Tank Army under Bagramyan's 1st Baltic Front tore a gap through the German defenses just north of Vitebsk. The break occurred through the German *IX. Armeekorps,* where *Korpsabteilung D* was positioned.[12] During this summer offensive, the 6th Tank Army performed so well that in September 1944 Stalin bestowed the honorary 'Guards' title on the formation. A day after the offensive began, 1st Belarusian Front had broken through along a thirty-five-mile-wide front and had advanced approximately ten miles. From the north of Vitebsk, 6th Tank Army tore a wide gap through the defense lines of *Korpsabteilung D* and quickly reached the Duna River, west of Vitebsk.[13] The only force that was available for employment against this thrust was *schwere Panzerjäger-Abteilung 519,* which had been directly under *3. Panzerarmee* control as a reserve. This unit was immediately sent to the area of Shumilino, where it fought to desperately hold back the attack.

The Germans had regrouped in and around the town of Shumilino and held the Red Army tanks and infantry for two days, but in the end, the Soviet wave was just too strong. In the city of Vitebsk itself, German stragglers were already arriving from north, east, and south of the city limits. The German military field

**Figure 5.** Author's silhouette drawing of the Nashorn (Rhinoceros) tank destroyer. The armored reserve for *3. Panzerarmee, Panzerjäger-Abteilung 519* was outfitted with this armored vehicle. The vehicle carried the accurate and very deadly 88 mm Pak 43 anti-tank gun. The anti-tank gun of this tank destroyer had outstanding piercing capabilities. When fired, the muzzle velocity of the round was 1,030 meters per second (3,400 feet per second). With that kind of kinetic energy, the round could penetrate the armor of any enemy tank. It could, at a great distance, penetrate the frontal armor of even the super-heavy Soviet IS-2 tank. The most effective killing range of the gun was 1,500 meters (1.5 kilometers), or one mile. This made it a perfect weapon to destroy enemy tanks before the opponent's armor could come into range. The one drawback to this tank destroyer was its thin armor plating, which made it an easy target to destroy once the enemy was close enough.

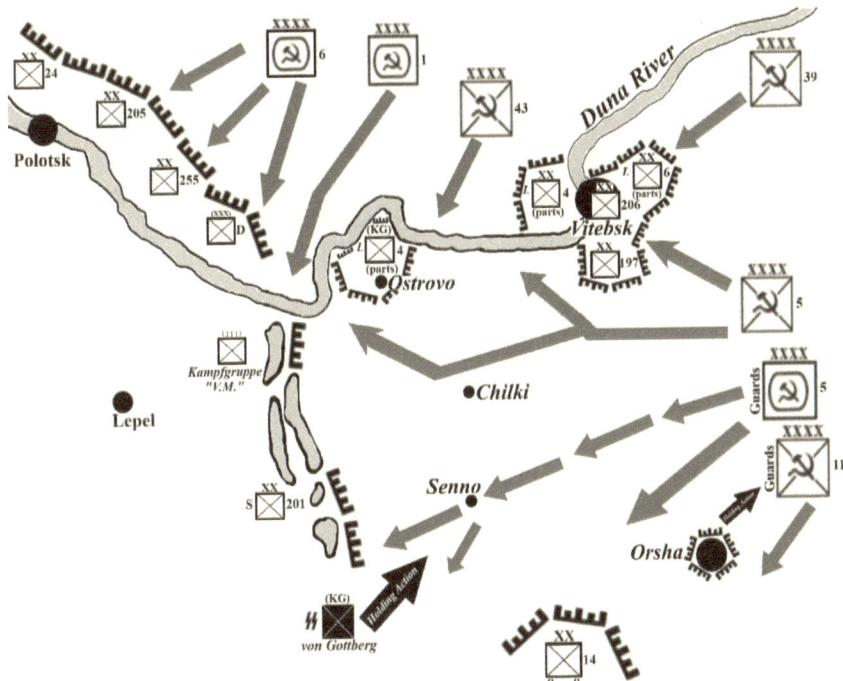

**Figure 6.** The advance of Russian forces occurred very rapidly, trapping a significant number of German divisions.

police in the city were soon overwhelmed with stragglers. To the east of Vitebsk and immediately south, the Soviets employed four armies: 5th Army, 39th Army, 5th Guards Tank Army, and 11th Guards Army. Against this huge striking force, the divisions comprising the German *LIII. Armeekorps* and *VI. Armeekorps* collapsed. Only the *14. Infanterie-Division (motorisiert)* and *95. Infanterie-Division* were able to make a fighting withdrawal in a southwesterly direction, but the divisions of *LIII. Armeekorps* were quickly encircled and cut off in what was called the Vitebsk pocket. Hitler had actually relented and agreed to order the bulk of *LIII. Armeekorps* to try and break out of the city on 25 June, so long as one division was chosen to remain and hold Vitebsk. This order made no military sense whatsoever, since leaving a single division behind would not stop the enemy from capturing the city. Nevertheless, Hitler's order was followed, and *Generalleutnant* Hitter's division, *206. Infanterie-Division,* was chosen as the sacrificial lamb that would remain behind to hold the city.[14] However, by then the ring of steel around Vitebsk was too strong, and the breakout attempt failed. When the city fell to the Red Army on 26 June, another 38,000 Germans were taken off the chessboard.

General Hitter didn't wait to be taken so meekly into captivity. He ordered *206. Infanterie-Division* to try and break out. His division's regiments never made it farther than nine miles from the city before they were caught and overwhelmed.

A few stragglers made it through the dense forests to eventually reach German aid stations, where they told the story of their division's demise.[15] While *3. Panzerarmee* and *9. Armee* were getting pummeled, *4. Armee* did not go unscathed. *Generalleutnant* Vincenz Müller's *XII. Armeekorps (4. Armee)* was surrounded by Soviet armored troops east of Minsk and cut off. This is the pocket that would eventually contain German divisions from both the *9. Armee* and *4. Armee* (see Figure 9). On 3 July, Müller was given command of the approximately 100,000 to 130,000 men of the now mostly cut off *4. Armee*, given that the existing commander, *General der Infanterie* Kurt von Tippelskirch, was farther west and therefore outside the pocket. The *4. Armee* had been holding a defensive line east of Orsha and Mogilev when the Russians attacked. Since then, it had been badly mauled by the Red Army and forced to retreat. The siege of Orsha and Mogilev didn't last long and cost the Germans another two divisions. The strategy of *Feste Plätze* was proving a failure. A breakout from the pocket that had developed just east of Minsk was attempted by *Generalleutnant* Müller, with *18. Panzergrenadier-Division* leading the effort, but the attack mainly failed due to superior Russian forces and the fact that the German front line was now 100 kilometers from the pocket. The distance was simply too great.

**Figure 7.** A destroyed Panzer IV tank, sometime in 1944. The destruction of the *Ostheer* involved the employment of overwhelming forces combined with the tactics of blitzkrieg pioneered by the Germans. A key factor to this strategy was the destruction of the enemy's armored reserve. Another part of this strategy was constant offensive operations, which would keep the enemy off-balance. These repeated offensives cost the Soviets a considerable number of men and materiel, but it also propelled the Red Army closer and closer to the Reich. While the USSR could afford to take heavy losses the Germans could not. MINSK STATE ARCHIVE.

Most of the *18. Panzergrenadier-Division* perished in the pocket, but its replacement and training battalion, which was located in Germany, survived. It was sent to *Wehrkreis I* (Military District No. I) and was redesignated as *Panzergrenadier-Bataillon 2105* (five companies), as part of *Panzer-Brigade 105*—a new unit which was created on 28 July 1944, at Troop Training Ground Mielau, in East Prussia.

**Figure 8.** The disposition of German forces under Army Group Center on 2 July 1944. The most noticeable thing that one can gather from this German wartime situation map is the chaos that still existed in Army Group Center at the time and the apparent disintegration of an organized front line. As the next map (Figure 9) indicates, two days after this situation map was created by the staff of Oberkommando des Heeres, German forces had been pushed back to a line roughly bordering Daugavpils, Molodechno, Baranówichi, Stolbtsy, and Pinsk.

The two motorized regiments of *18. Panzergrenadier-Division* attempted to break out from the pocket located just east of Minsk. *Grenadier-Regiment 51 (motorisiert)* tried to make their way to the southwest but failed. The remnants of *Grenadier-Regiment 30 (motorisiert)* actually managed to breakthrough the Soviet armored ring. They had headed northwest from the pocket. On 7 July, the divisional commander, *Generalleutnant* Karl Zutavern, fell while leading his division during the breakout attempt.

The remnants of *18. Panzergrenadier-Division*, some 2,160 men in total, were sent to Troop Training Ground Mielau, in East Prussia. They arrived on 16 July 1944. On 28 July 1944 the division was officially disbanded. However, on 7 September 1944 the division was once again reestablished by using *Panzer-Brigade 105* as a basis for the new division. In addition, another 1,500 men who had served with the division on the Eastern Front but were currently in replacement units in Germany later joined the newly reestablished division at Troop Training Ground Neuhammer, located near the Silesian town of Neuhammer am Queis. By 28 June 1944 there was no solid, coherent front line in the region of *Heeresgruppe Mitte*. That same day Hitler appointed *Generalfeldmarshall* Otto Moritz Walter Model as supreme commander of the army group. The first thing that Model did was to ask Hitler's permission for the units under *4. Armee* and *9. Armee* that were trapped east of Minsk, to break out. Again, Hitler vacillated until it was too late. The second thing Model did was to order the army group into a mobile defensive posture.

To this end he ordered *201. Sicherungs-Division* and *170. Infanterie-Division* to act as a screen against Red Army forces moving toward Vilnius, Lithuania. Hitler also commanded that *5. Panzer-Division* (under *Gruppe von Saucken*) to cover the region between Molodechno and Minsk, while *12. Panzer-Division* would cover the area from Stolbtsy to Minsk. The *4. Panzer-Division*, whose men came from the Würzburg region of Germany, along with the Silesian *28. Jäger-Division*, defended the west bank of the Nieman River by Stolbtsy. The *52. Sicherungs-Division* was made responsible for the area between Baranówichi and Pinsk. The 5th Hungarian Reserve Division would cover the northern banks of the Pripyat River west of Pinsk. On 3 July 1944, Minsk fell. On 17 July 1944, the Red Army paraded approximately 57,000 German POWs through the streets of Moscow, culminating in their march past the Kremlin building, where Stalin stood, watching the whole spectacle with an expression of satisfaction.

*Generalleutnant* Hans Speidel had recently been appointed as chief of staff to Field Marshal Erwin Rommel, the commander in chief of *Heeresgruppe B* (Army Group 'B') in the West, and privately remarked to his new superior, referring to the events unfolding in Belarusia, "We're in a pickle. . . . the floodgates are creaking."[16] He was correct in his estimation of the military situation facing the *Ostheer*. Speidel was one of only a few anti-Hitler plotters who avoided the wrath of the SS after the failed assassination attempt on Hitler's life on 20 July 1944. Trained as a historian, he would survive the war and eventually serve in the *Bundeswehr*.

Between 22 June and 19 August 1944, the Red Army caused *Heeresgruppe Mitte* the loss of close to 400,000 men killed, wounded, missing, or taken prisoner. Between 6 June and 23 July 1944, the Allies fighting in France had caused 116,863 German soldiers killed, wounded, missing, or taken prisoner.[17] In Italy, between September 1943 and April 1945, another 100,000 German soldiers

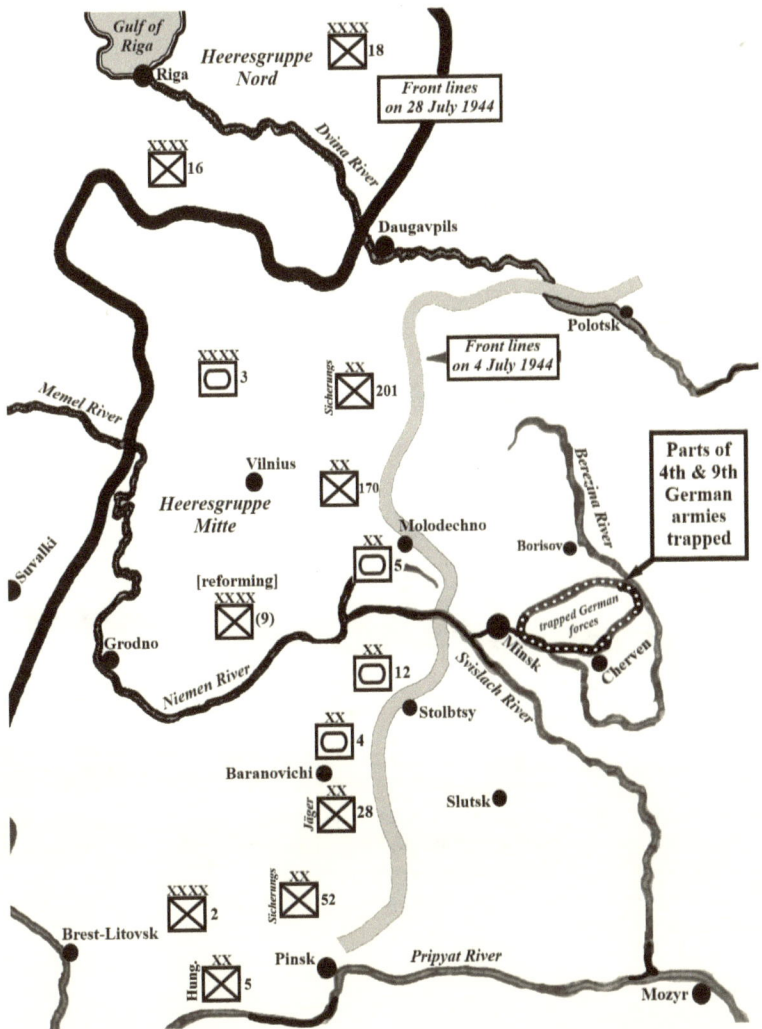

**Figure 9.** By 4 July 1944, Army Group Center had been able to establish a semi-contiguous front line, but both the right and left flanks were not firmly tied to the neighboring German army groups, and the divisions holding this line were in no condition to resist a determined Russian assault. Walter Model, the new commander of Heeresgruppe Mitte, now opted for a mobile defense. The problem however, was a lack of mobile divisions.

would be killed and approximately 300,000 would be listed as wounded, missing, or taken prisoner. That means that, on average, every month the Germans were losing 20,000 men in Italy. Thus, the number of casualties between June and July were around 40,000 men. If you include August, the figure was around 60,000. In Yugoslavia, German combat losses was close to 10,000 between June and August 1944. Thus, from June to August 1944, the *Wehrmacht* lost on the principal battlefronts around 586,863 men. This number does not even include losses incurred in other regions of the Eastern Front. If you factor in German losses from the entire Russian Front between June and August 1944, that number rises to almost 935,000 men. That amount is close to one million casualties between a two-and-a-half- to three-month period. This high attrition rate could not be sustained by Nazi Germany. If anyone wants to know when the German Army in the East began to fall apart, the answer is the summer of 1944.

**Figure 10.** Above, a German *Sturmgeschütz IV* prepares to fire on the enemy. As the Red Army offensives continued to pound the *Wehrmacht* front lines, the German panzer arm, always the last mobile defense, was employed more and more. More engagements meant a larger loss of armored fighting vehicles, which the *Ostheer* could ill afford to lose. MINSK STATE ARCHIVES.

*Chapter 2*

# THE LVIV-STANISLAV-SANDOMIERZ OFFENSIVE, 13 JULY–29 AUGUST 1944

### THE MILITARY SITUATION

In mid-July, as the destruction of Army Group Center was taking place, approximately 840,000 men, 14,000 pieces of artillery, Katyusha rockets and mortars, and around 1,800 tanks and assault guns of the 1st Ukrainian Front attacked *Heeresgruppe Nordukraine* (Army Group Northern Ukraine).[1] This Red Army attack came to be known as the 'Lviv-Stanislav-Sandomierz' offensive and involved three separate operations:

1. The Lviv offensive (13–27 July 1944)
2. The Stanislav offensive (13–27 July 1944)
3. The Sandomierz offensive (28 July–29 August 1944)

However, the overall operation has been more commonly referred to as the 'Lviv-Sandomierz' offensive. For the operation, the commander of the 1st Ukrainian Front, Marshal Ivan S. Konev, could count on seven infantry armies (1st Guards, 3rd Guards, 5th Guards, 13th, 18th, 38th, and 60th), three tank armies (1st Guards Tank,[2] 3rd Guards Tank, and 4th Guards Tank), and two cavalry-mechanized groups under Lieutenant-General V. K. Baranów and Lieutenant-General S.V. Sokolov.[3] Konev had recently been promoted to Marshal of the Soviet Union (in February 1944), for his actions during the Battle of Kursk a year earlier, in July 1943. Now he would lead his front against German and Hungarian forces under *Heeresgruppe Nordukraine* (Army Group Northern Ukraine). Commanding *Heeresgruppe Nordukraine* was *Generaloberst* Josef Harpe.[4] Harpe could only count on about 420 tanks, assault guns, and tank destroyers. That included the armored vehicles of 2nd Hungarian Armoured Division (thirty Hungarian and six German tanks). In July 1944, *Heeresgruppe Nordukraine* was composed of *1. Panzerarmee, 4. Panzerarmee*, and 1st Hungarian Army. The Hungarians were located

on the southern flank of the army group, along the Carpathian Mountains, while
*1. Panzerarmee* and *4. Panzerarmee* were strung out along a roughly 400-kilometer-long front between Stanislav and Zamosc. The Hungarians were linked with units of *1. Panzerarmee* under *Armeegruppe Rauss*. The Hungarians would remain attached to the Germans throughout 1944 and up until February 1945:

> 7 April to 21 July 1944: *Heeresgruppe Nordukraine*
>
> 22 July to 15 August 1944: *Armeegruppe Raus (1. Panzerarmee* + 1st Hungarian Army), *Heeresgruppe Nordukraine*
>
> 16 August to 22 September 1944: *Armeegruppe Heinrici (1. Panzerarmee* + 1st Hungarian Army), *Heeresgruppe Nordukraine*
>
> 23 September to 20 October 1944: *Armeegruppe Heinrici (1. Panzerarmee* + 1st Hungarian Army), *Heeresgruppe A*
>
> 23 October to 17 December 1944: *Armeegruppe Wöhler (8. Armee* + 1st Hungarian Army), *Heeresgruppe Süd*
>
> 18 December 1944 to 25 January 1945: *Armeegruppe Heinrici (1. Panzerarmee* + 1st Hungarian Army), *Heeresgruppe A*
>
> 26 January to 1 February 1945: *Armeegruppe Heinrici (1. Panzerarmee* + 1st Hungarian Army), *Heeresgruppe Mitte*

On 13 July 1944, the German and Hungarian forces under *Heeresgruppe Nordukraine* were organized as follows:

Directly under army group control for special employment: *schwere Panzerjäger-Abteilung 88* (thirty-five *Nashorn* tank destroyers), and *schwere Panzer-Abteilung 506* (forty-four *Tiger-I* tanks).[5]

1st Hungarian Army:[6]

    *z.b.V. (zur besondere Verwendung):* 2nd Hungarian Mountain Brigade (mass), 19th Hungarian Reserve Division (mass), part of 2nd Hungarian Armoured Division, part of *19. Waffen-Grenadier-Division der SS (lettische Nr. 2)*.[7] At this time, these units were performing an anti-partisan operation.

    Army Reserve: 2nd Hungarian Armoured Division (mass, with thirty Hungarian tanks and six German *Panzerkampfwagen IV* tanks),[8] 27th Hungarian Light Division, 6th Hungarian Infanterie Division (in transit), 7th Hungarian Infantry Division, and the bulk of *19. Waffen-Grenadier-Division der SS (lettische Nr. 2)*.

    6th Hungarian Army Corps: 19th Hungarian Reserve-Division (part), 1st Hungarian Mountain Brigade, 2nd Hungarian Mountain Brigade, (part). Later, 19th Hungarian Reserve Division would be attached to this corps.

    7th Hungarian Army Corps:[9] 16th Hungarian Reserve Division (part), *68. Infanterie-Division, 168. Infanterie-Division*.

    *XI. Armeekorps: 101. Jäger-Division,* 18th Hungarian Reserve Division, 24th Hungarian Infantry Division, 25th Hungarian Infantry Division.

1. *Panzerarmee:*

z.b.V. (zur besondere Verwendung): *20. Infanterie-Division (mot.)* (in the process of being withdrawn), *14. Waffen-Grenadier-Division der SS (Galizien Nr. 1),*

*LIX. Armeekorps: 1. Infanterie-Division,*[10] *208. Infanterie-Division,* 20th Hungarian Infantry Division.

*XXIV. Panzerkorps: 254. Infanterie-Division* (mass),[11] *75. Infanterie-Division, 371. Infanterie-Division.*

*XLVIII. Panzerkorps: 96. Infanterie-Division, 349. Infanterie-Division, 359. Infanterie-Division.*

*III. Panzerkorps: 1. Panzer-Division* (sixty-two tanks), *8. Panzer-Division* (fifty-seven tanks)

*XIII. Armeekorps: Korpsabteilung C,*[12] *361. Infanterie-Division, 454. Sicherungs-Division.*

Part of the Russian preparations for the offensive included the creation of fake artillery positions, false radio communication from non-existent Russian formations, and even the placement of inflatable balloons that resembled a Russian armored vehicle. The Soviet command also attempted to create fake assembly areas immediately behind the lines, as a deception, although the Germans soon discovered they were false. For the most part, however, the deceptions worked. The Russians estimated that the Germans wasted somewhere in the neighborhood of 2,900 artillery shells on Russian artillery positions that were fake. The Soviet 13th Army, in particular, was successful in convincing the Germans that an attack would take place farther south along the Russian lines than it actually did. The Germans were not exactly sure of when or where the Red Army attack would come, but they took proactive measures to prepare for the coming assault by preparing a defense in depth in the most likely area of attack:

> The main battle position was mined in depth up to fifteen miles to the rear. Prior to the major offensive the area east of Lviv during the summer of 1944, the sector where the main attack thrust was expected, was mined with 160,000 antipersonnel and 200,000 antitank mines within the zone defense. This was the first time that the Germans applied zone defense tactics.[13]

## BREAKTHROUGH

The first phase of the offensive began on 13 July in the direction of Rava-Ruska. The Soviets began to envelop *XIII. Armeekorps* when they broke through the defense lines of *340. Infanterie-Division* north of Dubno and the *454. Sicherungs-Division*, whose frontline positions were located southwest of Kremianez. The 1st Ukrainian Front forces quickly broke through in and around the town of

20   *The Bitter End*

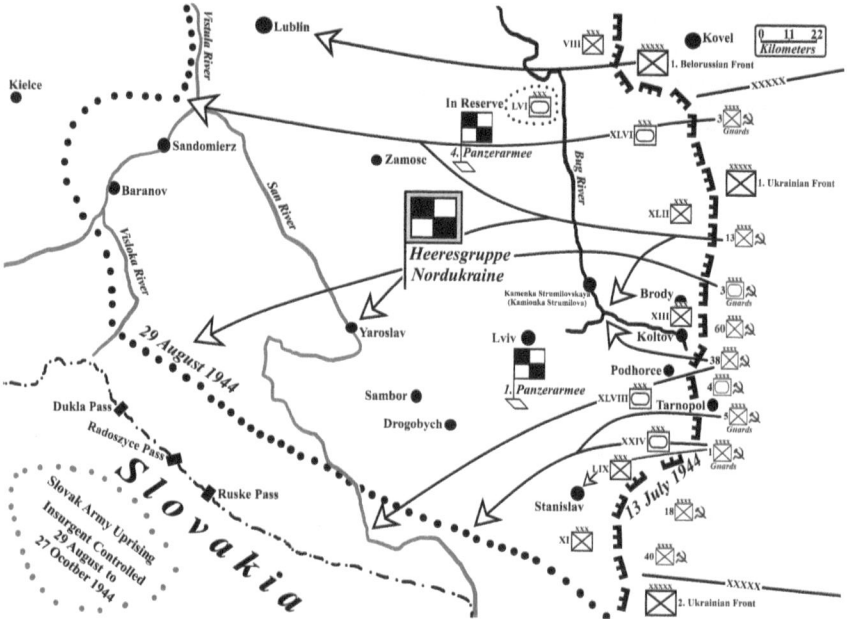

**Figure 11.** Between 13 July and 29 August, the 1st Ukrainian Front broke through the lines of Army Group Northern Ukraine and, in the process, destroyed the German *XIII. Armeekorps*. By the end of August, Red Army forces had reached the lower Vistula River in Poland and the Czechoslovak border.

Horokhiv. On the first day of the offensive, the Red Army was able to penetrate a little over thirteen miles. The breakthrough occurred in the region of *XLII. Armeekorps*, just north of the positions held by *XIII. Armeekorps*. A day later, the offensive began all across the front lines of 1st Ukrainian Front. The panzer divisions of *XLVI. Panzerkorps*, *16. Panzer-Division* (seventy-five tanks), and *17. Panzer-Division* (sixty-eight tanks) counterattacked several times against the leading elements of 3rd Guards Army and 13th Army, but the Soviet advance was merely slowed down. Both panzer divisions were attacked on their flanks, threatening their encirclement. The *XLVI. Panzerkorps*, therefore, opted for a fighting withdrawal. Both the *16. Panzer-Division* and *17. Panzer-Division* were then assigned to *III. Panzerkorps* at the beginning of August.

## THE BRODY POCKET

As 38th Army and 60th Army pressed their attack against *XIII. Armeekorps*, keeping its German units tied down, on 15 July, the 3rd Guards Tank Army and 4th Tank Army pressed home an attack near the town of Koltov that broke the back of the German defense there. Through this five-kilometer-wide gap poured the tanks and motorized infantry of both tank armies. Elements of 3rd Guards Tank Army and 38th Army closed the trap shut on *XIII. Armeekorps*, when they linked up just south of Kamenka Strumilovskaya. Inside the trap were approximately 45,000 Germans comprising the following units: *349. Infanterie-Division, 361. Infanterie-Division, Korpsabteilung C* (the remnants of *183. Infanterie-Division, 217. Infanterie-Division*, and *339. Infanterie-Division*), and the *14. Waffen-Grenadier-Division der SS (Galizien Nr. 1)*.

The order to break out was authorized on 18 July 1944. It was understood that the *XLVIII. Panzerkorps* with *1. Panzer-Division* and *8. Panzer-Division* would cross the lower Bug River and attack from outside the pocket, while simultaneously the divisions of *XIII. Armeekorps* would attempt to break out. The problem was that the panzer divisions of *XLVIII. Panzerkorps* needed to hack their way through fifteen to twenty miles of enemy-held territory to break the pocket. The terrain was also a problem, since the area they were to counterattack through was heavily wooded, with many swamps. Frankly, the probability of a successful

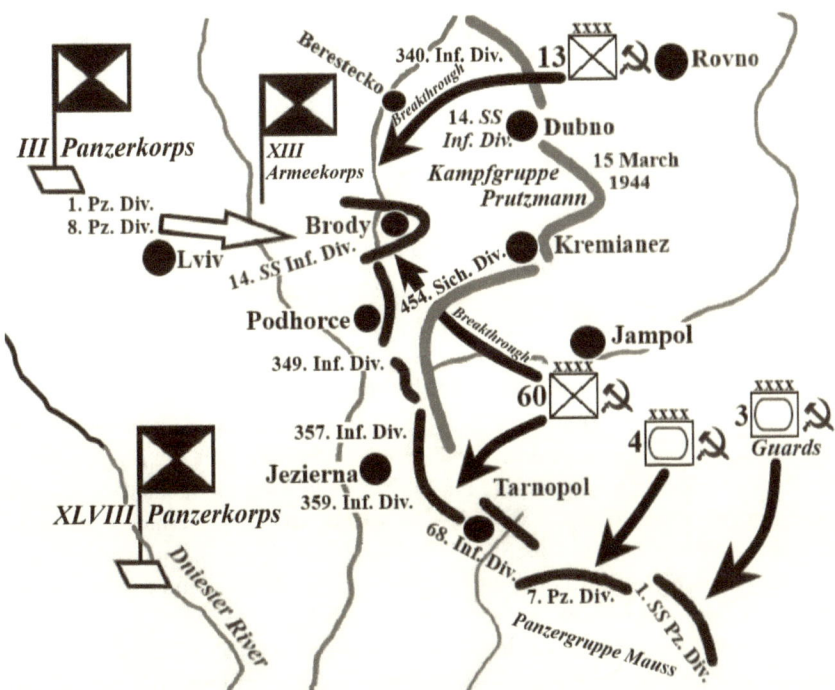

**Figure 12.** Encirclement of the *German XIII. Armeekorps* in July 1944. The group named as *Panzergruppe Mauss* in the map is named after *Generalleutnant* Emil Karl Hans Mauss, who was the commander of *7. Panzer-Division* and one of only twenty-seven men to receive the much-coveted Knight's Cross with Oak Leaves, Swords, and Diamonds. *Panzergruppe Mauss* included both the *7. Panzer-Division* and *1. SS Panzer-Division* 'Leibstandarte Adolf Hitler'.

operation was extremely low. The progress was impeded by the enemy, who kept the pressure up, as well as by the terrain, and the fact that *XIII. Armeekorps* wished to save as many of their vehicles as they could, which cluttered the few narrow roads and blocked traffic.

Army Group North Ukraine also employed *schwere Panzer-Abteilung 506* and its forty-four Tiger I tanks to the relief effort. In spite of much bravery, *schwere Panzer-Abteilung 506*, alongside *1. Panzer-Division* and *8. Panzer-Division*, could not break the ring of Soviet forces to relieve the trapped German corps. By 17 July, this heavy Tiger tank battalion was down to forty operational Tiger I tanks. Shortly thereafter, most of the Tiger tanks had to be destroyed to prevent their capture, after being abandoned for lack of fuel. Only seven survived to be transferred to *schwere Panzer-Abteilung 508*, which, at the time, was operating in Italy. German radio communication inside and outside the pocket was also interrupted, so the only possible alternative form of contact from unit to unit were runners and messengers. The first to make contact with one of the units outside the pocket (*1. Panzer-Division*), was a regiment of *217. Infanterie-Division*, which had attacked in a southwesterly direction. On 21 July, *Korpsabteilung C* and *349. Infanterie-Division* finally broke through the Russian lines just south of the Lviv-Tarnopol rail line. The rest of *XIII. Armeekorps*, however, was doomed. During the battle of the Brody pocket, German and Ukrainian losses were 25,000 killed and 17,000 captured. Of the 12,000-man *14. Waffen-Grenadier-Division der SS (Galizien Nr. 1)*, only 3,000 survived the battle, while 9,000 men were either killed or taken prisoner.

## THE CAPTURE OF LVIV

On 5 July 1944, the Polish Home Army ordered a mobilization of AK forces in and around Lviv. This was in anticipation of a nationwide uprising (code-named Operation Tempest). For this operation, the Home Army would employ its entire force of just over 336,000 men. In total, the Lviv region contained approximately 14,400 AK soldiers.[14] On 18 July the Ukrainian auxiliary police withdrew from the city, alongside and escorting the Nazi civilian administration. The city was left under the command of the *Wehrmacht*. On 19 July, the *4. Panzerarmee* committed three divisions: the *16. Panzer-Division, 20. Infanterie-Division (motorisiert)*, and *168. Infanterie-Division* in the area of Zholkov, in order to attempt to block the advance of 1st Guards Tank Army toward Lviv.[15] These German divisions held the Red Army for a day, then they began to give way. The *16. Panzer-Division* made a fighting withdrawal via Lviv and reached the Sambor area, in Galicia. Various *kampfgruppen* from the division offered a mobile defense in the area south of Przemyśl up to the Furka Pass.

By 22 July, the Red Army 29th Tank Brigade (under 10th Tank Corps of 4th Tank Army) entered the eastern part of the city limits. That was the signal for the Home Army to attack. Between 23 and 27 July 1944, the Germans in

Lviv were assaulted by a combination of AK forces inside and north of the city and Russian forces entering from the east. The city was taken on 27 July. A day later, the Red Army, following Joseph Stalin's orders, began disarming all Home Army units that they encountered in and around the city. In addition, the NKVD (People's Commissariat for Internal Affairs) began arresting all AK officers as well as Polish Home Army civilian officials. On 1 August, *16. Panzer-Division* moved to the region of Kraków in order to press a Russian bridgehead that had been established near Sandomierz and Baranów.

## THE CAPTURE OF STANISLAV

With the seizure of Lviv, the way was open for the advance on Stanislav (now known as Ivano-Frankivsk). The Germans immediately realized the threat to their flanks that this posed. The Red Army had already placed a large wedge between *4. Panzerarmee* and *1. Panzerarmee*. Now they were increasing the danger that both German armies could soon be enveloped. The pressure on Stanislav had begun to be felt by the Germans as early as 20 July, when 1st Guards Army had finally broken through the stubborn defenses of *XXIV. Panzerkorps* to the north and northeast of Stanislav and was now swinging south to cut off *LIX. Armeekorps*. The commander of *Heeresgruppe Nordukraine, Generaloberst* Josef Harpe, gave the order for a general withdrawal west from the Stanislav area to the San River. On 23 July, the 18th Army finally went on the offensive, placing pressure on the German rear guard as their forces withdrew west. Nine days later, on 27 July, the Red Army entered the city of Stanislav. When they did, they found approximately 1,500 Jews who had managed to hide in the city until its liberation. Out of the prewar Jewish population of around 24,000 Jews, only 6.25 percent had survived the Nazi occupation.

## THE CAPTURE OF SANDOMIERZ AND THE SANDOMIERZ-BARANÓW BRIDGEHEAD

The Red Army halted for a few days in the last week of July in order to allow its supply and support units to catch up. The Russians had managed to reach the Vistula River and had been able to establish a small bridgehead in the region of Baranów and Sandomierz. The Germans, realizing the danger that the bridgehead posed, had begun to attack it almost from the very moment that the Red Army had established it. By the end of August, the bridgehead was roughly forty kilometers deep by seventy kilometers wide. On 29 July, in a surprise attack, the Red Army 350th Rifle Division had surprised a German *flak* unit in the town of Baranów and overwhelmed it, crossing the Vistula River and establishing what was initially a small bridgehead. By 30 July the bridgehead was approximately nine miles wide and seven miles deep. In the small town of Anapol, some thirty-seven miles south along the Vistula River, the 3rd Guards Army also established a bridgehead on 30 July. By 1 August, a sufficient number of pontoon bridges had been built which could accommodate even the heavier Russian tanks and assault guns. During that first week in August, the Russians poured into the bridgehead. For example, it only took twenty-one hours for the entire Red Army 11th Guards Tank Corps to cross the Vistula. By 10 August 1944, the *III. Panzerkorps,* containing *3. Panzer-Division, 16. Panzer-Division,* and *20. Infanterie-Division (motorisiert),* had advanced to the vicinity of Khmelnik.

In order to add weight to this counterattack, *schwere Panzer-Abteilung 509* and *schwere Panzer-Abteilung 501* (Tiger I & II tanks) were sent to bolster the armored and motorized divisions of *III. Panzerkorps.* The Germans chose two attack vectors for the counterattack. The main brunt of the German counterattack centered on German forces which had been staging in and around the town of Szydłów. One attack vector was made by units of *III. Panzerkorps* straight toward the bridgehead from the Szydłów area, along the highway to the crossings at Baranów. The other was made by the divisions of *LIX. Armeekorps* directly against Baranów, along the eastern bank of the Vistula River. It was intended for the bridgehead to perish with the capture of the main crossings and the cutting off of communications. Additionally, connecting two strike groups would hopefully result in encircling at least a portion of the 5th Guards Army. Unfortunately for the Germans, the Russians had gotten wind of the coming counterattack from a prisoner they had captured the night before—a member of *3. Panzer-Division.* Thus, when the German attack began on the evening of 10 August, the Russian units on the bridgehead were on the alert. By 12 August, the German counterattack had petered out.

The German employment of two entire Tiger tank battalions to bolster the German offensive had proved insufficient. The *Luftwaffe* had even made an effort to support the attack, claiming over 300 sorties between 10 and 12 August, but they were to no avail. The Russians were simply too numerous and were well dug in. During the counterattack, the Tiger tank battalions were badly mauled because the Soviets had employed their Joseph Stalin tanks against the Tiger II tanks of *schwere Panzer Abteilung 501.* In fact, of the thirty-nine Tiger II tanks that the battalion had before the battle, only eleven were still operational by 17 August. The other heavy tank battalion—*schwere Panzer Abteilung 509,* which had begun the counterattack with twenty-nine Tiger I tanks—also suffered heavy losses. In September 1944, it was withdrawn from the front lines and refitted with the new Tiger II heavy tank.

With both sides exhausted, the front lines in the area stabilized as the Germans and Russians settled in and entrenched. The front there would remain relatively quiet until the January 1945 Red Army winter offensive. Both sides had taken heavy losses. The German lost around 144,000 men, while the Hungarians claimed about 30,000 killed, wounded, captured, or missing. Russian losses were heavier, given that they were on the offensive. Just over 224,000 Red Army soldiers were wounded, with another 65,000 killed, captured, or missing. Red Army armored losses were said to be 1,269 tanks, assault guns, and tank destroyers. Most of the armored losses were in tanks (840). Exact German tank losses are not available, but from all accounts, it appears that over 400 armored fighting vehicles were lost by the Germans. The Red Army had lost twice as many men and three times as many armored fighting vehicles. However, the operation proved to be a success because it brought the Red Army to the frontiers of Slovakia and Romania and the Red Army up to the Vistula River in Poland. In addition, the Red Army caused further heavy German losses. While the Red Army could afford to lose the men and equipment, the Germans could not.

As the Lviv-Stanislav-Sandomierz offensive came to an end, another problem faced the German forces operating in the region of the Balkans and southern Ukraine. On 29 August 1944, major units of the Slovak Army rebelled—further

**Figure 13.** Position of German forces under *Heeresgruppe Nordukraine* on 2 August 1944.

endangering German forces operating in the region. Because of the successful Soviet offensive against *Heeresgruppe Nordukraine*, the OKW made the decision to reorganize their command structure in the region. As a result, *Heeresgruppe Südukraine* (Army Group South Ukraine) was created on 5 September 1944. It was formed from the southern portion of *Heeresgruppe Süd* (Army Group South) and was part of the German military's reorganization efforts in response to the Soviet offensives that were pushing into Eastern Europe. The creation of *Heeresgruppe Südukraine* was a strategic adjustment aimed at bolstering the German defense in the southern part of the Eastern Front. This reorganization came in the wake of significant Soviet advances, including the Slovak Army uprising, the Lviv-Stanislav-Sandomierz offensive, and the broader Soviet push into Ukraine.

## THE SLOVAK ARMY UPRISING

As the Red Army approached the three principal passes into Slovakia, the Slovak Army mutinied and joined the Slovak partisans. The center of the Slovak Army uprising was the town of Banská Bystrica. In early September 1944, a *kampfgruppe* was created from the *XXIV. Panzerkorps*, employing three reinforced battalions from the *68. Infanterie-Division*, *96. Infanterie-Division*, and *208. Infanterie-Division*. This battle group, named *Kampfgruppe Mathias*, was used in eastern Slovakia in order to help quell the Slovak Army uprising, which had begun on 29 August. Beginning on 3 September, a unit of the *18. SS-Freiwilligen-Panzergrenadier-Division "Horst Wessel"* was added to the *kampfgruppe*.

Other *kampfgruppen* were established in order to send forces into Slovakia to help put down the uprising. These included *Kampfgruppe Schill*, *Kampfgruppe Ohlen*, *Kampfgruppe Junck*, *Kampfgruppe Major Volkmann*, *Kampfgruppe Mathias*, *Kampfgruppe Rintelen*, and units from *Korück 531*. By late October 1944, the Germans had effectively crushed the uprising. The resistance fighters faced brutal reprisals, and many were killed or captured. The uprising was somewhat supported by the Soviets, who provided limited aid. However, the assistance was not enough to turn the tide against the better-equipped and more organized German forces. The Germans conducted punitive operations against civilian populations suspected of supporting the uprising, which further intensified the suffering in the region. The course of the uprising was as follows:

*1. Beginning of the Uprising*

On 29 August 1944, the Slovak National Uprising officially began. The resistance attacked German military installations, police stations, and government buildings. The uprising initially took place in central and eastern Slovakia, with key battles around the city of Banská Bystrica. A large portion of the Slovak Army took part in the uprising, which was geared to help open the way for the Red Army to enter the country. Although the rebels had been preparing since the beginning of 1944, the German reaction to the uprising was swift and punitive.

*2. Key Battles and Expansion (Late August–September 1944)*

Initially, the rebels gained control of several cities, including the strategic center of Banská Bystrica, where the heart of the uprising would be centered. Rebels also pushed back German forces in some areas. Soviet support was crucial, providing the Slovak partisans with some air-dropped arms and supplies. The presence of Soviet advisers, brought in by air, also played a key role. Nevertheless, the Germans quickly mobilized all available forces in order to suppress the uprising, sending significant forces to crush the resistance. This included ground troops supported by *Luftwaffe* air attacks.

*3. The German Counteroffensive (October–November 1944)*

In October 1944, German forces launched *Unternehmen Sturm* ('Operation Storm'), a major counteroffensive aimed at retaking the territory and crushing the uprising. German forces surrounded and heavily bombed the city of Banská Bystrica, weakening the partisan stronghold. The German SS troops carried out brutal reprisals against civilians suspected of aiding the rebels. Thousands of people were killed, and dozens of villages were destroyed in what was known as the 'burning' of Slovakia. By late October, the uprising had been largely defeated, and German forces recaptured the majority of the territories held by the partisans.

*4. The End of the Uprising (December 1944)*

With German forces closing in, many of the resistance fighters withdrew into the mountainous regions of eastern Slovakia. Although the uprising was militarily crushed, surviving Slovak Army rebels joined partisan bands and continued guerrilla warfare in the forests and hills of eastern Slovakia. The Soviets had made an attempt to bring in the Czechoslovak Corps operating as part of the Red Army, but German resistance was too strong. This Nazi resistance limited the uprising's ability to gain traction. By December 1944, organized fighting in the form of large units essentially ended, although isolated partisan groups continued to fight the Germans as well as the pro-German Hlinka Guard for several months.[16]

# Chapter 3

# THE BALTIC STATES

### THE RACE TO RIGA: THE LENINGRAD OFFENSIVE

The race to reach the Baltic States and capture the Estonian, Latvian, and Lithuanian capitals of Tallinn, Riga, and Vilnius (respectively) began with the Leningrad-Novgorod offensives, of which the Leningrad offensive was the first. Launched on 14 January, and expanded south to Novgorod, where a second offensive took place to coincide with the Leningrad attack. The Leningrad-Novgorod offensives lasted until 1 March 1944. On 14 January, the 2nd Shock Army, employing 366 tanks, struck the frontline defenses of *9. Luftwaffen-Feld-Division,* redesignated as *9. Feld-Division (L),* and *10. Luftwaffen-Feld-Division,* similarly renamed as *10. Feld-Division (L),* beginning November 1943. Soon after they began to appear on the Eastern Front, the Russians very quickly discovered that German air force field divisions were, for the most part, poorly trained and equipped. These divisions were not the elite German parachute divisions but instead had been created from excess air force ground personnel. They also received very little training. Their smaller organization and lack of training meant that they could be attacked and destroyed more easily than regular German army divisions. The Soviets would thus, if at all possible, organize their offensives to coincide with a heavy assault at the location where these air force field divisions were stationed. The result would invariably be a breakthrough in the German line.

This tactic would work again and again. In addition to concentrating on the weaker air force field divisions, by the beginning of 1944, most of the German divisions along the Eastern Front were greatly reduced in strength and stretched thin. For example, the *SS Nederland Brigade,* which had around 6,000 men total, was covering a front line of some fifteen kilometers (ten miles). The *SS-Panzer-Grenadier-Regiment 'Nordland',* with 14,500 men, held a front line that was twenty-four kilometers long (sixteen miles). Both *9. Feld-Division (L)* and *10. Feld-Division (L)* contained around 10,000 men each. While *10. Feld-Division (L)* had to defend

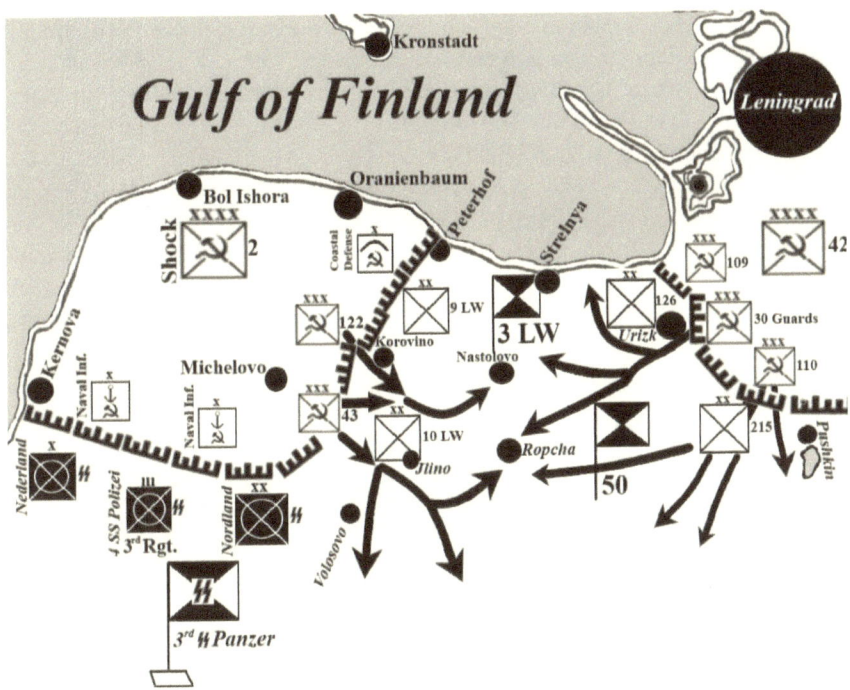

**Figure 14.** In mid-January 1944, the Red Army finally launched their much-anticipated offensive to remove the German stranglehold on the city of Leningrad. The attack, as well as future Soviet offensives, would eventually culminate with the capture of most of the Baltic States by the end of the year.

a front line that was seventeen kilometers long (just over eleven miles), *9. Feld-Division (L)* was slightly better off, having to control a front line of some fifteen kilometers. The problem for the Germans came to a head on the night of 13–14 January 1944, when 2nd Shock Army began its breakout from the Oranienbaum pocket with an initial artillery barrage which amounted to just over 100,000 shells. These landed on German positions within a span of a few hours. This huge artillery barrage pounded the positions of *III. (germanisches) SS-Panzerkorps* as well as *III. Luftwaffen-Feldkorps*.[1]

In addition, the Soviets mobilized forty-two rifle divisions and nine tank corps from their Leningrad Front and threw them against the lines of *18. Armee*. The bombardment of the positions of *III. (germanisches) SS-Panzerkorps* was a deception, however. The commander of 2nd Shock Army, Lieutenant-General I. I. Fedyuninsky, planned his attack very well. Employing two naval infantry brigades and a coastal brigade to cover forty-three kilometers (almost twenty-nine miles) of the Oranienbaum front, Fedyuninsky was able to mass eight rifle divisions and one tank division on a front only ten and a half kilometers wide (seven miles). The sector of attack was in front of *III. Luftwaffen-Feldkorps*. Additionally, the Soviets created unremitting false radio messages and troop movements to make the Germans think that large Russian forces were massing on the sector of *III. (germanisches) SS-Panzerkorps,* when in reality Fedyuninsky only had two naval infantry brigades in that sector.² This is what allowed the Russian general to concentrate such massive firepower on both *Luftwaffe* field divisions, whose low combat efficiency, no doubt, had not remained concealed from the Soviet command.³ On the German side, confusion reigned. While *III. (germanisches) SS-Panzerkorps* braced for an attack which never came, almost immediately the lines of the *Luftwaffe* soldiers, already greatly weakened, simply melted away under the concentrated Russian assault. The recipe for disaster that had been previously simmering for months suddenly came to a boil. A heavy price was paid for the German's disregard of this problem. One report described it this way:

> The full weight of the attack fell on the 9. Luftwaffen Feld-Division to the east of the pocket. Remnants of the 9. Luftwaffen Feld-Division escaped the Soviets but fell back in a wild retreat and were not combat worthy. The net result was that a major, unrepairable breakthrough was made in the northern wing of 18. Army within a few hours of the beginning of the attack.⁴

The Soviets had concentrated the bulk of their 43rd & 122nd Corps between Korovino and Zasstrove, leaving only the 50th Coastal Brigade to man the front lines facing *9 Feld-Division (L)* from Peterhof to Korovino. This allowed the 11th and 43rd Rifle Divisions and the 152nd Tank Division to hit the left flank of the division. When the Soviets brought up the 131st, 168th, and 196th Rifle Divisions to quickly follow up the initial attack units, it formed an overwhelming force that simply steamrollered through the *Luftwaffe* positions. Now the Soviets concentrated these six divisions in a six-kilometer-wide front of *9. Feld-Division (L)* between Korovino and Jlino, guaranteeing a successful breakthrough.⁵ The other four and a half kilometers of front lines out of the total ten and a half kilometers designated as the breakout point were assigned to divisions that were to attack *10. Feld-Division (L).* The *SS-Pionier-Bataillon 11,* which had been stationed between both air force units, was quickly surrounded and had to fight its way out of this sea of Red Army tanks and infantry. They took heavy losses before part of the battalion was able to extricate itself and rejoin its parent division. One source described their predicament:

> The Nordland units that had been deployed in the vicinity of the Luftwaffe field divisions suffered most on the first day of the offensive. This was particularly true for SS Pionier Bataillon 11, which had been engaged in building up defensive positions between the Luftwaffe 9. Feld-Division (L) and 10. Feld-Division (L). Parts of the battalion absorbed the full force of the initial Soviet attack, but they held on to their positions in vicious hand-to-hand fighting against tank-supported infantry. The cost however, was terrible: 2. Kompanie, SS Pionier Bataillon 11 lost 100 men killed and

wounded alone on 14 January. Despite this, the Waffen-SS troops held on doggedly by themselves even as the inexperienced neighboring Luftwaffe troops fell back rapidly—often in near panic.[6]

In *18. Armee* headquarters, intelligence estimates that had been written months before, and had been based on combat intelligence, had now proven all too prescient. Extensive warnings had been made regarding enemy preparations to launch a double envelopment operation against the German forces arrayed around Leningrad—probably during the winter of 1943 to 1944. The focal points of this probable Soviet offensive had been identified as being three key areas of the front:

(1) The Novgorod region south of Leningrad.[7]
(2) The area on the western part of the Leningrad region between Urizk and Pulkovo.
(3) The Oranienbaum pocket, where *9. Feld-Division (L)* and *10. Feld-Division (L)* covered the rearward positions of *126. Infanterie-Division* and *215. Infanterie-Division* on the westernmost part of the Leningrad front.

However, the army group commander failed to replace with more reliable formations these *Luftwaffe* field divisions which were not, coincidentally, committed in these regions.[8] On 17 January 1944, OKH, *Oberkommando des Heeres*, or (German) Army High Command, approved measures geared for the withdrawal of Army Group North to more tenable positions. One of these measures called for the withdrawal of *9. Feld-Division (L)* and *126. Infanterie-Division* from the Urizk-Strelnya-Peterhof region, where the remnants of both divisions had been pushed by the dual Russian drive from Oranienbaum and Leningrad.[9] The attempt to break out of the encirclement began on 18 January, but Soviet forces simply sliced into the withdrawing columns of both divisions. An Army High Command report for 19 January presented a clear summary of the situation. It stated that communications with *9. Feld-Division (L)* had been lost:

> 19 January 1944: 3. SS-Panzerkorps attack with tank support on Popscha, employing six tanks. With attacks on highway to the south of Kipen, four enemy tanks were destroyed. Kipen was lost. Over the activity of Feld-Division 9 (L), no news is available.[10]

In reality, *9. Feld-Division (L)* had been wiped out between 14–18 January 1944. It simply ceased to exist. The unit was recorded officially destroyed on the night of 19 January, north of Krasnoye Selo and Ropscha, while it was attempting to reach the lines of General Wegener's *L Armeekorps*.[11] Command of what remained of *9. Feld-Division (L)* fell to the leadership of *Oberst* Fischer, the commander of the *126. Infanterie-Division*. This was because *Oberst* Michael, the commander of *9. Feld-Division (L)*, had fallen in combat on that same day, while leading his men.[12] A naval artillery unit, *Marine-Artillerie-Abteilung 530,* under

*Korvettenkapitän* Erich Schenke, had tagged along as well. The *Grenadier-Regiment 424* of *126. Infanterie-Division* had led the assault group for the breakout. All that remained of the regiment was a greatly weakened infantry battalion of 150 men (a company in strength) and a few remaining anti-tank guns. This, however, contradicts one source that stated:

> The majority of 126. Infanterie-Division, as well as Feld-Division 9 (L), and Marine Artillerie Abteilung 530 made it through.[13]

Losses for *9. Feld-Division (L)* between 14 January and 1 March 1944 included 315 killed, 1,196 wounded, and 1,548 missing—most of whom were probably captured.[14] Since the division began the battle with strength of some 10,000 men, we can surmise that perhaps around 6,500 men survived to be distributed to other German units.[15] These men then survived to be employed in other units once the division was disbanded. Most likely, the majority of these 'survivors' were rear area support troops, since the 'bayonet' strength of the division on 14 January was at around 2,000 men. By 23 January, the front lines had been dramatically altered, and there was no question that the Russians had succeeded in breaking out of the Oranienbaum pocket, linking up with the Leningrad Front, and finally releasing the German grip around the city of Leningrad.

In the wake of the Russian drive, the German forces of Army Group North were reeling back, heading toward the borders of Estonia and Latvia. Many units from the Oranienbaum and Leningrad sectors were not intact. In fact, numerous battle groups were common. One such group was called *Kampfgruppe Helling* and was made up of men from the *SS-Pionier-Bataillon 11* and survivors of *10. Feld-Division (L)*.[16] By 26 January 1944, III. *(germanisches) SS-Panzerkorps* had withdrawn to positions in and around Narva, along the Estonian-Russian border. The *11. SS Panzergrenadier-Division 'Nordland'* and the survivors of *10. Feld-Division (L)* dug in around Kingisepp and prepared to attempt to stop the 2nd Shock Army from gaining further ground.[17] The breakout from the Oranienbaum pocket was a key turning point in the northern sector of the Eastern Front. It directly led to the lifting of the siege of Leningrad and the collapse of German defenses in the region, leading to the eventual liberation of the Baltic states. The operation underscored the growing dominance of the Red Army and the declining ability of German forces to hold their positions in the face of coordinated Soviet offensives.

## THE RACE TO RIGA: THE NOVGOROD OFFENSIVE

Just as in the Leningrad offensive, the Red Army chose to concentrate their main breakthrough in the sector where a *Luftwaffe* field division was stationed. The Russians had more than a year to study these *Luftwaffe* field divisions and derive an estimation of their abilities and deficiencies. I don't believe it was a surprise that the Soviets began to direct the focal point of their offensives in the front lines of these air force field divisions. When launching future offensives, they would do this whenever possible. *1. Feld-Division (L)*, in particular, was woefully unprepared to hold back a determined Soviet assault. The assault guns of the division's anti-tank battalion had long been withdrawn in order to help form another air force field division. The only form of anti-tank protection that the division had were a mere fifteen anti-tank guns. The unit didn't even have any flak guns to fall back on, since they, too, had been withdrawn on Göring's orders.[18] The scene was thus set for the eventual defeat of this air force field division and another important Russian breakthrough.

Lacking enough heavy weapons with which to defend itself against an armored attack, the only thing that favored the unit was the natural water barrier that Lake Ilmen and the Volkhov River afforded it. But in mid-January 1944, the temperature dropped dramatically, and these natural water obstacles became frozen. The Soviets managed to insert Major-General Sviklin's 58th Rifle Brigade across Lake Ilmen, just south of the city of Novgorod, and proceeded to attack the rear area positions of the *1. Feld-Division (L)*. The thrust cut the western and southern roads leading into the city, leaving the northern road as the only exit. Inside the city, *Grenadier-Regiment 503, II. Artillerie-Abteilung, Artillerie Regiment 290*, as well as units of *1. Feld-Division (L)* took up defensive positions at the outskirts of the city and in the city itself.[19]

Lieutenant-General Korovnikov, who was in overall charge of the attack, saw a window of opportunity open up when his initial forces drove westward from the city as far as the *Rollbahn* (runway) and decided to commit the 372nd and 225th Rifle Divisions as well. Eventually, Korovnikov also sent into the breach the 299th Rifle Regiment and the 34th and 44th Rifle Brigades. Now the German defenders were being attacked from three sides: west, south, and east. Eventually, the 225th Rifle Division would cut the northern escape route from the city. Inside the city of Novgorod, panic began to set in. The riflemen of *1. Feld-Division (L)* had been thrown off guard by this sudden flanking maneuver, but their officers now tried to establish some sort of a revised defense. In the ruins of the city, they were joined by *Kampfgruppe Furguth*, which had been brought up and, as stated earlier, was the only available corps reserve.[20] In the city, *II. Artillerie-Abteilung/290. Artillerie Regiment* would provide covering fire. After two days of intense fighting, the order to withdraw was given.

The last intact ammunition dump in the city was blown up during the night of 19 January 1944 so the Russians would not capture it. Afterward, a breakout order was received. Not many German soldiers were able to escape the Soviet encirclement. *Kampfgruppe Furguth*, for example, reached the German lines with only one officer and around 100 men. The remnants of *1. Feld-Division (L)* were combined with the survivors of *28. Jäger-Division* and *Kavallerie-Regiment Nord* (Cavalry Regiment 'North'). This battle group, nicknamed *Kampfgruppe Speth*, numbered only about 2,200 men. In effect, *1. Feld-Division (L)* had ceased to

34  *The Bitter End*

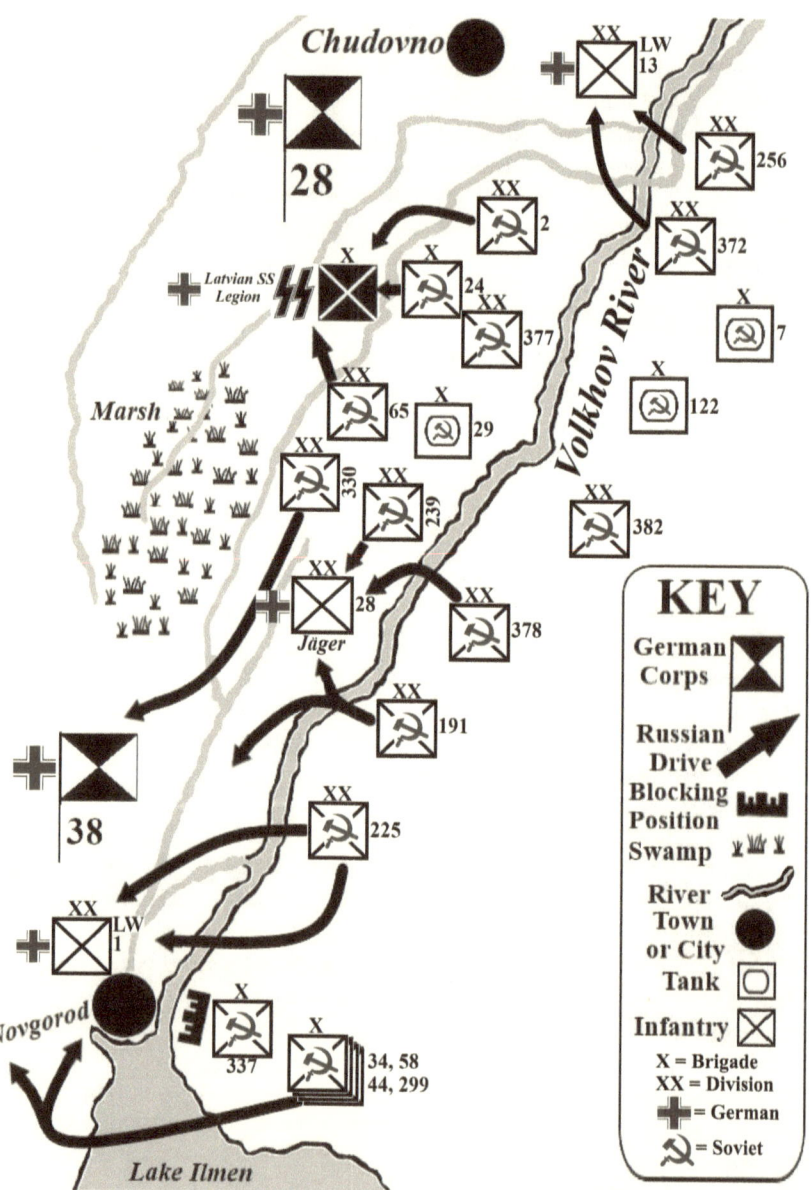

**Figure 15.** The Soviet Leningrad-Novgorod Offensive, January 1944. The map shows the Soviet attacks in the Novgorod-Chudovno region. The Russians were able to outflank *1. Feld-Division (L)* by crossing through a frozen section of Lake Ilmen.

exist. By 2 February 1944, the battle group represented about a quarter of the total 'bayonet' strength of *XXXIV. Armeekorps*. This corps now had about 9,100 combat troops, not including support personnel. At the beginning of February 1944, the entire front line from the Volkhov River by Lake Ilmen to Kirishi was held by the *XXVIII. Armeekorps*, with *21. Infanterie-Division*, *96. Infanterie-Division*, and *13. Feld-Division (L)*.

The 9,000 or so survivors of the much-reduced *XXXVIII. Armeekorps* were now attached to *XXVIII. Armeekorps*.[21] The infantrymen from *1. Feld-Division (L)* continued to serve under *Kampfgruppe Speth* until April 1944 when the division was officially dissolved. In reality, *1. Feld-Division (L)* had ceased to function as a division around the time of the breakout from the city of Novgorod, between 19–21 January 1944. The remnants of the *Luftwaffe* infantry from *1. Feld-Division (L)* were eventually reassigned to the Silesian *28. Jäger-Division*, which was also virtually wiped out and was in the process of reforming.

## THE RACE TO RIGA: RETREAT TO THE PANTHER-WOTAN LINE

On 24 January, *XXVIII. Armeekorps* began to experience Soviet infantry attacks of regimental size. It was clear that the entire German northern army group would have to withdraw. The plan was to retreat to the so-called Panther-Wotan line, which had been nicknamed the *Ostmauer* (Eastern Wall). The positions had begun to be constructed in the fall of 1943, but its fortifications were nowhere close to completion or depth. The date of 24 January was the same day that a breakthrough occurred in the defense lines of *12. Feld-Division (L)*. However, a rapid counter-attack, led personally by the divisional commander with a *Jäger* battalion that was in reserve, managed to temporarily stabilize the front lines.[22] One day later, *12. Feld-Division (L)* experienced enemy breakthroughs in the areas by Drosdovo and Dubrovy.[23] On 26 January 1944. it withdrew to the region of Grushino and Schudovo.[24] On that same day, Red Army tank units once again penetrated the lines of the division at Tschudski-Bor and Dubrovy, affirming the correctness of the divisional commander, Gottfried Weber, to order the withdrawal of his division, lest it be surrounded.[25]

The Soviet attack had been particularly heavy against the divisions of *XXVIII. Armeekorps*, but losses were even greater in the neighboring positions of *XXXVIII. Armeekorps*. In fact, by the last week of January 1944, the divisions under *XXXVIII. Armeekorps* had been reduced to mere battle groups. Those included *Kampfgruppe Schuldt*: five battalions from *2. (lettische) SS Brigade*, plus one regiment from *12 Feld-Division (L)*, and parts of *13 Feld-Division (L)*. *Kampfgruppe Speth* could count on the remnants of *1. Feld-Division (L)*, *28. Jäger-Division*, and parts of *Kavallerie Regiment Nord*, plus a few Estonian *Schuma* battalions. *Kampfgruppe Bock* was the remnants of the *4. SS-Panzergrenadier-Division 'Polizei'*. This SS division had been mauled as well and was withdrawn from heavy fighting on 21 January 1944. It was transferred to *XXXVIII. Armeekorps*. *Kampfgruppe Pohl*, like *Kampfgruppe Bock*, was at regimental strength, but its composition is unknown. In total, the strengths of these battle groups included 4,500 men for *Kampfgruppe Schuldt*, 2,200 for *Kampfgruppe Speth*, and 1,200 each for *Kampfgruppe Bock* and *Kampfgruppe Pohl*. By 28 January 1944, *12. Feld-Division (L)* had withdrawn to Drosdovo and Dubrovy. On 30 January, half of the 9,100-man strength of *XXXVIII. Armeekorps* was withdrawn when *Kampfgruppe Schuldt* was shifted to *XXVIII. Armeekorps*.[26] On 2 February, the division was located by the rail line between Ssalzy and Baleskaya. It then moved to Oredesh on 8 February, and was by Luga on 9 February. From 10–13 February, it defended Luga. The German forces stood in a semicircle around that important north Russian city. On 3 February, *12. Feld-Division (L)* was detached temporarily from the front lines and was moved to cover the connection between *XXVIII. Armeekorps* and *I. Armeekorps*.[27]

The Soviet 2nd Shock Army played a significant role in the battle for Luga. The Germans, under the command of *Generalfeldmarschall* Ernst Busch (commander of Army Group North), had their forces stretched thin and were now retreating from several positions in the region. The German defense was buckling, and the Soviet forces had superior manpower and artillery, which made their attacks increasingly effective. The Soviet forces launched a series of attacks on the German defensive positions around Luga, encircling the town and cutting off German supply lines. After intense fighting, including heavy artillery bombardments and airstrikes, Soviet forces were able to break through the German defenses.

Similarly, the remnants of *13. Feld-Division (L)* were shifted to the same locality and placed on the western flank in the area between the Luga positions and *58. Infanterie-Division*. A German document dated 7 February 1944 listed the division as having incurred heavy losses during the fighting withdrawal from the Volkhov front. In almost one month of heavy fighting, the entire division had been reduced to a mere 7,424 men, out of which only 1,481 men were the actual bayonet strength.[28] It had begun the withdrawal with around 11,000 men, and during the withdrawal, the division had lost around 3,576 men. On 13 February, *12. Feld-Division (L)* lost some ground on its left flank while fighting alongside *21.* and *58. Infanterie-Division*. Red Army attacks against these three German divisions were particularly heavy on this date. In addition, the German units also had to deal with Soviet guerrilla bands that were attacking many German rear area units and positions.[29]

Three days later, on 16 February, it was the turn of the line companies defending the right flank of *12. Feld-Division (L)* to feel the brunt of the enemy attack.[30] One day later, the division was reporting heavy enemy tank attacks with some T-34 tanks destroyed by the *Landsers*.[31] The withdrawal of *Heeresgruppe Nord* continued throughout February. The retreat to the so-called *Bamberg Verteidigungs-sline* (Bamberg Defense Line) began on 19 February 1944. During this withdrawal, the Red Army placed heavy pressure on the units of *XXVIII. Armeekorps*. Continued heavy pressure on the right flank of *Feld-Division 12 (L)* continued throughout that day.³² As if targeted, *12 Feld-Division (L)* was particularly hard-hit.³³ By 23 February, the division had withdrawn to Pleskau (Pskov). On 25 February, *Feld-Division 12 (L)* and other units of *XXVIII. Armeekorps* began to launch local counterattacks that managed to keep the attacking Red Army units temporarily off-balance.³⁴

## THE CONSEQUENCES OF THE NOVGOROD OFFENSIVE

The Soviet Novgorod Offensive, launched between 14–27 January 1944, was part of the broader Leningrad-Novgorod strategic offensive, which aimed to lift the siege of Leningrad, push German forces out of the region, and begin to advance into the Baltic states. The operation had significant military consequences. The *Panther-Linie* (Panther Line), designed as a defensive line for *Heeresgruppe Nord*, was breached during the Novgorod Offensive. The Soviet 59th Army launched a powerful assault, forcing the Germans to abandon Novgorod and to retreat toward the Luga River. This compromised the overall German defensive strategy in the region. The offensive forced Army Group North, particularly *16. Armee*, to abandon key positions. The Germans withdrew westward to avoid encirclement, losing strategic ground they had held since 1941. This withdrawal marked the beginning of a broader retreat into the Baltic states.

The Red Army liberated Novgorod, an important historical and logistical center, on 20 January 1944. Its recapture symbolized a significant morale boost for Soviet forces and the civilian population. The retreating German forces suffered substantial losses in manpower and equipment. Many rear-guard actions resulted in heavy casualties due to Soviet pressure. The destruction of infrastructure during the retreat also impeded the Germans' ability to regroup. The success of the Novgorod offensive set the stage for subsequent Soviet advances in the Baltic region. By destabilizing the positions of *Heeresgruppe Nord*, the Soviets created opportunities for further offensives, including the eventual liberation of Pskov and Narva. The operation reinforced the shift in strategic initiative to the Red Army on Leningrad Front. The Germans were increasingly forced into a defensive posture, conducting only localized counterattacks rather than major offensives.

Finally, the loss of Novgorod and the disruption of the Panther Line shook German morale and strained command relationships within *Heeresgruppe Nord*. The constant pressure from Soviet forces left German commanders with limited options and heightened the sense of impending defeat. In summary, the Novgorod offensive was a decisive step in the Soviet expulsion of German forces from northern Russia and (eventually) the Baltic States. It contributed to the liberation of Leningrad, accelerated the collapse of Army Group North, and set the stage for Soviet operations and eventual conquest of the Baltic region later in 1944.

**Figure 16.** Positions of *18. Armee* as of 4 March 1944.

## THE BATTLE FOR PSKOV

By 27 February, *18. Armee* was located around Pskov and Lake Peipus. North of Pskov, Lake Peipus offered protection from enemy attacks. Between 23 February and 14 August 1944, *18. Armee* successfully defended Pskov. This was quite an achievement, given that many of its divisions were actually the strength of a regiment or brigade. The *12. Feld-Division (L)* continued to remain split up into two groups, one fighting alongside *8. Jäger-Division,* while another part fought alongside parts of *126.* and *212. Infanterie-Division* just south of Pskov. Two days later, units of the division were shifted north and placed under *L. Armeekorps.*[35] The division remained north of Pskov until August 1944. During all that time, it successfully blocked all Red Army attempts to break through there.

The second battle for Pskov occurred between 30 March and 17 April 1944. The Red Army initially gained a span of territory in the area of the greatly weakened *212. Infanterie-Division,* whose lines cracked in four different places. The men of one of the *Luftwaffe jäger regiments* of *Feld-Division 12 (L)* were immediately employed in a counterattack and succeeded in reaching the Lobany-Vanukha line, closing the hole in the line. The other, a *Luftwaffe jäger regiments*, stationed farther north, was also employed in the counterattack but only managed to gain a few hundred meters of ground.[36] In March, *13. Feld-Division (L)* was finally disbanded, and parts of this unit were used to reinforce the weakened *12. Feld-Division (L)*. During March, the division was attached to *L. Armeekorps.* In March, the remnants of *13 Feld-Division (L)* were under *XXVIII. Armeekorps.* On 3 April, the Soviets launched a total of four army corps, with a further three corps in reserve against *215. Infanterie-Division, 8. Jäger-Division,* and *12. Feld-Division (L)*. The Soviet 53rd, 86th, and 326th Rifle Divisions, which attacked the defense lines of the *215. Infanterie-Division* in the region of Krapivinka and Letovo, were repulsed by the exhausted Swabian line companies from Wurtemberg.[37] The *12. Feld-Division (L)* was holding the right flank of *215. Infanterie-Division.*

On the right flank of the *Luftwaffe* infantrymen was *8. Jäger-Division,* in the region of Vernavino. There, *8. Jäger-Division* managed to give some ground to the six Red Army rifle divisions of 6th and 119th Rifle Corps. The greatest amount of territory lost occurred in the middle of these three divisions, that is, the front lines of *12. Feld-Division (L)*. The division, which was holding the region of Poddvorov and Sapatkino-Pavlona, was hit by no less than six rifle divisions (18th, 46th, 56th, 224th, 275th, and 311th Rifle Division). A small bulge developed in the center, and for a time, it seemed that *215. Infanterie-Division* and *8. Jäger-Division's* flanks would be enveloped. The town of Poddvorov exchanged hands several times before the grenadiers of the *12. Feld-Division (L)* held on and finally halted the enemy assault.[38]

This victory was not without heavy losses, however. Eighteenth Army had employed *12. Feld-Division (L)* in the hardest positions, and it desperately needed to be replenished. That fact alone meant that the German Army High Command considered this former *Luftwaffe* division as a reliable unit. Between 4–8 April, the

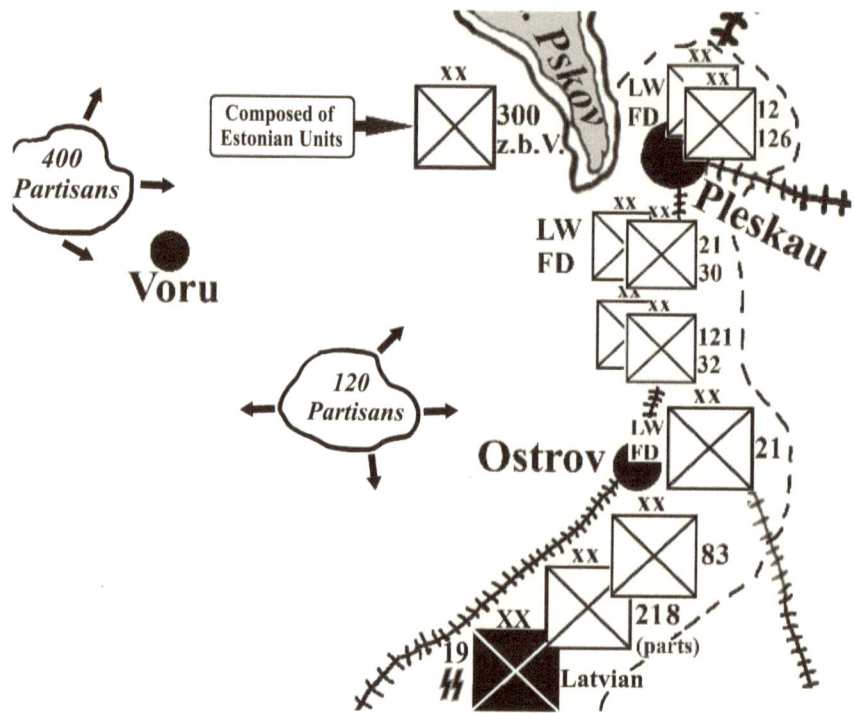

**Figure 17.** German positions around Pleskau (Pskov) in June 1944.

Pomeranian regiments of *32. Infanterie-Division* assumed the frontline positions which had recently been held *215. Infanterie-Division* and *12. Feld-Division (L)*.[39] The division now shifted its location again, when *21. Infanterie-Division* switched positions with it on 9 April 1944. By 15 April, *12. Feld-Division (L)* was back under *XXVIII. Armeekorps*. Mid-April was also the time that *13. Feld-Division (L)* ceased to exist.[40] It was then that *18. Armee* used the existing parts of *13. Feld-Division (L)* to replenish and reinforce *12. Feld-Division (L)*.[41] The special *Division z.b.V. 300*, which controlled several regiments of Estonian frontier guard units, also received parts of *13. Feld-Division (L)*.[42] The divisional headquarters for *Division z.b.V. 300* was actually formed using the staff from *13. Feld-Division (L)*.[43] The line regiments could no longer sustain three *Jäger* battalions. There simply weren't enough replacements to support a three-battalion regiment. The decision was, therefore, made to reduce the size of *Jäger-Regiment 23 (L)* and *Jäger-Regiment 24 (L)* to two battalions apiece.

In order to make up for the loss of the third battalion in each of the two regiments, the First Battalion of *Jäger-Regiment 25 (L)* and First Battalion of *Jäger-Regiment 26 (L)*, from the now-defunct *13. Feld-Division (L)*, were merged to become *I. Jäger-Bataillon* and *II. Jäger-Bataillon* of *Jäger-Regiment 25 (L)*. In addition, *I. Bataillon/ Grenadier-Regiment 374* was now redesignated as *Fusilier-Bataillon 12 (L)* of *12. Feld-Division (L)*.[44] The divisional artillery regiment, *Artillerie-Regiment 12 (L)*, was also reinforced by the addition of a fourth artillery battalion. All these efforts made it possible for *12. Feld-Division (L)* to continue to remain as one of the most effective formations of *18. Armee*. It is certain that if the division had not been an effective formation, Army Group North would have simply disbanded the unit. On 2 May 1944, *12. Feld-Division (L)*, alongside *126.* and *215. Infanterie-Division*, were still holding Pskov in a semicircle. Estonian frontier guard regiments, under the command of *Division z.b.V. 300*, were now guarding the left flank of the city, behind the west bank of Lake Pskov. *21.* and *30. Infanterie-Division* covered the right flank of Pskov, while *Heeresgruppe Nord* assigned *XXVIII. Armeekorps* two armored units as reserves: *schwer Panzer-Abteilung 502* and *Sturmgeschütz Abteilung 184*. On 13 May, the records of *Heeresgruppe Nord* listed that only seven out of its thirty-two divisions, including infantry, armor, security, etc., were at full combat readiness.[45] The *12. Feld-Division (L)* was one of those seven divisions.[46]

The rest of the divisions of *Heeresgruppe Nord* were in various stages of effectiveness. This report on the condition of *12. Feld-Division (L)* was confirmed on 18 July when *Heeresgruppe Nord* stated in their daily War Diary that *12. Feld-Division (L)* was considered one of the best of the seven divisions in the entire army group.[47] There is no clear explanation for this, given that most of the *Luftwaffe* field divisions performed so miserably. Was it because the division had a higher caliber of officers and NCOs? Was it weaponry? We will never really know, but we can speculate as to why it performed as well as it did. Perhaps it was due to the influx of experienced army veterans when the division was inducted into the *Heer* in November 1943. Perhaps it was on account of the fact that the division kept receiving replacements and reinforcements, which kept its regiments mostly up to strength. Perhaps it was on account of the fact that the Red Army did not plan any major offensives in its sector of the front line. Or maybe the induction of entire army units, like one battalion from *Grenadier-Regiment 374* becoming the new *Fusilier-Bataillon 12 (L)* within the division, also had something to do with it. Perhaps it was a combination of all of these factors. Whichever is the case, on 24 July 1944, Army Group North listed their divisions according to combat worthiness as follows:[48, 49]

**Table 1. Combat readiness of divisions under Army Group North.**

| COMBAT EFFECTIVENESS | DIVISIONS UNDER ARMY GROUP NORTH |
|---|---|
| Fully Combat Effective: | *11., 21., 30., 58.,61., 227. Infanterie-Division* and *12. Feld-Division (L)*. |
| Partially Combat Effective: | *126., 225., 263., 389. Infanterie-Division, 20. Waffen-Grenadier-Division der-SS (estnische Nr. 1) 21. Feld-Division (L)*. |
| Exhausted, Only Partially Effective: | *24., 32., 81., 83., 87., 93., 121., 132., 205., 215., 218., 290., 329. Infanterie-Division* and *281. Sicherungs-Division*. |
| Completely Combat Ineffective: | *23. Infanterie-Division, 15.* and *19. (lettische) Waffen-Grenadier-Division der SS*. |

42    The Bitter End

## EFFECTS OF THE BATTLE FOR PSKOV

The second battle for Pskov had begun on 30 March 1944, with the Soviets launching a series of attacks to encircle and isolate the city from the German defenses. Soviet forces advanced rapidly, exploiting weaknesses in the German defensive lines, which had been weakened by the Leningrad and Novgorod offensives. The fighting in the area was intense, with Soviet forces utilizing artillery and air support to break through German defenses. The Soviet 2nd Shock Army, Soviet 3rd Guards Tank Army, and other units focused on surrounding Pskov and cutting off German supply routes effectively isolated the city. Despite strong German resistance, the Soviets were able to gradually gain ground, liberating surrounding towns and encircling German garrisons in the area. As the battle progressed, the German forces within Pskov faced mounting pressure and began to retreat. The final stages of the battle were marked by Soviet forces pressing into Pskov itself. The city was heavily bombed, and house-to-house fighting broke out. By 17 April 1944, after fierce resistance, the Soviet forces successfully liberated Pskov. Its capture signaled yet another German withdrawal westward and the loss of the defensive advantage which Lake Peipus and Lake Pskov offered.

**Figure 18.** Positions of *Armee-Abteilung Narwa* on 1 March 1944.

## THE RACE TO RIGA: THE BATTLE FOR NARVA

The battle for Narva would last from 2 February to 10 August 1944. For the Red Army, breaching the Narva Isthmus—which sits between the Gulf of Finland and Lake Peipus—was crucial from a strategic standpoint. If the Narva operation had been successful, there would have been no obstacles in the way of advancing up the coast to Tallinn, the Estonian capital. For its defense, a total of three German corps ended up being employed. These included: *III. (germanisches) SS-Panzerkorps, XXVI. Armeekorps,* and *XLIII. Armeekorps.* The Order of Battle for the Soviet Leningrad Front on 1 March 1944 was as follows:

> 2nd Shock Army (Lieutenant-General Ivan Fedyuninsky): 43rd Rifle Corps, 109th Rifle Corps, and 124th Rifle Corps.
> 8th Army (Lieutenant-General Filip Starikov): 6th Rifle Corps and 112th Rifle Corps.
> 59th Army (Lieutenant-General Ivan Korovnikov): 117th Rifle Corps and 122nd Rifle Corps.

Directly under Leningrad Front control: 8th Estonian Rifle Corps, 14th Rifle Corps, 124th Rifle Division, 30th Guards Rifle Corps, 46th, 260th and 261st Guards Heavy Tank Regiment, 1902nd Self-propelled Artillery Regiment, 3rd Breakthrough Artillery Corps, 3rd Guards Tank Corps. At the start of the Narva Offensive, the Leningrad Front could count on 136,830 men, 150 tanks, 2,500 assault guns, and over 800 fighters and bombers. At the start of the battle, the German order of battle for *Armee-Abteilung Narwa* (created in February 1944) was the following:

> Directly under army group control: *schwere Panzer-Abteilung 502* (Tiger-I tanks), *Landesschützen-Bataillon 752,* and *Infanterie-Bataillon 540 z.b.V.*[50]
> *III. SS (germanisches) Panzerkorps,* led by *SS-Obergruppenführer* Felix Steiner: *11. SS Panzergrenadier-Division 'Nordland', 4. SS Panzergrenadier-Brigade 'Nederland', 20. Waffen-Grenadier-Division der SS (estnische Nr. 1).*
> *XXVI. Armeekorps,* led by *General der Infanterie* Anton Grasser: *11. Infanterie-Division, 58. Infanterie-Division, 214. Infanterie-Division, 225. Infanterie-Division, (estnische) Grenzschutz Regiment 3* (beginning 15 April).
> *XLIII. Armeekorps,* led by *General der Infanterie* Karl von Oven: *61. Infanterie-Division, 170. Infanterie-Division, 227. Infanterie-Division, Panzergrenadier-Division Feldherrnhalle, Gnesen (Genesenden) Grenadier-Regiment.*[51]

In the months of February and March 1944, the Red Army tried several times to break through the Narva front. In the south, the small remnants of some divisions collapsed shortly afterward under a new Soviet offensive, so that by 24 February, the Red Army took control of the main railway line that ensured the supply of munitions and other materials for the Narva defenders. The capture of the rail line also threatened to encircle the *III. (germanisches) SS-Panzerkorps*. The remnants of the *61. Infanterie-Division* could not stop the Russian advance, so *Panzergrenadier-Division 'Feldherrnhalle'* and *schwere Panzer-Abteilung 502* (with twelve remaining operational Tiger-I tanks) had to be employed to correct the situation. On 26 March 1944, *XLIII. Armeekorps* began a counterattack with the *11. Infanterie-Division* and *227. Infanterie-Division*. In the course of fierce fighting, Soviet troops were pushed back toward the Narva River in the south. Only the Soviet bridgehead southwest of Narva could not be eliminated even after heavy fighting. In the following months, the front in the area calmed down.

As of 1 March 1944, the strength of *Armee-Abteilung Narwa* was 123,541 men. However, the requirements of other sectors of the Eastern Front soon forced a reduction of troops. The attack against Army Group Center, which began on 22 June 1944, soon drew away eight divisions totaling 101,291 men; these numbers including the seasoned and battle-hardened *Panzergrenadier-Division 'Feldherrnhalle'*. This withdrawal of forces left only around 22,250 men to defend the Narva isthmus. It was at this point that the Red Army took the opportunity to launch another wave of attacks against the Narva defenders. On 24 July, the new Russian offensive began. Heavy fighting lasted until the end of July, throughout which the Germans were able to hold and maintain the front. However, once *Armee-Abteilung Narwa* transferred the bulk of its forces to the south, in order to support the beleaguered southern wing of *Heeresgruppe Nord*, the front began to give way. The Red Army renewed its attacks on 21 August. *Panzer-Kampfgruppe Graf von Strachwitz* was brought up to support *Armee-Abteilung Narwa* in order to help repel the Russian attacks. In this, he was assisted by the Prussian regiments of *11. Infanterie-Division*. The Russian formations managed to break through between *Armee-Abteilung Narwa*, and *18. Armee* and advanced toward Pernau.

Under heavy fighting, *Armee-Abteilung Narwa* was able to hold its positions. However, on 18 September, the *III. (germanisches) SS-Panzerkorps* was ordered to withdraw to Pernau, while some of its units were ordered to pull back to Reval. On 25 September 1944, *Armee-Abteilung Narwa* was renamed *Armee-Abteilung Grasser*.[52] In October, *Armee-Abteilung Grasser* was ordered to withdraw from Estonia and withdraw toward Riga, Latvia. German losses for the Battle of Narva included about 54,000 wounded and around 14,000 killed, missing, or taken prisoner. Russian losses stood at around 380,000 wounded and about 100,000 killed, missing, or taken prisoner. The battle proved to be a tactical success for the Germans, given that they delayed the Russian advance by several months. The ratio of men killed, wounded, or taken prisoner was 7:1 in favor of the Germans. Thus, the Russians lost seven men for every German loss. However, while the Russians could afford to take these losses, the Germans could not.

South of Lake Peipus and Lake Pskov, the Germans had prepared a defense line that included wooden as well as some cement bunkers, trenches, wooden roads, and prepared artillery positions. However, the Panther Line had not been completed and lacked the depth to hold back a determined Soviet offensive. The

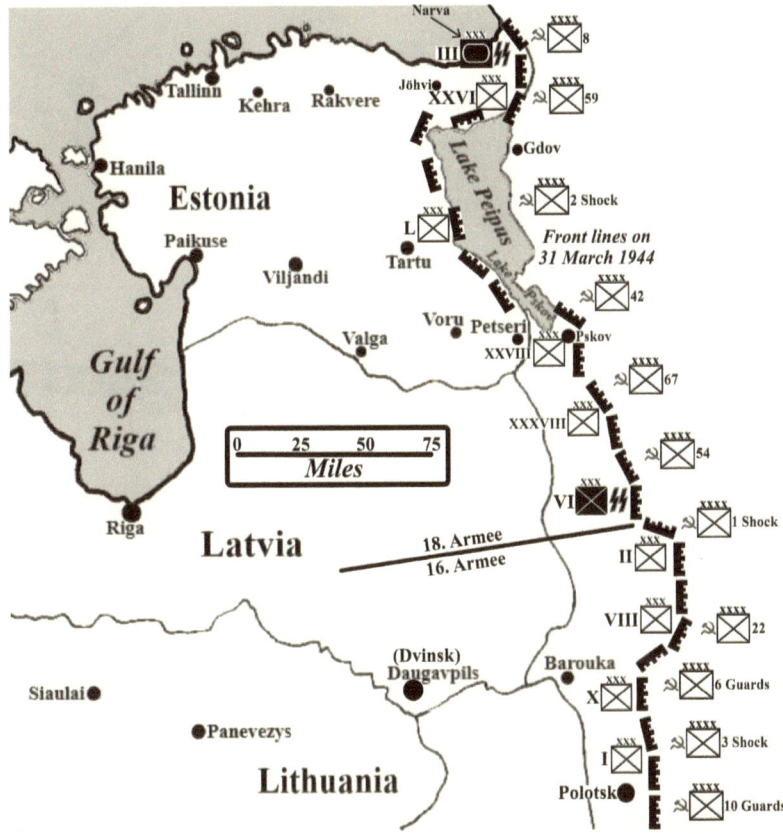

**Figure 19.** Positions of Army Group North on 31 March 1944.

line was to be thousands of kilometers long and, in theory, stretched all across the Russian Front, from Narva in the north to the Black Sea in the south. However, the reality was that the *Panther Linie* was more hope than reality. It was nowhere near completed. The positions around the *Panther Linie* were adjusted between 25–27 February 1944, when *Gruppe Herzog,* formerly known as *Gruppe Friessner,* was ordered to withdraw to the so-called *Darmstadt Linie* (Darmstadt Line). General Herzog was the current commander of *XXXVIII. Armeekorps*. It was this corps to which *21. Feld-Division (L)* was now attached. The front lines of *XXXVIII. Armeekorps* extended southeast, where *VI. SS-Freiwilligen-Armeekorps* was operating.[53] By 4 April 1944, *12. Feld-Division (L)* and *21. Feld-Division (L)* were still fighting around Pskov (Pleskau, in German). The division was located south of Ostrov, north of Opochka, and west of Novorzhev.

To the north of its positions was *Kampfgruppe Schulz*, which contained the remnants of *12. Feld-Division (L), 126. Infanterie-Division, 212. Infanterie-Division,* and *8. Jäger-Division*. Farther north, by Pskov, was *Gruppe Generalmajor Gothsche,*

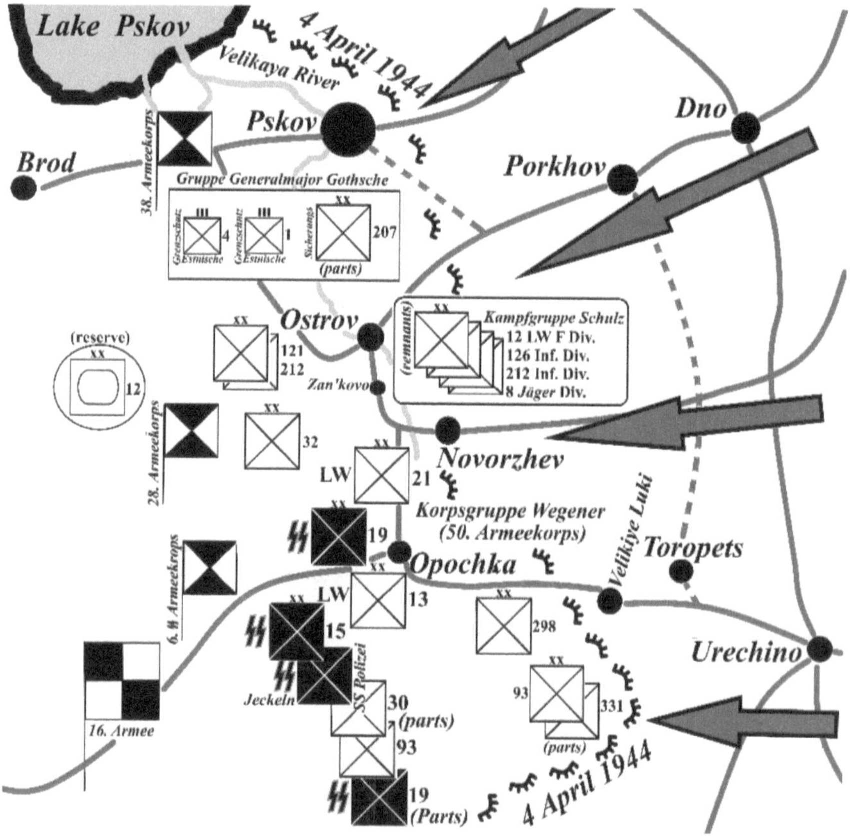

**Figure 20.** Positions of *16. Armee*, 4 April 1944.

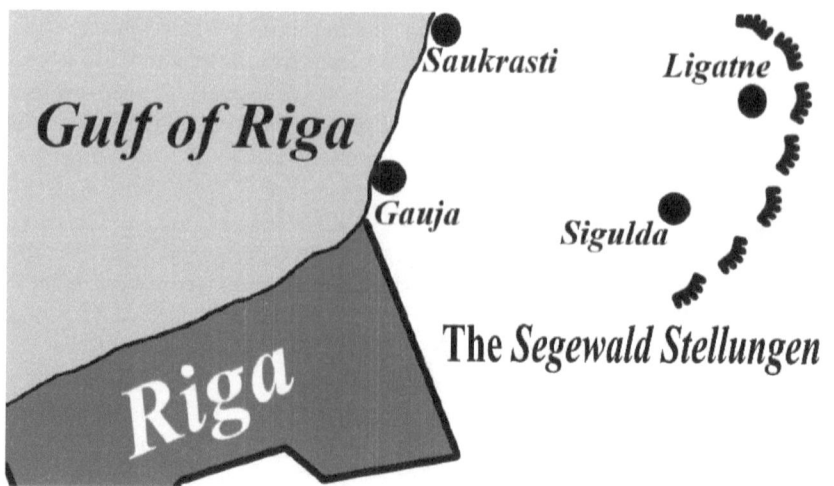

**Figure 21.** The so-called *'Segewald stellungen'* (Segulda positions).

which contained what remained of *207. Sicherungs-Division*, as well as *Grenzschutz-Regiment 1 (estnisch)* and *Grenzschutz-Regiment 4 (estnisch)* (Estonian 1st and 4th Frontier Guard Regiment). It was clear that by the beginning of April, *16. Armee* had taken a heavy beating. Many of its divisions had been reduced to mere battle groups.

In May, *21. Feld-Division (L)* continued to serve under *XXXVIII. Armeekorps*. By June, the divisional front lines were still located south of Ostrov. The left flank of the division was now manned by men of the Pomeranian *32. Infanterie-Division*, while the right flank was held by the greatly reduced Hanoverian regiments of *83. Infanterie-Division*. By July, the front lines of *16. Armee* now stretched from Pskov to as far south as Volki. In July 1944, the Red Army once again attempted to outflank the German defenses in and around Pskov. The Soviets concentrated their effort on the front lines of *XXXVIII. Armeekorps*, which they knew had been

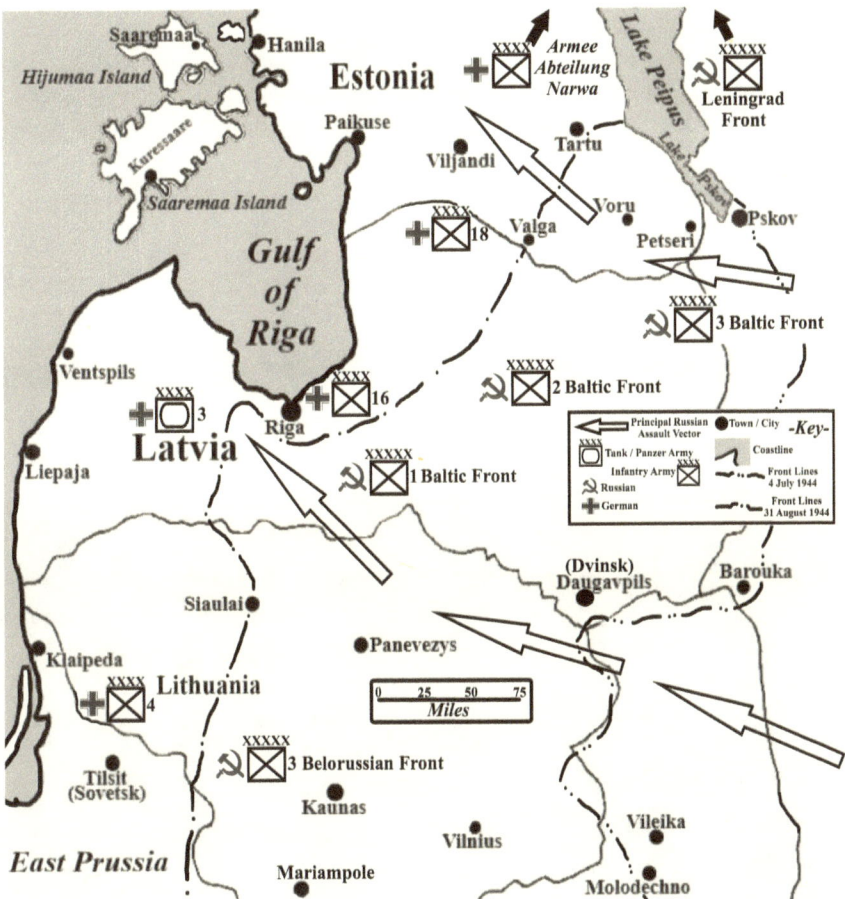

**Figure 22.** Advance of Red Army in the Baltic States between 4 July and 31 August 1944.

battered and greatly weakened. In particular, they sent armored units to try and break through the lines of *21 Feld-Division (L)*. The division had begun to take heavy losses as early as February 1944, as it withdrew from positions along the Lovat River, between Cholm and Staraya Rusa. A chronicler writing the combat history of *32. Infanterie-Division* described the situation thusly:

> Actually, the front of 21. Luftwaffen Feld-Division cracked under strong enemy pressure during the evening of July 20. As the advanced elements of 32. Infanterie-Division arrived in the Utroya sector, early on 21 July, they found it occupied by enemy forces. The crossings were either destroyed or in the hands of the enemy. The regiments crossed the river under difficult conditions, fighting their way through enemy troops and occupying a position between Utroya and Kukhva, in which they continued to fight bitterly with the enemy. 21. Luftwaffen Feld-Division was completely exhausted, and there was also spotty contact with the 121. Infanterie-Division, which was also in heavy combat.[54]

The Soviet offensive had its intended consequence, which was to force a break through the lines of *XXXVIII. Armeekorps*. Four days after the Red Army

**Figure 23.** Military situation of Army Group North on 4 October 1944.

launched its attack, the headquarters of Army Group North rated *21. Feld-Division (L)* as only partially combat effective.⁵⁵

That description meant that the division was only capable of limited defensive action. By 2 August, the division had withdrawn into northeastern Latvia, between Alüksne (Marienberg), by Lake Alüksnes, and Ape (Hoopendorf). The next major movement for the divisions of *18. Armee* occurred in early October, when the army was ordered to withdraw to the so-called *Segewald stellungen* (Sigulda positions).⁵⁶ This was a defensive area which resembled a half-circle and began north of the town of Ligat (Ligatne), near the Gulf of Riga, and stretched just north of Segewald (Sigulda).⁵⁷ It was *XXXVIII. Armeekorps* which covered the withdrawal to these new positions. *11. Infanterie-Division, 30. Infanterie-Division, 32. Infanterie-Division, 225. Infanterie-Division,* and *21. Feld-Division (L)* covered the withdrawal of German forces to the *Segewold Stellung*. The *21. Feld-Division (L)* played a major role in covering the withdrawal and suffered accordingly.

## THE RACE TO RIGA: THE RIGA OFFENSIVE— 14 SEPTEMBER TO 24 OCTOBER 1944

The Red Army advance had halted at the end of August. Simply put, the Russians had outrun their supplies. Both sides were exhausted after months of fighting. However, it only took the Soviets two weeks to replenish their arms and units, receive replacements, and prepare for the next phase of the Baltic campaign: the capture of the Latvian capital of Riga. The offensive began on 14 September with 43rd Army, 6th Guards Army, 4th Shock Army and 22nd Army attacking *16. Armee* south and southeast of Riga.

Farther west, 5th Guards Tank Army aimed at cutting off the retreat of the entire northern German army group by attacking west of Dobele in an attempt to reach the Gulf or Riga just west of the Latvian capital. This Russian tank army was engaging the left wing of *3. Panzerarmee* and right wing of *16. Armee*. The resulting battle of Memel was launched on 5 October 5 by the 1st Baltic Front. This attack shattered *3. Panzerarmee* and temporarily cut off *Heeresgruppe Nord* from *Heeresgruppe Mitte*. The *16. Armee* and *18. Armee* that were squeezed in and around Riga were now almost completely surrounded. *Heeresgruppe Nord* only had one option: move its divisions out of the Riga cauldron and establish a defensive position in the Courland region of Latvia. To that effect the entire army group was quickly withdrawn. On 10 October, the *227. Infanterie-Division,* with the support of the heavy flak guns of *6. Flak-Division* (stationed in Riga), acted as a rear guard. The race for Riga was now over. The six battles for the Courland pocket now lay ahead.

# Chapter 4

# FINLAND LEAVES THE WAR

For close to three years, the German *20. Gebirgsarmee* had been fighting the Russians in Lapland, the northernmost region of Finland. The Finnish Army's front zone had been relatively quiet from January to June 1944, but in February, the Russians began to deploy more forces against *20. Gebirgsarmee*. The Red Army was obviously building up its forces for a major attack. The Red Army facing the Germans in Lapland had grown from 100,000 men to around 150,000. All indications pointed to a Russian offensive that would begin by the end of June 1944. The *XXXVI. Gebirgs* sector was the area most in danger, where four brigades and two new Red Army divisions had been brought up. This also included additional artillery and rocket launcher batteries. In addition, the Soviets had extended their right flank substantially. Their closest front line was now located northwestward of the German positions. This provided the Red Army a good starting point from which to later encircle *20. Gebirgsarmee*.[1]

Farther south, the Red Army was planning a surprise for the Finns. Beginning on 9 June, the Finnish 4th Army Corps defending the Karelian Isthmus began to be probed. A day later, a massive Soviet artillery barrage heralded the arrival of the Red Army offensive. The Finnish 3rd Army Corps stood on the flank of the 4th Army Corps, but together, these two Finnish corps only possessed three infantry divisions and one infantry brigade acting as a reserve.

The truth was that the Finnish front lines were too thin.[2] Most importantly, the Finns also lacked adequate anti-tank weaponry. For the offensive in Karelia, the Red Army had assembled ten infantry and three tank divisions. When the bombardment began, approximately 350 Russian guns were positioned for every kilometer of front. The Finns, who were not expecting the attack, were taken by surprise. By 13 June, the Finnish were planning to give up the defense lines along the Svir and Maaselka River and pull back from eastern Karelia to a shorter defense line northeast of Lake Ladoga. By 20 July 1944, the Russian summer offensive against the Finns in eastern Karelia ended. Two weeks later, on 4 August,

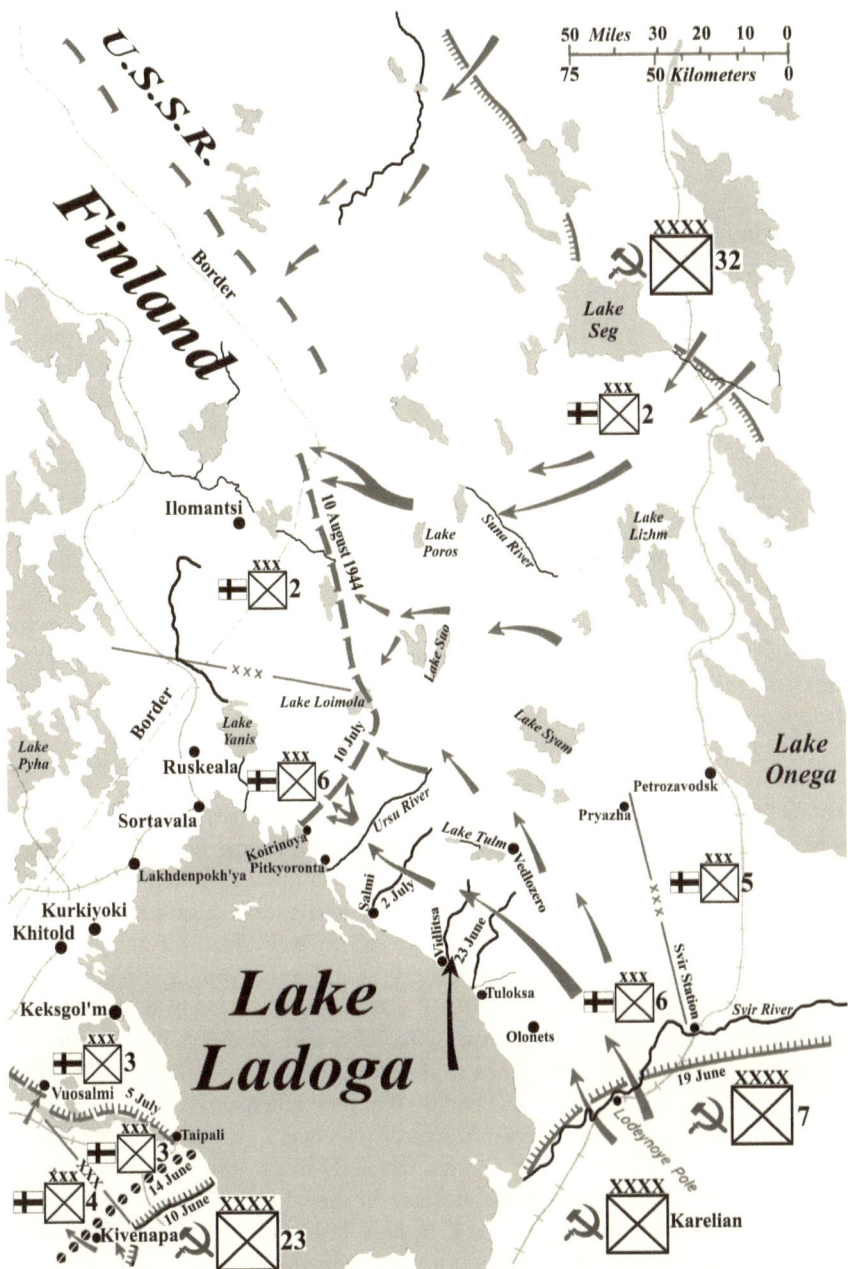

**Figure 24.** This map depicts the Soviet offensive against the Finnish Army between Lake Seg, Lake Onega, and Lake Ladoga, from June-August 1944. The German defeat in the Leningrad sector and subsequent withdrawal of the *Ostheer* through the Baltic States clearly indicated to Finland that Nazi Germany was on the ropes. The summer offensive against the Finnish Army convinced the country's chief military leader, Marshal Mannerheim, of the need to sue for peace.

Marshal Mannerheim became the leader of Finland after the resignation of President Risto Ryti and a special act by the Finnish parliament, which conferred the presidency to Mannerheim. This allowed Finland to end the agreement that had recently been signed between Ryti and Germany's foreign minister, Joachim von Ribbentrop.[3]

On 2 September 1944, Marshal Mannerheim informed the Germans of the Finnish intention to leave the war. The Finns entered into negotiations with the Russians on 5 September. Two weeks later, on 19 September, the Moscow Agreement was signed. This agreement effectively ended the Continuation War between the two countries and outlined the terms of peace. The treaty required Finland to cede territory to the Soviet Union, including the region of Karelia. It also forced the Finns to agree to physically expel the German Army from Finnish territory if they had not withdrawn by 15 September 1944. Obviously, the time allotted for the withdrawal of German forces was insufficient for a full departure from Finland. The Russians knew this, and merely wished to see the Finns fighting their former ally. In addition, the Germans themselves created the circumstance for actual conflict between the Finnish Army and the *Wehrmacht*, when they attempted to capture the island of Suursaari, as a prerequisite to implementing a withdrawal from Finland. The German attempt on 15 September failed, and some 1,000 Germans—out of an original force of 1,400—were captured by Finnish forces on the island. Once the Germans initiated hostilities, previous friendships disappeared, and all bets were now off.

In 1941, the pool of men eligible for military service had been around 855,000 men, out of a population of 3.8 million people. By June 1941, approximately 300,000 Finnish men had been mobilized for the war. From the 855,000 men, we must deduct 15 percent of males between the ages of eighteen to fifty who could not serve. The reasons included physical or mental disabilities, criminal activity, including imprisonment, antisocial behavior, exclusion from military service on account of a specialized trade vital to the war effort, accidental deaths, and so on. This amounted to some 128,250 men, leaving roughly 555,000 men who could still be mobilized. We must also factor in 15,000 men who served in the Navy and 20,000 in the Air Force. That left a pool of about 392,000 men of recruiting age that could be mobilized after June 1941. Between June 1941 and December 1943, the Finnish Army had 70,000 men killed and 35,000 wounded, of which about 18,000 could return to military service.

That left 87,000 men who were permanently lost to the war. Thus, of the original 300,000 troops in the Finnish Army in June 1941, only around 213,000 had survived to the beginning of 1944. In June 1944, the Finnish Army stood at 425,000 men. That means that (counting replacements) between June 1941 and June 1944, 212,000 men from the pool of 392,000 had been inducted. By 1 July 1944, only 180,000 men of military age could still be drafted into the Finnish Armed Forces. While the Russians suffered heavy losses during their summer offensive, by 11 July 1944, Finnish casualties for the year stood at just over 32,000 men, leaving (at best) 393,000 men in the Finnish Armed Forces by 1 August 1944. Deducting Finnish air force and navy personnel, the actual strength of the Finnish Army on 1 August was around 358,000 men divided into some thirty-four divisions (counting independent brigades).

In early July 1944, barely 12,000 men were available from the recruit training centers to replace these heavy losses. The point of citing these figures is to illustrate that, by the summer of 1944, Finland was at the breaking point. The war could no longer be sustained for an indefinite period of time. There just weren't enough Finnish men of military age. This was another reason why the Finns decided to sue for peace. Frankly, the small nation of Finland had reached its limit, militarily speaking.[4] The Germans had attempted to aid the Finns when the Russian summer offensive had begun. On 23 June, the Germans had sent *Sturmgeschütz-Brigade 303* to help the Finns. On 28 June, the *122. Infanterie-Division* had arrived as well. This was in addition to the Germans gifting the Finns 9,000 single-shot *Panzerfaust* anti-tank weapons and 5,000 *Panzerschreck* (bazookas). All of this aid, however, was insufficient to push back the Red Army. But the aid helped to halt the Soviet offensive by late July. Soon, however, the German loss of Pskov (on 23 July) and Narva (on 28 July) forced the OKW to order the return of *122. Infanterie-Division* from Finland back to *Heeresgruppe Nord*.

Farther north, in Lapland, where the German *20. Gebirgsarmee* was fighting, preparations for a possible German withdrawal from the nickel-rich mines of Petsamo had actually been prepared. The code name for this operation was *Unternehmen Birke* (Operation Birch). The majority of the stores which had been accumulated were not only munitions and weaponry but also vast amounts of raw nickel that was vital for the war effort. This hoard amounted to approximately 135,000 short tons. Throughout the summer, these stores were slowly withdrawn, so by the end of September 1944, they had been safely taken to Norway. The importance of the Petsamo nickel mines was further reduced when, in the late summer of 1944, a new deposit of nickel was discovered in eastern Austria. This allowed *Generaloberst* Lothar Rendulic to convince Hitler that there was no further need to hold on to the nickel mines at Petsamo. On 4 October 1944, the German dictator gave permission for *20. Gebirgsarmee* to begin its withdrawal toward northern Norway.[5] Immediately, *Unternehmen Birke* (Operation Birch) was put into action. The order of battle for *20. Gebirgsarmee* in early September 1944 was as follows:

XIX. *Gebirgs-Armeekorps*:
  2. *Gebirgs-Division*
  6. *Gebirgs-Division*
  210. *Infanterie-Division*
  *Divisionsgruppe van der Hoop (Divisions Stab z.b.V. 613)*:
    Grenadier-Brigade 193 (ex-Grenadier-Regiment 193)
    Grenadier-Brigade 503 (three battalions of *Luftwaffe* infantry)

*XXXVI. Gebirgs-Armeekorps:*
  163. *Infanterie-Division*
  169. *Infanterie-Division*
*XVIII. Gebirgs-Armeekorps:*
  6. *SS Gebirgs-Division 'Nord'*
  7. *Gebirgs-Division*
  *Divisionsgruppe Kräutler (Divisions Stab z.b.V. 140)*[6]

This last division, *Divisionsgruppe Kräutler,* had been recently established in April 1944. On 7 September, it was given the designation *Divisions Stab z.b.V. 140.* This divisional group was led by *Oberst* Mathias Kräutler. In keeping with German Army standards for a divisional commander, he was promoted to *Generalmajor* on 1 October 1944. *Divisions Stab z.b.V. 140* was organized as follows:

*Skijäger-Bataillon 13*
*Jäger-Bataillon 6*
*Jäger-Bataillon 3*
*Gebirgsjäger-Brigade 139*
  *I. Gebirgsjäger-Bataillon (1.–5. Kompanie)*
  *II. Gebirgsjäger-Bataillon (6.–10. Kompanie)*
  *III. Gebirgsjäger-Bataillon (11.–17. Kompanie)*[7]
*Pionier-Bataillon der Divisionsgruppe Kräutler*
*Artillerie-Regiments Stab z.b.V. 931* with:
  II. *Artillerie-Abteilung des Artillerie-Regiments 82*
    *Artillerie-Abteilung 124*
    *Leichtgeschütz-Abteilung 424*
*Nachschubtruppen 818.*

Opposing *20. Gebirgsarmee* was the Russian 14th Army, which, at this time, contained 31st Corps, 99th Army Corps, 126th Army Corps, 127th Army Corps, 131st Army Corps, and Corps Group Pigarevich. In addition, a special Russian naval landing division eventually landed on the Srednii Peninsula. Guarding this small peninsula was *Divisionsgruppe van der Hoop,* composed of two German grenadier regiments. This divisional group immediately withdrew from the peninsula and positioned itself at the neck of the peninsula, which was a far shorter and therefore better defensive position because it offered a bottleneck which would prove difficult for the Russians to break through. When the Russians realized that the Germans were about to withdraw, they launched what would be referred to as the Petsamo-Kirkenes offensive. The offensive would last from 7–29 October 1944.

## THE LAPLAND WAR 1944–1945

Initially, the *20. Gebirgsarmee* had struck a deal with the Finns that would permit German forces to withdraw in order, destroying roads and rail bridges as they retreated. This would give the Finnish Army, which was to follow closely behind, the excuse needed to tell the Russians that they were making progress, but also that the Germans were impeding their advance. It was hoped that this trick would hopefully prevent conflict between the Germans and the Finns. This arrangement, however, was not rock solid—meaning that it would most likely not hold up forever, as the Finns were very determined to abide by the Russian terms for peace. In fact, beginning on 28 September, incidences of Germans and Finns firing on one another began to occur. South of the *20. Gebirgsarmee* boundary line, Marshal Mannerheim had moved the Finnish 6th Infantry Division and a border *Jäger* brigade to Kajaani. The Finnish Armored Division, the 3rd Infantry Division, and the 11th Infantry Division were sent to Oulu. All of these forces were under a Finnish corps grouping under the command of General Siilasvuo. To follow up the German withdrawal from Lapland, Marshal Mannerheim had allocated several divisions. Initially, the Finnish Armored Division and, later, the Finnish 3rd Infantry Division advanced on Rovaniemi, the capital of Lapland. The town was important because it was on the withdrawal route for *XVIII. Gebirgs-Armeekorps*. If the town was taken by either the Finns or the Russians, the retreat of this German mountain corps would be blocked. Rovaniemi was also important because it was the headquarters for *20. Gebirgsarmee* and the airfield there was where the headquarters for *Luftflotte 5* was stationed.

On 1 October, fighting broke out between German and Finnish troops in and around the towns of Tornio and Kemi. At Tornio, a Finnish landing went undetected at the port of Röyttä, which lies on the outer region of the town of Tornio. The battles there lasted until 8 October, when the Finns forced the Germans to withdraw, giving up that vital road and rail link to northern Sweden. Finnish forces lost 375 killed, 1,400 wounded, and twenty-three captured. German losses totaled 500 killed, 1,600 wounded, and 400 taken prisoner. Four German tanks were also lost in the fighting, given that the Finns were well equipped with the *Panzerfaust* and *Panzerschreck* anti-tank weapons, which, ironically, the Germans themselves had recently supplied to the Finns. This battle would be the fiercest fight that would occur between the former Axis allies. In retribution, General Lothar Rendulic, the commander of *20. Gebirgsarmee,* now ordered a scorched-earth policy in Lapland, seeing the capture of Tornio as a betrayal by the Finns. The battle of Tornio had demonstrated to the Soviet Union that the Finnish government was actively trying to remove the Germans by force. Furthermore, the Finnish army had shown that it was prepared and ready to use force against their former military ally.

The next conflict to occur between the Germans and the Finns was the battle for Rovaniemi, which took place from 12–13 October 1944. The fighting at Rovaniemi actually began by accident. Originally, General Rendulic had given strict orders that the only facilities that should be destroyed at Rovaniemi were administrative buildings, rail and road bridges, the stores in warehouses that could not be withdrawn, and the local airfield, which was to be made unusable. Private homes and the town hospital were to be left alone. However, a Finnish commando unit saw a German ammunition train at the town station. Without consult-

**Figure 25.** After the successful Red Army offensives by Lake Ladoga and Lake Onega, the Russians launched their Petsamo-Kirkenes offensive that would last from 7–29 October 1944. The operation was meant to push the Germans back to the Norwegian-Finnish border region.

ing his superior, the Finnish commander of this unit made a split-second decision to blow up the munitions train. The train was filled with so much ammunition that the resulting explosions set off an uncontrolled fire that gutted most of the town. Whether the Germans were still intending to burn down the whole town after the fighting at Tornio is basically a moot point, given the explosion that resulted from the destruction of the German ammunition train. At the time, no one knew what had happened, so the Finnish command assumed that the Germans had orders to destroy the entire town. The subsequent fighting there cost around 141 Finnish men killed, wounded, or missing. The Germans had fifty-two dead, 164 wounded, and nine missing. The Germans also lost one tank in the fighting.

### PETSAMO-KIRKENES OFFENSIVE

The initial Russian attempt to breakthrough near the port of Petsamo was met with coordination problems and bad weather which delayed the capture of the city for a week. The Germans themselves were directed to give up Petsamo on 15 October. On that very day, the first Russian troops entered the city around noontime. The commander of the 14th Army, General Kirill Meretskov, had approximately 113,200 men, plus 20,300 men of the Soviet Northern Fleet in support. The brunt of the offensive would be placed on two Russian 'light' infantry corps: 126th Rifle Corps and 127th Rifle Corps. These two Red Army corps were composed of a combination of ski troops, light infantry, and naval infantry. The attack would be backed up by 1,000 artillery pieces comprising howitzers, Katyusha rockets and mortars, 750 fighters and bombers, 110 tanks, thirty battalions of engineers, and two transport battalions equipped with the following American amphibious vehicles:[8]

- DUKW: a six-wheel-drive amphibious modification of the two-and-a-half-ton GMC truck.
- LVT-4 'Alligator': the first landing vehicle tracked employed by the United States.
- LVT(A)-4 Amtrack: basically the 'Alligator' tracked vehicle with an armored superstructure and the Stuart tank turret attached on top.[9]

In spite of a slow start to the offensive due to inclement weather and poor artillery coordination, the Red Army was eventually able to break through the German lines along the Titovka River. It was then that an amphibious operation was launched by the Soviets, who landed naval infantry on the Srednii Peninsula. In response, *Divisionsgruppe van der Hoop* was withdrawn from the peninsula and *163. Infanterie-Division,* which was in the process of retreating toward northern Norway, was recalled and sent to bolster the defenses at Petsamo. The attack on

Petsamo itself began on 13 October, with the Russians attempting to bypass the town and therefore cutting off the route of retreat for the German forces. The Germans quickly saw the danger and ordered a withdrawal. The leading unit during the breakout was *2. Gebirgs-Division*. The Germans managed to escape, and on 15 October, Petsamo was captured by the Red Army. Delaying the Russian advance was the effective German effort of destroying roads, bridges, laying mines, and creating obstacles that slowed down the Red Army advance to a crawl. Despite harsh weather conditions, tough terrain, and an effective German scorched-earth policy, Soviet forces managed to push the Axis powers back and eventually captured Petsamo and Kirkenes by the end of October. Kirkenes was taken on 25 October.

General Meretskov ordered an end to the offensive on 29 October 1944. From then on, the 14th Army would only send out troops to perform reconnaissance on the withdrawing German forces. From the Russian point of view, the operation was deemed a military success because it succeeded in removing the danger that the Russian port of Murmansk had been under for three years. In addition, the Germans were pushed out of Lapland and withdrew to northern Norway. The nickel mines of Petsamo were captured and more territory liberated. For his part in this operation, General Meretskov was promoted to marshal of the Soviet Union and was posted to the Far East command, where he was assigned a vital role in the Red Army offensive against the Japanese Army in early August 1945. The Petsamo-Kirkenes offensive turned out to be the last major battle fought during World War II that took place above the Arctic Circle. As such, it is still studied at Russian military academies and has been written about in Russian military circles as part of what has come to be termed as 'Stalin's Ten Blows'—one of ten Red Army offensives that were launched in 1944, which Stalin apologists like to claim led to the destruction of the *Ostheer* and, therefore, the eventual collapse of the Third Reich. From the German point of view, most historians agree that General Rendulic achieved a successful withdrawal of *20. Gebirgsarmee* because the Russians were delayed long enough for an orderly withdrawal to occur and the fighting between Finnish forces and German troops was relatively limited.

## Chapter 5

## ROMANIA

Between March and May 1944, the 2nd and 3rd Ukrainian Front had attempted to force a crossing of the Dniester River in an overly ambitious plan to enter Romania and the Balkans before the start of the summer season. Traditionally poor weather—*Rasputitsa,* likewise referred to as *Bezdorizhzhia,* the muddy season—as well as stiff German and Romanian resistance worked to cause these attacks to falter short of complete success. Soviet operational planning during this time period often proved too grandiose. As a result, the forces allocated and the time allotted for these actions to take place often were insufficient to complete the assigned operational goals. That, in turn, caused tactical failures to change into strategic disappointments. On 30 March 1944, the Germans established *Heeresgruppe Südukraine* in southern Russia. This Army Group had been created by simply renaming *Heeresgruppe A* (Army Group 'A'). The army group was created as a response to the Soviet advances and the changing dynamics of the war. The reorganization aimed to better respond to the evolving threat from the Soviets. At the time of its creation, the German *8. Armee* was located in northern Moldova, the German *6. Armee* was in Bessarabia, and the German *17. Armee* was defending the Crimea. In addition, Romanian forces in these areas were made subordinate to the army group.

Romania was now within striking distance of the Red Army. To defend it, two army groups were created. The first was *Heeresgruppe Moldau* (Army Group Moldova), comprising *8. Armee* and the Romanian 4th Army. This force was led by *General der Infanterie* Otto Wöhler. The second army group was located in Bessarabia and named *Gruppe Dumitrescu*. It was composed of *6. Armee* and the Romanian 3rd Army. This force was led by Colonel-General Petre Dumitrescu. Both *Heeresgruppe Moldau* and *Gruppe Dumitrescu* were subordinate to *Heeresgruppe Südukraine*. From 31 March to 24 July 1944, *Generalfeldmarschall* Ferdinand Schörner led *Heeresgruppe Südukraine*. When Schörner left to assume command of *Heeresgruppe Nord, Generaloberst* Johannes Frießner assumed the post. He held that

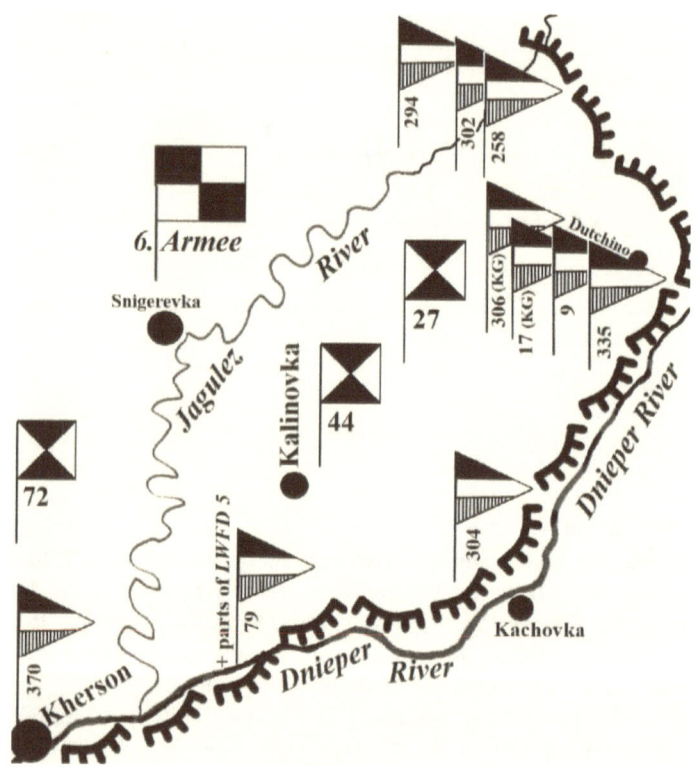

**Figure 26.** Positions of 6. Armee in March 1944.

**Figure 27.** The borders of Romania as they appeared in 1944.

**Figure 28.** *Heeresgruppe Südukraine* on 2 August 1944.

**Figure 29.** *Heeresgruppe Südukraine* on 2 August 1944.

position from 25 July to 23 September 1944. At the start of August, the following Russian forces were facing this combined German and Romanian defense: 2nd Ukrainian Front, with 4th Guards Army, 7th Guards Army, 5th Shock Army, 6th Tank Army, 27th Army, 40th Army, 52nd Army, 53rd Army; and 3rd Ukrainian Front, with 37th Army, 46th Army, and 57th Army. The Red Air Force was represented by the 17th Air Army.

Combined, *Gruppe Dumitrescu* could count on twenty-one German and twenty-three Romanian divisions. *Heeresgruppe Moldau* could count on the equivalent of eight Romanian divisions and three German divisions. The state of these forces, however, varied. Altogether the combined German and Romanian strength for what would come to be known as the Second Jassy-Kishinev offensive (20–29 August 1944) was some 500,000 Germans, 405,000 Romanians, 400 tanks and assault guns, 7,600 guns of all calibers, plus 810 aircraft (all types and models) from *Luftflotte 4* and the Romanian Air Force, which could field about 250 fighters.[1] That represented the entire strength of *Heeresgruppe Südukraine*. Facing this German-Romanian force were 2nd and 3rd Ukrainian Front with 1,314,000 troops, 16,000 guns, 1,870 tanks and assault guns, and 2,200 aircraft of the 17th Air Army.

## SECOND JASSY-KISHINEV OFFENSIVE

The first Jassy-Kishinev offensive, which had begun on 5 April 1944 and was aimed at capturing all of Romania, had ended by 6 June. As stated earlier, the problems that plagued the first attempt to enter the Balkans through Romania was overambition on the part of the planners, an extended supply line, and a strong Axis defense, along with poor weather. The Germans, too, had problems which were particular to where they were operating. For example, the *Wehrmacht* divisions in Romania had to depend heavily on the Hungarian and Romanian railroads, both of whom were overburdened and notoriously inefficient.[2] While the Red Army supply system had finally caught up to the advances made by the 2nd and 3rd Ukrainian Front, and the muddy season had given way to fine summer campaign weather, the German supply difficulties still remained. As a result, and in spite of Axis hopes for stalling the Russians yet again, the second Jassy-Kishinev offensive would play out in a different manner. Two other factors had conspired to initially defeat the Red Army offensive. The first was ineffective Soviet combat performance.[3] The second reason was a successful German defense plan, which took into account the terrain of the region. The Germans defeated Soviet forces attacking in the direction of Târgu Frumos (9–12 April) and Podu Iloaiei (12 April). Red Army losses during this drive included over 150,000 men, while the Germans and Romanians combined suffered approximately 45,000 casualties. Thus, the initial Jassy-Kishinev offensive failed, boosting the morale of the German and Romanian forces.

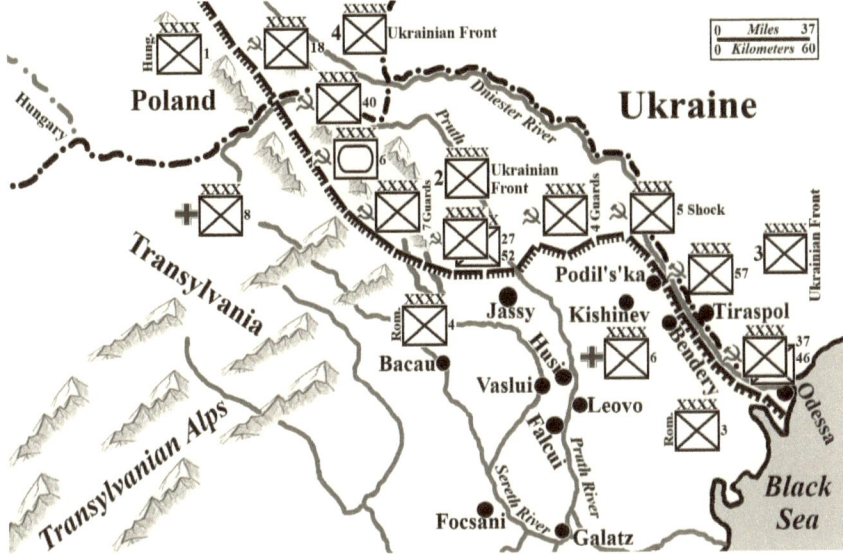

**Figure 30.** Red Army and Axis positions on 20 August 1944.

Although the first battle for Jassy and Kishinev had failed, the Red Army had advanced beyond Romania's prewar border region during the Uman-Botoșani offensive in early April 1944. This allowed both Ukrainian fronts to position themselves for a second attempt at breaking fully into Romania and, therefore, enter the Balkans proper. Waiting for the arrival of the Red Army in Yugoslavia was the communist partisan leader, Josip Broz Tito, who was battling around 450,000 German and Croatian troops. Like Finland, Stalin hoped that a series of offensive blows in 1944 would bring about the collapse of Romanian, Bulgarian, and Hungarian resistance. In the case of the Romanians and Bulgarians, his plans were eventually realized, but a German-inspired coup against the Admiral Horthy government in Budapest in the fall of 1944 assured that the Hungarians would fight alongside Nazi Germany until the bitter end. Nevertheless, Romanian and Bulgarian forces took up arms against the Nazis in the second half of 1944. They fought their former German ally until end of the war, as per the peace agreements that Romania and Bulgaria made with the Soviet Union.

The planning for this second offensive went smoothly, with Red Army units positioning themselves immediately behind the front lines chosen as the breakthrough points. The 6th Tank Army was selected as the main attack unit that would follow up after the initial breakthrough. It would seize the Siret River crossings and the Focșani Gate.[4] Surprisingly, Romanian intelligence regarding the upcoming Red Army attack was more precise than that of the Germans, who believed that the Bagration offensive in the region of Army Group Center had drawn most of the available reserve forces from STAVKA. When Romania's leader, Marshal Antonescu, suggested that Romanian and German divisions be withdrawn to a more defensible position, along the Focșani-Nămoloasa-Brăila line, the new commander of *Heeresgruppe Südukraine, Generaloberst* Johannes Frießner, absolutely refused to consider the idea. Frießner had recently been fired by Hitler after serving only nineteen days (4–23 July) as commander of *Heeresgruppe Nord* because he had ordered a retreat without the Führer's permission. If he were to have requested that Marshal Antonescu's withdrawal plan be considered, he would have likely been removed again by Hitler from his new post as commander of *Heeresgruppe Südukraine.*

At the start of the second Jassy-Kishinev offensive, Frießner's combined German and Romanian force was twenty-three German and twenty-three Romanian divisions. The total number of men amounted to some 440,000 Romanian and 360,000 German troops. The Germans had made an effort to reinforce *6. Armee* and *8. Armee* since the devastating losses incurred between March and July 1944. Some divisions were even above the authorized strength of 10,000 men. Unfortunately for the Germans, 85 percent of the soldiers in both of these German armies were recent replacements or reinforcements that had been sent from the German Replacement Army in the Reich. Only about 15 percent of the men were veterans of previous campaigns. This meant that both armies were at a disadvantage in combat experience. New soldiers tend to die quicker than the older, more seasoned troops who have learned how to survive the trials and tribulations that occur in combat.

For armored protection, the Germans had *10. Panzergrenadier-Division* and *13. Panzer-Division,* while the Romanians had their 1st Armored Division stationed north of the town of Roman. This was the staging area of the division. At the start of the Russian offensive, this Romanian armored division had forty-eight *Panzer IV-H* tanks, twelve *Sturmgeschütz III.-G* assault guns, twenty-four German armored halftracks of the series 250 or 251 variety, and ten TACAM T-60 tank destroyers.[5] When the Russian attack began on 20 August, some elements of 1st Armored Division were still far behind the staging area. The *13. Panzer-Division* would eventually be committed piecemeal when the fighting began. The main *kampfgruppe* of this division would see heavy fighting at Popovka, just south of Bendery. Its armored complement on 13 August, a week before the offensive, was forty-one *Panzer IV-H* tanks, five *Panzer III.-L* tanks, seventeen *Marder II* tank destroyers,[6] and around eighty *Schützenpanzerwagen 250* and *251* armored halftracks. Not counting the assault guns, when the Soviet offensive began, half of the tanks that faced the Red Army were manned by Romanian tank crews.

The Germans also had four assault gun brigades, one of which was *Sturmgeschütz-Brigade 228* under *8. Armee,* and a heavy tank destroyer battalion, *Panzerjäger-Abteilung 93* with a total of some 280 assault guns. Of that number, *Panzerjäger-Abteilung 93* possessed twenty-five *Nashorn* tank destroyers that carried the deadly 88 mm L-43 anti-tank gun. This left 255 vehicles between the four assault gun brigades, which roughly equates to sixty-three to sixty-four vehicles per brigade. Obviously, some brigades had more assault guns than others, so the distribution of the armored fighting vehicles was uneven. Regarding *Sturmgeschütz-Brigade 228*, it lost all of its assault guns during the battles in Romania.[7] The other two assault gun brigades that fought in Romania in August were *Sturmgeschütz-Brigade 236* and *Sturmgeschütz-Brigade 278*. On 10 June 1944, *Sturmgeschütz-Brigade 236* was renamed *Heeres-Sturmartillerie-Brigade 236*. It arrived in the Jassy area on 20 August 1944. The brigade was immediately committed to the fighting and was destroyed there between 20–28 August 1944. The eighty-seven survivors of this brigade were eventually withdrawn and sent to Posen (Poznan) in German annexed Polish territory. They reached the city on 6 October. Another assault gun unit, *Sturmgeschütz-Brigade 278*, which was also attached to *8. Armee*, was completely destroyed in August fighting under *LVII. Panzerkorps* in the region of the Pruth River. *Heeres-Sturmgeschütz-Brigade 286* fought in the area of Kishinev but miraculously survived the Russian onslaught. It would later operate in Transylvania, before withdrawing to Hungary. Later on, it operated in the area of the Gran Bridgehead near Bratislava, Slovakia.

*Heeresgruppe Dumitrescu*, comprising the Romanian 3rd Army and German *6. Armee*, had two divisions as a reserve: *13. Panzer-Division* and the Romanian 1st Cavalry Division. *Heeresgruppe Wohler*, which included the Romanian 4th Army and German *8. Armee*, also had two divisions in reserve: *10. Panzergrenadier-Division* and *153. Feldausbildungs-Division*. These four divisions placed in reserve represented an insufficient quantity of Axis forces that would have been needed to properly stop any Red Army offensive. However, the Germans and Romanians simply had no other forces available. The destruction of Army Group Center

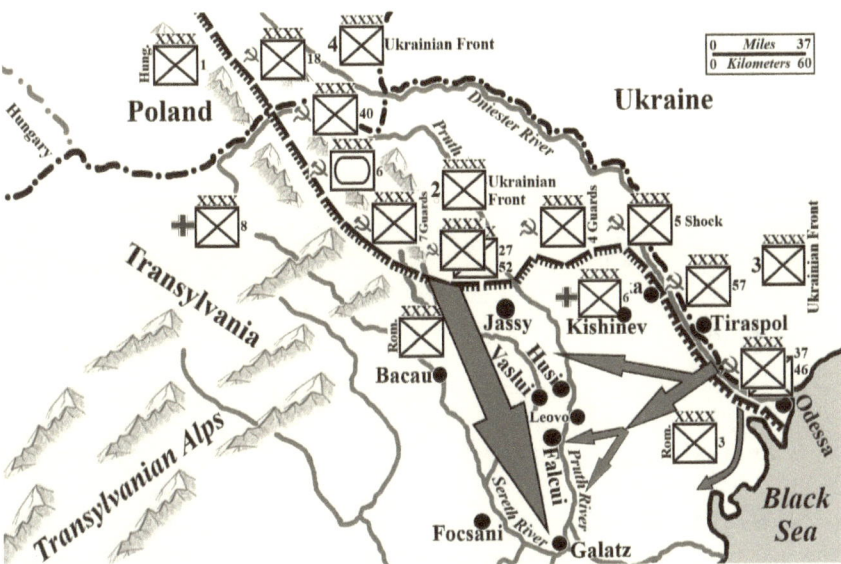

**Figure 31.** The second Jassy-Kishinev offensive, 20–29 August 1944.

and the battles in western Ukraine and eastern Poland between March and early August 1944 had substantially weakened the *Ostheer*. As the battle developed, the employment of these four divisions would prove to be insufficient to stop the Soviet steamroller.

The Russian plan was to breakthrough at four main points in the German and Romanian front line, with the northernmost pincer aiming to capture many crossing points along the Pruth River, once the assaulting units had broken through the Axis line. It only took two days of violent attacks before the Russians broke through the line just west of Jassy (Iasi).

The reserve divisions were thrown into the battle beginning on the first day of the offensive, as were most of the assault gun brigades which *Heeresgruppe Südukraine* possessed. Unfortunately for the Germans, these forces were basically swept aside. By 23 August, for example, *13. Panzer-Division,* which had been committed piecemeal, was no longer a coherent fighting force. As the Russian attack vectors developed, they turned into a double envelopment that trapped a portion of *8. Armee* and most of *6. Armee,* as well as a sizable number of Romanian divisions. The battle was the second time that *6. Armee* had been trapped and virtually destroyed by the Red Army. On 20 August 1944, its order of battle was as follows:

*VII. Armeekorps:*
   *106. Infanterie-Division*
   *370. Infanterie-Division*
   *Romanian 14th Infantry Division*
*XLIV Armeekorps:*
   *62. Infanterie-Division*
   *258. Infanterie-Division*
   *282. Infanterie-Division*
   *335. Infanterie-Division*
*LII. Armeekorps:*
   *161. Infanterie-Division*
   *294. Infanterie-Division*
   *320. Infanterie-Division*
*XXX. Armeekorps:*
   *15. Infanterie-Division*
   *257. Infanterie-Division*
   *302. Infanterie-Division*
   *306. Infanterie-Division*
   *384. Infanterie-Division*

Part of the reason why a double envelopment developed was not merely the speed of the Soviet advance, especially by its tank and mechanized forces, but instead the relatively slow speed of the German and Romanian infantry divisions, which could not withdraw fast enough. In fact, the pressure that the Russian attack placed on the Axis forces also worked to destroy divisional cohesion within these horse-drawn divisions. This, in turn, facilitated the Axis collapse. Shortly after the battle, the Germans took stock of their losses. In total, the *Ostheer* had lost between 150,000 to 200,000 soldiers killed, wounded, or taken prisoner.

The collapse at the front coincided with a coup against Marshal Antonescu in the Romanian capital of Bucharest. This coup was led ostensibly by the Romanian king, Michael, but behind it lay other fingerprints. Michael immediately sued for peace and withdrew from the Axis. A day later, on 24 August, fighting broke out among the former Axis allies between Ploesti and Bucharest. Romanian forces now laid down their arms. As part of the peace treaty, the Russians demanded that the Romanian Army take up arms against the Germans. This is how the Romanian 1st and 4th Army ended up fighting the Germans from September 1944 until the end of the war. Between 22 June 1941 and 8 May 1945, the Germans lost 8,980,000 men killed, wounded, taken prisoner, or missing on the Eastern Front. Of that number, about 900,000 were lost between June and August 1944. That is just over 10 percent of total losses for the entire war on the Eastern Front, taken over a three-month period. This indicates that those months saw very heavy fighting. It also points to the theory that the *Ostheer* began to unravel in the summer of 1944.

## Chapter 6

## THE RED ARMY IN THE BALKANS

### BULGARIA

As early as 17 August 1944, the Bulgarians had informed the German command that they intended to withdraw their forces from Yugoslav-Macedonia and Greek-Thrace. For many months prior, the Bulgarian occupation forces there had either ignored German requests for cooperation or had ceased launching their own anti-partisan drives. The Germans soon learned that the Bulgarians had secretly made a *pactum de non aggrediendo* ('agreement of nonaggression'), or modus vivendi, if you will, with the partisans. Once Romania surrendered and switched sides, the Bulgarians became more belligerent and standoffish. Given this attitude, *Generalfeldmarshall* Maximilian von Weichs, the commander of *Heeresgruppe 'F'*, thought it best to order the Greek islands to be evacuated (except for the vitally important islands of Crete and Rhodes).[1] In addition, his army group was to withdraw to a defensive line running from the island of Corfu, to Ioannina, then to Kalabaka and finally to Olympus.[2]

On 5 September 1944, the Soviet Union declared war on Bulgaria, even though the Bulgarians had never declared war on the USSR. Three days later, elements of the 3rd Ukrainian Front entered Bulgarian territory. Communist-inspired general strikes, as well as mini-revolts led by pro-communist forces in the army and civilian population, broke out all over the country beginning on 6 September. A day after the Russians entered Bulgarian territory, a military coup toppled the existing Bulgarian government. A year earlier, King Boris III had died of natural causes. He was succeeded by his six-year-old son, Simeon II. Due to his young age, a regency was established to rule in his place. The regent was Lieutenant-General of the Artillery Nikola Mihov. It was Mihov's government that was overthrown on 9 September. In its place, a communist regime was installed. Immediately, Bulgaria joined the Allies and began military operations against the Germans.

**Figure 32.** The route of withdrawal for *Army Group 'F'* out of Greece in the fall of 1944. The advance of Russian and Bulgarian armies threatened to cut off the withdrawal route for *Army Group 'F'* in Greece.

In September 1944, three armies from Bulgaria, numbering some 455,000 troops, invaded Yugoslavia. They joined forces with Soviet and Yugoslav forces and advanced to Niš and Skopje with the strategic objective of obstructing the German forces' withdrawal from Greece. Within a month, most of southern and eastern Serbia, plus the Macedonian regions, were liberated. The Bulgarian 1st Army (130,000 strong) later even advanced into Hungary.[3] Beginning in early September, Tito, the leader of the Yugoslav communist partisans, began to threaten German forces stationed in Belgrade from the west, while 3rd Ukrainian Front threatened the Serbian capital from the east. The Bulgarians advanced into Serbia and Macedonia, taking Niš, Krusevac, Pazar, Pec, and Prizren. If the withdrawal route for *Heeresgruppe 'E'* out of Greece could be cut, the Germans would be trapped. The fate of an entire army group hung in the balance. If *Heeresgruppe 'E'* were to have been cut off, approximately 200,000 German troops would be lost. In September 1944, *Heeresgruppe 'F'* (which comprised *2. Panzerarmee* and *Heeresgruppe 'E')* was composed of the following units:

*2. Panzerarmee: General der Artillerie* Maximilian de Angelis
   *XV. Gebirgs-Armeekorps: General der Infanterie* Ernst von Leyser
      *264. Infanterie-Division*
      *373. Infanterie-Division (kroatische Nr. 2)*
      *392. Infanterie-Division (kroatische Nr. 3)*
      *1. Regiment Brandenburg (motorisiert)*
      *4. Regiment Brandenburg (motorisiert)*

   *XXI. Gebirgs-Armeekorps: General der Panzertruppen* Gustav Fehn
      *21. Waffen-Gebirgs-Division der SS 'Skanderbeg'*
      *181. Infanterie-Division*
      *297. Infanterie-Division*
      *SS-Polizeiregiment 14*
      *2. Regiment Brandenburg (motorisiert)*

   *LXIX. Armeekorps: General der Infanterie* Helge Auleb
      *1. Kosaken-Kavallerie-Division*
      *Reserve-Jäger-Regiment 1* (beginning 1944 it was stationed in Karlovac. The regiment was destroyed there in February 1945)[4]

   *V. SS-Freiwilligen-Gebirgs-Armee-Korps: SS-Obergruppenführer und General der Waffen-SS* Artur Phleps
      *7. SS-Freiwilligen-Gebirgs-Division 'Prinz Eugen'*
      *118. Jäger-Division*
      *369. Infanterie-Division (kroatische Nr. 1)*
      *13. kompanie der SS-Polizei-Gebirgsjäger-Regiment 18* (part)

*Heeresgruppe 'E': Generaloberst* Alexander Löhr
   *XXII. Gebirgs-Armeekorps: General der Gebirgsjägertruppen* Hubert Lanz
      *104. Jäger-Division*
      *Festungsbrigade 1017*
      *Festungsbrigade 966*
   *LXVIII. Armeekorps: General der Flieger* Hellmuth Felmy
      *41. Festungs-Division*
      *117. Jäger-Division*
      *SS-Polizei-Gebirgsjäger-Regiment 18* (bulk)
   *XCI. Armeekorps: Generalleutnant* Ulrich Kleemann (18 September to 9 October 1944). Then *General der Infanterie* Werner von Erdmannsdorff.
      *Festungs Brigade 968*

*Kommandeur der Truppen Festung Kreta: General der Infanterie* Friedrich-Wilhelm Müller
    22. Luftlande-Infanterie-Division
    133. Festungs-Division

*Wehrmachtbefehlshaber Südost: General der Infanterie* Hans-Gustav Felber
    Responsible for German forces in Croatia, Serbia & Greece. Then from 26 September to 27 October 1944 Felber became the *Kommandeur des Gebiets des Militärbefehlshabers in Serbien* with the following troops:[5]
    Feldkommandantur 599 (Belgrade)
    Feldkommandantur 809 (Nis)
    Serbisches-Freiwilligen-Korps[6]
    Russisches-Gardekorps[7]

*Wehrmachtbefehlshaber Mazedonien: Generalleutnant* Heinz Scheurlen (appointed in October 1944)
    11. Feld-Division (L)—arriving from Greece

The German supreme command in the Balkans included:
    *Oberbefehlshaber Südost: Generalfeldmarschall* Maximilian von Weichs[8]
    *Befehlshaber Serbien*
    *Befehlshaber Saloniki-Ägäis*
    *Befehlshaber Süd-Griechenland*
    *Befehlshaber Kroatien*
    *Kommandant der Festung Kreta*

## SERBIA

While 2nd Ukrainian Front had turned north upon capturing Bucharest on 30 August, and was advancing through the Transylvanian Alps toward Hungary, 3rd Ukrainian Front was rapidly advancing into Serbia, with the intent of taking Belgrade, the Yugoslav capital. By 25 September, *General der Infanterie* Hans Felber was trying to organize a defense of Serbia. He was able to obtain troops from the following units:

    *4. SS Panzergrenadier-Division 'Polizei'*
    *1. Gebirgs-Division (die Edelweiß-Division)*
    *4. Regiment Brandenburg (motorisiert)*
    *Heeres-Sturmartillerie-Brigade 191* (four batteries)
    *SS-Polizei-Gebirgsjäger-Regiment 18* (Bulk)
    *Grenadier-Regiment 92 (motorisiert)*
    *20. Flak-Division* (spread out between Belgrade, Serbia, and the Albanian border).

**Figure 33.** General reference map of the Balkans in 1941. The major mountain ranges are listed.

On 26 September, a German battle group, *Kampfgruppe Fischer*, comprising *2. Regiment Brandenburg* (minus its First Battalion), plus a battalion of the *1. Gebirgs-Division*, found themselves fighting elements of the Soviet 57th Army five kilometers north of Negotin. The *I. Bataillon, 2. Regiment Brandenburg (motorisiert)*, together with the *I. Reiter-Abteilung, 1. Kavallerie-Regiment, Russisches-Gardekorps*, defended the heights east of D. Milanovac against attacking Soviet units. Soviet attacks against the combined German and Czarist-era Russian force continued into 27 September. As late September wore on, however, more and more pressure was placed on the Axis defenders until slowly they were pushed from their positions. By the time this battle had ended, the Axis forces had engaged not only the Soviet 57th Army but the Yugoslav Partisan 14th Corps as well. The main reason for the German withdrawal was not merely the superiority in numbers of the enemy but also that the Germans and their allies were facing strong Russian armored units. Against them, the German and Czarist Russians only had obsolete French R35 tanks—totally useless against the modern Russian armored vehicles.

As the battle of Belgrade began to develop, more German forces were drawn to the Yugoslav capital. The leading battalion of *SS-Polizei-Gebirgsjäger-Regiment 18* reached Kragujevac, some sixty miles from the capital, as the crow flies. By 25 September, the leading elements of the SS police mountain infantry regiment reached the outskirts of Belgrade. No sooner had they arrived then the unit was ordered to Jabuka. The regiment got there on 25 September, where they were assigned to protect the mountain pass that led to Romania, near the town of Szaskabanya. Soon, however, the Soviet 4th Guards Mechanized Corps appeared. By 28 September, the Germans withdrew to Carbunari. Also defending Belgrade was *Grenadier-Regiment 92 (motorisiert)*. It, too, would suffer heavy losses during the battle for Belgrade. In October, it would withdraw into Bosnia. By 30 September, Straza was captured by elements of 3rd Ukrainian Front. According to one account, as the Germans withdrew toward the Yugoslav capital, they did not have time to bury their dead, nor attend to the wounded, who were left to the tender mercy of the Red Army.[9]

By 3 October, both *SS-Polizei-Gebirgsjäger-Regiment 18* and *Grenadier-Regiment 92 (motorisiert)* were located in Pancevo, just a little over fifteen kilometers (nine and a half miles) from Belgrade. By then, *SS-Polizei-Regiment 5* had returned to Belgrade, after taking part in *Unternehmen Margarethe* in Hungary. This SS police regiment, alongside *SS-Polizei-Gebirgsjäger-Regiment 18* and *Grenadier-Regiment 92,* took part in the defense of Belgrade in October 1944. The 1st Guards Army attacked Pancevo beginning on 4 October. The Germans held the town until they were forced to withdraw on 6 October. The garrison commander for Belgrade, *General der Infanterie* Hans Felber, was demanding that both units hold back the Red Army in order to have sufficient time to organize a defense of the city. After falling back from Pancevo, both regiments (now referred to as *Kampfgruppe Hillebrandt*), were located in Borcsa, just north of the Serbian capital. There they encountered a *Luftwaffe* flak battery that happened to be in the town. With the 88 mm flak guns acting in an anti-tank role, the battle group held off the Russians until 10 October, when they were forced to withdraw into the Serbian capital. It was then that German sappers blew the bridges over the Danube River, giving the defenders a measure of protection. However, moving rapidly from the south were two partisan corps who were bent on liberating Belgrade.

The German defenders were trapped in a slowly closing vise. Inside the city, General Felber had a heavy (105 mm) *Luftwaffe* flak battalion from *20. Flak-Division*, what remained of *SS-Polizei-Gebirgsjäger-Regiment 18* (about 600 men), and *Grenadier-Regiment 92, SS-Polizei-Regiment 5,* plus the equivalent of a regiment of troops, made up from supply, communications, and support units that were stationed in the city. The battle for Belgrade began on 11 October, with 1st Guards Army throwing a heavy barrage of artillery fire from across the Danube

74   *The Bitter End*

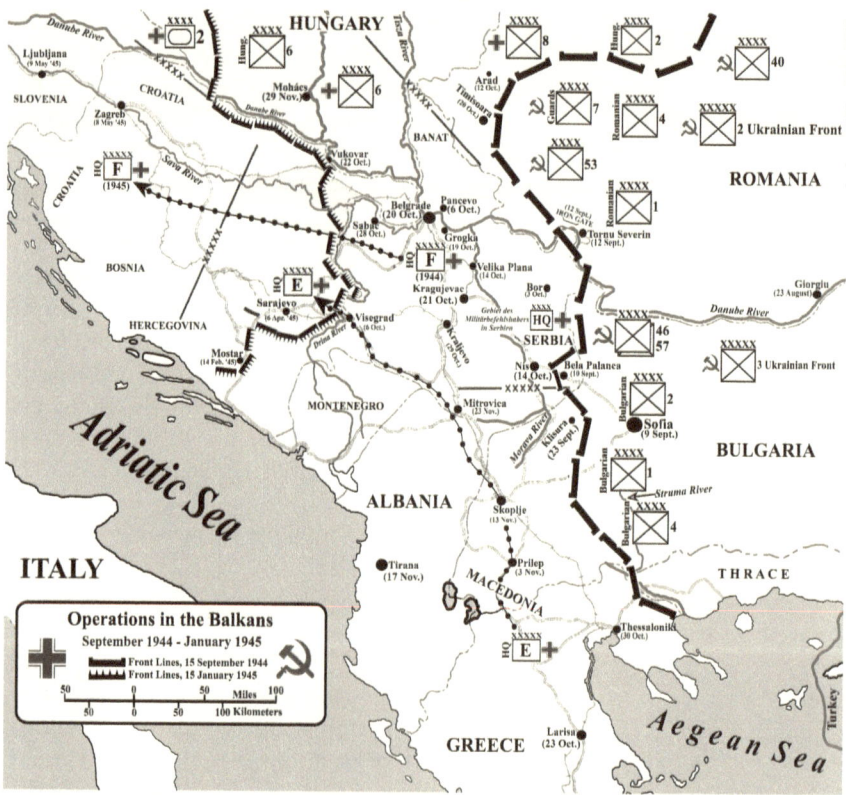

**Figure 34.** Red Army operations in the Balkans, 15 September 1944 to 15 January 1945. The dates listed in parenthesis alongside the town/city name is the date when the locality was liberated by Tito's partisans, the Red Army, or the Bulgarian or Romanian Army.

River. Meanwhile, Russian engineer units were rapidly building pontoon bridges downriver from the city that could support Red Army tanks. The Partisan 1st Army Corps and Partisan 14th Army Corps were also making progress toward the Yugoslav capital. On the afternoon of 14 October, Soviet tanks appeared southeast of the city, supported by motorized infantry. Once again, the call went out for German tanks to stop the Red Army tank advance. However, the only available 'armor' which the German command had were (once again) obsolete French or Italian tanks. Six days later, on 20 October, the Russians entered Belgrade.

It was at this point that Joseph Stalin made a strategic decision. He left the reconquest of the rest of Yugoslavia to the Bulgarians and to Tito's partisan army. The 3rd Ukrainian Front now turned north, skirting Belgrade on its way to the Yugoslav-Hungarian border. Army Group 'E', which was withdrawing from Greece, was saved. Stalin obviously considered the defeat of Hungary far more important than the liberation of Yugoslavia. He reasoned (rightly), that

Tito's partisan army would eventually accomplish the job of expelling the Axis from Yugoslavia and, therefore, did not need Russia's help. Stalin, however, also understood that after the war he would have to tread lightly when it came to Yugoslavia. While the USSR could invade a Warsaw-Pact nation (as it did during the Czech spring of 1968), taking over Yugoslavia in a similar fashion was out of the question. The numerous mountain ranges and vast woods of Yugoslavia meant that any occupying power would suffer the same fate that the Germans were now experiencing. Yugoslavia, therefore, was a different matter and required a different approach than brute military force. Tito knew this, and this fact allowed the Croatian communist leader to sometimes go against the interest of the USSR without suffering any consequences.

## Chapter 7

# INTO CENTRAL EUROPE

### THE CARPATHIAN-DUKLIANSKY OFFENSIVE: 8 SEPTEMBER TO 28 OCTOBER 1944

On 8 September 1944, the Soviet 38th Army (1st Ukrainian Front) aimed to break the German front at Krosno, push through the Dukliansky Pass, and advance one hundred kilometers to Prešov and Poprad in less than a week. This operation was launched in order to support the Slovak Army uprising. This rapid timetable, however, was contingent upon the cooperation of the now-defunct East Slovak Army. The East Slovak Army had been effectively defeated by 1 September, during the early stages of the Slovak National Uprising. This occurred after the Germans launched *Unternehmen Katzenkopf* (Operation Cat's Head), aimed at disarming the East Slovak Army. The operation unfolded with a surprise attack by Wehrmacht forces. Due to poor coordination, lack of preparation, and divided loyalties among the Slovak forces, the Germans quickly neutralized the East Slovak Army. The 1st Ukrainian Front, which had been consolidating after a protracted advance over the preceding two months, now lacked sufficient manpower and supplies. Because of the unanticipated developments in Slovakia, its attack plan had to be hastily planned in less than a week. Thus, on a narrow front and with little preparation, the 38th Army was attacking frontally into the defensively formidable Carpathian Mountains.

Nevertheless, by 11 September, the German second line of defense had been broken and a two-kilometer-wide breach was made. The town of Krosno was taken by the Red Army that same day. By nightfall on 12 September, the Russian 38th Army reconnaissance units had successfully crossed into Slovak territory. Taking a risk, the 1st Guards Cavalry Corps was sent through this narrow corridor behind the German lines. On 14 September, the Germans successfully sealed the breach in their front line, effectively cutting off 1st Guards Cavalry Corps. The Germans were able to achieve this because of the timely arrival of the Saxon *357*.

*Infanterie-Division.* The area was extremely mountainous, which was not conducive for cavalry operations. Soon, most of the horses began to tire, get hurt, or die. The corps' mobility was thus affected. To make matters worse, 1st Guards Cavalry Corps had not carried extra ammunition or supplies. Cut off from further provisions, the corps had to make a breakout attempt to reach the Russian lines. After the battle, 1st Guards Cavalry Corps was so badly shaken that it had to be withdrawn from the front and reorganized.

On 6 October, Soviet and Czechoslovak forces eventually captured the southern tip of Dukla Pass. From 17–18 October, approximately 35,000 German troops crossed the border from Hungary into Slovakia. Stalin took advantage of the situation and ordered 2nd Ukrainian Front to Budapest. By focusing his attention on Hungary and Austria instead of Slovakia, Stalin effectively ended support for the Slovak uprising. As a result, the battle for the Dukla Pass was a fight that need not have taken place. The decision by the Red Army to enter Slovakia when it did, accompanied by the 1st Czechoslovak Corps (operating under Russian auspices), now appeared more a political decision than military strategy. The problem with this was that when Russian and Czechoslovak losses began to pile in the face of a stiff and hardened German defense, no one had the nerve to tell Stalin that the attack should be called off. Only after the Germans crushed the uprising was the offensive ended.

The forces involved in the fighting included elements of 1st Ukrainian Front (Marshal Ivan Konev), including the 1st Czechoslovak Corps. Specifically, the 1st Guards Army of 1st Ukrainian Front was committed. Elements of 4th Ukrainian Front (38th Army) were also used. The German and Hungarian forces that took part in the battle were all grouped under one command: *Armeegruppe Heinrici.* It included units from *1. Panzerarmee* and 1st Hungarian Army. In turn, *Armeegruppe Heinrici* formed part of *Heeresgruppe A (4. Panzerarmee, 17. Armee,* and *Armeegruppe Heinrici). Heeresgruppe A* was created on 23 September 1944 in southern Poland and the surrounding Carpathian Mountains by simply renaming *Heeresgruppe Nordukraine.* The army group was deployed to defend southern Poland and Slovakia. It was responsible for *1. Panzerarmee, 4. Panzerarmee, 9. Armee,* and the newly reformed *17. Armee.*[1] The particular German and Hungarian divisions that took part in the defense of what the Soviets referred to as the Carpathian-Dukliansky offensive included:

German: *1. Panzer-Division, 68. Infanterie-Division, 75. Infanterie-Division, 254. Infanterie-Division,* and *357. Infanterie-Division*
Hungarian: 16th Infantry Division, 20th Infantry Division, and 24th Infantry Division

Russian and Czech divisions that took part in the battle were as follows:

Russian: 1st Guards Cavalry Division, 2nd Cavalry Division, 3rd Cavalry Division, 67th Guards Rifle Division, 107th Rifle Division, 129th Rifle

Division, 140th Rifle Division, 183rd Rifle Division, and 271st Rifle Division

Czech: 1st Czechoslovak Infantry Division, 2nd Czechoslovak Parachute Brigade, 3rd Czechoslovak Infantry Brigade, and 1st Czechoslovak Tank Brigade

The 67th Guards Rifle Division was one of the leading divisions earmarked for the main breakthrough effort during the offensive. As a result, it took part in some of the fiercest fighting and took losses accordingly. The 107th Rifle Division played a significant role in the battle, pushing through German defensive lines.

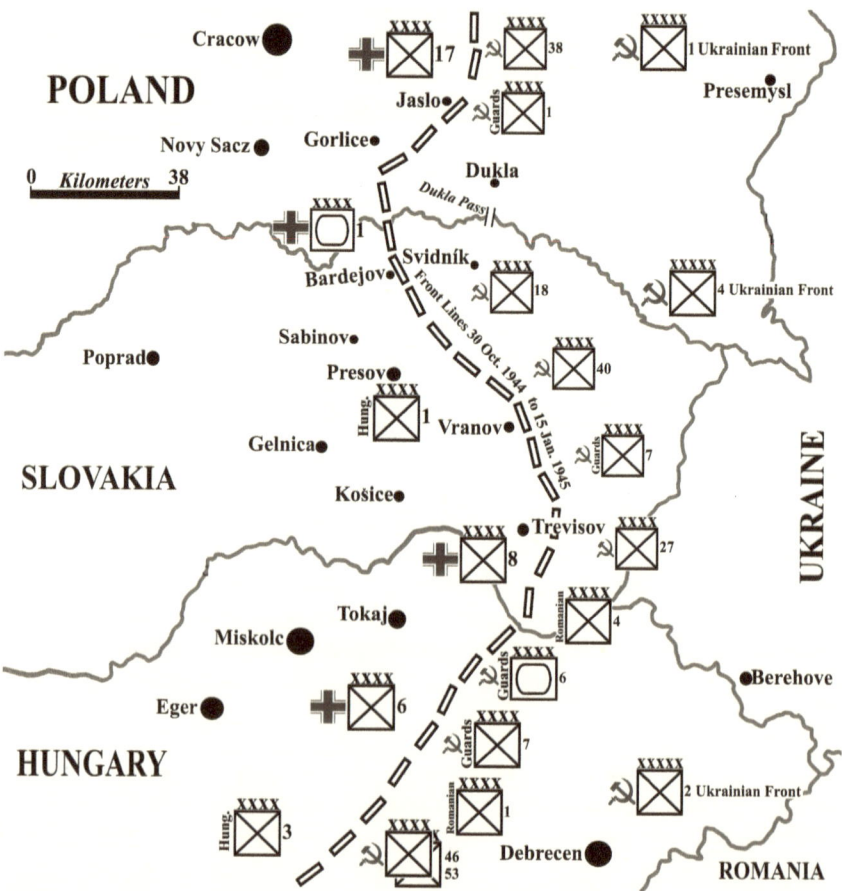

**Figure 35.** German and Russian positions at the end of October 1944 along the western Carpathian Mountains. The front line in this region remained static until about the middle of January 1945, when the Russians renewed their offensive across the expanse of the Eastern Front.

107th Rifle Division also took heavy losses. The 140th Rifle Division was also heavily involved in the offensive, contributing to the Soviet efforts to capture the high ground and pass through. It, too, sustained heavy casualties. The 183rd Rifle Division was actually operating under the 1st Ukrainian Front but was eventually committed to the fighting as well. The 271st Rifle Division, like 183rd Rifle Division, was part of the Soviet 1st Ukrainian Front's reserve forces. This division was eventually brought into the battle to support the main assault after initial Soviet advances were slowed by stiff German and Hungarian resistance.

The Soviet 38th Army was led by General Kirill Moskalenko. It was tasked with breaking through the pass. The previously mentioned divisions, along with additional support from other rifle divisions and artillery units, fought in grueling conditions. The battle resulted in heavy casualties for both sides, with the Soviets and Czechoslovak forces suffering significantly higher losses as they tried to break through the strong German and Hungarian defenses. Despite these challenges, the Soviets eventually captured the pass, although at a great cost in lives. During its East Carpathian offensive from 8 September to 28 October, the Red Army lost 126,211 men. This amounted to just over a third of the total number of troops that it had employed in the operation. As for the Czechs, the 1st Czechoslovak Corps, which at the time was part of the 1st Ukrainian Front (Marshal Ivan Konev), worked closely with Soviet forces. It played a major role in securing a path through the Carpathian Mountains into Slovakia. As a result, it saw intense combat as well, and accordingly sustained heavy casualties. When the Red Army finally captured Dukla Pass, the Germans slowly withdrew into eastern Slovakia, giving stiff resistance as they retreated. Thereupon this area of the front quieted down. During the period from the end of October 1944 to about the middle of January 1945, the front line remained relatively static, with little or no progress being made by Soviet forces. During this time, the Red Army once again waited for its supply and support services to catch up and for new replacements to arrive. The plan was to drive into Germany and central Europe at the start of 1945 and end the war.

## THE BATTLE FOR DEBRECEN

The Battle of Debrecen (6–29 October 1944) was a bellwether to see if the Red Army could reach Budapest before 1945. It was also a battle where both forces employed large numbers of tanks. It was also very costly. Between 6 October to 6 November, German and Hungarian losses included 100,000 killed or wounded and 42,000 men captured by the Red Army.[2] The 2nd Ukrainian Front (General Rodion Malinovsky) was ordered to capture Budapest. Malinovsky was to attack through a region south of the city of Arad. The 53rd Army, 6th Guards Tank Army, and Cavalry Mechanized Group Gorshkov were to attack near Oradea, in the direction of Debrecen. If a breakthrough occurred, the rest of 2nd Ukrainian

Front (Cavalry Mechanized Group Pliyev, the 46th Soviet Army, and the 1st Romanian Army) would take advantage of the tear in the German lines and exploit it. Facing the attacking forces of 2nd Ukrainian Front was the weakened 3rd Hungarian Army. When the attack began on 6 October, the first Hungarian unit to feel its fury was the Szekler Border Guard Division. This division was involved in protecting the Hungarian-Romanian border and was called into action as the Red Army approached. It was largely composed of troops recruited from the Székely population, an ethnic Hungarian group from Transylvania. The division almost disintegrated on the first day of the attack. Hastily put together from border guard units, it could not withstand the Soviet onslaught. The other divisions of 3rd Hungarian Army included three infantry divisions.

The 6th Hungarian Infantry Division was one of the key infantry units deployed in defense around Debrecen. The 20th Hungarian Infantry Division played a role in defending the region around Debrecen and was involved in heavy combat. The 25th Hungarian Infantry Division was another unit tasked with holding back the enemy assault. Like its sister divisions, it was understrength and faced difficulties maintaining cohesive lines due to the overwhelming Soviet forces. The 3rd Hungarian Army possessed two mobile divisions: the 1st Cavalry Division and 1st Armored Division. The 1st Cavalry Division was one of the few remaining mounted units, used mainly for mobility in difficult terrain. However, cavalry units were increasingly motorized by this stage of the war, but the 1st Cavalry Division depended principally on horses.

The 1st Armored Division was one of Hungary's few armored divisions, though by October 1944, it had been heavily depleted and had perhaps fifty to sixty operational tanks and assault guns.[3] By then, the division had suffered heavy attrition during previous engagements and was struggling to replace lost equipment due to shortages in production and supplies. The difficult terrain and lack of adequate maintenance facilities also contributed to the reduction in operational tanks, as many were lost or rendered inoperable due to mechanical issues rather than direct combat. The division was equipped with some German *Panzer IV* tanks and *Sturmgeschütz III.* assault guns. What few assault guns there were were parceled out to the division's infantry as a way to bolster their defense. However, most of its armor was composed of the Turán I and II tanks. The division would operate in conjunction with German panzer divisions around Debrecen throughout the battle. Although it fought with great bravery, it would prove insufficient to stop the Soviet armored assault.[4] On 6 October, two armored corps and five mechanized corps of 2nd Ukrainian Front attacked along a 160-kilometer front stretching from Mako to Nagyvarad. The 3rd Hungarian Army, which possessed only seventy tanks and assault guns, would face off against the twenty-two cavalry and infantry divisions of 2nd Ukrainian Front, supported by 627 tanks.

By 7 October, the leading elements of 2nd Ukrainian Front had advanced about forty miles when it encountered the German *III. Panzerkorps (1. Panzer-Division, 23. Panzer-Division)* of *1. Panzerarmee*. The two panzer divisions did their best to stop the Soviet attack, but all they managed to do was to delay the northern pincer of the Russian attack by making the Red Army advance slow down to less than seven miles by the morning of 8 October. The Germans, seeing that a breakthrough along the lines of 3rd Hungarian Army had occurred near Arad, brought up the *76. Infanterie-Division* to replace *23. Panzer-Division,* which was now ordered south to the area of Arad in hopes that it could plug the gap there. While *1. Panzer-Division* delayed the lead elements of 6th Guards Tank Army, playing for time, the line regiments of the Brandenburg *76. Infanterie-Division* were able to establish a hastily built defense line that slowly held. Eventually, this Red Army northern attack group was stalled near the town of Oradea.

In addition, *Panzer-Division Feldherrnhalle* was ordered to the Tisza River crossings to defend against any Red Army unit that might slip through the German and Hungarian defenses. The *Panzer-Division Feldherrnhalle* was a recent creation. Its original unit, *60. Panzergrenadier-Division,* had been destroyed during the Soviet 1944 summer offensive against Army Group Center. The remnants of that division were brought first to Germany, where it received replacements and new divisional units. It was then sent to Mezőkövesd in Hungary to reform. The division didn't really change its name from *60. Panzergrenadier-Division* until 27 November 1944, when it officially became known as *Panzer-Division Feldherrnhalle.* One of the reasons why the divisional title was not changed immediately was to help deceive enemy intelligence. This division would also feature prominently during the battle for the Hungarian capital.

The tank battle of Debrecen, which took place from 9 to 20 October, was caused by the Soviet Union's advance and the German army's quick reaction and concentration in the great Hungarian plain to that threat. The German-Hungarian forces took up their positions with eleven divisions and 227 tanks and assault guns against the mechanized Pliyev and Gorskov Groups and the Soviet 53rd Army and 6th Guards Tank Army. These Red Army forces were markedly superior, given the employment of not only the T-34/85 tanks but also JS-1 and JS-2 (Joseph Stalin) tanks as well. The Soviets had a total of thirty-nine divisions and brigades, supported by 773 tanks and assault guns. However, Malinovsky's units were weak because they were divided into multiple tactical groups that were also attacking in different directions.

In spite of a stiff German and Hungarian defense, by 10 October, the 2nd Ukrainian Front had established several bridgeheads along the Tisza River. Now the leading Soviet columns were less than forty-seven miles from the Hungarian capital, Budapest. The next day a combined Hungarian and German counterattack forced the Russians back to the Tisza River area. In response to increased enemy counterattacks, the Soviets ordered the deployment of four Romanian divisions to the Tisza River bridgeheads below the town of Szolnok. However, these Romanian troops fared poorly against a revitalized German and Hungarian counterattack. Newly arriving forces, including two mobile divisions, *24. Panzer-Division,* and *4. SS Panzergrenadier-Division 'Polizei',* plus a heavy tank battalion *(schwere Panzer-Abteilung 503),* caused havoc among the Romanian divisions.

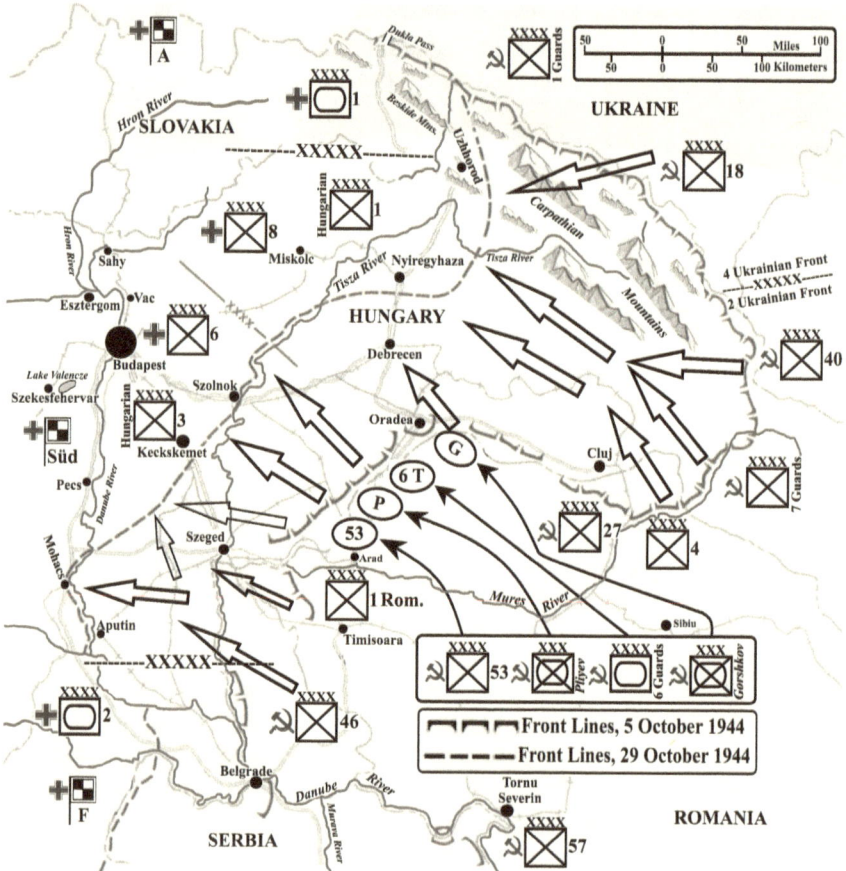

**Figure 36.** Operations along the Romanian-Hungarian border, 8–29 October 1944.

On 8 October, elements of Cavalry Mechanized Group Pliyev and *23. Panzer-Division* clashed near the town of Hajdúszoboszló. By 9 October, the town was in Russian hands. The *23. Panzer-Division* thereupon turned toward Debrecen, where it became part of its defense. On 14 October, 2nd Ukrainian Front captured Oradea after a vicious tank battle that cost both sides over a hundred tanks. After this tank battle, the panzer divisions of *1. Panzerarmee* were depleted. It was in the middle of October that 4th Ukrainian Front, which had been idle during the first week of the offensive, opened up with a massive artillery barrage. With German and Hungarian forces fully committed, several Romanian divisions were committed to the fighting at Debrecen, reinforcing the divisions of 6th Guards Tank Army and 27th Army. With this influx of fresh troops, Debrecen was captured between 19–20 October. At this point, the German *8. Armee* (*General der Infanterie* Otto Wöhler) became cut off. The Germans, however, reacted quickly and counterattacked with a large force that included the Bavarian *3. Gebirgs-Division*, the Saxon *15. Infanterie-Division*, the *8. SS Kavallerie-Division 'Florian Geyer'*, the *1. Panzer-Division*, and *23. Panzer-Division*. A breach was made in the Red Army encirclement on 24 October through which the survivors of *8. Armee* were able to withdraw (26–28 October).

The German armored counterattack at Nyíregyháza had saved the *8. Armee* from encirclement and eventual destruction. The German front line was also (temporarily) stabilized and a new front line established. The German and Hungarian forces had stopped the Red Army advance on Budapest, but only temporarily. For example, Nyíregyháza was recaptured by the Red Army on 30 October. Still, the Germans had bled the Russians, especially several corps' commands under 2nd Ukrainian Front. This did not come cheaply. The Hungarian and German forces suffered 53,000 casualties, while the Russians (including their new Romanian allies) had lost more than 117,000 men killed, wounded, missing, or captured. Of that number, approximately 33,500 were Romanian casualties.[5]

Tank losses were about 500 for the Soviets and around 200 for the Germans and their Hungarian ally. The Germans and Hungarians had lost around 490 guns while the Red Army and Romanian Army lost a total of 1,656 guns. Although the losses were far greater on the Russian side, the battle was seen ultimately as a victory for the Red Army, even though the Germans were able to halt the offensive short of Budapest. While the Russians could afford to take such heavy losses, the Germans could not. The offensive had not been the blitzkrieg that the Russians wanted, but it did get them to within 60 to 120 miles (depending on the location of the Red Army units) from Budapest. This was well within striking distance of the Hungarian capital. The Red Army would eventually reach Budapest on 7 November 1944. By 24 December, the Soviets would encircle Budapest. A siege now began of the city, which lasted fifty days, until the capital's surrender on 13 February 1945.

## THE WESTERN CARPATHIAN OFFENSIVE, 12 JANUARY TO 18 FEBRUARY 1945

During the winter of 1944–1945, STAVKA, the Soviet Supreme High Command, had time to plan the next blow against German and Hungarian forces in the western Carpathian Mountains. STAVKA left the details of just exactly how the Red Army was to accomplish this to the local front commanders. The 4th Ukrainian Front, 2nd Ukrainian Front, together with together with the 1st Czechoslovak Corps and 1st and 4th Romanian Army, were to clear the enemy from the region. For the offensive, a total of 482,000 Soviet troops would be used. The 1st Czechoslovak Corps, recently reinforced to a strength of 11,500 men, was also to be used. Finally, the Romanian 1st and 4th Army would deploy 99,300 men for the operation.

The principal German force in the region was *1. Panzerarmee,* but before the offensive was over, it would involve *8. Armee,* the 1st Hungarian Army, as well as part of *17. Armee.* The *1. Panzerarmee* had been bled in the previous battles between August and October 1944. At the start of the offensive, the army likely had some 100,000 to 110,000 soldiers, though this varied as units were reinforced or transferred to other sectors. This was significantly lower than its estimated strength of around 160,000 men in October 1944. Many of its troops were now understrength divisions or hastily formed units. The *8. Armee* consisted of a mixture of infantry divisions, panzer divisions, and panzergrenadier divisions, as well as other supporting units. It had perhaps around 90,000 to 100,000 men. By January 1945, these divisions were understrength, with some infantry divisions operating with only 50 to 70 percent of their authorized manpower. The 1st Hungarian Army had perhaps 80,000 men. The *17. Armee,* which was positioned in southern Poland and partially in Slovakia, possessed about 100,000 men. Similarly, its divisions were also badly depleted. Although they took more losses, the Russians slowly advanced. By 31 January, the 4th Ukrainian Front had reached the Soła River, along a line stretching through the towns of Liptovský Mikuláš, Liptovský Hrádok, Jablonka, and Żywiec. By early March 1945, the 3rd Ukrainian Front had advanced up to the Gran (Hron) River. Because of this, Germany lost control of the Ore Mountains in Slovakia (in the Spiš and Gemer region), which were important to the German war industry.

## Chapter 8

## BUDAPEST AND VIENNA

### THE SIEGE OF BUDAPEST,
### 24 DECEMBER TO 13 FEBRUARY 1945

The Second and Third Ukrainian Fronts resumed their push to encircle Budapest on 5 December, as the Fourth Guards Army neared the northern end of Lake Balaton. The 3rd Ukrainian Front, employing the 46th Army, launched an assault from Csepel Island over the Danube River's west channel to Ercsi. Simultaneously, the 6th and 7th Guards Tank Armies tore through the area beyond Hatvan. Malinovskiy's advance (2nd Ukrainian Front) reached Vac on the Danube River bend, north of Budapest on the eighth, while Tolbukhin's closed the line Lake Balaton-Lake Velencze to the southwest of the settlement. The Axis forces were so stretched thin, that between Budapest and Lake Valencze there were only 2,500 German and Hungarian troops holding a nineteen-mile-long front. Clearly these forces were insufficient. By 23 December, 4th Guards Army had taken Bicske, thus cutting the road and rail line running west out of Budapest. A day later, it was no longer possible for the German and Hungarian divisions to withdraw from Budapest. This had occurred because the Führer wanted the Hungarian capital, as well as a small bridgehead over the Danube River, to be held for a possible future counteroffensive. On 26 December, 3rd Ukrainian Front reached Esztergom, completing the encirclement of Budapest.

Five days after Budapest was surrounded, on 29 December, Adolf Hitler declared the city a *'Festungsstadt'* (fortress city). The German forces defending Budapest were under the control of *IX. Waffen-Gebirgs-Armeekorps der SS*, whose commander was of *SS-Obergruppenführer und General der Waffen-SS* Karl Pfeffer-Wildenbruch. The units trapped in the city included: *13. Panzer-Division* (much reduced), *271. Volksgrenadier-Division, 8. SS-Kavallerie-Division 'Florian Geyer', 22. SS-Freiwilligen-Kavallerie-Division 'Maria Theresia', schwere Panzer Abteilung 503, SS-Polizei-Regiment 1,* plus other smaller forces. Hungarian troops trapped in the city were

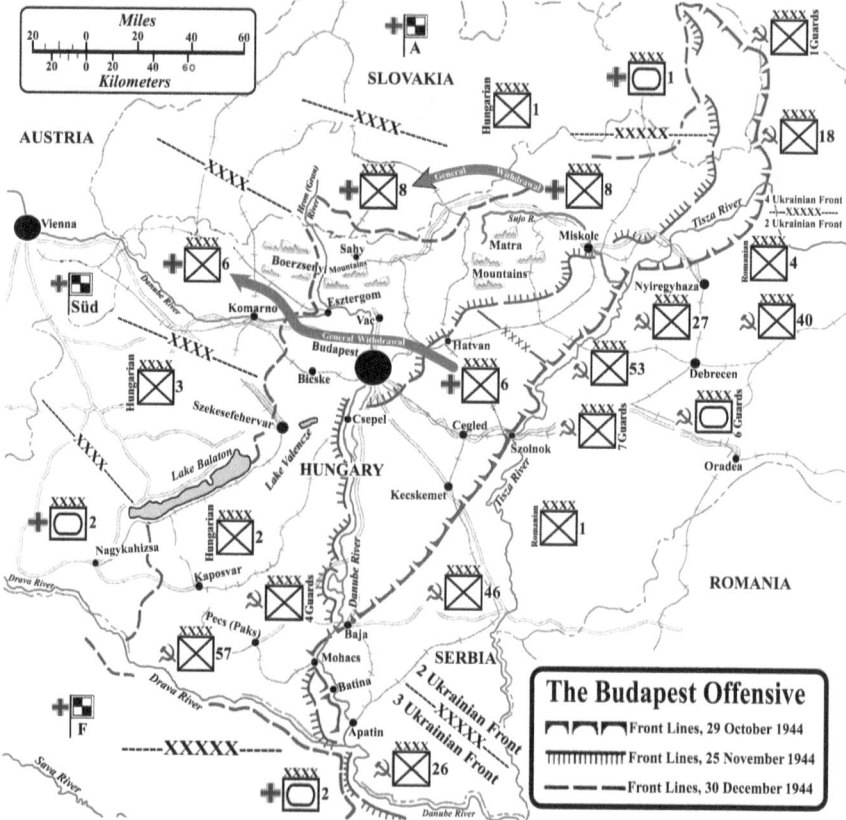

**Figure 37.** Operations in Hungary during the Budapest Offensive. The map covers operations from 29 October to 30 December 1944.

primarily from the 3rd Hungarian Army and included remnants of various divisions, many of which were already weakened from earlier fighting. For the defense of their capital, the Hungarians could count on 1st Armored Division, 1st Cavalry Division, 10th Infantry Division, 12th Reserve-Division, plus other smaller odds and ends. Roughly some 80,000 men were now surrounded in the Hungarian capital. Of this number, slightly more than half were Hungarian troops. The defenders could count on 117 anti-tank guns and about 125 tanks and assault guns.

The threat that the capture of Budapest posed was not merely to the collapse of Hungarian resistance, but also the loss of around 80,000 men. *Generaloberst* Johannes Friesner, the commander of *Heeresgruppe Süd,* was relieved of his command by Hitler, who claimed he was unable to stop the Red Army advance. It didn't matter to Hitler that no German general could have prevented the Soviet advance, given the weakened German and Hungarian forces. The Führer was looking for an excuse to explain the current military reversal, and Friesner was best positioned to be the fall guy. He was relieved on 22 December, and in his place, Hitler placed *General der Infanterie* Otto Wöhler. Determined to try and relieve the trapped Budapest garrison, Wöhler planned *Unternehmen Konrad*, a plan he devised that would eventually involve three separate attacks. Hitler had given permission for *IV. SS-Panzerkorps* to be transferred from *Heeresgruppe Mitte* so its forces could be used for the attack. The corps contained 3. SS-Panzer-Division 'Totenkopf' and 5. SS-Panzer-Division 'Wiking'. This SS panzer corps would be the principal strike force of the relief attempt. The operation was planned in three phases, named Konrad I, II, and III:

> *Unternehmen Konrad-I.* This first phase of the operation was launched on 1 January 1945 and was led by the panzer divisions of *IV. SS-Panzerkorps* from the area around Tata. The attack was eventually halted by a combination of anti-tank units and Soviet armor near Bitschke (Bicske).
> *Unternehmen Konrad-II.* This second phase of the operation was launched on 7 January 1945. It was also led by *IV. SS-Panzerkorps,* which now attacked from Esztergom. The attack was also halted by the Red Army, this time near Hohenberg (Pilisszentkereszt).
> *Unternehmen Konrad-III.* This third phase of the operation was launched on 17 January 1945 and was likewise led by *IV. SS-Panzerkorps,* with an additional armored element: *III. Panzerkorps.* The attack was launched south of Budapest near Stuhlweißenburg (Székesfehérvár). The Germans were aiming to encircle no less than ten Soviet divisions while also trying to break the siege of Budapest.

The German divisions involved in *Konrad III* stopped just south of Ertschi (Ercsi). It was actually *General der Infanterie* Wöhler who ordered a halt to the offensive. He did so because he feared (rightly) that his flanks would be exposed to Soviet flanking attack, given that *IV. SS-Panzerkorps* was short on supporting infantry. Although it was a militarily sound decision, the order infuriated the commander of *IV. SS-Panzerkorps, SS-Obergruppenführer und Generale der Waffen-SS* Herbert Otto Gille, who now realized that the sacrifices his men had made advancing deep into the enemy line were now for naught. The operation had begun with high hopes. When the offensive began, the Germans had been able to concentrate around fifty to sixty tanks per kilometer of front line. This concentration of armor had not been achieved by the *Ostheer* since the Kursk offensive, almost a year and a half ago. Faced with a determined and well-planned assault, 3rd Ukrainian Front employed the same tactic which, ironically, had defeated the German *Zitadelle* offensive in July 1943. The Russians quickly organized a defense in depth, some twenty-five to thirty kilometers deep. In it, they dug trenches, placed anti-tank obstacles covered by machine gun and anti-tank fire, placed anti-tank and anti-personnel mines, prepared deadly ambushes, and held their armored reserves in case the Germans managed to get through. As was attested during the

Russo-German War, and Putin's current war on Ukraine, the Russians were, and still are, masters of defense.

During the fighting for the city, approximately 70,000 Hungarian Jews were living in appalling conditions in the Budapest Ghetto. The German and Hungarian garrison, including the civilian population, was starving. The condition of these Jewish people in the ghetto was even worse, but most survived the siege and the war. About 15,000 either starved to death, were killed during the siege by artillery fire, or were shot by the Nazis. What likely saved the majority of them was the rapid Soviet advance, which prevented their annihilation at the hands of their enemies. That the Nazis did not complete the mass execution of this large Jewish population is puzzling at first, given their track record and the fact that a good portion of the Budapest garrison was composed of *Waffen-SS* troops.

The likely reason why they were spared probably has to do with the fact that, from the very beginning of the siege, the Red Army continued to press their attacks against the German and Hungarian defenders. It would have been almost impossible for the SS to organize and implement the mass murder by shooting, of some 70,000 people in the midst of the siege. In addition, the writing was clearly on the wall. Even to the most fanatical SS trooper had to know that retribution would soon come to those who had been involved in war crimes. That, too, likely held back the Nazis and Hungarian fascists from murdering these people. In the concentration camps, however, the opposite proved to be true. As the Allied front lines came closer to the Reich, the SS in these camps increased their tempo of murder, all in an attempt to kill as many people as possible before the arrival of Allied forces could put a stop to it.

Although the siege of Budapest only lasted around fifty days, approximately 38,000 Hungarian civilians died of starvation or were killed or maimed from the effects of the constant Russian artillery barrage and air bombardment. Stalin wanted Budapest captured quickly, so the Red Army was ordered to storm the city, regardless of losses. Pest, which was on the east bank of the Danube River, was taken between December 1944 and the first week of January 1945. Csepel Island, which lay in the southern part of the city, was captured by Soviet marines on 9 January. By 18 January, the defenders had withdrawn from the eastern half of Budapest. Resupply proved difficult and eventually impossible given the limited space. The Russians never ceased firing rounds at the city. By early February 1945, the defenders were on the verge of breaking.

Lieutenant Colonel Oskar Varikhazi, the commander of the 6th Hungarian Infantry Regiment, alongside 300 other officers and men of what remained of the unit, crossed the lines and surrendered to Russian forces on 11 February 1945. The surrender of this regiment was like a signal notifying the garrison commander that the discipline of the defenders was quickly slipping away. Acknowledging that the end was in sight, *SS-Obergruppenführer und General der Waffen-SS* Pfeffer-Wildenbruch ordered his men to prepare a breakout from the city. To do this, they needed to cross the Russian lines in order to escape the closing Red Army

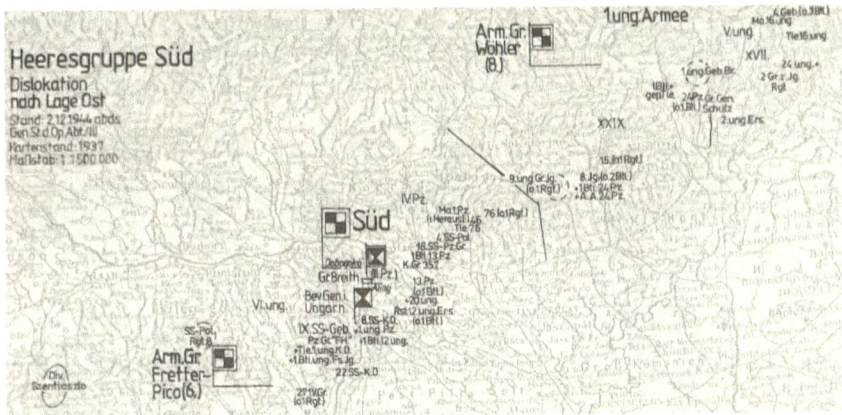

**Figure 38.** This German *Kriegsgliederung Karte* shows the northern and central sectors of Army Group South as of 2 December 1944. The remaining part of Army Group South as it stood on that date is shown in the next figure (Figure 39).

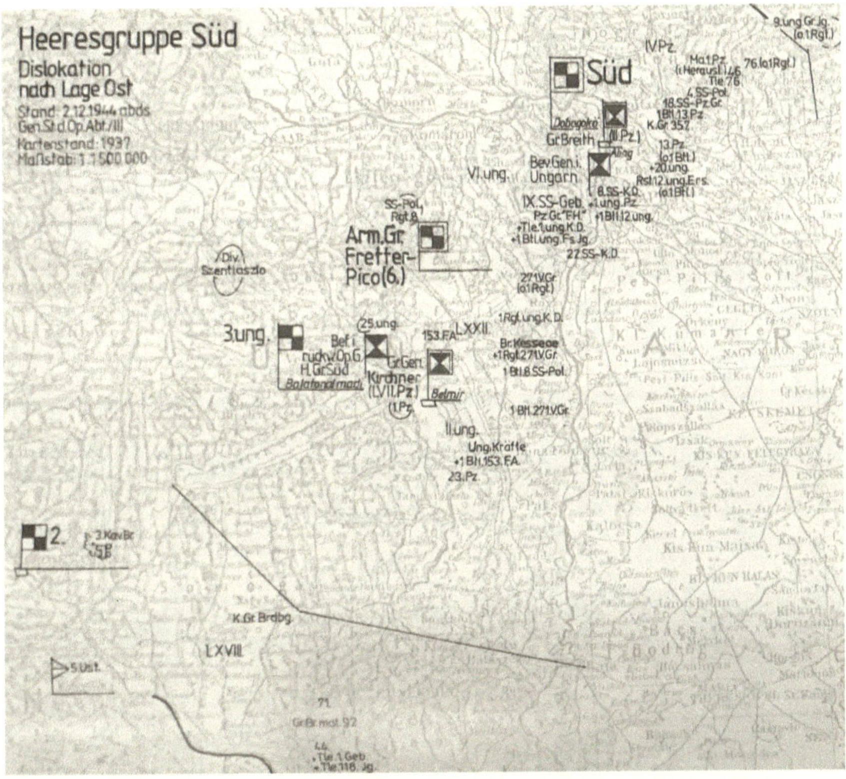

**Figure 39.** This German map overlaps the *Kriegsgliederung Karte* shown in Figure 38, and also shows the southern sector of Army Group South on 2 December 1944.

vise. On the night of 11 February, most of the remaining 28,000 German and Hungarian defenders attempted a breakout from Budapest. Only a small number of troops chose to stay behind in the doomed city. The breakout was poorly planned and met with heavy Soviet resistance.

The troops attempted to break out in small groups under the cover of darkness, but they had to traverse difficult terrain, including hilly and wooded areas, which slowed them down and exposed them to Soviet fire. Only a small fraction, around 600 to 800 soldiers, managed to escape and reach the German lines. The vast majority of the German and Hungarian troops, along with some civilians who attempted to flee with them, were either killed during the breakout or captured by Soviet forces. Many were taken prisoner and sent to Soviet labor camps in Siberia. Some leading members of the Hungarian fascist 'Arrow Cross' movement, like László Endre, were caught in the escape attempt, and were later tried and executed for treason. The failed breakout attempt marked the final collapse of Axis resistance in Budapest. Two days later, on 13 February 1945, the city officially surrendered, and Soviet forces gained complete control of the Hungarian capital, which was acknowledged by the raising of the flag of the Soviet Union atop Castle Hill (Buda Castle).

**Figure 40.** Positions of 6. *Armee* in Slovakia on 1 February 1945

## DER LETZTE ANGRIFF

The last phase in the eventual capture of Vienna really began on 16 March, with the Soviet counteroffensive launched against a German attack, called *Unternehmen Frühlingserwachen* (Operation Spring Awakening). This was the last German counterattack of World War II. It took place south of Budapest, around Lake Balaton. The purpose of the offensive was to protect the Hungarian oil field at Großkanizsa (Nagykanizsa), which lay close to the border with Croatia. A secondary objective was to delay the Red Army advance on Vienna. The German plan, led by *SS-Oberstgruppenführer und General der Waffen-SS* Sepp Dietrich's *6. Panzerarmee*, involved pushing Soviet forces back from the area and thus protecting the oil fields. The offensive began on 6 March 1945, with German forces attacking Soviet positions along the Danube River and Lake Balaton.

The *6. Panzerarmee*, consisting of elite *Waffen-SS* units like the *Leibstandarte-SS 'Adolf Hitler'* and *'Totenkopf'* panzer divisions, spearheaded the attack, aiming to break through Soviet lines near Nagykanizsa. The offensive also involved the *2. Panzerarmee* and the *6. Armee*, which aimed to advance toward Székesfehérvár and the southern sector of the front. Initially, the Germans made some progress, benefiting from tactical surprise and poor weather that limited Soviet air support. However, despite local successes, their advance soon began to bog down due to the combination of tough Soviet defenses, muddy terrain, and logistical difficulties (not enough gasoline and not enough supplies). The German forces earmarked for the offensive were as follows:

*6. Panzerarmee:*
- *I. SS-Panzerkorps*
  - *1. SS-Panzer-Division 'Leibstandarte Adolf Hitler'*
  - *12. SS-Panzer-Division 'Hitler Jugend'*
- *II. SS-Panzerkorps*
  - *2. SS-Panzer-Division 'Das Reich'*
  - *9. SS-Panzer-Division 'Hohenstaufen'*
  - *23. Panzer-Division*
  - *44. Reichsgrenadier-Division 'Hoch und Deutschmeister'* (initially in reserve)
- *I. Kavallerie-Korps* (army reserve)
  - *3. Kavallerie-Division*
  - *4. Kavallerie-Division*

*6. Armee:*
- *IV. SS-Panzerkorps*
  - *3. SS-Panzer-Division 'Totenkopf'*
  - *5. SS-Panzer-Division 'Wiking'*
  - *96. Infanterie-Division*
  - *711. Infanterie-Division*

  III. Panzerkorps
   1. Panzer-Division
   3. Panzer-Division
   356. Infanterie-Division
   25th Hungarian Infantry Division
 From 2. Panzerarmee:
  LXVIII. Armeekorps
   71. Infanterie-Division
   16. SS-Panzergrenadier-Division 'Reichsführer-SS'
  XXII. Gebirgs-Armeekorps
   1. Volksgrenadier-Division
   118. Jäger-Division
 Heeresgruppe 'E'
  XCI. Armeekorps
   1. Kosaken-Kavallerie-Division
   11. Feld-Division (L)
   104. Jäger-Division
   297. Infanterie-Division

  In spite of high hopes and preparation, Operation Spring Awakening turned into a disaster for the Germans. The failure of the offensive left them with no armored reserves. Because of this, they were unable to halt the Soviet advance on Vienna. It also weakened their already decimated forces on the Eastern Front. When the Red Army began its drive toward Vienna on 16 March, they were able to encircle a portion of 3rd Hungarian Army north of Bicske. Hitler was fuming at the defeat of the offensive and, as usual, looked for a scapegoat. This time, he turned his fury on his own SS. He blamed the *Waffen-SS* divisions under Sepp Dietrich for the failure. He accused them of lacking loyalty and commitment to the war. In a furious rage, the Führer ordered the infamous 'Stand Fast' order and on 31 March, and he stripped the SS units of their divisional cuff bands. The SS cuff band was a source of pride for the men who wore them on the lower-left sleeve of their field blouse. Dietrich responded to Hitler's punishment with disgust and defiance. He reportedly remarked that if Hitler wanted the cuff bands removed, he should come and remove them himself from the corpses of the fallen soldiers who had died fighting for him.
  Despite his anger, Dietrich did not take any overt action against Hitler. He remained loyal to his command, but the incident further widened the rift between some *Waffen-SS* officers and Hitler during the final months of the war. By 24 March, German forces were decisively defeated in western Hungary. The failure of the offensive to achieve its objectives not only marked the collapse of the attack but also led to the near-total decimation of many of the best German armored

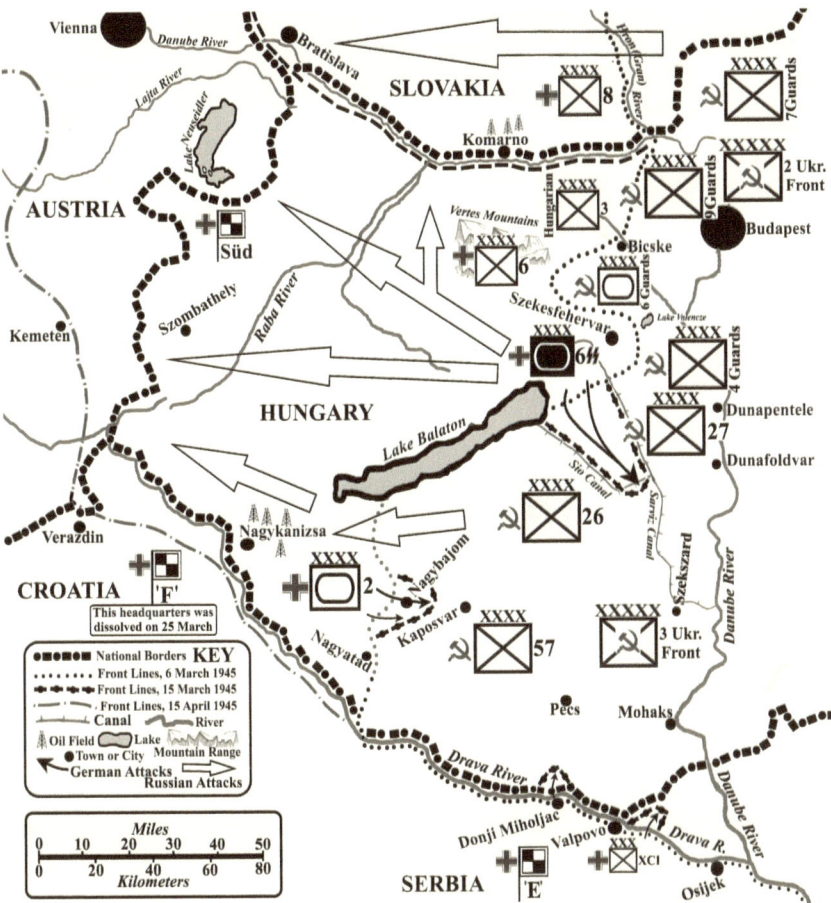

**Figure 41.** German and Soviet operations between 6 March and 15 April 1945. In early March, the Germans launched their last offensive of the war. A little over a week later, it ended in failure. The Germans spent their last reserves on that offensive, which allowed the Red Army to advance on Vienna against minimal resistance.

divisions. The Soviets wasted little time and counterattacked rapidly, recapturing lost ground and pushing the Germans back toward Austria. By April, the remnants of German forces were in full retreat, and the collapse of their southern front paved the way for the final Soviet push into Vienna, which would fall on 13 April 1945. The defeat at Lake Balaton marked the last German offensive of the war, and it accelerated the collapse of Nazi Germany. Less than two months later, on 8 May 1945, the war in Europe ended with Germany's unconditional surrender.

**Figure 42.** A German motorized column on the move in the spring of 1945. In March, the Germans would launch a final counteroffensive in Hungary, aimed at protecting the Hungarian oil fields and keeping the Red Army from reaching Vienna. Both goals would not be achieved. BUNDESARCHIV.

## THE VIENNA OFFENSIVE, 16 MARCH TO 15 APRIL 1945

For the offensive against the Austrian capital of Vienna, Stalin assigned the 2nd and the 3rd Ukrainian Front for the operation. The offensive began on 16 March, with the main Soviet attack vector between Lake Balaton and Esztergom. It was *IV. SS-Panzerkorps* and the right flank of the 3rd Hungarian Army that felt the heaviest brunt of the Soviet attack. On the second day of the offensive, the right flank of the Hungarians collapsed. By 18 March, the two leading Soviet armies—4th Guards Army and 9th Guards Army—broke through the defense lines of *IV. SS-Panzerkorps* just west and southwest of Lake Velence. In the meantime, *6. Panzerarmee* was attempting to extricate itself from the bulge it had created during the recent 'Spring Awakening' offensive. The German *6. Armee* was given the difficult, if not impossible, task of covering their retreat. At this point, there was a break in the line between *6. Panzerarmee* and *6. Armee* that spanned more than ten miles.

The commander of *6. Armee* communicated that they needed reinforcements to plug the gap. Army Group South headquarters responded that there were no reserves to be had. Soon, the 6th Guards Tank Army saw the redeployment attempt by *6. Panzerarmee* and attacked in the direction of Szekesfehervar, in an attempt to cut off the entire German panzer army. The Soviets wanted to cut off the German route of retreat between the northern tip of Lake Balaton and the town. Szekesfehervar was captured by the Red Army on 20 March. A week later, the Red Army forced a crossing of the Raba (Raab) River in four points. Through these bridgeheads flowed the divisions of 4th Guards Army, 9th Guards Army, and 6th Guards Tank Army. Immediately this move threatened *8. Armee,* whose right flank was being covered by *LXXII. Armeekorps.* This German army was also protecting the remaining oil fields located near Komarno, north of the Danube River. On the left flank of *LXXII. Armeekorps* were two more corps belonging to *8. Armee: XXIX. Armeekorps* and *IV. Panzerkorps* (which had recently been renamed *Panzerkorps 'Feldherrnhalle'*). Facing *8. Armee* was 1st Romanian Army. The composition of *8. Armee* at this time included the following units:

- *LXXII. Armeekorps* with: *Divisionsgruppe Kaiser* (odds and ends),[1] *8. Jäger-Division,* and a battle group of the *76. Infanterie-Division.*
- *IV. Panzerkorps* with: *10. SS-Panzer-Division 'Frundsberg', 46. Volksgrenadier-Division, 357. Infanterie-Division, 271. Volksgrenadier-Division,* plus a battle group of the *211. Volksgrenadier-Division.*
- *XXIX. Armeekorps* with: *101. Jäger-Division,* the 24th Hungarian Infantry Division, parts of the 5th Hungarian Infantry Division, plus a battle group of the Bavarian *15. Infanterie-Division.*

By 29 March, the 6th Guards Tank Army had reached the frontier between Austria and Hungary. Three days later, on 1 April, the 1st Guards Mechanized Corps of 4th Guards Army reached the town of Deutschkreuz (Sopronkeresztúr), ninety kilometers, or about fifty-six miles, from the Austrian capital. By 3 April, 5th Guards Tank Corps and 9th Guards Mechanized Corps, belonging to 6th Guards Tank Army, reached Wollersdorf and, a day later, Baden. Now the leading elements of 6th Guards Tank Army was just twenty-six kilometers (sixteen miles) from Vienna. In the meantime, farther north, the Russian 46th Army had reached the Leitha River and forced a crossing near the town of Bruck. Three armies were now poised to capture Vienna. On 8 April, the leading Russian units began to attack the German defenders of the city from the south, east, and northeast. On 13 April, the Red Army cut off any possible retreat from the city by taking Deutsch Wagram, Langenzersdorf, and Korneuburg.

In and around the Austrian capital, elements of five German divisions attempted to hold the Russians. These included *2. SS-Panzer-Division 'Das Reich', 3. SS-Panzer-Division 'Totenkopf', 44. Infanterie-Division 'Hoch und Deutschmeister', Führer-Grenadier-Division,* and the *271. Volksgrenadier-Division.* In addition, the city contained over a dozen *Volkssturm* and *Hitler Jugend* battalions whose military value was limited. There were also several flak battalions from the *17. Flak-Division,* which were stationed in the city. Some of these antiaircraft guns were employed against the Red Army tanks, but others, stationed on rooftops and high buildings,

96    *The Bitter End*

**Figure 43.** Location and disposition of 8. Armee as of 1 March 1945.

were useless against ground targets. On the day that Vienna was surrounded (13 April), the Soviet Danube Fleet brought into the western half of the city two more divisions using the river. Units from these two divisions managed to capture the remaining bridge in the city, spanning the Danube River, that had not yet been blown. By 7 April 1945, *Heeresgruppe Süd* could no longer claim that it held anything resembling a front line. The floodgates had been torn open at the end of March, and through it flowed the entire Russian Army. If Hitler had not launched Operation Spring Awakening in March 1945, squandering what armored reserves he still possessed, and instead, husbanded his armor, the Red Army might have been delayed from taking Vienna by another month or two. On the afternoon of 13 April, the remaining defenders of Vienna, mostly from the *2. SS Panzer-Division 'Das Reich'*, surrendered.

## Chapter 9

# BRATISLAVA AND PRAGUE

### THE BRATISLAVA-BRNO OFFENSIVE, 25 MARCH TO 5 MAY 1945

The 2nd Ukrainian Front launched the Bratislava-Brno offensive beginning on 25 March 1945 after an eight-hour-long artillery barrage where hundreds of cannons levelled its fire in and around the town of Levice. The objective of such a thunderous barrage was to force a crossing over the Hron (Gran) River. This was done at several points along the front. Units from 7th Guards Army (153rd Rifle Division and 357th Rifle Division) crossed first and established the bridgehead. In this effort the Soviet Danube Fleet proved particularly helpful in silencing enemy artillery fire. On 27 March, the Hungarian 24th Infantry Division, which the Germans considered still battle-worthy, simply disbanded and its men began marching home. On 28 March, Vráble was taken by elements of 49th Rifle Corps. Within forty-eight hours, the bridgehead had expanded twenty-two miles west of the Hron River.

On the right flank of 7th Guards Army was 40th Army and 53rd Army, which were having a tough time advancing, not so much because of German resistance but more so because of the mountainous topography of the region. On the left flank of 7th Guards Army was 46th Army. On 26 March, Banská Bystrica, which had been the center of the Slovak Army uprising in the summer and fall of 1944, was captured by units of the 4th Romanian Army.

The primary goal of the offensive was to capture the cities of Bratislava, the capital of Slovakia and Brünn (Brno), a major Czech city located twenty-six miles north of Vienna, along the banks of the Svartka River. This offensive was planned to clear the way for further advances into Czechoslovakia and to secure the central region of Europe. Following the attack on Bratislava, beginning on 2 April, fighting for the city lasted about 48 hours. By 4 April, Soviet forces controlled the Slovak capital and immediately ordered a continuance of their advance toward

Brno. Heavy fighting occurred as the Germans attempted to hold their positions. On 3 April, the bridges over the Danube River, that were located in Vienna, as well as immediately north and south of the city, were blown up. That meant that any German or Hungarian troops east of the river could no longer escape. After four years of fighting, the Red Army had learned how to conduct a combined arms operation, employing infantry, armor, and air support to break through the German defenses.

However, forcing a river crossing was not conducive to mobile warfare tactics. This slowed the Russian advance by about a month, as the Red Army once again needed to force a crossing, this time over the Danube. On 6 April, advanced elements of the Red Army crossed the Morava River near the town of Lanžhot. The fighting there proved to be intense, with the Germans not only employing a regular army unit but also youths from the *Hitler Jugend* and a few *Volkssturm* battalions as well. To make matters worse for the Russian attackers, the town was defended by what remained of *11. Panzer-Division*, which still possessed around sixty tanks. The battle lasted until 11 April, when resistance was finally broken. While the Red Army fought this pitched battle at Lanžhot, the Soviet 53rd Army managed an easier crossing near the town of Hodonin on 13 April.

After crossing the Morava River, the next significant river obstacle was the Jihlava River. *Panzer-Division 'Feldherrnhalle 1'*, created on 27 November 1944 by simply renaming *Panzergrenadier-Division 'Feldherrnhalle'*, had taken up defensive positions behind this river and was blocking the advance on Brno. In addition, *16. Panzer-Division*, together with more *Volkssturm* battalions and *SS Ersatz- und Ausbildungs-Bataillon 13*, made their appearance on 19 April. The defense by the Germans centered on the town of Ořechov. Taking this town would open the

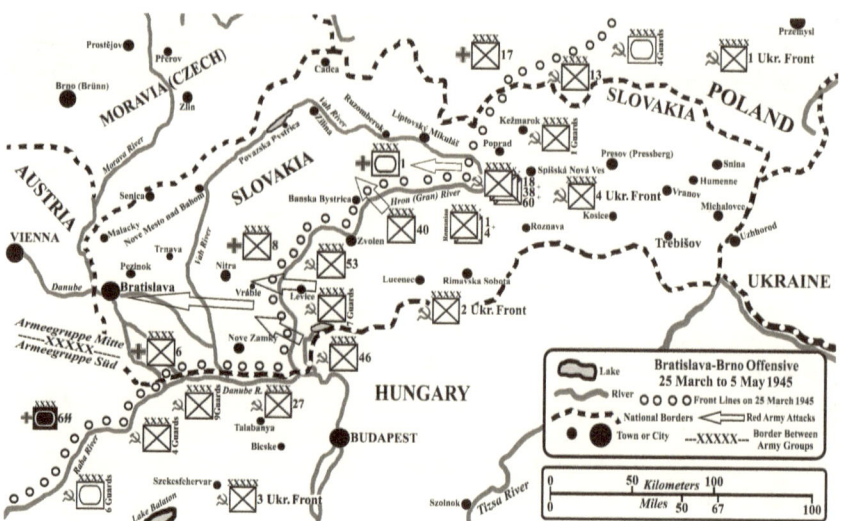

**Figure 44.** The Bratislava-Brno Offensive, 25 March to 5 May 1945.

way for the capture of Brno by the Red Army. The Germans utilized the terrain of the region and the urban environment to their advantage, leading to heavy casualties on both sides. A counterattack was launched by the Germans that temporarily surrounded a Red Army mechanized unit; however, by the evening of 23/24 April, the Russians were able to break the encirclement. The assault on Brno intensified in late April. As the Soviet forces tightened their grip on Brno, the German defense began to crumble under the pressure. On 26 April 1945, after several days of bitter fighting, the Soviet 2nd Ukrainian Front entered Brno. German forces withdrew from the city or were taken prisoner, leaving the city under Soviet control. The fighting culminated in the final capture of the city on 5 May 1945. The fall of Brno, which was an important transportation and industrial hub, was crucial for the Soviet advance into western Czechoslovakia.

## *HEERESGRUPPE ÖSTMARK*

On 2 April 1945, as the military situation for *Heeresgruppe Süd* was rapidly deteriorating, the German high command once again tried to reorganize in order to attempt to stabilize the military situation in Austria and lower Germany. On that day, *Heeresgruppe Östmark* was created from the remaining command staff of *Heeresgruppe Süd* and *Heeresgruppe 'F'*. The initial headquarters for the new army group was Vienna.[1] However, with the fall of the Austrian capital on 13 April, the forming staff were forced to withdraw westward with the rest of the retreating German Army. The headquarters was relocated to the town of Zell am See, in western Austria. Zell am See, located in the Austrian Alps, became a temporary base for the command. It was expected that if Hitler and the Nazi leadership made a final stand in the Austrian alps, the remnants of the German forces in the region would be drawn there for its defense. Hitler had chosen *Generaloberst* Dr. Lothar Rendulic to lead this new command.[2] The Chief of the General Staff was *Generalleutnant* Heinz von Gyldenfeldt. The first general staff officer for the headquarters ('Ia') was *Oberstleutnant i.G.* Gunther Bang. The headquarters had a few troops that it controlled directly. These were *Nachrichten Regiment 530* (530th Communications Regiment) and *Grenadier-Ersatz-Bataillon 67* (67th Grenadier Replacement Battalion).

*Heeresgruppe Östmark* was created to control what remained of *6. Panzerarmee*, *6. Armee*, and *8. Armee*. The mission assigned to it was the impossible task of defending western and central Austria, as well as southern Germany. By late April, the *8. Armee* was located around Gaubitsch, in the Mistelbach district of lower Austria. The remnants of *6. Panzerarmee* were more or less located west of Vienna, along the Danube River, while *6. Armee* was holding the city of Graz. In April 1945, these armies still amounted to some 400,000 men. The Red Army entered Graz on 30 April but would continue to fight German troops in the city until 8 May, when the city garrison finally surrendered. On 7 May, American troops belonging to the U.S. 3rd Army reached Zell am See, in western Austria, and captured the headquarters. As the supreme commander responsible for Austria and southern Germany, Rendulic negotiated the surrender of all German forces in the area. German forces under the command of *Heeresgruppe Östmark* surrendered to British and American troops as they encountered them. In the meantime, more and more scattered German units attempted to withdraw west in order to surrender to American or British forces. Justifiably, no one wanted to be captured by the Red Army.

## THE PRAGUE UPRISING AND THE PRAGUE OFFENSIVE, 6–11 MAY 1945

When the Prague uprising began on the morning of 5 May 1945, initially the Czechs employed passive resistance, like tearing down German flags and replacing them with Czech flags. Conductors refused to accept Reichsmarks on trams and to call out the tram stops in German as was required. Soon, individual German soldiers and in groups of two to four were being attacked and murdered on the streets. The Germans responded with rifle and machine-gun fire. Prague and its surrounding environs were an armed camp. The Germans knew that American and British bombers were ordered not to target Czech lands for bombing, like German territory was experiencing on a daily basis. However, Czech territory did experience several significant air raids, particularly toward the end of the war. These bombings were primarily aimed at disrupting Nazi war production and transportation networks.

As a result of this, the German military had placed numerous warehouses and ammunition depots in the city of Prague and in the surrounding outskirts of the city because they would likely not be targeted by Allied bombers. There were also several German military training bases, an SS officer's academy, and other military installations close to the Czech capital. The youth of Prague took advantage of this and stormed warehouses in the city that were guarded by a skeleton crew of security guards or soldiers. They began to arm themselves. The Czech patriots even managed to capture five armored vehicles—a few of the Hetzer tank destroyers, at least one French AMR-35 tank, and some halftracks. What they did find in abundance were hundreds of German *Panzerfaust* anti-tank weapons.[3] In addition, the Czech resistance contacted Major-General Sergei Kuzmich Bunyachenko and requested the assistance of the Russian Liberation Army against the Germans.[4]

Bunyachenko, realizing the end of the Nazi regime was near, feared retribution by Stalin's regime that would follow Germany's defeat. He knew what awaited every man who had volunteered to serve in the Russian Army of Liberation (ROA). The Russian turncoat reasoned that if his troops were to assist the Czechs to liberate their capital, then perhaps the western powers might intercede on their behalf. The ultimate hope was to receive asylum in the West.[5] There were two ROA divisions near the city of Prague. The first was the *600. Infanterie-Division (russische Nr. 1)*, which on 1 April 1945 was behind *9. Armee* lines. The division, however, left the Oder battlefront without permission in late April and headed south to Prague. Another ROA unit, the *650. Infanterie-Division (russische Nr. 2)*, was located west of Prague. These two divisions would eventually be brought into the city to help expel the Germans.

For the Germans, the betrayal of the ROA was particularly stinging. They had lavished a lot of effort, training, and outfitted both divisions with ample rifles, mortars, artillery, anti-tank guns, and engineering equipment. For 1945 German standards, both divisions were overstrength and magnificently equipped. The irony is that aside from an ROA anti-tank brigade, which briefly fought along the Oder, the men of the ROA never fired a shot in anger against the Red Army.

**Figure 45.** Positions of *4. Panzerarmee* between Guben and Görlitz, 1 April 1945.

A postwar writer, Jürgen Thorwald, called the Russian Army of Liberation 'an illusion'.⁶ On the German side, as soon as the Prague garrison realized that they were facing two full-strength infantry divisions in addition to the city rebels, a call went out to all available German forces in the vicinity of Prague for assistance. The various depots, school, and training and replacement units were immediately mobilized. Several *kampfgruppen* (battle groups) were organized for the relief of the city. These included:

> *SS-Kampfgruppe Demes*: This battle group contained three battalions of the Fascist Slovakian Hlinka Guard. The regiment was named *Slowakisches Grenadier-Regiment Nr. 1 'Hlinka Garde'*. Its commander was *SS-Obersturmbannführer* Walter Demes.
>
> *SS-Kampfgruppe Klein*: This battle group was created using the *SS Pionier-Schule 4* (SS Engineer School Nr. 4), located near the town of Hradischko. The commander was the head of the school, *SS-Standartenführer* Emil Klein.
>
> *SS-Kampfgruppe Jörchel*: Led by *SS-Standartenführer* Wolfgang Jörchel, the commander of the *SS-Junkerschule Prag* (SS Officer Candidate School 'Prague'). Together with the personnel from *SS-Truppenübungsplatz Böhmen*, they became a part of *SS Regiment 'Mahren'*. This SS infantry regiment also contained *SS Flak Batterie Prag*.
>
> *Kampfgruppe Reimann*: In the area of Český Brod were elements of what remained of *I. Flak-Korps*, under the command of *General der Flakartillerie* Richard Reimann.
>
> *SS-Kampfgruppe Wallenstein*: This emergency formation was put together on 13 April employing training and reserve units from *SS-Truppenübungsplatz Beneschau*. It was ordered to move north, toward the Czech capital, which was under attack. According to the available literature, this formation was to form the basis for the creation of another SS division: *44. SS-Panzergrenadier-Division 'Wallenstein'*. The end of the war put an end to this plan. However, it should be noted that by this time period in the war, the Germans were creating 'divisions' by simply putting together whatever scratch units were available in a locality and assigning whatever available command there was. These became the 'instant divisions' that Allied troops faced more and more as they entered the Reich. When the *kampfgruppe* was engaged south of Prague, only the reconnaissance battalion, *SS-Aufklärung-Abteilung 'Wallenstein'*, managed to get to the city center.

*SS-Kampfgruppe Wallenstein* contained sixty tanks and assault guns plus 100 motor vehicles of all types. The tanks and assault guns were the older models that had been withdrawn from frontline service and were now used to train new tank and assault gun crews. For example, there were several *StuG III* assault guns of various models (A, B, C, D, and E). Some of these vehicles carried the outdated

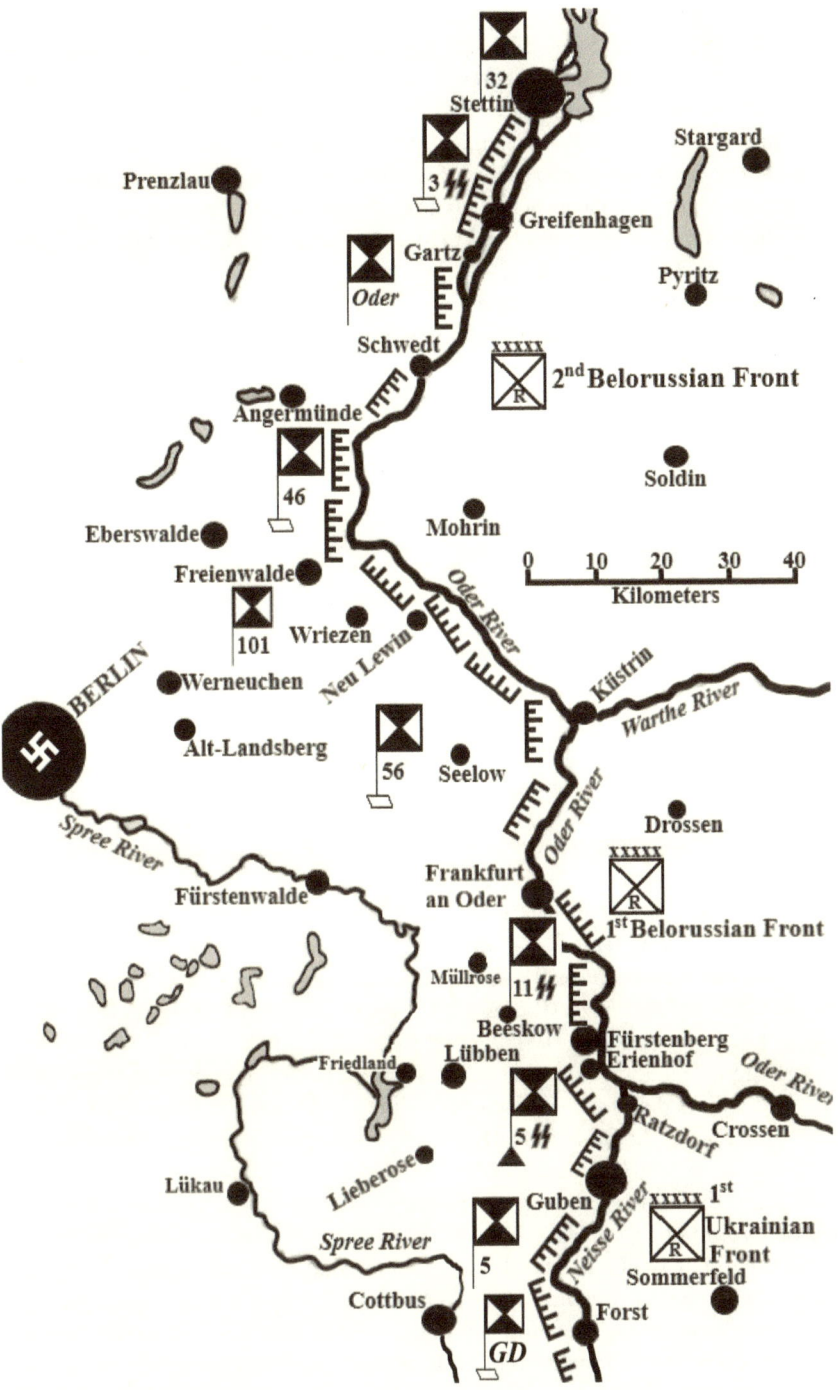

**Figure 46.** The army corps of *3. Panzerarmee*, *9. Armee*, and *4. Panzerarmee* along the Oder River, 16 April 1945.

short-barreled 75 mm StuK 37 L/24 anti-tank gun. The battle group also contained a variety of the older Panzer II, III, and short-barreled Panzer IV tanks. While the Germans had this motley assortment of outdated AFVs, the two ROA divisions they would confront in and around Prague were equipped with captured T-34 tanks. To make matters worse for the Germans, some of the tank rounds were fake. Many had the stenciled marking that read 'for training purposes only,' indicating that when the round was fired, it would create the noise of a tank gun but no projectile would be shot. The best that the tank crews could expect from these rounds was to scare the enemy into cover. In any event, most of these tanks and assault guns never got to the fighting in Prague, as the decision had been made to transfer most of them using several trains (because of a lack of petrol). Unfortunately for the Germans, the trains were stopped at Čerčan by Czech patriots, who blew up the rail tracks. Most of the SS battle groups listed here were to become a part of the never officially created *44. SS-Panzergrenadier-Division 'Wallenstein'*. On paper, the division was organized as follows:

> *SS-Grenadier-Regiment Nr. 1 'Wallenstein'* (*SS-Standartenführer* Wolfgang Jörchel)
> *SS-Grenadier-Regiment Nr. 2 'Wallenstein'* (*SS-Obersturmbannführer* Karl Schlamelcher)
> *Slowakisches Grenadier-Regiment Nr. 1 'Hlinka Garde'* (*SS-Obersturmbannführer* Walter Demes). This unit was acting as the third regiment in the proposed SS division, though it was probably on a temporary basis, given that it was composed completely of Slovakians.
> *SS-Pionier-Regiment 'Wallenstein'* (*SS-Oberführer* Emil Klein)
> *SS-Panzerjäger-Abteilung 'Wallenstein'* (*SS-Sturmbannführer* Erich Sinn)
> *SS-Aufklärung-Abteilung 'Wallenstein'* (*SS-Hauptsturmführer* Erhard Körner)
> *SS-Fusilier-Bataillon 'Wallenstein'* (*SS-Sturmbannführer* Leander Hauck)
> *SS-Sturmgeschütz-Abteilung 'Wallenstein'* (*SS-Sturmbannführer* Klaus von Allwörden)
> *SS-Nachrichten-Abteilung 'Wallenstein'* (*SS-Sturmbannführer* Helmut Bäume)
> *SS-Nachschub-Bataillon 'Wallenstein'* (*SS-Sturmbannführer* Arno König)
> *SS-Sanitäts-Abteilung 'Wallenstein'* (*SS-Sturmbannführer* Dr. Hans Lucha)[7]

I should mention here that if the war had been a few months longer, the 'Wallenstein' SS division may have been officially created. However, we should take note that by doing so, the *Waffen-SS* was gutting many of its training and replacement units. This circumstance—resorting to training and reserve units and employing them in frontline combat—indicated two things. First, that the Nazi regime had no other available forces to throw at the enemy, and two, that the regime knew they would not need these training, replacement, and reserve units in the future, as the war was already lost. The Third Reich was merely buying a little more time by throwing these forces into the breach. The SS *'Wallenstein'* division, such as it was, never fought completely as one unit but rather in three to four segmented parts. One final battle group was established for the relief of Prague:

*Kampfgruppe der 2. SS-Panzer-Division 'Das Reich'*. On 5 May, the remnants of this SS division were located in Hořovice, about twenty-nine miles southwest of Prague. However, when the unit began to move toward the Czech capital, to help relieve the German garrison, it was stopped cold by elements of the ROA *650. Infanterie-Division (russische Nr. 2)*. The SS division, now a mere shadow of its former self, quickly withdrew and headed southwest, in the direction of Pilsen (Plzeňský), in search of American troops that they could surrender to.

The first units of the *600. Infanterie-Division (russische Nr. 1)* entered Prague on 6 May, about noontime. Elements of the division would fight until 7 May. By then, it had disarmed thousands of German troops in the city. Nevertheless, when the Czechs realized that they were not going to be liberated by western forces, and that the Red Army was going to occupy Czechoslovakia, they understood that associating with members of the Russian Liberation Army would harm future Czech-Soviet relations. It was then that the Czech National Council made it clear to the Russian turncoats that they were no longer welcome in the city. The ROA withdrew that very day and headed west, in a vain attempt to do what most Germans were trying to do: surrender to western Allied forces. Once the Russian ROA troops abandoned the city, the tables turned against the insurgents, and the Germans began to get the upper hand. By 8 May, only one section of the city was still under control by the Czech patriots.

In the beginning of May 1945, divisions from Army Group Center that were still resisting the advance of 1st and 4th Ukrainian Front in Czechoslovakia and 2nd Ukrainian Front in Austria were ordered by *Generaloberst* Alfred Jodl, the chief of staff for the Armed Forces High Command, to continue to resist the Russian

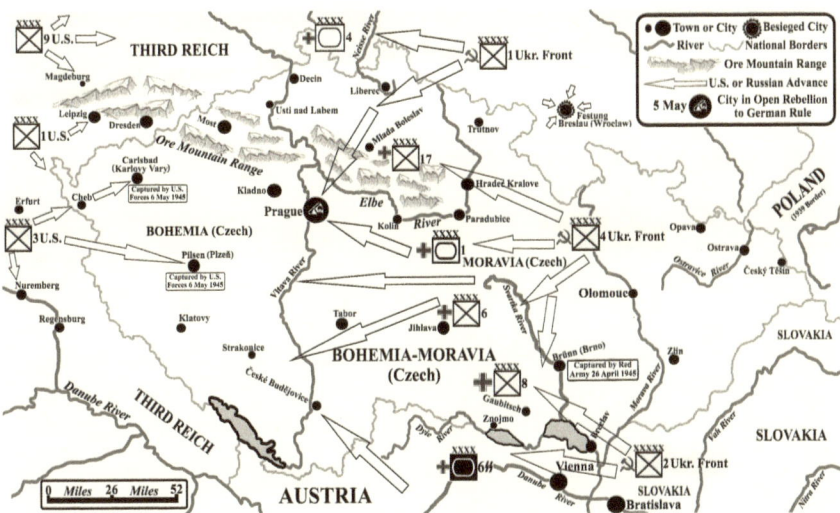

**Figure 47.** Advance of American and Soviet forces into western Czechoslovakia, April–May.

advance. Jodl also ordered that all German units should try and make an orderly withdrawal west. They were to do this in order to surrender to western Allied forces. Jodl's instruction was issued on 2 May 1945 but was basically a redundant order, given that this is exactly what every single German unit belonging to the *Ostheer* wanted to do at all costs. This sentiment was felt by all, from private or high-ranking general. Everyone wanted to avoid being captured by the Soviets and only wished to surrender to either American, British, or French forces.[8] On 9 May, fighting between the insurgents and the Germans continued in the city. In order to stop the killings, the Czech National Council offered a truce. They would allow German forces retreating from the Russians free passage through the city. The one caveat was that they had to surrender their arms as they left. They contacted the *Wehrmachtbefehlshaber, General der Infanterie* Rudolf Toussaint, and offered him the deal. The general quickly accepted. Toussaint was desperate to get as many German units to the west as possible. The agreement allowed for the rapid transport of German forces fleeing the Russians. He also wished that the German civilians leaving the city could do so unmolested by the insurgents. By the early morning of 9 May, the Czech capital had been emptied of Germans. Shortly thereafter, soldiers from the 1st Ukrainian Front entered Prague. According to one account, the Russians only lost ten men taking the city.[9]

# Chapter 10

## DIE SCHLACHT UM KURLAND, 1944–1945

### SETTING THE STAGE

The battle for Courland developed when *Heeresgruppe Nord* (Army Group North) became surrounded in the region of the Courland peninsula (Latvia) following the Red Army capture of Memel (Klaipėda) on 10 October 1944. The capture of this port city was accomplished by employing the Soviet 4th Shock Army and 51st Army of 1st Belarusian Front. The Russians had previously almost trapped *Heeresgruppe Nord* during the battle for Riga, the Latvian capital. The 5th Guards Tank Army thrust northwest of the town of Dobele, threatening to cut off the entire army group by reaching the Gulf of Riga and sealing off its route of retreat. This occurred within the context of what the Russians called the Riga offensive, which lasted from 14 September to 24 October 1944. This offensive involved all three Russian Baltic fronts (1st, 2nd, and 3rd) against the German *16. Armee, 18. Armee,* and parts of *3. Panzerarmee*. In total, this amounted to some 200,000 to 240,000 frontline soldiers comprising twenty-six infantry divisions, two panzer divisions, and four separate tank and assault gun brigades. Including noncombatants, the army group numbered about 400,000 men.

The offensive to capture Memel on the Lithuanian coast began on 5 October and involved units of *3. Panzerarmee* facing 4th Shock Army and 51st Army. Having been almost wiped out during Operation Bagration in the summer of 1944, *3. Panzerarmee* could only offer token resistance. By 10 October, it was clear that *Heeresgruppe Nord* was in serious trouble. On that day the Russian front line was so close to the city that Russian artillery could now fire directly into the Latvian capital. The army group successfully evaded the Russian trap west of Riga by leaving a screening force behind that allowed the other divisions to retreat. The Red Army entered Riga on 13 October. The army group had avoided being cut off in Riga, but the capture of Memel three days earlier meant that the only place Army Group North could go was the Courland peninsula. It was in that Latvian peninsula that

108    The Bitter End

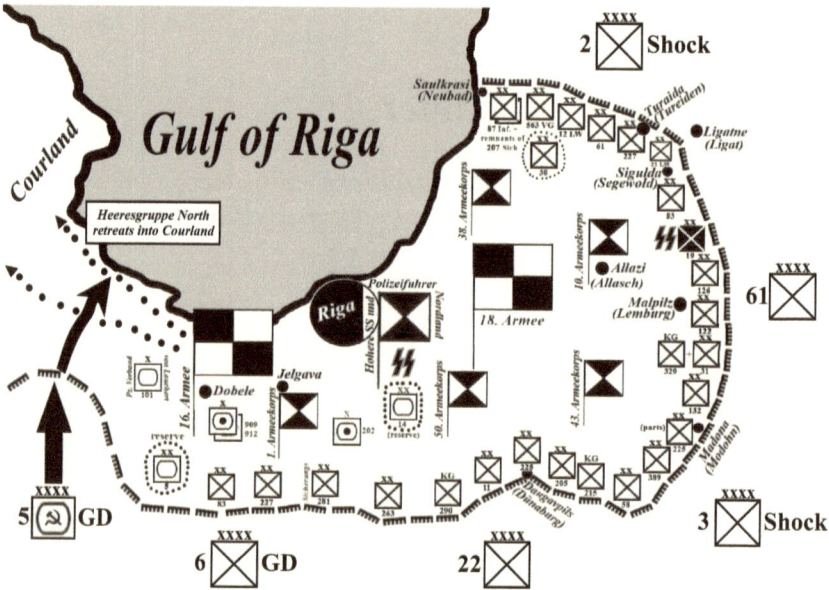

**Figure 48.** At the start of the second week in October 1944, the rapid advance of 5th Guards Tank Army threatened to cut off the entire German northern army group.

the trapped divisions of Army Group North would remain for the rest of the war. This group of divisions came to be known as the Courland pocket. The German troops in the peninsula faced south, with the cities of Liepāja on the Baltic coast and Tukums on the Gulf of Riga serving as the anchors of the German defense. The front line was a 240-kilometer-long land front, plus a 320-kilometer-long coastline that also needed monitoring in case of amphibious attack.

Of course, there was an attempt to reestablish a land link to the trapped army group, but after the summer battles, *Heeresgruppe Mitte* was in no condition to launch a successful counterattack. In the port of Memel, the German *XXVIII. Armeekorps* was caught and surrounded. The situation had become critical because a new division, the Pomeranian *551. Volksgrenadier-Division* (home base: Stettin), had collapsed on the first day that they encountered Russian forces heading toward the coast. By 7 October, there was no coherent front in the region. Defending Memel were three formations: the Prussian *7. Panzer-Division,* whose nickname was the *Gespensterdivision* (Ghost Division), *Panzergrenadier-Division 'Gross Deutschland',* and the Saxon *58. Infanterie-Division.* Later in the siege, the Germans brought in by sea the Brandenburg *95. Infanterie-Division* and withdrew the '*Gross Deutschland*' and *7. Panzer-Division,* both of which had been seriously battered.

There followed a long siege which lasted until 27 January 1945, when the Germans withdrew from the port city with the help of the *Kriegsmarine.* In total, *Heeresgruppe Nord* was besieged and cut off from the regular German front lines from 10 October 1944 to 8 May 1945. During that time period, the army group would experience six major Russian offensives. These were named, sequentially, the 1st, 2nd, 3rd, 4th, 5th, and 6th Battle for Courland. There was actually a plan in the works, devised in the fall of 1944, to reestablish a land link with the trapped army group. However, this planned counterattack was conditioned on a successful German offensive in the Ardennes. The Ardennes offensive, a plan devised and ordered by Adolf Hitler, was launched on 16 December 1944. This was an act of desperation on the part of the German dictator. The plan had five basic goals. These were as follows:

1. Split the Allied Forces: Hitler aimed to divide the American and British armies by driving a wedge between their forces, particularly between British troops in the north and American units in the south. This would cripple the Allies' ability to coordinate their operations.
2. Capture the Belgian port of Antwerp: Antwerp was a crucial Allied supply hub. By seizing it, the Germans hoped to cut off the Allies' supply lines, disrupt their logistics, and create a critical shortage of fuel and ammunition. The Allies would then have to bring in supplies through French ports, which were far from the front lines.
3. Encircle and destroy Allied units: The Germans planned to encircle and annihilate large numbers of Allied troops, which would delay their advance into Germany and which Hitler hoped could potentially force the Allies into a negotiated peace.
4. Boost German morale: After a series of humiliating and devastating defeats in 1944, Hitler wanted to restore the fighting spirit of the German military and civilian population by achieving a major victory.
5. Redirect forces east: It was also hoped that if the offensive would have succeeded completely, according to Hitler's plan, the Allies would have been forced to make a separate peace (Hitler's fantasy wish), or more realistically, the timetable of the Allied armies would have been pushed back by as much as eight to ten months. Hitler hoped that this delay would be sufficient to produce enough jet fighters which, he reasoned, would allow the *Luftwaffe* to regain aerial dominance over Germany. With dominance of the sky, the Allied bomber offensive would come to a screeching halt and war production would continue.

If the Ardennes offensive succeeded, Hitler was planning to replace *6. Panzerarmee* with lesser units and redeploy this large panzer force to East Prussia. The plan was to launch a Hail Mary–style offensive in the spring of 1945, with the attack vector curving in a northeasterly direction, much akin to a giant hook. The date for the operation was estimated to be sometime in March or April. The weather would not be a major factor because the tanks would be operating in East Prussia, Lithuania, and Latvia. Therefore, the *Rasputitsa* of the spring weather cycle that so impeded the Germans in Russia would not be a major obstacle as the roads and the weather conditions would be significantly more manageable in the

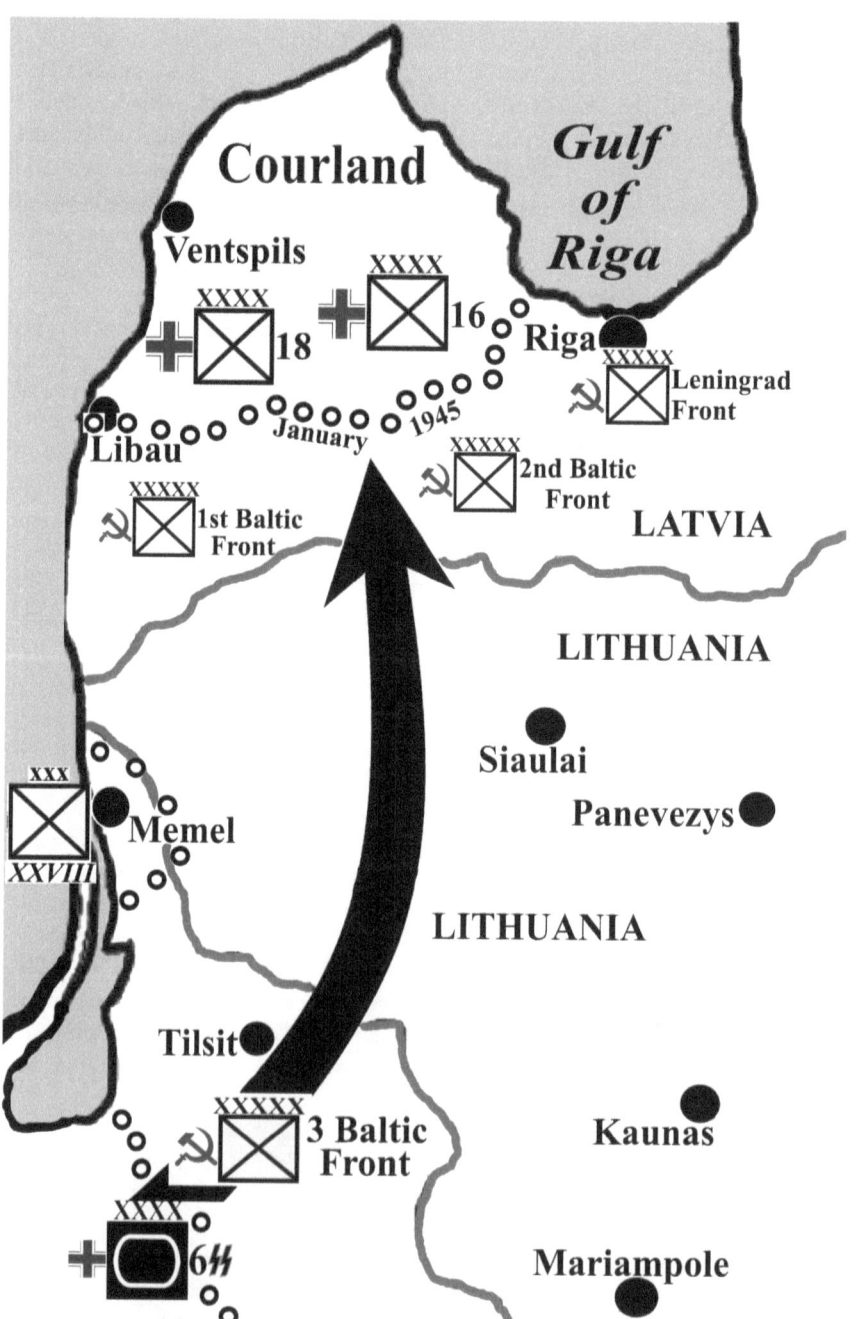

**Figure 49.** If the Ardennes offensive in December 1944 had proved successful, Hitler planned to employ the *6. Panzerarmee* on the Russian front, in an attempt to relieve *Heeresgruppe Kurland* in the spring of 1945.

Baltic States. Like the Ardennes offensive, this operation would have been a highly risky move. Such an offensive would have certainly entailed much peril, with the potential for catastrophic failure if the gamble did not succeed.

The Ardennes offensive was another such highly risky Hail Mary move. These operations are often undertaken when a force is in a dire state, running out of time, resources, or options, with the hope that a bold, risky move might reverse the military situation. The attack usually relies on surprise, speed, or exploiting a perceived weakness in the enemy to achieve success. It is obvious that Hitler was prepared to take such a highly risky move in the fall of 1944. It is also interesting to consider that the Führer would have been tempting fate yet again, with this 'Baltic offensive', had the Ardennes operation worked out as he had planned. It shows us that Hitler understood the calamitous military situation that he was facing in the fall of 1944. He behaved like a cornered animal when trapped: He lashed out in one final attempt to escape the vise that was slowly strangling the Third Reich.

The chances that this planned but never executed offensive would have succeeded is very low. The *6. Panzerarmee* would have had to advance a distance of some 150 to 200 kilometers (about ninety-three to 124 miles), depending on the location of the front lines when the offensive would start. In addition, even if *6. Panzerarmee* would have been assisted by both *4. Armee* and *3. Panzerarmee*, the Germans would have had to fight a total of four Soviet fronts: 1st Baltic, 2nd Baltic, 3rd Baltic, and the Leningrad Front, which was now in the Baltic States. Put together, these four fronts numbered between 1,350,000 and 1,700,000 men. There is no doubt that the generals leading *Oberkommando der Wehrmacht* (Armed Forces High Command) would have tried to discourage such an obviously risky plan, but it likely would have taken place anyway, given that Hitler always had the final say in all military and political matters. As it happened, the Ardennes offensive, that highly chancy operation Hitler was willing to take, failed.[1] The Führer now set his sights on smaller designs. He sent *6. Panzerarmee* to Hungary in order to help protect the Hungarian oil fields. There *Heeresgruppe Süd* would launch one final offensive from 6–15 March 1945 that would also falter. Having expended his final armored reserves in two failed offensives, by mid-March 1945, Hitler lacked any mobile force that could in the immediate future plug gaps in the German front line. Soon after, the German lines began to tear apart, both on the Western Front and the Eastern Front. With no substantial armored reserves available to stop enemy breakthroughs, Soviet and western Allied troops poured in, like water gushing through a broken dam.

## NECESSARY WITHDRAWALS

With no substantial reserves available in the fall of 1944, Hitler had to resort to stopgap measures. Approximately six German divisions were eventually evacuated from the Courland pocket between October 1944 and early 1945 to be employed

**Figure 50.** Tiger-I tanks of the 510th Heavy Tank Battalion, somewhere in Courland, Latvia, in the spring of 1945. Two entire German armies would be surrounded for the rest of the war in what would become the Courland pocket. BUNDESARCHIV.

along the main battlefront between the Vistula and Oder rivers. These evacuations took place during the early stages of the siege, before Hitler largely forbade further troop withdrawals from the pocket. These troops were sent to East Prussia and the Oder Front to defend against the advancing Red Army. Hitler became reluctant to withdraw further German divisions from the Courland pocket. The sea route was the only way in or out of the pocket and was constantly being harassed by Russian warships, submarines, and bombers, all looking to sink a juicy troop transport ship. Because the Soviets knew this, the main target of attack in all of the six major battles launched against the trapped army group was the major port city of Libau (Liepāja). Hitler was also under the mistaken belief that the Courland pocket could still serve a strategic purpose for Nazi Germany, either as a potential launching point for future operations in the East or as a base from which German forces could continue to threaten the Soviet Union's northern flank. He saw the area as a symbolic stronghold that should be defended at all costs. On 25 January 1945, Adolf Hitler finally renamed *Heeresgruppe Nord* as *Heeresgruppe Kurland* (Army Group Courland).

## THE FIRST BATTLE FOR COURLAND, 15–20 OCTOBER 1944

The first battle for Courland, as this initial attack came to be known, began on 15 October and lasted eleven days, until 20 October 1944. The main point of attack centered between the towns of Auce and Zeitweilig (Īslaicīgi). The principal Red Army force earmarked for the main assault was 5th Guards Tank Army (2nd Belarusian Front). Ferdinand Schörner, the current commander of *Heeresgruppe Nord*, had prepared for the expected Russian attack. Several divisions had been placed in reserve behind the German lines. These included from left to right (where left began in the port city of Libau) the following forces: *4. Panzer-Division*, at Grobin (Grobina), *61. Infanterie-Division*, between Dürban (Durbe) and Schründen

(Skrunda), the bulk of *215. Infanterie-Division*, fifteen kilometers south of Frauenburg (Saldus), *12. Panzer-Division*, at Hasenpoth (Aizpute), and *83. Infanterie-Division*, which was located near the Gulf of Riga, about twenty kilometers north of the town of Tukums. In this first battle, the Russians lost 522 armored fighting vehicles (tanks and assault guns).[2] Elements of 2nd Belarusian Front attacked in the direction of Moscheiken (Mazsalaca) and Autz (Auce). This placed three divisions, *21. Feld-Division (L)*, *329. Infanterie-Division*, and *81. Infanterie-Division* at the center of the Red Army assault. In mid-October 1944, before the start of this first offensive, *21. Feld-Division (L)* had received some badly needed replacements when *Waffen-Grenadier-Regiment der SS (lettische Nr. 7)*, mustering two battalions of Latvian SS infantry, was temporarily attached.[3]

There is no mention of this Latvian SS regiment being officially incorporated into the ranks of either *15. Waffen-Grenadier-Division der SS (lettische Nr. 1)* or *19.*

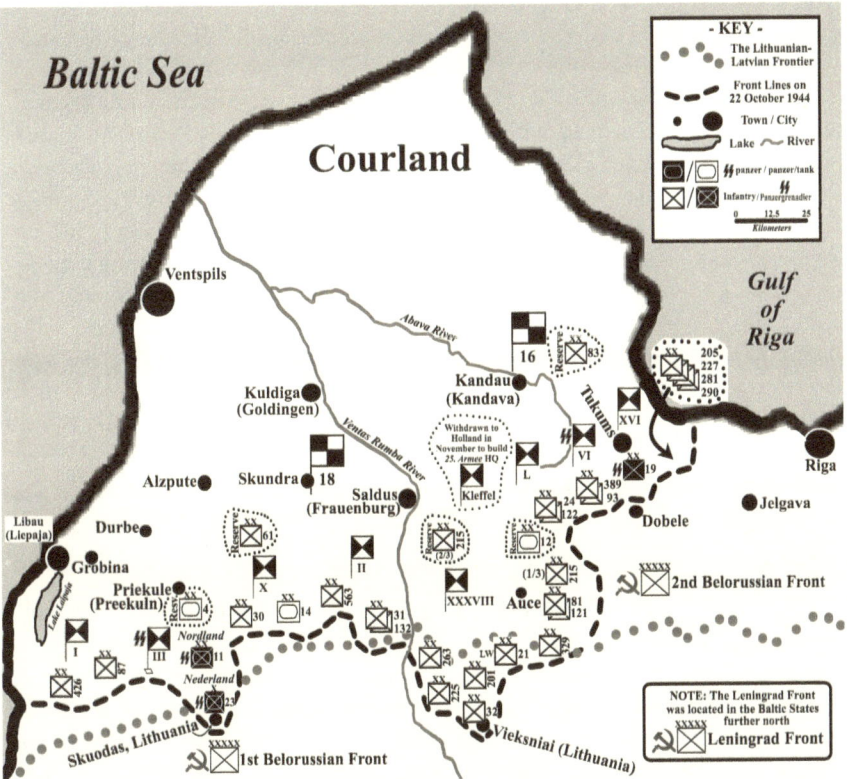

**Figure 51.** Positions of Army Group North on 22 October 1944, just prior to the start of the First Battle of Courland. Korps Gruppe Kleffel, which was a renaming of Korps Gruppe Grasser, was basically the headquarters for *Armee-Abteilung Narwa*. In November 1944, it was withdrawn from Courland via Libau and sent to The Netherlands, where it was used as the basis for the headquarters of the newly established *25. Armee*.

*Waffen-Grenadier-Division der SS (lettische Nr. 2)*. Most likely, sometime during the fall of 1944, it was disbanded, and its men were used as replacements for both Latvian SS divisions. The Latvian volunteers appear to have gotten along quite well with the men of *21 Feld-Division (L)*, but I digress. The attack against Mazsalaca and Auce was eventually blunted by *12. Panzer-Division*, which had been in reserve just behind the front lines.

The drive in this sector of the front lines was centered on capturing Frauenburg (Saldus). In particular, three divisions were pummeled heavily by 122nd Mechanized Corps and 12th Tank Corps. As a result, in a span of just of seventy-two hours, the *24. Infanterie-Division*, *93. Infanterie-Division*, and *122. Infanterie-Division* suffered over a thousand casualties.[4] After two days of relative inactivity, the Soviets once again continued their attacks. This time they concentrated on two key points. The first was at Doblen (Dobele), where *93. Infanterie-Division, 389. Infanterie-Division,* and *19. Waffen-Grenadier-Division der SS (lettische Nr. 2)* were located. The second was centered between Siksni and Kaletl, southeast of Libau and southwest from Priekule. These two attacks were also halted after fierce fighting.

Although the first battle for Courland ended on 20 October, the Russians renewed their assault locally. On 24 October, they concentrated their attack against the *215. Infanterie-Division*, which had recently replaced *121. Infanterie-Division* just southeast of Auce.[5] Although badly mauled, the Württemberg regiments of *215. Infanterie-Division* were eventually able to stop the Russian advance. Sporadic fighting continued along the breadth of the front lines of *I. Armeekorps, III. (germanisches) SS-Panzerkorps,* and *XXXVIII. Armeekorps*. During the fighting between 15 and 26 October, around 1,150 Soviet tanks and assault guns were destroyed but at a high cost in German lives. For example, *X. Armeekorps* alone recorded almost 50 percent losses. For another example, a regiment of the *4. SS-Freiwilligen-Panzergrenadier-Brigade 'Nederland'* was reduced to a platoon of twenty-five men. In essence, the regiment had been wiped out. The First Battle of Courland (15–20 October) had come to an end. This first battle had cost the Germans 21,292 soldiers killed, wounded, or taken prisoner.

## THE SECOND BATTLE FOR COURLAND, 27 OCTOBER TO 2 NOVEMBER 1944

For this second assault against the lines of Army Group North, the Red Army had prepared a preliminary artillery and air bombardment. The Russians employed over 1,800 planes. The vital port of Libau (Liepāja) was targeted and subject to an intense aerial bombardment that damaged some small German ships in the port and set most of the city on fire. The artillery barrage against the selected battle lines lasted an hour and a half. During that time, hundreds of artillery pieces and rocket launchers of all types and sizes fired into the German defense lines. The front line chosen for this second attack was between Auce and Dobele. Once again, the leading Russian force was 5th Guards Tank Army, whose 400 tanks and assault guns were concentrated between these two towns. A good portion of those tanks were the new super-heavy Joseph Stalin II tanks, which were markedly superior to every German armored fighting vehicle, except the King Tiger tank. A day after the attack began, the town of Dobele was captured by the Red Army.

Simultaneously, units from 1st Belarusian Front launched a furious artillery and air barrage between Skuodas and Preekuln. Together with 8th Guards Army, the front lines of *4. SS-Freiwilligen-Panzergrenadier-Brigade 'Nederland'*, *30. Infanterie-Division*, and parts of the *11. SS-Freiwilligen-Panzergrenadier-Division 'Nordland'* was flattened by the massive artillery barrage. Southwest of Auce, 10th Guards Army employed all of its component assault guns in the region of *21. Feld-Division (L)*. The men of this air force field division could not prevent a breakthrough and were forced to withdraw. Only by the timely arrival of the Bavarian *12. Panzer-Division* and a regiment of the Silesian *389. Infanterie-Division* was the front temporarily stabilized. In the region of *X. Armeekorps*, the *14. Panzer-Division* did its best to stop the Red Army attack. It had recently been reinforced by twenty Tiger-I tanks of *schwere Panzer-Abteilung 510*. Four of those tanks were sent to help the beleaguered *30. Infanterie-Division*, which was located on the right flank of *14. Panzer-Division*.

The fighting was so intense that in two days of fighting (29–30 October), about 1,400 men were lost between *14. Panzer-Division, 11. SS-Freiwilligen-Panzergrenadier-Division 'Nordland'*, and *30. Infanterie-Division*. The East Prussian *4. Panzer-Division* was again committed to this offensive and managed, temporarily, to halt the Russian advance. Fighting all along the front lines let up around 1 November, with a fresh rainfall coming down that again turned the ground to mush. The Russians had made some progress but at a great cost. In the entire month of October 1944, the Red Army had lost 1,143 tanks and assault guns while trying to break through the lines of Army Group North.[6]

The Germans took the time to reposition its forces to prearranged positions. In particular, the flanks of *XXXVIII. Armeekorps* were too exposed. The order was given to withdraw its divisions to a new defensive line between Lake Zebres and Lake Lielauce. In the meantime, 5th Guards Tank Corps tried once again to batter its way through the defense lines of *X. Armeekorps*, only to be stopped in its tracks. Nevertheless, the Germans took heavy casualties. The *X. Armeekorps*, for example, which had begun the second Russian offensive with over 8,000 troops, could now only count 4,012 men between its battered divisions. Altogether the second Courland offensive had cost the Germans about 44,000 men killed, wounded, or taken prisoner. Two German divisions—the Silesian *23. Infanterie-Division* and East Prussian *218. Infanterie-Division*—were bled so much that the only duty they could perform was coastal watch. Two additional divisions—the West Prussian *207. Infanterie-Division* and the Westphalian *285. Sicherungs-Division*—now had to be disbanded.

Some divisional losses were great, like within *32. Infanterie-Division*. By 28 November, *Infanterie-Regiment 4* had been reduced to eighty men in its *I. Bataillon* and forty men in its *II. Bataillon*. The regiment was now the size of a small company. Another regiment in the division, *Infanterie-Regiment 94*, only contained its *I. Bataillon*, which could count on only ninety men. Finally, the third regiment in the division, *Infanterie Regiment 96*, only had its *I. Bataillon*, with a strength of 105 men. Thus, the total 'bayonet' strength of *32. Infanterie-Division* on 28 November 1944 was just 315 men. Between 1–30 November, *Heeresgruppe Nord* lost 33,181 men killed, wounded, or taken prisoner. From September to the end of November, the army group had suffered 68,000 men killed, wounded, or taken prisoner. During the first two battles for Courland, the *Luftwaffe* there claimed to have shot down 293 Red Air Force fighters, fighter-bombers, and bombers. But in spite of these heavy losses, the Soviets controlled the skies over Latvia. On 1 December, the paper strength of the army group was 505,546 men. This number included all branches of service: *Heer, Luftwaffe, Kriegsmarine,* and *SS*.

## THE THIRD BATTLE FOR COURLAND, 21–31 DECEMBER 1944

In the third week in December, frost set in, and the muddy ground froze, allowing for the Soviets to attack again. On 21 December 1944, at 07:20 a.m., a heavy Russian artillery barrage began that eventually landed 170,000 shells on a narrow front of the German line. Hundreds of Russian guns bellowed, unleashing their deadly shells at the German positions. The Soviets employed the 3rd Shock Army, 4th Shock Army, 10th Guards Army, and the 42nd Army over a front line of just over twenty-three miles. The temperature in the open was only 5 degrees Fahrenheit. With the windchill factor, it was minus 10 degrees Fahrenheit. Simultaneously, the Red Air Force sent hundreds of bombers and fighter bombers to try and flatten what the immense artillery barrage had missed.

Approximately 170,000 artillery shells struck the front line of *I. Armeekorps* and *XXXVIII. Armeekorps*. The *205. Infanterie-Division, 215. Infanterie-Division, 225. Infanterie-Division,* and *563. Volksgrenadier-Division* were pummeled like rag dolls. At 8:30 a.m., 2nd Belarusian Front unleashed the first-wave units: 3rd Shock Army, 42nd Army, and 10th Guards Army. Simultaneously, 4th Shock Army from 1st Belarusian Front attacked. The objectives in the region of 1st Belarusian Front were Libau and Saldus. The small village of Pampali, which lay southwest of Saldus, turned out to be the focal point of the Red Army attack. The *329. Infanterie-Division* was hit head-on by the leading Russian tank division, with Soviet tanks and mechanized troops also attacking the *205. Infanterie-Division* on the left flank of *329. Infanterie-Division*.

Late in the morning of 21 December, *205. Infanterie-Division* collapsed. On the right flank of *329. Infanterie-Division*, the *225. Infanterie-Division* and *132. Infanterie-Division* did not collapse, but their front lines were broken, allowing enemy forces to pierce their lines. On the left flank of *205. Infanterie-Division*, the *215. Infanterie-Division* was also pushed back. It was at this time that the Germans

**Figure 52.** Army Group North on 2 December 1944.

sent in *227. Infanterie-Division* and *12. Panzer-Division* in a counterattack around Saldus. In addition, *Sturmgeschütz-Brigade 912* was also committed at Saldus.[7] However, these forces proved incapable of halting the Red Army advance. Another reinforcement, *11. Infanterie-Division,* was brought up to fill in the gap that had occurred between *132. Infanterie-Division* and *225. Infanterie-Division*.

On 22 December, the 4th Shock Army, with nine divisions, renewed its attack against Pampali after another artillery and air barrage covered the German front lines in and around the village. The brunt of this assault fell on the positions of *225. Infanterie-Division*. The army group now released *4. Panzer-Division* from reserve and committed it between *225. Infanterie-Division* and *329. Infanterie-Division*. However, various circumstances dealing with the weather, congested roads, poor radio communication, and lack of sufficient petrol caused 40 percent of the Panther tanks of *4. Panzer-Division,* 50 percent of its Tiger-I tanks, and 75 percent of its *Panzer IV* tanks were unable to reach the selected location.

As a result, only a small battle group, with twenty Panther tanks, ten Tiger-I tanks, and two Panzergrenadier companies of *4. Panzer-Division* counterattacked.

**Figure 53.** Positions of *Heeresgruppe Kurland* on 24 January 1945.

Unfortunately for the Germans, the attacked force proved too small. In addition, the *kampfgruppe* was subject to a Red Army anti-tank ambush that finally halted their advance.[8] By 23 December, *4. Panzer-Division* could count on only thirteen tanks. Another forty-nine tanks were being serviced in the rear and were, therefore, not operable at this time.[9] Nevertheless, the employment of this panzer division did manage to temporarily hold the line.

On 24 December (Christmas Eve), the 22nd Army (2nd Belarusian Front) attacked the position of *VI. SS-Armeekorps* north of Dobele in an attempt to capture the town of Dschegsten (Džūkste), which lay to the northwest. In a strange twist of fate, Latvians serving in the Red Army 130th Infantry Corps, attacked Latvians who were serving in the *19. Waffen-Grenadier-Division der SS (lettische*

Nr. 2).[10] The SS division, as well as *281. Sicherungs-Division* on its left flank, were slowly pushed back about eight kilometers. The fighting between the Latvian SS and the Red Army Latvians would continue until the end of the year. On the left flank of *VI. SS-Armeekorps, XVI. Armeekorps* held. That evening, the Red Army ceased its attacks. On the morning of 25 December, however, the fighting for Džūkste continued.

Meanwhile, 6th Guards Army attacked in the direction of Bunkas, eastsoutheast of Grobina. This move again threatened to encircle Libau. By 26 December, the German army group claimed to have destroyed 111 enemy tanks and assault guns between 1 and 26 December. On 28 December, the Red Army 5th Tank Corps and 19th Tank Corps finally broke through the German lines at Džūkste. The situation was temporarily saved when the Latvian SS division counterattacked on 29 December. Next, it was the turn of *93. Infanterie-Division* to be hit hard, but the arrival of the now replenished *4. Panzer-Division* saved the day. The Germans also brought in *12. Panzer-Division*, which helped to halt the Red Army offensive in and around Džūkste. By 31 December, the third battle for Courland ground to a halt. The modest estimate of Russian armored fighting vehicles destroyed in the whole of December 1944 was probably around 400. The Red Army also took somewhere between 16,000 to 18,000 men killed, wounded, or captured. German losses were perhaps 10,000 to 12,000 men.

## THE FOURTH BATTLE FOR COURLAND, 23 JANUARY TO 3 FEBRUARY 1945

At the end of the third battle for Courland, the army group contained 405,000 men, of which 375,000 were frontline soldiers and 20,000 were *Luftwaffe* troops, with about 12,000 *Waffen-SS* and *SS-Polizei* forces. Around 71,000 soldiers had been evacuated from the Courland pocket in December 1944 alone. At the beginning of January 1945, four German divisions in the Courland pocket—*19. Waffen-Grenadier-Division der SS (lettische Nr. 2), 4. Panzer-Division, 12. Panzer-Division*, and *12. Feld-Division (L)*—counterattacked in the area of Džūkste against the 42nd Army. This was a limited counterattack, geared to create more space for maneuver. By 6 January, the Germans had advanced about three kilometers of ground. The attack did not occur without losses. In fact, *4. Panzer-Division* had to be withdrawn when all of their tanks were either destroyed or rendered unusable due to mechanical reasons.

The Fourth Battle of Courland began on 23 January 1945 with the Soviets attacking at two distant focal points in the German line simultaneously. One was an attack on both sides of the town of Prekuln, followed by further attacks between Frauenburg and Tukkum. The Russians were hoping to capture Libau, Prekuln (Prekule), Saldus, and Džūkste. The *215. Infanterie-Division* and *205. Infanterie-Division*, both of which were located south of Saldus and were neighbors along the front line, were hit particularly hard by the initial Soviet artillery barrage that heralded this fourth offensive. Then the nine rifle divisions, supported by tanks of 10th Guards Army, attacked. The front line began to buckle, until the divisional commander of *215. Infanterie-Division* ordered a counterattack. Employing handheld anti-tank weapons backed up by some guts, the Swabian grenadiers of *215. Infanterie-Division* held the Soviets long enough for the Pomeranian *12. Panzer-Division* to arrive. The fighting here continued until 3 February, with no significant breakthrough being made by the Red Army.

In the meantime, the 6th Guards Army launched eleven Red Army divisions against the German defenders near Prekuln. In the way were three German divisions: *121. Infanterie-Division, 263. Infanterie-Division,* and *126. Infanterie-Division.* Supporting these divisions were the *Stug. IV L 48* assault guns of *Sturmgeschütz-Brigade 912.*[11] On the right flank of *121. Infanterie-Division* were the *11. SS-Freiwilligen-Panzergrenadier-Division 'Nordland'* and *30. Infanterie-Division.* These two divisions now took the brunt of the attack by the Soviet 51st Army. The same day that the Red Army launched its fourth offensive, the *X. Armeekorps* requested the release of the *14. Panzer-Division,* which had been under *18. Armee* reserve. However, the division did not arrive to help the grenadiers of *30. Infanterie-Division* and the Norwegian, Dutch and Danish volunteers of *11. SS-Freiwilligen-Panzergrenadier-Division 'Nordland'* until 25 January. Supporting *14. Panzer-Division* was the heavy Tiger tank battalion, *schwere Panzer-Abteilung 510*. This heavy tank battalion was initially outfitted with Tiger-I tanks.

A seesaw battle now erupted with the front lines moving back and forth, depending on who was counterattacking at any particular time. This continued for several days. The fighting persisted until 3 February, when heavy snows made further operations virtually impossible. The fighting that took place during this fourth offensive showed no clear breakthrough being made by the Red Army. Only the positions along the Vartaja River had to be abandoned as the Red Army front lines reached the river at the beginning of February 1945.[12] The Soviets managed to take the bridgeheads on the Bārta and Vārtāja Rivers, but later counterattacks stabilized the situation. The Silesian regiments of *87. Infanterie-Division,* belonging to *II. Armeekorps* of *18. Armee,* had to establish a defensive line along the Vārtāja River.

The *14. Panzer-Division* was again placed in reserve, this time near Berzkrog. These preparations were part of safeguarding the Liepāja–Saldus railway line. On 17 February 1945, the *215. Infanterie-Division* was ordered out of the front lines and directed to travel to Libau (Liepāja) for its planned evacuation from the Courland pocket. The Thuringian *24. Infanterie-Division* was brought up to replace it on the front lines. The division embarked and was transported to Gotenhafen and Danzig-Neufahrwasser.[13] Between 23 January and 3 February, the Red Army lost about 42,000 troops killed, wounded, or taken prisoner. In addition, according to the Germans, the Soviets lost 541 tanks and assault guns during the same period. On 20 February, *Heeresgruppe Kurland* had 354,600 men of the *Heer*, 21,000 men from the *Luftwaffe*, 12,000 men of the *Waffen-SS*, and 12,600 men of the *Reichsarbeitsdienst* (Reich Labor Service).

## THE FIFTH BATTLE FOR COURLAND, 20 FEBRUARY TO 10 MARCH 1945

On 20 February 1945, at exactly 7:00 a.m., more than 2,000 Red Army artillery, heavy mortar, and Katyusha rockets began to rain down steel fire on the German positions between Dzukste (Džūkste) on the eastern side of Courland and Preekuln (Priekule) on the western side of Courland. The Fifth Battle of Courland had begun. Five German divisions in and around Prekuln were now attacked by twenty-one Red Army divisions belonging to 51st Army and 6th Guards Army, supported by several tank brigades. This fifth offensive came with a renewed Russian effort to destroy the port facilities of both Libau (Liepāja) and Windau (Ventspils) by air bombardment. In spite of the fact that some Soviet infantry units were late in starting the offensive, by 21 February, the Red Army had surrounded Prekuln. The trapped German forces inside the town managed to break out on 22 February. To restore the front line there to some sort of cohesive defense, the Germans sent in *14. Panzer-Division, 11. Infanterie-Division,* and *Heeres-Sturmartillerie-Brigade 912* (the old *Sturmgeschütz-Brigade 912* renamed). Eventually this effort also required the employment of *132. Infanterie-Division* and *225. Infanterie-Division*. This took about a week to accomplish.

On 1 March, it was the turn of the German defenders at Saldus to feel the Soviet wrath, when 42nd Army launched its attack. The *122. Infanterie-Division* was hit hard, falling back to the town of Dzukste, which quickly fell. On the right flank of *122. Infanterie-Division,* both the *19. Waffen-Grenadier-Division der SS (lettische Nr. 2)* and the *24. Infanterie-Division* were able to hold on to their positions in the forest. It was then that *Panzer-Brigade 'Kurland'* was employed there to stabilize the German front. The Red Army persisted in trying to break the German lines for another week until the offensive was called off on 10 March 1945. The Fifth Battle for Courland had now come to a halt. The Germans held the line and did not allow any serious breakthrough to occur, but this came at a cost. The *121. Infanterie-Division* was so weakened from the fighting that for a time it had to be withdrawn from the front lines. This division later switched positions with *87. Infanterie-Division,* which had covered a quieter sector of the front. After-action reports noted that during this fifth offensive the Red Army had lost 70,000 men killed, wounded, or taken prisoner and lost 600 tanks and assault guns.

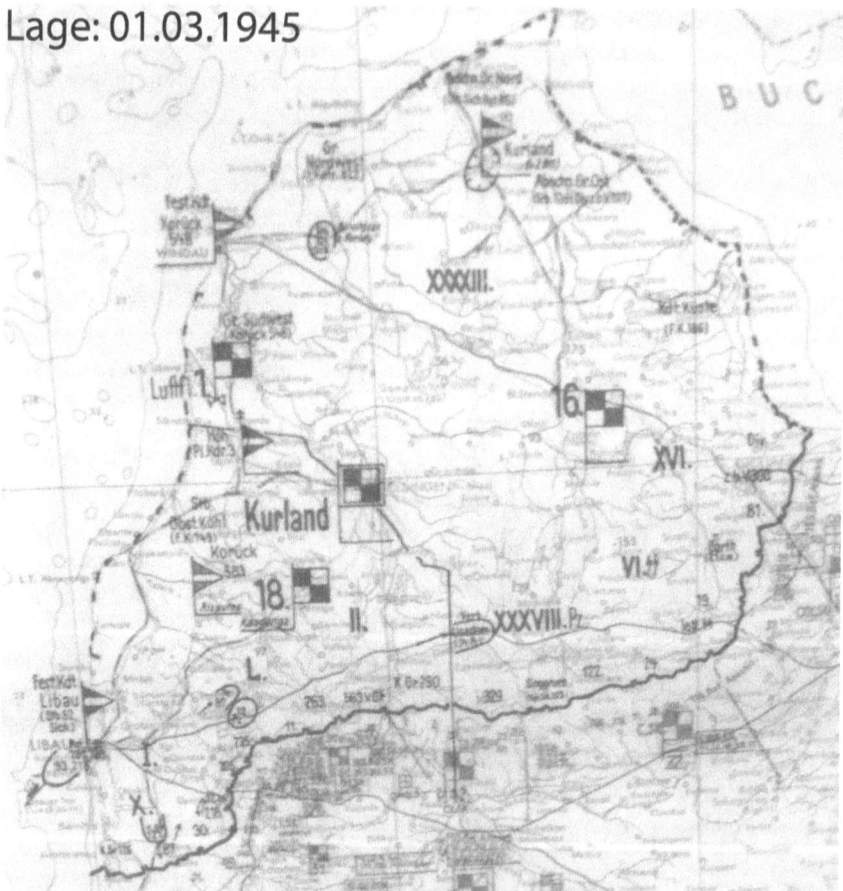

**Figure 54.** Location of units under Army Group Courland on 1 March 1945.

## THE SIXTH BATTLE FOR COURLAND, 18–31 MARCH 1945

Around mid-March, the snow and ice began to melt, turning what had been hard surfaces into a quagmire of mud. Many roads and trails were under water. The Soviet 10th Guards Army was selected to be the lead force in a renewed Russian attempt to capture Libau. On the first day of the offensive, the Soviets lost ninety-two tanks. Once again, the army group brought in the divisions that had become known as the 'fire brigades' that could extinguish the enemy's attack: *11. Infanterie-Division, 12. Panzer-Division,* and *14. Panzer-Division*. This time, however, these divisions had been replenished after the losses that they incurred from the fifth Russian offensive. The line began to give way and soon was broken at Saldus. The *122. Infanterie-Division* and *218. Infanterie-Division* were pushed back. Meanwhile the Red Air Force was once again targeting the port of Libau and Ventspils. This time, communications hubs and supply lines were targeted with greater brevity than had been seen previously.

The fighting became more intense, as communication among the German divisional and regimental headquarters began to falter. This, in turn, caused commands to be delayed, misinterpreted, or not acted upon at all. The result was the fragmentation of the German lines, as gaps appeared through which Soviet troops move toward the rear of the German line. Battalions were cut off from their regiment, strong points were surrounded, and even the German artillery batteries came under direct enemy tank and infantry attack. The fighting centered on the forests and local villages and houses located just south of Saldus. In this type of close-quarters fighting, the *218. Infanterie-Division* from Berlin-Brandenburg quickly became cut off and had to break out.

Once again, the *14. Panzer-Division* was sent in to assist *218. Infanterie-Division* to extricate itself from the trap, but it spent its final strength in achieving this success. For some reason, the Red Army offensive stopped on 23 March. By then the Soviets had lost another 263 tanks and assault guns. Fighting continued into the beginning of April, with no sizable territory being captured by the Red Army. By then, Soviet losses for this sixth offensive numbered around 70,000 men killed, wounded, or taken prisoner. On 1 April, the commander of *Heeresgruppe Kurland* wrote a report in which he rated the divisions under his command. These were rated as follows:

**Table 2. Combat Rating of German Divisions in Courland, 1 April 1945.**

| Division | Rating |
|---|---|
| 11. Infanterie-Division | Very Good |
| 12. Panzer-Division | Good |
| 24. Infanterie-Division | Good |
| 81. Infanterie-Division | Good |
| 121. Infanterie-Division | Good |
| 126. Infanterie-Division | Sufficient |
| 205. Infanterie-Division | Sufficient |
| 225. Infanterie-Division | Sufficient |
| 263. Infanterie-Division | Sufficient |
| 329. Infanterie-Division | Sufficient |
| 30. Infanterie-Division | Barely Adequate |
| 122. Infanterie-Division | Barely Adequate |
| 132. Infanterie-Division | Barely Adequate |
| 218. Infanterie-Division | Barely Adequate |
| 290. Infanterie-Division | Barely Adequate |
| 19. Waffen-Grenadier-Division der SS | Barely Adequate |
| 14. Panzer-Division | Barely Adequate |
| 563. Volksgrenadier-Div. | Insufficient |

124    *The Bitter End*

Given that reinforcements were no longer arriving from the Reich, the commander of the army group requested that the *Luftwaffe* in Courland make available men that could serve as infantrymen. The *Luftwaffe* provided 7,000 men divided into seventeen battalions (a little over 400 men per battalion). These *Luftwaffe* battalions, although of limited use given their lack of infantry training, nevertheless filled in some gaps in the army group.

## THE TALLY SHEET

On 1 May 1945, the Red Army announced over loudspeakers that the Führer was dead. Since no German troops surrendered after the news was announced, the Soviet command ordered their artillery to begin to plaster the German front lines. This occurred on 3 May, with a simultaneous announcement that Berlin had fallen and the war for Germany was lost. On 7 May, Admiral Karl Dönitz, who

**Figure 55.** Location of German and Russian units in Courland on 1 April 1945.

was the new head of government for what remained of the Reich, was forced to sign unconditional surrender. The commander of *Heeresgruppe Kurland* contacted the Russians and between them they agreed that hostilities would cease beginning at 2 p.m. on 8 May 1945. A final wave of 14,400 men left by boat from Libau (Liepāja), and another 11,300 troops managed to escape Courland in the early morning hours of 9 May from the port of Windau (Ventspils). Their destination: Allied-controlled Germany. On the evening of 9 May, 203,112 Germans (of which 189,000 were combat troops), including forty-two generals and 14,000 Latvians, surrendered to the Red Army. Between October 1944 and May 1945, somewhere between 25,000 to 30,000 German soldiers were killed in Courland. Over the same period of time, another 80,000 to 100,000 were wounded, and around 207,000 were captured. That figure of 207,000 includes the 203,112 that surrendered on 9 May 1945. Over the entire campaign in Courland, around 170,000 soldiers and 200,000 civilians were evacuated to the Reich. Some fanatical Nazi officers and men preferred to kill themselves rather than surrender.

## WITHDRAWALS AND REINFORCEMENTS

Throughout the campaign in Courland, the Kriegsmarine kept the army group there supplied with sufficient arms and ammunition. Only toward the end of March 1945 did munitions and supplies for Courland begin to falter. This reflected the decreasing effectiveness of the German Navy. Although there had been a plan to evacuate Courland, Hitler had forbidden it, most likely because withdrawing so many men was a logistical impossibility. Nevertheless, other German army groups, particularly Army Group Center and then Army Group Vistula, continued to receive divisions from Courland. Officially Army Group Courland could not withdraw, but realistically, a part of the army group did just that. The following German units were withdrawn from Courland between November 1944 and March 1945:

- *290. Infanterie-Division*—withdrawn in November 1944.
- *4. Panzer-Division*—withdrawn on 17 January 1945.
- *32. Infanterie-Division*—withdrawn in late January 1945. At the beginning of February 1945, the division stood between Jastrow (Jastrowie) and Camin (Camin powiedział) in Poland.
- *III. (Germanisches) SS-Panzerkorps*—withdrawn in late January 1945.
- *11. SS-Freiwilligen-Panzergrenadier-Division 'Nordland'*—withdrawn in late January 1945.
- *4. SS-Freiwilligen-Panzergrenadier-Brigade 'Nederland'*—withdrawn 28 January 1945 to Stettin to form into a new unit: *23. SS-Freiwilligen-Panzergrenadier-Division 'Nederland'* The strength of this new 'division' was only 5,700 men—the size of a reinforced brigade.
- *215. Infanterie-Division*—withdrawn in February 1945.

*93. Infanterie-Division*—withdrawn in February 1945. Located in Samland (northwest of Königsberg) on 1 March 1945.

*schwere Panzer-Abteilung 510*—withdrawn in February 1945. Donated its remaining twenty-two Tiger-I tanks to *Panzer-Brigade 'Kurland'*.

*12. Feld-Division (L)*—withdrawn in early March 1945.

Also evacuated were the remnants of:

*15. Waffen-Grenadier-Division der SS (lettische Nr. 1)*—withdrawn in January 1945.

*31. Volksgrenadier-Division*—battle group withdrawn in late January 1945. Arrived in Schwetz (Siwecle), northeast of Bromberg (Bydgoszcz), on 4 February 1945 without heavy weapons and vehicles.

*227. Infanterie-Division*—withdrawn in January 1945.

*389. Infanterie-Division*—withdrawn in February 1945.

The following formations were created at the end of January and beginning of February 1945 for employment in Courland:

A. *Fahnenjunker-Grenadier-Regiment 'Kurland'* (Officer Candidate Regiment 'Kurland')
   *I. Bataillon*
   *II. Bataillon*
B. *Feldausbildungs-Division 'Kurland'* (ex-*Feldausbildungs-Division Nord*)
   *Feldausbildungs-Regiment 639*
   *Feldausbildungs-Regiment 640*
C. *Panzer-Brigade 'Kurland'* (created from parts of *12. Panzer-Division, 14. Panzer-Division,* and excess army personnel from *16. Armee*):[14]
   Brigade commanders: *Oberst* Horst von Usedom, then: *Major* Graf von Rittberg

Organization:

*Brigade-Stab 'Kurland'* (from the staff of *Panzer-Regiment 29*)
   *Panzer-Bataillon 'Kurland'* (twenty-two Tiger-I tanks donated by *schwere Panzer-Abteilung 510*, when it was withdrawn from Courland in February 1945) with:
      *Panzer-Bataillon Hauptquartier* (two Tiger-I tanks)
      *1. Panzer-Kompanie* (ten Tiger-I tanks)
      *2. Panzer-Kompanie* (ten Tiger-I tanks)
      *3. (Beute) Panzer-Kompanie* (ten captured T-34/76 and T-34/85 tanks)
   *Divisions-Füsilier-Bataillon 12* (formerly *Panzer-Aufklärungs-Abteilung 12*)
   *Divisions-Füsilier-Bataillon 14* (formerly *Panzer-Aufklärungs-Abteilung 14*)
   *Grenadier-Sturm-Bataillon 'Kurland'*—simply a renaming of *Sturm-Bataillon AOK 16*

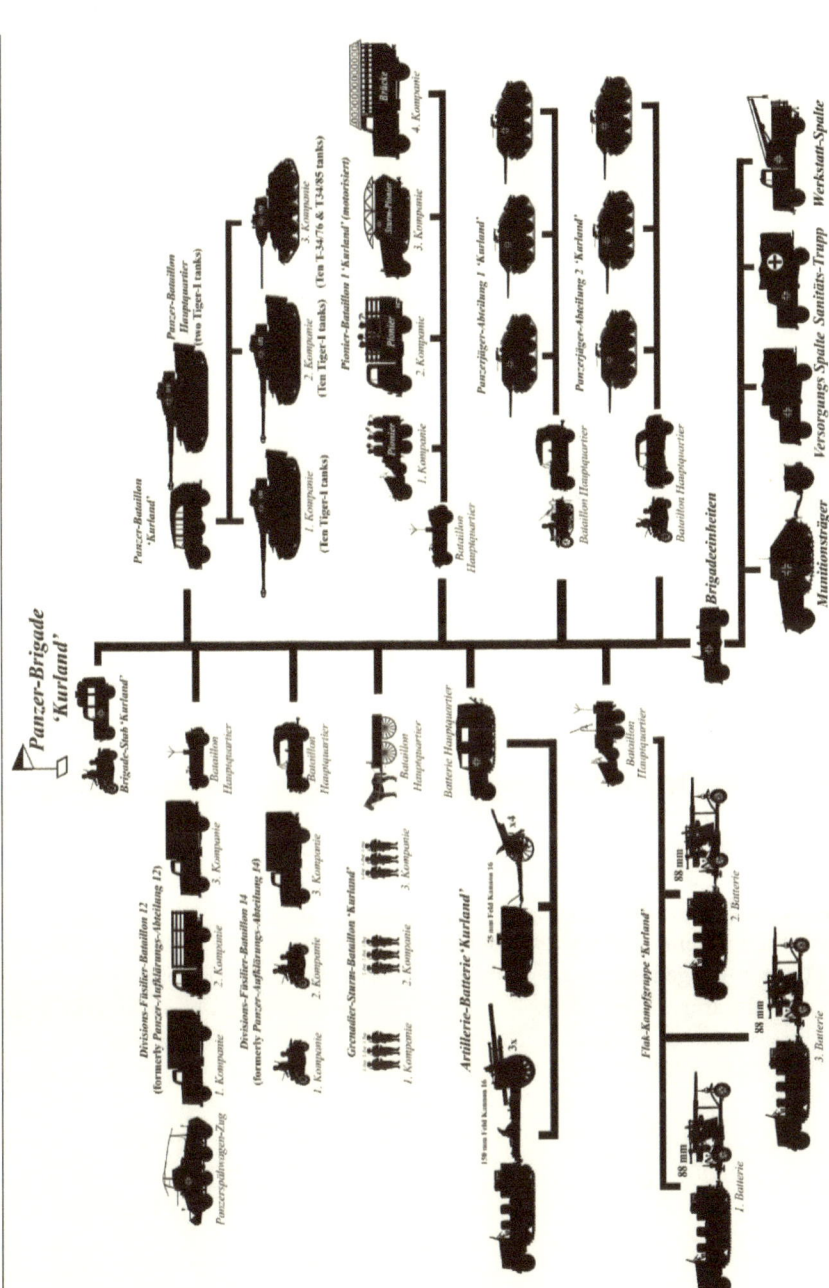

**Figure 56.** Organization of Panzer-Brigade 'Kurland' in March 1945. AUTHOR'S LINE DRAWING.

(The assault infantry battalion for *16. Armee*)

*Pionier-Bataillon 1 'Kurland' (motorisiert)*—from *Heeres-Pionier-Bataillon 44 (16. Armee)*

*Panzerjäger-Abteilung 1 'Kurland'* (28x *Panzer. 38(t) Hetzer* tank destroyers)[15]

*Panzerjäger-Abteilung 2 'Kurland'* (25x *Panzer. 38(t) Hetzer* tank destroyers)[16]

*Flak-Kampfgruppe 'Kurland'* (three batteries of 88 mm flak guns in an anti-tank role)

*Artillerie-Batterie 'Kurland'* (three heavy 150 mm and four light 75 mm field howitzers)

*Panzer-Brigade 'Kurland'* was employed as a whole unit in February 1945 around Itzried-Bunka, about forty kilometers southeast of Libau. The reason that this armored brigade was created was because of the withdrawal from Courland of *III. (Germanisches) SS-Panzerkorps* and its two component units: *11. SS-Freiwilligen-Panzergrenadier-Division 'Nordland'* and *4. SS-Freiwilligen-Panzergrenadier-Brigade 'Nederland'*.

## A FINAL WORD ON ARMY GROUP COURLAND

Some authors have claimed that Adolf Hitler's whim or lack of military expertise was the reason why *Heeresgruppe Nord*, aka *Heeresgruppe Kurland*, was left to fend for itself while the rest of the *Ostheer* fought it out with the Red Army between the Vistula and Oder rivers from 12 January–30 April 1945. My research has concluded that there were three reasons possibly why Hitler may have wanted to keep the army group where it was. First, the Führer probably believed that this large force in the Baltic States, although surrounded, was tying down a sizable force of Soviet troops that would otherwise be used against Berlin, the final Russian goal. Secondly, as prefaced in this chapter, Hitler actually had plans, no matter how fantastical and impossible to achieve, to reestablish a land link with *Heeresgruppe Kurland* if the Ardennes offensive would have succeeded as Hitler wished. Thirdly, Hitler (rightly) judged that it was virtually impossible for the *Kriegsmarine* to evacuate most of the army group safely. This, however, did not prevent him from taking some divisions out of the pocket to reinforce the main German front lines.

## Chapter 11

## *FESTUNGEN*: BREAKWATERS IN THE EAST

### BLITZKRIEG WARFARE BUT SIEGE MENTALITY

A factor that helped to shorten World War II was Adolf Hitler's 'Stand Fast' directive, forcing German units to freeze and hold their ground where they happened to be. The reason why Hitler gave this absurd military order was because he hated giving up ground. This most often made it easier for Allied forces to bypass German units. Surrounded German formations where then destroyed. The best example of this is Hitler's decision not to permit *6. Armee* to withdraw from Stalingrad. When the Red Army broke through the front lines of the 3rd Romanian Army, northwest of Stalingrad (on 19 November 1942), and the 4th Romanian Army, southeast of Stalingrad (on 20 November 1942), an encirclement of *6. Armee* was a forgone conclusion. The 'Stand Fast' order was issued to *6. Armee* on 24 November 1942. That directive was the death knell for all German soldiers fighting at Stalingrad. Unfortunately for the Germans, Hitler's decision to order the *Ostheer* to 'stand fast' during the Soviet 1941–1942 winter counteroffensive had proven to be the best option, given the military situation that he himself helped to create. This, in turn, solidified in Hitler's mind the mistaken belief that *always* standing fast was the best course of action.

Thus, Hitler's penchant for employing World War I–style tactics was encouraged and affirmed in what was clearly a war of maneuver. He took this idea a step further with his decision to create what he termed *festungen* (fortresses). The theory behind these 'fortresses' was that certain strategically important cities would be declared as strongholds, where German troops were ordered to hold their positions to the last man, even though surrounded. Hitler believed this would stiffen resistance, bolster morale, and buy time for German forces to regroup or mount counteroffensives. Hitler likened these so-called fortress cities to breakwaters which would fragment or at least slow down enemy offensives. This was a throwback to his experiences as a corporal in the 16th Bavarian Reserve Infantry Regiment during World War I.

What Hitler failed to factor in his calculation to employ this tactic was that military forces during World War I moved significantly slower than their later counterparts in World War II. Speed made creating 'fortresses' in towns and cities behind the enemy advance superfluous. All they did was tie up German troops that the Third Reich could ill afford to lose. But, as stated previously, Hitler had the final say in all matters political and military. No one could countermand a *Führerdirektiv* without risking his life in the process. These directives formed a part of Hitler's centralized control over military decisions. These orders and commands often bypassed or overrode sound advice given by professional military officers. In a real sense, Hitler was his own worst enemy. He was not a trained military tactician and many, if not most, of his military decisions showed him to be an amateur on the battlefield. These imprudent decisions also helped cost him the war. The following were the major cities that Adolf Hitler labeled as a *'festung'* (fortress) on the Eastern Front:

1. Glogau: The siege of the Silesian city of Glogau began on 11 February 1945 and ended on 1 April 1945 with the fall of the city. Glogau is now known as Glogów and is in western Poland.
2. Breslau (now Wrocław, Poland): August 1944. Declared a fortress and held out under siege by Soviet forces until 6 May 1945, just two days before Germany's surrender.
3. Posen, spelled Poznań in Polish:10 February 1945. Declared a fortress to slow down the Soviet advance. It was captured on 23 February 1945 after a thirteen-day siege.
4. Königsberg (now Kaliningrad, Russia): 24 January 1945. Designated a fortress, it withstood a Soviet siege until its fall on 9 April 1945.
5. Heiligenbeil (East Prussia, now called Mamonovo, Russia)—24 January 1945. Declared a fortress in the defense of East Prussia against the Soviets. Fell to the Red Army on 25 March 1945.
6. Danzig (now Gdańsk, Poland)—12 January 1945. Declared a fortress during the Soviet advance, it fell on 30 March 1945.
7. Vienna (Austria): 10 April 1945. Declared a fortress but fell to Soviet forces after intense fighting on 13 April 1945. The fighting for the city only lasted three days, so it does not warrant mention. For more information, please see chapter 8, 'Budapest and Vienna'.
8. Berlin (Germany): 16 April 1945. In the final days of the war, Berlin was effectively designated a fortress, defended fiercely in the Battle of Berlin before its fall on 2 May 1945. This city will be discussed within the context of the chapter on the Russian Oder offensive and the capture of Berlin, ending the war.

The above list does not even include the fifteen French and German cities that the western Allies also labeled as fortresses, the most important of which were the following: Brest, Lorient, Saint-Nazaire, Dunkirk, and Metz.

## Glogau

The siege of Glogau lasted from 11 February to 1 April 1945. The 3rd Guards Tank Army, commanded by General Pavel Rybalko, took part in surrounding the city. However, it was the 5th Guards Army, led by General Aleksei Zhadov, which was assigned the task of reducing the fortress. In addition, the Soviet 13th Army played a supporting role in the siege. Leadership over the garrison was initially entrusted to *Oberst* Schön. Soon after, it was handed to *Oberst* Jonas Graf zu Eulenburg, who became the final *Festungskommandant* (fortress commander). Colonel Eulenburg had won the German Cross in Gold on 7 December 1944, while leading *Grenadier-Regiment 67* of the Thuringian *23. Infanterie-Division*. He had earned this award for the actions of his regiment on the Baltic islands of Moon and Sworbe, on 19 October 1944. For his stiff defense of Glogau, Eulenburg was awarded the Knight's Cross of the Iron Cross on 22 March 1945. The garrison defending Glogau consisted of the following units:[1]

*Festungs-Infanterie-Bataillon 1445*
*Landesschützen-Bataillon 1091*
*Pionier-Ersatz und Ausbildungs-Bataillon 213*
*Pionierkompanie 61 (Festungs-Pionierstab 9)*
*Festungs-Artillerie-Abteilung 61*
*Reserveoffiziersanwärterschule*

In addition, the garrison commander of Glogau could count on five *Volkssturm* battalions made up from the male inhabitants of Glogau and the surrounding villages, whose ages ranged from sixteen to sixty years old. In total, *Festung Glogau* had perhaps 6,000 to 7,000 men. By German Army 1945 standards, that equaled about one division. However, only about 1,500 were actual veterans, and the rest were basically unproven in combat. The city did have the added benefit of being surrounded by forts. Because of the way that the forts were designed and built, they provided excellent enfilade fire that could rain down on enemy troops attempting to take the strongholds. In fact, Soviet troops found it frustratingly difficult to reduce these fortresses. These defensive works allowed the garrison to last for as long as it did. Between 28 January and 3 April, the OKW *(Oberkommando der Wehr-macht)* mentioned the siege of Glogau a total of seventeen times. The last mention of the Glogau defenders (3 April) was the following transcript from the OKW:

> The garrison of the fortress of Glogau, which has been encircled since 12 February, under the leadership of its commander, Colonel Graf zu Eulenburg, has closed the important Oder crossings to the enemy for more than six weeks of fighting and has tied up strong forces of the Soviets. Crowded together in a confined space, the brave defenders were overwhelmed by the enemy after the last ammunition had been fired.[2]

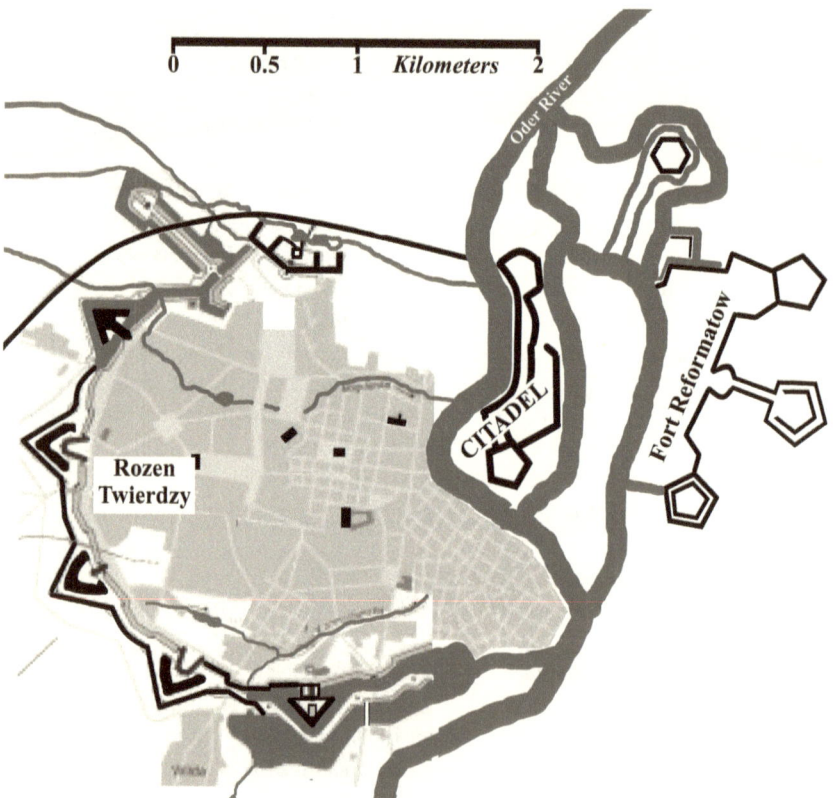

**Figure 57.** Glogau in 1945, with its fortifications.

The garrison of Glogau never surrendered. Instead, it was overwhelmed by superior Red Army forces on 1 April 1945. In a last-ditch attempt to avoid capture, Colonel Eulenburg and about 800 men attempted a breakout to the west, in hopes of reaching the German lines. Only a handful made it. The rest were either killed or captured. German losses during the siege numbered about 3,000 people, including civilians killed in the crossfire. Soviet losses were 3,500 killed or wounded.

*Breslau*

On 17 January 1945, as the Russian juggernaut neared Breslau, the provincial capital of Silesia, *Gauleiter* Karl Hanke gave the order for the code word '*Gneisenau*' to be broadcast on local radio and to be published on the front page of the local newspapers. This command immediately placed into motion the activation of all reserve, replacement, convalescent, *Volkssturm, Hitler Jugend*, and training units in the region of the city and surroundings to muster. Soldiers who were in transit and awaiting trains were also directed to report. From these diverse sources, five grenadier regiments were initially created by the end of the month. While the city was gathering its troops for a defense, the *269. Infanterie-Division*, which was fighting just east of the city, sacrificed itself to buy Breslau some time. For seven days, from 21–28 January, these grenadiers from north Germany threw themselves at the advancing Russian tanks and infantry.[3] Using teller mines, the handheld *Panzerfaust*, plastic charges, and even hand grenades wrapped in a bundle, they were able to knock out seventy-six Red Army tanks.[4] On 29 January, *269. Infanterie-Division* was ordered to new positions just south of Breslau. During the fighting, as the Red Army was attempting to encircle Breslau, part of this division would end up getting trapped in the city.

By 13 February 1945, the Red Army had effectively surrounded Breslau. For the defense of Breslau, Hanke promised fifty *Volkssturm* battalions, but only thirty-eight took part in the battle. Given that preparations for the defense of the Silesian capital had begun in the fall of 1944, a substantial force of Home Guard troops had been made available. In late January 1945, a *Hitler Jugend* regiment was organized and also employed for Breslau's defense. Then in February 1945, *SS-Festungs-Regiment 1*, more commonly known as *SS-Regiment 'Beßlein'*, after its commander, *SS-Obersturmbannführer* Georg-Robert Beßlein, was created from rear-area SS training and replacement units and schools. This SS regiment would feature prominently in the defense of the city. It was created partly from *1. SS-Infanterie-Geschütz-Ausbildungs und Ersatz-Bataillon 1*, a training unit stationed in Breslau. Another rear-area school that formed part of this SS regiment was

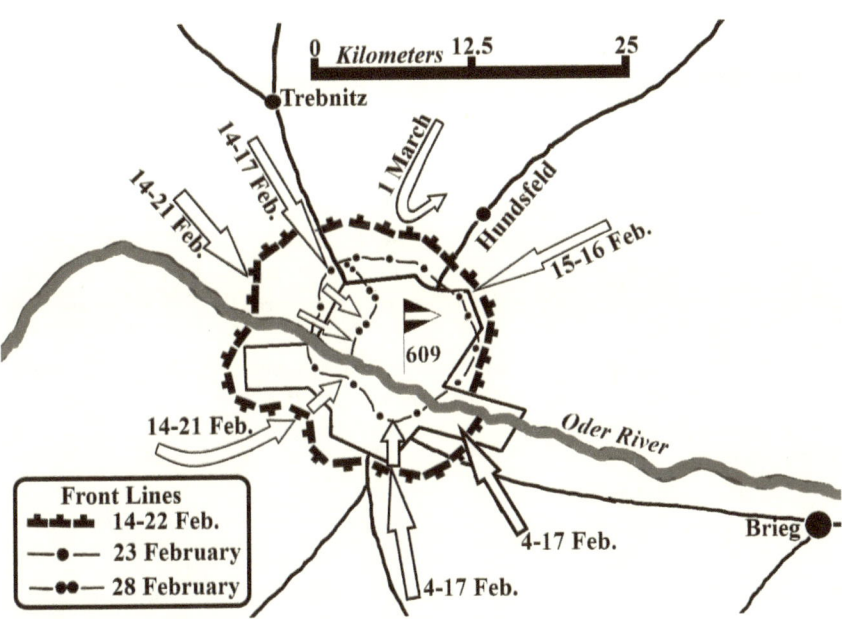

**Figure 58.** The siege of Breslau, February to March 1945.

*SS-Panzergrenadier-Ausbildungs und Ersatz-Bataillon 1*. Finally, the regiment had also been created from *SS-Unteroffizier-Verwaltungsschule* (SS NCO Administrative School), which was also located in Breslau. The regiment contained four battalions numbered using Roman numerals: *I., II., III.,* and *IV. Festungs-Bataillon 'Beßlein'*.

*Festung Grenadier-Regiment Breslau* (Fortress Grenadier-Regiment Breslau), another unit created to defend the Silesian capital, was established using men who were in the city in transit along with the following three army schools: *Heer-Unteroffizier-Schule 'Striegau', Heer-Fahrausbildung und Ersatz-Bataillon 28,* and *Heer-Veterinär-Ausbildungs und Ersatz-Bataillon 8*.[5] There was also to be an artillery regiment that was to be created in February 1945 for the defense of the city. However, this was never created given the lack of artillery guns. Instead, the men from *Artillerie-Regiment 15* were turned into infantrymen. The regiment contained four battalions of three batteries each and was named *Grenadier-Regiment 'Mohr'*, after its commander, *Major der Reserve* Otmar Mohr. Mohr had been the commander of the regiment's third artillery battalion in 1943, when he was a captain. Later *Major* Karl-Heinz Reichert replaced him in 1944 as the new commander of the third artillery battalion in the regiment. This new regiment was created in February, while the other regiments had been established in January 1945.[6]

That same month, a battle group of the *269. Infanterie-Division* became trapped in Breslau and fought as part of the garrison until the city's surrender on 6 May. For flak support, one flak regiment, stationed in Breslau, was employed against enemy ground forces. The regiment was raised in Breslau in March 1944 and was initially a part of *14. Flak-Division*. However, it was later assigned to *11. Flak-Division* when *14. Flak-Division* was transferred to Mecklenburg. As the Russian army attacked Breslau, *Flak-Regiment 150* (led by *Oberst der Luftwaffe* Joachim Quodbach)[7] took part in the city's defense.[8] Not all of the flak guns in the regiment were able to be employed against enemy ground targets, as some of the guns were stationary and/or placed on rooftops, which negated their use on the ground. Finally, on 26 January 1945, the army headquarters of *Wehrkreis IV* (4th Military District), located in Dresden, activated *Division z.b.V. 609*. The division was also referred to as *Festungs-Division 'Breslau'*. On 30 January 1945, *Generalleutnant* Siegfried Ruff was assigned as divisional commander. *Division z.b.V. 609* arrived in Breslau in February and was assigned to control the following units:[9]

*Regiment Reinkober*—*Oberst der Reserve* Fritz Reinkober[10] *(I., II., III. Bataillone)*
*Regiment Kersten*—*I. Bataillon, II. Bataillon, III. Bataillon*
*Regiment Schulz*—*I. Bataillon, II. Bataillon, III. Bataillon*
*Regiment Seybold*—*I. Bataillon, II. Bataillon, III. Bataillon*
*Nachrichten Kompanie 609*
*Nachrichten Kompanie 1609*

*Generalmajor* Hans von Ahlfen was initially assigned as commander in Breslau. For the defense of Breslau, von Ahlfen controlled all of the abovementioned units. In addition, he had command of the following additional forces in the city:

SS-*Festungs-Regiment 1*(*SS-Obersturmbannführer* Georg-Robert Beßlein)[11]
  I., II., III., IV. SS *Festungs Infanterie Bataillone*
*Regiment Breslau A*: I. *Bataillon*, II. *Bataillon*, III. *Bataillon*
*Regiment Breslau J*: *Volkssturm Bataillon 25, Volkssturm Bataillon 27, Volkssturm Bataillon 28*
*Regiment Frankenstein*: I. *Bataillon*
*Regiment Karlowitz*: I. *Bataillon*, II. *Bataillon*
*Regiment R. V. Breslau*: *Genesenden Bataillon Fischer, Volkssturm Bataillon 55*
*Artillerie-Regiment Breslau*, with:[12]
  *Festungs Batterie 3049* (renamed *Festungs Batterie 14*)
  10. *Batterie/Artillerie Regiment 269* (renamed *Festungs Batterie 15*)
  *Festungs Batterie 3075* (renamed *Festungs Batterie 16*)
  *Festungs Batterie 3076* (renamed *Festungs Batterie 17*)
  *Wanke Batterie* (renamed *Festungs Batterie 18*)
  *Festungs Batterie 3081* (renamed *Festungs Batterie 19*)
  *Festungs Batterie 3082* (renamed *Festungs Batterie 20*)
  *Artillerie Ersatz und Ausbildungs Abteilung 28*
    1. *Batterie*
    2. *Batterie*
  *schwere Artillerie Abteilung 859* (210 mm Mörser 18)
    1. *Batterie*
    2. *Batterie*
    3. *Batterie*

*Generalmajor* Hans von Ahlfen had just over 40,000 men to defend Breslau. The Russians, who would be attacking the city, had a little over 200,000 men. Frankly, the Russians should have employed more troops if they really wanted to capture the city quickly.

*Generalmajor* von Ahlfen could count on 30,000 soldiers plus 15,000 *Volkssturm*. These 45,000 men were now defending a built-up area (a city). German demolition teams and even foreign slave labor were put to work, creating bunkers and trenches that surrounded Breslau with several ringed defense lines. A portion of the city center was flattened so that an emergency airfield could be built. The reason why Breslau held out for as long as it did was because the city was defended by a large number of troops who were well-entrenched and motivated. Although the Russians had a five-to-one advantage in men and an overwhelming number of tanks and assault guns, these vehicles could not operate effectively in a built-up area such as a city, especially one that was partially demolished to create rubble and obstacles. It was in this environment that the German *Panzerfaust* worked most effectively at destroying Soviet armor. Finally, five Russian soldiers to one German soldier was not a sufficient ratio of troops needed to capture Breslau, even though a third of the garrison was composed of *Volkssturm* and *Hitler Jugend*. That was because the elaborate fortifications made up for their lack of training and experience.

136   *The Bitter End*

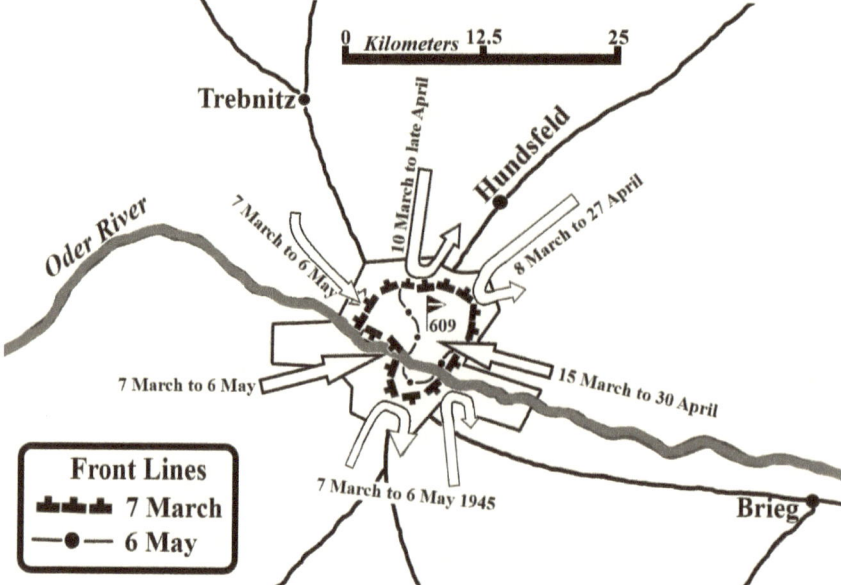

**Figure 59.** The siege of Breslau, March to April 1945.

Not all senior commanders in the city agreed on how best to defend Breslau. An argument soon broke out between von Ahlfen and *Gauleiter* Hanke over the airfield that was being built in the center of the city. From the beginning, both men did not get along. *Generalmajor* von Ahlfen saw Hanke as just another Nazi Party hack, with no real military experience. He chafed at having to hear Hanke's demands on how best to defend the city. *Gauleiter* Hanke saw von Alhfen as just another career officer—the same type of officer that had attempted to kill the Führer eight months earlier. Because of this growing rift between both men, von Ahlfen, who had been in charge of the city garrison since 30 January 1945, was eventually relieved of his command. Hanke, who had Nazi Party connections, got von Alhfen replaced. In his stead, *Generaloberst* Ferdinand Schörner, the commander of *Heeresgruppe Mitte*, assigned *General der Infanterie* Hermann Niehoff as the new garrison commander. Niehoff was appointed to this post on 5 March 1945. That same day, he was awarded the Oak Leaves to his Knight's Cross of the Iron Cross, which he had won on 15 June 1944, for his actions while leading *371. Infanterie-Division*.

*Posen (Poznan)*

The defense of Posen lasted about a month, from 25 January to 23 February 1945. In 1945, Posen had some advantages for a military force trying to defend the city. For one thing, the Warta River runs through Posen. The Warta flows from the Silesian Highlands to the south and eventually links up with the Oder River, which then empties into the Baltic Sea. The city also has old fortifications that were built in the nineteenth century. Although the forts and moats were from the past century, the Germans who would defend the city would make good use of them. When the siege began, the German garrison was somewhere between 15,000 and 20,000 men. They included *Luftwaffe* flak personnel conscripted to fight as infantry, several *Volkssturm* battalions, a company of *Sicherheitsdienst* personnel, the staff of the headquarters of the *Höhere-SS und Polizeiführer 'Warthe', General-SS Regiment 109* (which actually had the strength of a battalion), and even one SS police regiment. A small element of *Panzergrenadier-Division 'Großdeutschland'* also ended up fighting in the city. For the defense of the city, the Germans had two *Panther* tanks, one *Panzer IV* tank, and a few *Sturmgeschütz IV* assault guns. There was one *Tiger I* tank in the city that would become famous, because during the siege, this lone Tiger tank would be shifted from hot spot to hot spot, like a fire brigade. Eventually the Tiger tank was disabled by Russian fire, but even stationary, its crew continued to fight. The names of the crew members are as follows:[13]

> Commander: *Oberfeldwebel* Fritz Sander (later Richard Siegert would take command)
> Gunner: *Obergefreiter* Richard Siegert
> Driver: *Unteroffizier* Friedrich Heckmann
> Loader: *Schütze* Kurt Algner (later *Schütze* Everoth would assume this role)
> Radio operator/MG gunner: *Schütze* Kirrmeie

The initial garrison commander was *Generalmajor* Ernst Mattern, but he was replaced on 28 January 1945 by a fanatical Nazi general, *Generalmajor* Ernst Gonell. Mattern would now be second-in-command until Gonell killed himself on 23 February. Gonell's military background was mostly as regimental commander to various German infantry regiments. The principal forces defending the city were as follows:

> *Schule V für Fahnenjunker der Infanterie Posen*
> *Sturmgeschütz-Ersatz und Ausbildungs-Abteilung 500 (Major* Fritz Glossner*)*
> *Posen-Festungs-Infanterie-Bataillon 1442*
> *Posen-Festungs-Infanterie-Bataillon 1446*
> *Festungs-Maschinengewehr-Bataillon 82*
> *Festungs-Maschinengewehr-Bataillon 83*
> *Festungs-Maschinengewehr-Bataillon 90*
> *Festungs-Pionier-Bataillon 66*
> *Landesschützen-Bataillon 312*
> *Landesschützen-Bataillon 475*
> *Landesschützen-Bataillon 642*
> *Landesschützen-Bataillon 814*
> *1x Volkssturm Bataillon*
> *Kampfgruppe Lenzer (SS-Obersturmbannführer* Wilhelm Lenzer*)*[14]

The battle group contained around 500–600 men from the following units:

*Sicherheitsdienst-Kompanie der Höhere-SS und Polizeiführer 'Warthe'*
*General-SS Regiment 109* (actually a battalion in strength)
*Police Regiment Schallert* (*Oberst der Polizei* Hermann Schallert)
    *I. Bataillon* (actually a company in strength, CO: *Major der Polizei* Neufeld)
    *II. Bataillon* (actually a company in strength, CO: *Major der Polizei* Heine)
    *III. Bataillon* (actually a company in strength, CO: *Hauptmann der Polizei* Turban)

*Kampfgruppe Lenzer* also made use of six members of the *6. SS-Gebirgs-Division 'Nord'* and fifty members of the *19. Waffen-Grenadier-Division der SS* (lettische Nr. 2), which happened to be in the city. When the garrison surrendered, the Russians took 23,000 men prisoner. The Soviets had lost 6,000 men killed and many thousands more wounded.

Nothing in Gonell's résumé indicated that he was particularly brilliant or was an up-and-coming officer. Gonell was promoted to *Generalmajor* two days after becoming garrison commander of Posen (30 January). The Red Army forces that took the city included the following armies from the 1st Belarusian Front:

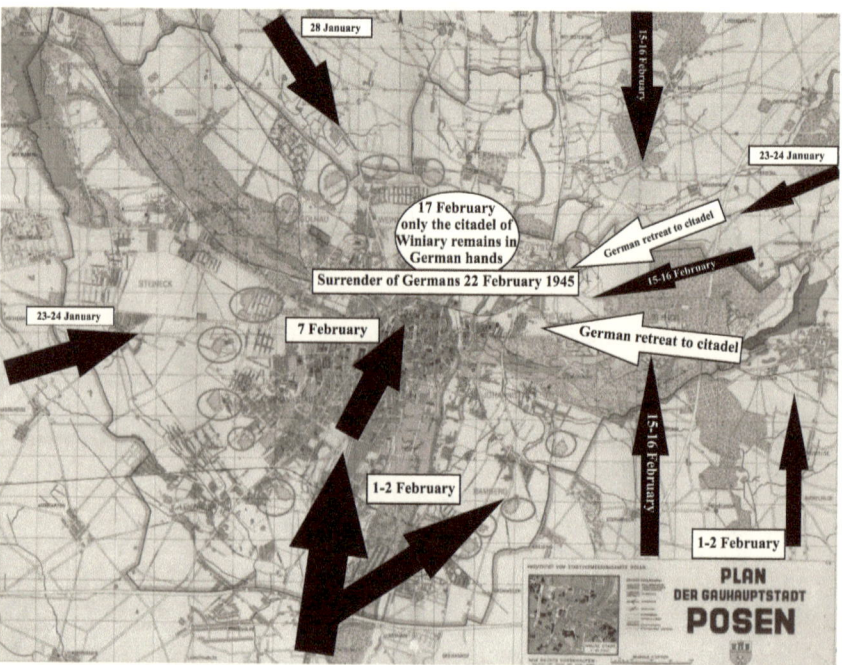

**Figure 60.** The capture of Posen (Poznan) by the Red Army in 1945.

8th Guards Army, commanded by General Vasily Chuikov
69th Army, under General Vasily Kryuchenkin
1st Guards Tank Army, led by General Mikhail Katukov

*Generalmajor* Gonell had been told to hold out because he was promised that he would be relieved. By 15 February, however, it was clear to Gonell that no relief was coming to the rescue of the trapped garrison. Apparently upset, that same day, he ordered that all German forces east of the Warta River were to attempt a breakout. On 18 February, the Red Army began its final assault on the redoubts and breastworks of the fortress at Posen. On 22 February, just a day before the garrison surrendered, Gonell was awarded the Knight's Cross of the Iron Cross. When the Posen garrison surrendered a day later, Gonell, who was forty-two years old, committed suicide. According to the story, he laid a Nazi flag on the floor of the headquarters bunker, laid down on it, then took out his Walther P-38 pistol and shot himself. The Red Army captured 12,000 German defenders who preferred to be taken prisoner rather than to die.

## Danzig

On 12 January 1945, the Red Army began their Vistula-Oder offensive. This offensive would break the back of Army Group Center, with Soviet forces traveling 300 miles west in a little over two weeks' time. On that same day (12 January), Danzig (Gdansk) was declared a fortress. Although the Red Army would threaten the city of Danzig as early as 7 March, the battle began a week later. The siege of Danzig would last two weeks, from 15–30 March 1945, and would involve a large number of German and Russian divisions. The siege of Danzig occurred within the context of a broader Russian offensive to liberate all of Pomerania. This was what the Red Army referred to as the East Pomeranian offensive. This offensive was split into several parts:

Konitz-Köslin offensive operation 24 February–6 March 1945
Danzig offensive operation 7–31 March 1945
Arnswalde-Kolberg offensive operation 1–18 March
Altdamm offensive operation 18 March–4 April 1945 (near Stettin)

On 24 January, Adolf Hitler ordered the creation of *Heeresgruppe Weichsel* (Army Group Vistula). Initially, Heinrich Himmler, the head of the SS, was appointed as its commander despite his limited military experience. The formation of Army Group Vistula was a desperate measure by the German High Command to consolidate their defenses in the face of the Soviet Vistula-Oder offensive.

The army group included remnants of other depleted units and newly formed divisions but struggled due to inadequate resources and leadership issues. The army group was tasked with defending the Oder River line from the advancing Soviet forces. It also assumed responsibility for the German divisions defending

140  *The Bitter End*

in and around Danzig. Seven German divisions were trapped in the city and eventually forced to surrender. They included *4. Panzer-Division, 32. Infanterie-Division, 203. Infanterie-Division, 542. Volksgrenadier-Division, 83. Infanterie-Division, 7. Panzer-Division,* and *18. Panzergrenadier-Division.* These divisions were

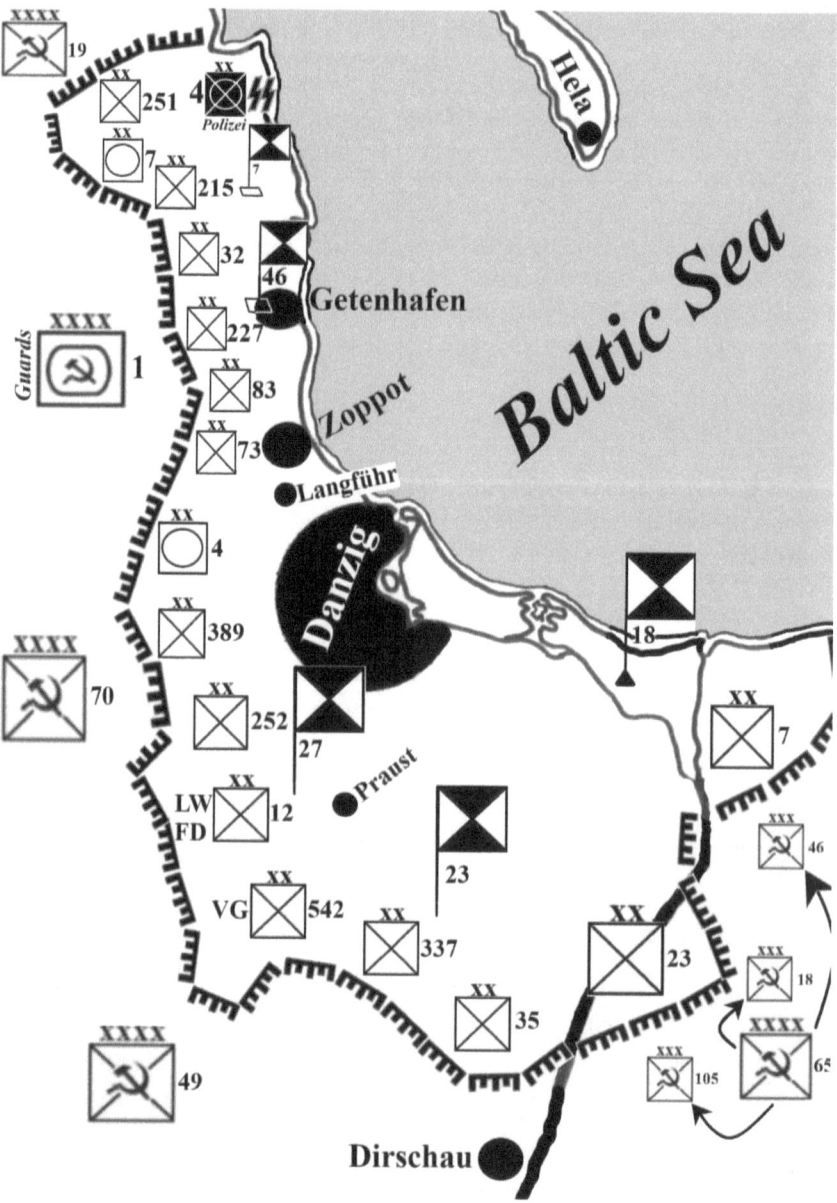

**Figure 61.** Second Army positions in and around Danzig, March 1945.

part of Army Group Vistula, under the command of General von Saucken. In the surrounded city were one and a half million terrified German civilians, about 100,000 wounded soldiers, and the remnants of the German *2. Armee*.[15] The units in this pocket extended in a semicircle from just northwest of Gotenhafen to southeast of Neustadt and east of Schönwalde. The lines then ran south to an area east of Karthaus and through the frontline towns of Rheinfeld and Löblau. On the eastern half of the pocket, the lines extended from Löblau to Dirschau then northeast to Neuteich, Tiegenhof, and finally Stutthof on the Bay of Danzig by the Frisches Haff. The city itself was captured on 30 March. The city had been surrounded for fifteen days. During that time, it was subject to intense and repeated artillery barrages.

### Königsberg

Between 12 and 14 January, the Soviets launched their winter offensive. The first units to begin the attack on 12 January were forces under the command of 1st Ukrainian Front. Using the bridgehead at Baranów, Red Army tanks and mechanized infantry were able to break through the German defense in half a day. The reserve for *4. Panzerarmee, XXIV Panzerkorps* was then committed on 14 January. The entire German line depended on the ability of *XXIV Panzerkorps* to halt the Russians. However, within twenty-four hours, Nehring's *XXIV Panzerkorps* was defeated. Now what lay in front of 1st Ukrainian Front was open ground. In the region of East Prussia, the 3rd Belarusian Front launched its attack on 14 January. The Soviet 43rd Army began to press the line held by *IX. Armeekorps*, taking Schlossberg (Pillkallen) on the fourth day of the offensive (18 January).

The 39th Army lent its support. The 5th Army, 28th Army, and 11th Guards Army attacked the weakened divisions of *XXVI. Armeekorps*. Despite intense pressure by the enemy, the Germans held Gumbinnen until it was taken on 22 January. Farther south, the 2nd Guards Army pushed forward toward Goldap, taking the town on 25 January. South of *XXVI. Armeekorps* lay the divisions of *XLI Panzerkorps*, which were facing the 31st Army. The 31st pushed forward beginning on 14 January and, by the afternoon of 24 January, had taken Lötzen (Giżycko).

To the west, Lake Niegocin was blocking the Soviet advance. Meanwhile, 6th Army had broken through the lines of *LV Armeekorps* and was threatening the right flank of *VI. Armeekorps*. By 27 January, four Soviet armies—43rd, 39th, 11th Guards, and 5th Army—were centering their attack vectors toward Königsberg. On 25 January, Hitler renamed those divisions belonging to Army Group Center who were now trapped in and around Königsberg and the area of the Frisches Hafe as Army Group North. Following this logic, Army Group 'A' was renamed as the new Army Group Center, and Army Group North became Army Group Courland. In spite of stiff resistance, the Red Army slowly squeezed the defenders in and around Königsberg belonging to *4. Armee*. The final assault on the city began on 6 April and ended on 9 April when the capital of East Prussia was captured.

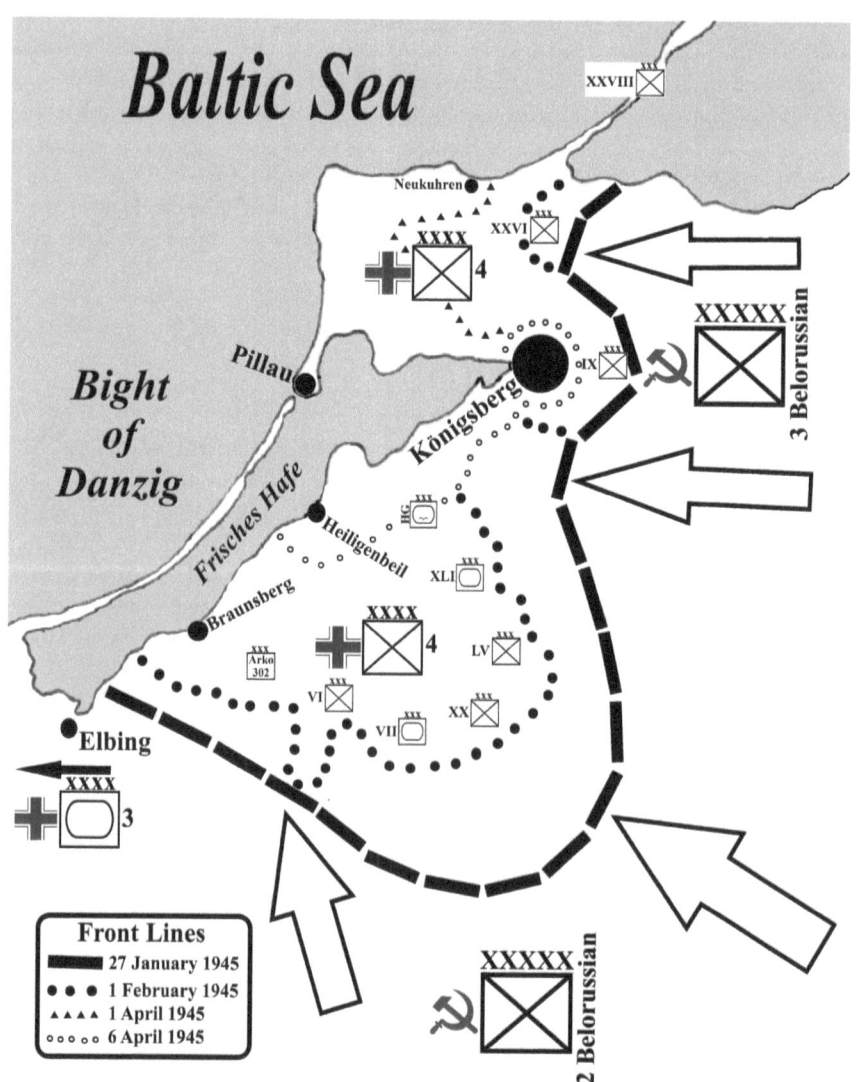

**Figure 62.** The siege of Konigsberg involved *3. Panzerarmee* and *4. Armee*. This map shows the front lines from 27 January to 6 April 1945. Most of *3. Panzerarmee* was able to withdraw into Pomerania, but *4. Armee* was unable to disengage and was destroyed in and around Königsberg.

Festungen: *Breakwaters in the East* 143

## THE HEILIGENBEIL POCKET, 26 JANUARY TO 8 APRIL 1945

Although not a siege of a city, the Heiligenbeil Pocket was the site of a major encirclement of German forces by the Soviet Red Army during the East Prussian Offensive in early 1945. It took place within the context of the capture of Königsberg by the Red Army. The pocket was formed around the area of Heiligenbeil (now Mamonovo, Russia) and included remnants of German Army Group Center, particularly the *4. Armee* under General Friedrich Hoßbach. The German divisions that were trapped and eventually destroyed or forced to surrender in the Heiligenbeil Pocket included the following: *28. Jäger-Division, 50. Infanterie-Division, 131. Infanterie-Division, 170. Infanterie-Division, 170. Volksgrenadier-Division, 286. Infanterie-Division, 349. Infanterie-Division, 558. Volksgrenadier-Division, 561. Volksgrenadier-Division, 563. Volksgrenadier-Division, 21. Infanterie-Division, 31. Infanterie-Division, 102. Infanterie-Division,* and *14. Infanterie-Division.*

These divisions, along with other smaller units and remnants of various formations, were encircled and eventually destroyed between late January and March 1945. The final collapse of the Heiligenbeil Pocket occurred in late March, and many of the remaining German forces were killed or captured or attempted to escape across the Baltic Sea via the port of Pillau.

**Figure 63.** German positions in and around Königsberg on 1 April 1945.

## THE SIEGE OF MEMEL (KLAIPEDA), 10 OCTOBER 1944 TO 28 JANUARY 1945

Like the Heiligenbeil Pocket, the siege of Memel was not considered one of Hitler's declared '*festungen*,' but it was an important part of the eastern campaign, so should be discussed. Basically, as the Red Army was advancing west, it launched what they called the Memel offensive from 5–22 October 1944. The attempt was to capture the port city and therefore help to seal off Army Group North from the main German front line. Although the Germans had launched two counter-offensives in August and September that temporarily halted the Red Army advance (*Unternehmen Doppelkopf* and *Unternehmen Casar*), by the beginning of October, the 1st Belarusian Front was on the verge of cutting off *Heeresgruppe Nord*. Half of the striking force of 1st Belarusian Front was concentrated in and around the northern Lithuanian town of Šiauliai. This huge force struck the northern wing of *3. Panzerarmee*, which, at the time, included *XXVIII. Armeekorps* (*Panzergrenadier-Division Großdeutschland, 7. Panzer-Division, 58 Infanterie-Division*) and *XL Panzerkorps* (*5. Panzer-Division* and *548. Volksgrenadier-Division*). The front at Šiauliai was held by the weak *551. Grenadier Division*.[16] On the first day of the offensive, the *551. Grenadier Division* collapsed under the weight of the Soviet attack. A ten-mile gap was now made through which 5th Guards Tank Army shoved as much armor and infantry as it could.

By 7 October, the cohesion of the entire northern wing of *3. Panzerarmee* collapsed, and a general withdrawal was ordered. The *XXVIII. Armeekorps* was pushed toward Memel, while *XL Panzerkorps* was pushed southwest, toward the East Prussian border, by the Soviet 43rd Army. Thereupon, the *XXVIII. Armeekorps* became besieged at Memel. This siege would last from 10 October, when the town was surrounded, to 28 January 1945, when *58. Infanterie-Division* withdrew as the rear guard from the town, by way of the Curonian Spit, a long sand dune that separated the Baltic Sea from the Curonian Lagoon. During the siege, the Germans managed to take out by sea *Panzergrenadier-Division Großdeutschland* and *7. Panzer-Division*. In their place, they brought into the pocket the *95. Infanterie-Division*.

## *FESTUNGEN:* FAILED BREAKWATERS

The idea behind establishing fortresses behind the enemy lines was a by-product of Hitler's faulty military thinking, based on his experiences in World War I. The belief that surrounded cities could act as breakwaters against a Soviet offensive proved flawed because the tactics of war had changed dramatically. The principal reason why this strategy was flawed was because armies during World War II moved considerably faster than armies had been able to maneuver in World War I. In addition, in emergencies, mobile forces could also be supplied by air. This

Festungen: *Breakwaters in the East* 145

**Figure 64.** German and Russian positions around Memel, 24 January 1945.

was something that was impossible during World War I. Simply naming a city a fortress, after it was surrounded by enemy forces, did not make that city any stronger than the defenses (if any) that existed at the time it was cut off. For the most part, leaving forces behind to be trapped in a city simply to slow down the enemy was a waste of much-needed manpower that the Third Reich could ill afford to lose. Any attempt by the German general staff to explain this to the Führer was usually drowned out by Hitler's accusation that the officers in the general staff were incompetent or defeatists.

Hitler proved to be an amateur when it came to military matters, no matter how much he immersed himself in the war and its prosecution. In addition, after the attempt on his life on 20 July 1944, Hitler became more suspicious of his generals and more paranoid. In the fall of 1944, he issued a directive that before a German division could make a decision such as to withdraw or even change its location on the battlefield, the Army High Command had to be informed and would then ask Hitler for a final yes or no on the move. Breaking this command order could get a general executed. What this created was literally a flood of requests from the divisional commanders for permission to move here or there. The Army High Command quickly became overwhelmed with hundreds of requests and could not process them all in a timely manner, as Hitler had to be made aware every time. This caused delays on the battlefield which affected the outcome of the war negatively for Germany. At one point in 1945, the Army High Command simply stopped processing these requests, and Hitler was too busy with other pressing matters to worry about it.

## Chapter 12

# BERLIN: THE RACE TO THE CAPITAL

*ES BEGANN ENTLANG DER WEICHSEL*

The senior lieutenant kept looking through his binoculars into the distance. The enemy was close, about 810 meters away (just a little over half a mile). He had seen many battles since joining the Red Army in the summer of 1943. At twenty, he was already a veteran of war. Earlier in the evening, he had warned his men, *'Get as much sleep tonight as you can, because beginning tomorrow, we will have little time for rest.'* The fall campaign season had seen his tank company whittled down to four tanks and nineteen troops. Now it had recently been brought up to full strength. He was always aware of the responsibility he had to his men. He had fought in too many battles to feel anything but the steady hum of dread in his bones. But something about tonight—something about the silence of the snow—felt different. Was it the cold, or the weight of everything yet to come? Every now and then he would lower the binoculars and stare out into the horizon, as if to see if dawn was breaking. His men were supposed to be in their trenches, deep in slumber, but many could not sleep on account of the cold or the nervous anticipation one gets just before you go into battle. Even lying down inside a tank was no guarantee that you would sleep well. As Lieutenant Vasili Mironov looked at his watch, he could barely make out the time. It was 21:15 in the evening.

The start of the offensive, when the Soviet artillery barrage was to begin, was to be at exactly 4:35 a.m., on the morning of 12 January 1945. Soviet forces under Marshal Georgy Zhukov (1st Belarusian Front) and Marshal Ivan Konev (1st Ukrainian Front) would start the day with a massive artillery barrage, which was now a common prelude to large-scale Soviet offensive operations, aimed at overwhelming German defenses. Within a few hours, the sky would be filled with large flashes of light, and the quiet of night would be replaced by the loud thunder of war, as thousands of artillery pieces would erupt, awakened from their slumber. For thirty minutes, they would unleash deadly projectiles without pause, ensuring the day would be soaked in violence. After the initial barrage, extended artillery fire was to continue intermittently as needed.

But right now, the sky was calm, and all Mironov could see were the thick snowflakes that would strike the ground at regular intervals, covering everything they would touch in a blanket of white. He tightened his coat around him, his breath fogging in the frigid air, as he watched the snow erase the world one flake at a time. The night seemed so tranquil that for a moment, perhaps, one could forget about the war. The night of the eleventh to the twelfth of January was a particularly cold one for central Poland. Much of the region was engulfed in freezing temperatures, heavy snowfall, and icy conditions. Tonight, the temperature had sunk to minus four degrees Fahrenheit. The cold, however, could not only be felt by Mironov, but he could also hear it. It was a soft hiss, as the wind blew the snow to and fro.

The quiet that prevailed was no accident. The army commanders had passed down the order for absolute silence to the corps commanders, who, in turn, relayed the command down to the first and second wave divisions earmarked for the offensive. Everyone had been warned by their officers that breaking silence would guarantee them a trip to a penal battalion. No one wanted to be sent to these punishment units because the attrition rate was five times higher than in normal combat formations. In addition, the penal battalions were always sent to the toughest sectors of the front line. Survival for a soldier in these battalions was measured in days, not in months. That is why everyone was being so careful not to drop a tank hatch or creak open an engine cover.

The Vistula-Oder offensive was hours away from starting, and the men of the 56th Independent Tank Regiment (attached to 5th Guards Army) were anxiously awaiting the arrival of dawn. Senior Lieutenant Mironov's tank regiment was part of the Russian Sandomierz-Baranów bridgehead. When 4:30 a.m. finally arrived, the early morning calm shattered like glass when the first shell tore through the sky. Mironov barely had time to blink before the ground trembled beneath him, his heart pounding in rhythm with the first thunderous blast. The snowflakes, once soft and floating, were now whipped into a frenzy, carried by the wind's sudden roar. What had been an evening of peace was now a morning swallowed up by the noise of war.

Other tank regiments attached to the three-rifle corps of 5th Guards Army included the 55th Independent Tank Regiment (T-34/85 tanks), 46th Guards Heavy Tank Regiment (IS-2 tanks), and the 71st Independent Guards Heavy Tank Regiment (IS-2 tanks). Additional armor was provided by the 1504th and 1505th Self-Propelled Artillery Regiments (SU-76 and SU-85 assault guns). They and the rest of the units in the bridgehead were to be the tip of the spear that was to break through the Nazi lines. Facing them was *XXIV. Panzerkorps*, with *16. Panzer-Division* and *17. Panzer-Division*. These two armored divisions were being held in reserve. They would be directly in the path of the Red Army advance toward Kielce. Holding the German front line in this sector of the battlefront were

**Figure 65.** Positions connecting *4. Panzerarmee* to *9. Armee* on 1 January 1945.

**Figure 66.** As the *Ostheer* withdrew, it destroyed rail and road links in order to slow the Soviet advance. This photograph was taken somewhere in Poland during the winter of 1944–1945. BUNDESARCHIV.

**Figure 67.** January 1945, a German column is seen retreating through a Polish road. The Soviet winter offensive of January 1945 would eventually propel the Red Army to the Oder River and the very gates of the Nazi capital. BUNDESARCHIV.

the Bavarian regiments of *68. Infanterie-Division* and Rhineland regiments of *168. Infanterie-Division*. The *168. Infanterie-Division*, in particular, was destined to be almost completely destroyed between 12–15 January 1945. The remnants of the division that escaped destruction at the Baranów bridgehead would try and reform in Silesia in February. It would then withdraw into Bohemia where it would surrender to the Red Army in early April, in the Kłodzko area.

Although the offensive had originally been planned to start on 20 January, the date for the attack had been moved up to 12 January on account of meteorological reports that warned of a thaw later in the month. If the Soviet high command had waited until 20 January to launch the offensive, the conditions would not be optimal, as tanks and assault guns would have to trudge through rivers of mud. Armored vehicles require firm ground on which to operate. Therefore, the attack needed to take place on the twelfth. For their part, the Germans were strung out too thinly along the entire front line. Hitler had long ago opted to keep calling remnants of units, whose strength was now that of a regiment, 'divisions'. Part of the reason was to deceive Russian military intelligence and partly out of Hitler's desire to see more German divisional flags on the situation map. Seeing all those little flags must have given the Führer comfort that he still commanded a large force able to fight toe-to-toe with an ever-growing and ever-stronger enemy. It was wishful thinking and a fantasy, but it pleased him.

Ever since 1943, the policy had been to form new divisions in lieu of replenishing the depleted ones. Gone were the days when a German division comprised

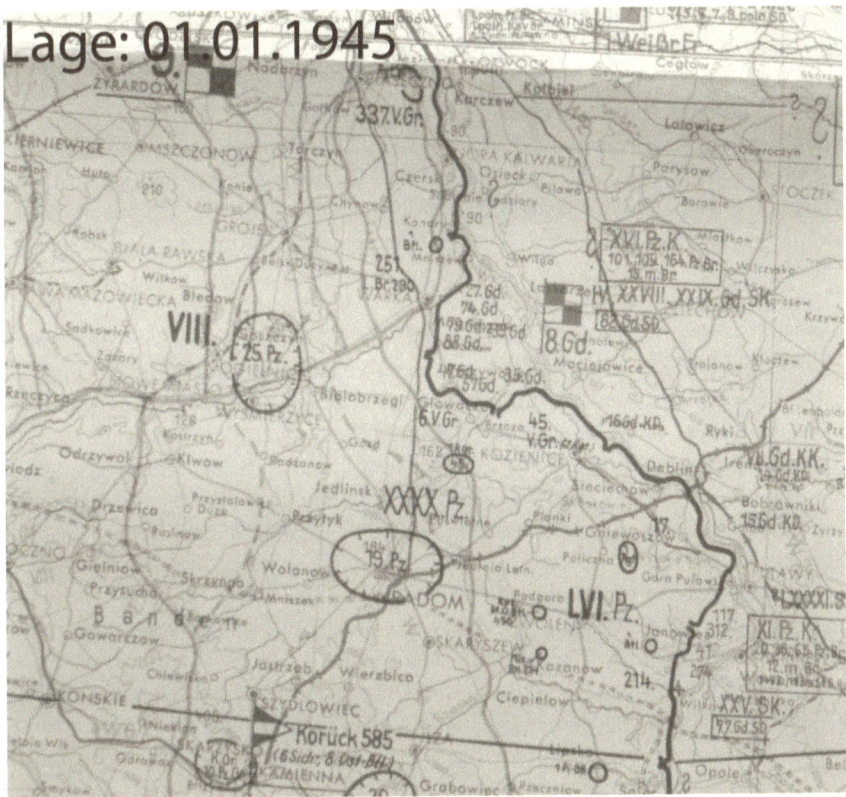

**Figure 68.** The positions of *9. Armee* on 1 January 1945.

nine infantry battalions. In 1943, the Führer had declared that henceforth the German infantry divisions would be called 'grenadier divisions.' By a stroke of the pen, Hitler had given regular infantry divisions the title of elite infantry formations, the likes of which had existed in the eighteenth and nineteenth century. Again, this was mere window dressing, but it made the Führer happy. In 1943, the nine battalion divisions were first replaced by three regiment divisions containing only two battalions per regiment, for a total of six battalions. Then, in 1944 Hitler, introduced the *Volksgrenadier* (people's grenadier) division, which only contained two regiments, with two battalions per regiment. Between 1939 and 1944, Germany's infantry division table of organization had been reduced from nine combat infantry battalions to just four. If the new *Volksgrenadier-Division* was lucky, it could field perhaps 6,000 to 7,000 men.

In January 1945, the German order of battle on the Eastern Front was composed of five army groups. In Courland, Latvia, you had *Generaloberst* Ferdinand Schörner's *Heeresgruppe Nord,* with *16. Armee* and *18. Armee.* Defending East Prussia and northern Poland along the Narew and Vistula River up to just north of Warsaw was *Generaloberst* Georg-Hans Reinhardt's *Heeresgruppe Mitte*, with *3. Panzerarmee*, *4. Armee*, and *2. Armee*. Farther south, defending the region of Poland from Warsaw along the Vistula River all the way down to the Carpathian Mountains along the Czechoslovak border, was *Generaloberst* Josef Harpe's *Heeresgruppe A*, with *9. Armee*, *4. Panzerarmee*, *17. Armee*, and *1. Panzerarmee*. Defending Hungary and the way to Austria was *Generaloberst* Otto Wöhler's *Heeresgruppe Süd*, with *6. Armee*, *8. Armee*, and what remained of 3rd Hungarian Army. In Yugoslavia, *Generalfeldmarschall* Maximilian von Weichs's *Heeresgruppe F* controlled *2. Panzerarmee* and *Heeresgruppe E*. The *2. Panzerarmee* contained *LXVIII. Armeekorps*, and *XXII. Gebirgs-Armeekorps*. *Heeresgruppe E* included *XXXIV. Armeekorps*, *XV. Gebirgs-Armeekorps*, *XXI. Gebirgs-Armeekorps*, and *V. SS-Freiwilligen-Gebirgs-Armeekorps* (in reserve). On 25 January, Hitler ordered a complete renaming of three army groups. *Heeresgruppe Nord* became *Heeresgruppe Kurland*, *Heeresgruppe Mitte* became *Heeresgruppe Nord*, and *Heeresgruppe A* became *Heeresgruppe Mitte*. That same month Hitler appointed Ferdinand Schörner as the new commander of *Heeresgruppe Mitte*.

The brunt of the Soviet Vistula-Oder offensive would be taken by the approximately seventy divisions comprising *Heeresgruppe Mitte* and *Heeresgruppe A*. Again, many of these 'divisions' were divisions in name only. The Germans under *Heeresgruppe A* were outnumbered five to one, while *Heeresgruppe Mitte* was outnumbered six to one. Altogether, the Soviet Vistula-Oder offensive would employ around 2,900,000 men. This amount also included the 1st Polish Army. Four Soviet fronts (1st Ukrainian Front, 1st–3rd Belarusian Fronts), with approximately 500 Soviet rifle divisions and 11,500 tanks and assault guns, were lined up against both German army groups. Altogether, *Heeresgruppe A* could count on no more than around 450,000 soldiers, 4,100 artillery pieces, and 1,150 tanks and assault guns. *Heeresgruppe Mitte* had even less, only around 250,000 men, 1,800 artillery pieces, and about 750 tanks and assault guns. The Red Army, therefore, had a four-to-one advantage in men and close to a six-to-one advantage in armored fighting vehicles. As far as artillery was concerned, the ratio was twenty Soviet artillery pieces to one German gun, overwhelmingly in Russia's favor. 1st Ukrainian Front could count on nine armies and one cavalry corps, while 1st Belarusian Front would employ ten armies (including the 1st Polish Army).

While 1st Ukrainian Front attacked on 12 January from the Sandomierz-Baranów bridgehead, the 1st Belarusian Front attacked from the Pulawy and Magnuszev bridgeheads two days later, on 14 January. This gave *9. Armee* a little time to readjust and prepare for the attack that was to come. In the north, *Heeresgruppe Mitte* could count on thirty-three infantry divisions and six panzer or *Panzergrenadier-Divisions* to hold a front line that was about 383 miles long. Most of these divisions were either bled white, exhausted, or both. The 3rd Belarusian Front joined in the offensive and began its attack against *Heeresgruppe Mitte* on 13 January, assaulting *3. Panzerarmee* north of Gumbinnen. The *4. Armee* attempted to assist *3. Panzerarmee* by pushing forward near Gumbinnen, but its divisions were slowly forced back.

*Berlin: The Race to the Capital* 153

**Figure 69.** Positions of *2. Armee* on 1 January 1945.

On 14 January, the 2nd Belarusian Front attacked from their bridgeheads at Rozan and Serock, between Ciechanow and Lomza, concentrating its forces against *2. Armee* in East Prussia. The 2nd Shock Army struck out toward Rozen while 70th Army pressed toward Modlin and 65th Army targeted Ciechanow. On the right flank of 2nd Shock Army, 48th Army and 3rd Army moved against *4. Armee* between Willenberg and Johannisburg, with 49th and 50th Armies lending their support. Meanwhile the six armies of 3rd Belarusian Front pressed their attacks against *3. Panzerarmee*. The goal was to reach the East Prussian capital of Königsberg.

For this effort, part of 1st Baltic Front also lent their support. To the south, 3rd Guard Army had broken out of the Sandomierz bridgehead and eventually turned north to trap German forces in Annopol and Ostrowiec Świętokrzyski. In the meantime, 4th Tank Army had already passed the city of Kielce and was heading toward the Warthe (Warta) River. Farther south, in the Baranów bridgehead region, 52nd Army, 5th Guards Army, and 60th Army were pressing their attacks against the weakened divisions of *17. Armee*.[1] By 17 January, Red Army forces were 150 kilometers deep behind the main German line, in open country, advancing along a 240-kilometer-wide front. At this point, it was clear that the *Ostheer* could no longer effectively defend the Eastern Front.

It was on 15 January that the weather finally cleared, allowing the Red Air Force the opportunity to pound the Germans. Up until then, icy fog and mixed

**Figure 70.** Positions of *3. Panzerarmee* and part of *4. Armee* on 1 January 1945, eleven days before the start of the Red Army winter offensive.

rain/snow had dominated the climate. North of Warsaw, on the border between *Heeresgruppe A* and *Heeresgruppe Mitte,* the 47th Army, which was the right flank of the 1st Belarusian Front, had breached the German defenses on 15 January. This was done with the support of fighter-bombers. Immediately the 61st Army began to flank Warsaw from the south, with the 47th and 70th Army moving from the north. This move placed the left flank of *Heeresgruppe A* in danger. On 16 January 1945, *Oberst* Bogislaw Oskar Adolf Fürchtegott von Bonin, who was

*Chef der operativen Abteilung des Generalstabs des Heeres* (Chief of the Operations Department of the General Staff of the Army), gave *Heeresgruppe A* permission to retreat from Warsaw. *Oberst* von Bonin did this to save part of the army group from encirclement.

When Hitler found out what this army colonel had done, he flew into a rage.[2] Colonel von Bonin was arrested by the *Gestapo* on 19 January and sent to a concentration camp. Miraculously, he survived the war. This order went contrary to the new Führer directive, which required all division, corps, and army commanders to contact the OKW in order to obtain Hitler's permission whether to move or not. Marshal Konev (1st Ukrainian Front) had noticed immediately that this new directive was having a detrimental effect on the German Army's ability to react quickly enough to Soviet moves. In his mind, he thanked Hitler for this 'gift.' The Soviet senior commander wondered in amazement at how the German General Staff could allow a former corporal to lead Germany into such a calamitous situation. Hitler and Stalin may have had many similar personality traits, like being ruthless, heartless, and manipulative. These traits had helped them take over their respective countries. But at least Stalin was no fool. He knew his military limitations and always allowed a little room for his generals to give him 'advice.' Hitler, on the other hand, only grew to believe that his generals were instigating defeatism. Further, he believed that this defeatism was affecting the conduct of the war. This was especially true after the attempt on his life by his own generals on 20 July 1944. Of course, it was his own poorly thought-out military and political decisions which had brought Germany to this present state.

Meanwhile, after being defeated in their staging area near the Baranów bridgehead, the *XXIV. Panzerkorps*, which had withdrawn west to Kielce, was forced to leave the city that same day. The panzer corps had been pushed out of the city by three armies from the 1st Ukrainian Front. Entire German corps-commands were now disconnected from one another as communication between forces broke down. Between 14 and 15 January, Kielce was liberated. Then on 16 January, Radom was captured by units from 3rd Guards Army. On Saturday, 17 January, the Red Army finally entered Warsaw. General Gotthard Heinrici's *9. Armee,* which had been defending Warsaw, had almost been destroyed and was retreating in disorder, like the rest of *Heeresgruppe Mitte*.[3] Faced with a broken and fractured front line, on 24 January, Hitler ordered the creation of *Heeresgruppe Vistula* (Army Group Vistula). From there, 1st Ukrainian Front fanned out in a wide area, with all armies heading toward the Oder River, where Army Group Vistula was to be organized. The 5th Guards Army and 13th Army headed for Breslau, while 3rd Guards Tank Army's main thrust vector was heading for Steinau and Glogau. While 1st Belarusian Front headed toward Küstrin on its left flank and Pomerania on its right flank, the 2nd Belarusian Front performed a drastic sweep in a northeasterly direction after breaking through Modlin, Mlawa, and Niedenburg. This set the stage for what would become the Heilignbeil Pocket, which was briefly discussed in chapter 11.

156   *The Bitter End*

This drive by the 2nd Belarusian Front was much akin to a Hail Mary move in American football terminology and was directed at capturing Marienburg and Elbing in West Prussia. This move aimed at trapping the bulk of *2. Armee, 4. Armee,* and *3. Panzerarmee* in East Prussia. Simultaneously, 1st Baltic Front pressed hard against *3. Panzerarmee*, while 3rd Belarusian Front hit *4. Armee* with all the weight that it could muster. By 26 January, a bulge, or pocket, of German troops had begun to form in Prussia, where Red Army forces were hemming in mainly elements of *4. Armee* and partly from *2. Armee* and *3. Panzerarmee*. This turned into what historians refer to as the Heiligenbeil Pocket. It's referred to as this because the pocket was located around the town of Heiligenbeil (present-day Mamonovo, Russia) near the Frisches Haff (Vistula Lagoon) on the Baltic Sea coast, southwest of Königsberg (now Kaliningrad, Russia).

This pocket was created when Soviet forces from the 3rd Belarusian Front, under the command of Marshal Ivan Chernyakhovsky (and later Marshal Aleksandr Vasilevsky), cut off German Army Group Center's forces. The Red Army's rapid advances left tens of thousands of German soldiers and civilians trapped in a narrow coastal strip, largely cut off from the rest of German-held territory. Inside the pocket were four German corps commands. Approximately fifteen German divisions were trapped in the Heiligenbeil Pocket. These divisions were part of the *4. Armee,* led by General Friedrich Hoßbach, along with some elements from *3. Panzerarmee.* As the Red Army's East Prussian Offensive progressed, these divisions were cut off from the main German lines and became encircled by Soviet forces. The German forces trapped inside included:

*4. Armee*
    VI. *Armeekorps* (*General der Infanterie* Horst Großmann)
        *349. Volksgrenadier-Division* (*Generalmajor* Karl Koetz)
        *24. Panzer-Division* (*Generalmajor* Gustav Adolf von Nostitz-Wallwitz)
        *14. Infanterie-Division* (*Generalleutnant* Erich Schneider)
        *28. Jäger-Division* (*Generalmajor* Ernst König)
    XX. *Armeekorps* (*General der Artillerie* Rudolf Freiherr von Roman)
        *Kampfgruppe der 102. Infanterie-Division* (*Generalleutnant* Werner von Bercken)
        *131. Infanterie-Division* (*Oberst* Nobiz)
        *Kampfgruppe der 61. Volksgrenadier-Division* (*Generalleutnant* Rudolf Sperl)
        *Kampfgruppe der 21. Infanterie-Division* (*Generalmajor* Heinrich Götz)
        *292. Infanterie-Division* (*Generalmajor* Rudolf Reichert)
    XLI. *Panzerkorps* (*General der Artillerie* Helmuth Weidling)
        *Divisionsstab z. b. V. 605*
        *170. Infanterie-Division* (*General* Siegfried Haß)
        Reserve: *547. Volksgrenadier-Division* (till February 1945: *Generalmajor* Ernst Meiners, then *SS-Standartenführer* Hans Kempin)

Reserve: 56. *Infanterie-Division* (*Generalmajor* Edmund Blaurock)
*Fallschirm Panzerkorps Hermann Göring* (*Generalleutnant* Wilhelm Schmalz)
562. *Volksgrenadier-Division* (*Oberst* Helmuth Hufenbach)
50. *Infanterie-Division* (*Generalmajor* Georg Haus)
*Fallschirm-Panzergrenadier-Division 2 'Hermann Göring'* (*Oberst* Söth)
*Panzergrenadier-Division 'Großdeutschland'* (*Generalmajor* Karl Lorenz)

The Heiligenbeil Pocket was one of the final, desperate stands of the German army on the Eastern Front. The significance of the battle is that it highlighted the collapse of German defenses and the massive human toll of the last stage of the war among both military personnel and civilians. The fierce fighting and evacuation efforts symbolized the chaotic and tragic final months of the war for Nazi Germany. The events leading up to and during this battle are a paragon of the events that occurred in the last year of the war that were repeated and whose consequences were felt by German forces and civilians alike. From 26 January, when 5th Guards Tank Army and 48th Army cut off the German retreat westward, to its end on 29 March 1945, the civilians in the pocket suffered as much as the soldiers, for there was no safe zone in the cauldron that was free of artillery salvos and air bombardment. To make matters worse, the severe winter increased the suffering tenfold.

**Figure 71.** A knocked-out *Jagdpanther* tank destroyer, somewhere in Pomerania, February 1945. While late-war German armored vehicle designs tended to be superior to Soviet tanks, they were fewer in number compared to the vast Red Army tank arsenal. Stalin thought as much when he famously said in 1943: 'Quantity is a quality all its own'.
MINSK STATE ARCHIVES.

## ARMY GROUP VISTULA

It was with these events, and other German military setbacks as a backdrop, that Hitler ordered that a new army group be built. This turned out to be *Heeresgruppe Vistula* (Army Group Vistula). Command of Army Group Vistula was initially given to *Reichsführer-SS* Heinrich Himmler. The official date in which he assumed command was 20 March 1945. Later, however, *Generaloberst* Gotthard Heinrici was given the post. He held this command from 21 March to 22 April, when he was relieved and *Generaloberst* Kurt Student assumed command. His tenure was brief and absentee, given that in late April he was captured by British forces in Schleswig-Holstein, near the Danish border.

For all intents and purposes, Heinrici was the last commander of the army group. In February 1945, the *2. Armee, 9. Armee,* and the ephemeral *11. SS Panzerarmee* were assigned to the army group. The *11. SS Panzerarmee* was an improvised headquarters with limited resources, meant to defend against Soviet advances in Pomerania.[4] Despite its designation as a 'panzer army,' it lacked significant armored forces and was primarily composed of understrength and hastily assembled units. In March, *3. Panzerarmee* was added to Army Group Vistula, and *11. SS Panzerarmee* was placed at the disposal of the army group. In April, the army group only contained *3. Panzerarmee* and *9. Armee.*[5]

Control of this new shadow army was given to *SS-Obergruppenführer und General der Waffen-SS* Felix Steiner, the commander of *III. (germanisches) SS-Panzerkorps.*[6] This army controlled *II. Armeekorps, Generalkommando Tettau, X. SS-Armeekorps,* and *XVI. SS-Armeekorps.* The *X. SS-Armeekorps* controlled the following forces: *Gneisenau-Regiment 1, Sturmgeschütz-Kompanie 'Reichsführer-SS', SS-Jagdverbände 'Mitte', Gruppe Voigt, Gruppe Lehmann, Division-Nr. 402,* and *Festung Schneidemühl.*[7] The *Division-Stab 402* was renamed *Division Nr. 402* when it

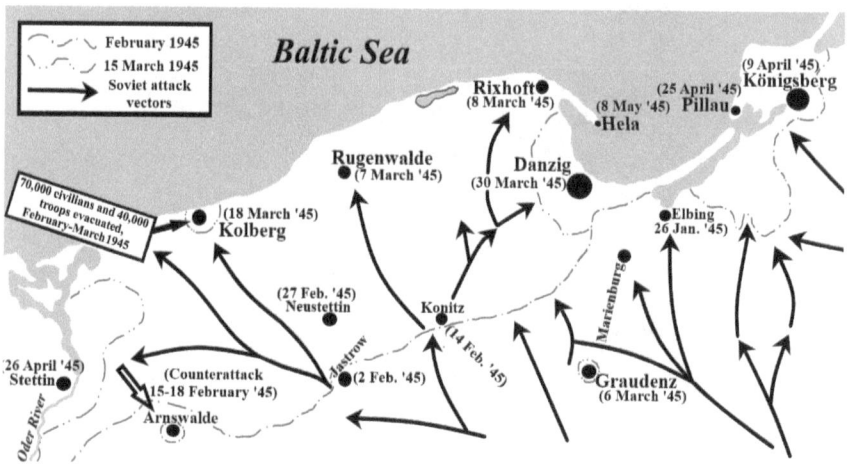

**Figure 72.** The conquest of Pomerania, February–March 1945.

was mobilized. Originally, it had been established in the city of Stettin *(Wehrkreis II)* on 25 September 1942. It had been created to control the various training and replacement troops as well as regional defense battalions located there. It was activated as a frontline unit on 20 January 1945 and assigned to the *X. SS-Armeekorps* in February 1945. Initially, the strongest corps in the army was *X. SS-Armeekorps*.

> *X. SS-Armeekorps* with:
> *SS-Jagdverbände 'Ost'* (an SS commando battalion)
> *Gneisenau-Regiment 1* (three battalions of infantry)
> *Sturmgeschütz-Kompanie 'Reichsführer-SS'* (one SS company of assault guns)

The following division *(Division Nr. 402)*, which also served under *X. SS-Armeekorps*, would be destroyed in Pomerania in March 1945:

> *Division Nr. 402* (*Generalleutnant* Siegmund Freiherr von Schleinitz) with:[8]
> *Grenadier-Ersatz-Regiment 258*
> *Grenadier-Ersatz-Regiment 522*
> *Heeres-Flakartillerie-Ersatz und Ausbildungs-Abteilung 272*
> *Aufklärungs-Ersatz-Abteilung 5*
> *Artillerie-Ersatz und Ausbildungs-Regiment 2*
> *Kavallerie-Ausbildungs-Abteilung 100*
> *Pionier-Ersatz und Ausbildungs-Bataillon 2*
> *Pionier-Ersatz-Bataillon 12*
> *Bau-Pionier-Ersatz und Ausbildungs-Bataillon 2*
> *Fahr-Ersatz und Ausbildungs-Abteilung 2*
> *Kraftfahr-Ersatz-Abteilung 2*

By late January 1945, *'Festung Schneidemühl'* (Fortress Schneidemühl) was on the front lines. Today, Schneidemühl is now known as Pila and is a part of Poland. This former German city was located 135 kilometers east-southeast of Stargard. Stargard itself is about 105 kilometers east of the city of Stettin, on the Oder River. In January 1945, the city of Schneidemühl had approximately 45,000 people. The city was captured by the Red Army on 14 February 1945. In January and February, the city was defended by the following German forces:

> *Festung Schneidemühl*
> *Volkssturm-Regiment 'Mentz'* (two battalions)
> *Volkssturm-Regiment 'Bonin'* (four battalions)
> *Volkssturm-Regiment 'Möring'* (two battalions)
> *Festungs-Maschinengewehr-Abteilung Schneidemühl I*
> *Festungs-Maschinengewehr-Abteilung Schneidemühl II*
> *Bataillon 'Kolberg'*, *'Eutin'*, & *'Treptow'* (*Heeres-Unteroffizier-Schulen*)
> *Bataillon Belgard*, *'Anklam'*, *'Schneidemühl'*, *'Hannover'*, & *'Feldherrnhalle'*

*(Heeres-Unteroffizier-Schulen)*
*Aufklärungs-Abteilung 'Stolp'* (a reconnaissance battalion)
*Marine-Bataillon (der 23. Schiffs-Stamm-Abteilung) Deutsch-Krone* (sailors acting as infantry)
*I. Artillerie-Bataillon/Artillerie-Lehr-Regiment 5 'Groß-Born'* (artillery battalion)
*Sturmgeschütz-Abteilung 'Graf Dohna'* (an 'assault gun' battalion that actually contained several *Wespe* and *Hummel* armored artillery vehicles)[9]

## GRUPPE LEHMANN (OBERST DR. CURT LEHMANN)

This was one of those 'instant' divisions which the Germans were creating in 1945. It was a jumble of four 'alarm' regiments made up of officer candidates from the Army Artillery School in Groß-Born. The initial designation of this 'division' was *Division Märkisch Friedland*. However, the unit began to be referred to as *Gruppe Lehmann* while a part of *Heeresgruppe Vistula* while serving under *11. SS Panzerarmee* in western Pomerania. This 'division' was destroyed by Soviet forces from 8–10 February 1945, in the area around Deutsch-Krone.
*XVI. SS-Armeekorps* controlled the following forces:

*15. Waffen-Grenadier-Division der SS (lettische Nr. 1)*
Parts of *SS-Panzergrenadier-Regiment 49 'de Ruyter' (23. SS-Freiwilligen-Panzergrenadier-Division 'Nederland')*
*Kampfgruppe Joachim* (formed from *SS-Grenadier-Ausbildungs und Ersatz-Bataillon 35*)

*Generalkommando Tettau* was composed of the following forces on 5 February 1945:[10]

*Infanterie-Division Köslin*
   *Regiment Krankewitz* (infantry)
   *Regiment Jatzinhen* (infantry)
   *SS-Waffen-Unterführerschule 'Lauenburg'* (infantry)
   *Baupionier-Ersatz und Ausbildungs-Bataillon 2* (engineer)
*Infanterie-Division 'Bärwalde'* (created from *Artillerie Schule II* in Gross Born, remnants of other units and *Volkssturm* battalions)
   *Regiment-Bärwalde 1* (infantry)
   *Regiment-Bärwalde 2* (infantry)
   *Regiment-Bärwalde 3* (infantry)
   *Regiment-Bärwalde 4* (infantry)
   *Regiment-Bärwalde 5* (infantry)
   *Artillerie-Regiment Bärwalde* (artillery)
   *Pionier-Bataillon Bärwalde* (engineer)
   *Fernmelde-Bataillon Bärwalde* (Telecommunications Battalion)

On 15 February, a third division was added: *163. Infanterie-Division*. It had 9,000 men. This division was reportedly destroyed near Stargard in early March 1945 by units from the 1st Polish Army. However, its remnants (4,500 officers, NCOs, and enlisted men) took part in the defense of Kolberg between 4–18 March 1945. It is there where the division was finally crushed. The remnants of this division were absorbed by the newly created *3. Marine Division* (an infantry division created from sailors).

*Wehrkreis II*: This command controlled the following units on 1 March 1945:

*263. Infanterie-Division*
*563. Volksgrenadier-Division*
*Kampfgruppe der 290. Infanterie-Division*

On 24 January 1945, *XVI. SS-Armeekorps*, which was operating against the western Allies, was moved from the Upper Rhine region to Pomerania. On 28 January 1945, the headquarters of *XVI. SS-Armeekorps* arrived in Märkisch Friedland. It was then moved to nearby Schönfeld airfield. *SS-Obergruppenführer* Eric von dem Bach-Zelewski retained control of the corps until 26 January 1945. At the beginning of February 1945, this SS corps command was renamed *X. SS-Armeekorps*. On 10 February, *Generalleutnant* Günther Krappe assumed temporary command. He was replaced by *SS-Standartenführer* Herbert Golz on 7 March 1945. Command of *XVI. SS-Armeekorps* (existed from February to March 1945) was finally given to *SS-Obergruppenführer* Karl-Maria Demelhuber. His chief of staff was *SS-Standartenführer* Adolf Ax. The 'Ia' of the corps was *Major* Ludwig Klöckner.[11] On 15 January, *General der Infanterie* Dr. Johannes Mayer assumed command of *Wehrkreis II*. For all intents and purposes, this German military district headquarters was acting as a corps command. Mayer was later replaced on 1 April by *Generalleutnant* Alfred Gause.

## UNTERNEHMEN SONNENWENDE

By the beginning of February 1945, the order of battle for *11. SS Panzerarmee* had changed completely. It was at this time that the one major event in the history of this rather brief and obscure army command took place. That turned out to be *Unternehmen Sonnenwende* (Operation Solstice). This counterattack was launched on 15 February 1945. The German forces initiated their attack on a thirty-three-mile-wide front from the city of Stargard. German forces advanced southeastward toward Arnswalde, where a small German garrison had been surrounded. The primary goal of this offensive was to relieve the Arnswalde and Küstrin garrisons. The attack began from the Stargard area, along the northern Oder River. The order of battle for *11. SS Panzerarmee* at this time was as follows:

11. *SS Panzerarmee* (*SS-Obergruppenführer und General der Waffen-SS* Felix Steiner)
   *XXXIX. Panzerkorps* (*Generalleutnant* Karl Decker)
      *Panzer-Division 'Holstein'* (forty-six *Panzer IV* tanks)[12]
      10. *SS-Panzer-Division 'Frundsberg'* (fifty-three *'Panther'* tanks and thirty-eight *Panzer IV* tanks)
      4. *SS-Polizei-Panzergrenadier-Division 'Polizei'*
      28. *SS-Freiwilligen-Panzergrenadier-Division 'Wallonien'* (twenty *'Hetzer'* tank destroyers)
   *III. (germanisches) SS-Panzerkorps* (*Generalleutnant* Martin Unrein)
      (*schwere*) *SS-Panzer-Abteilung 503* (twelve King Tiger tanks)
      11. *SS-Freiwilligen-Panzergrenadier-Division 'Nordland'* (twenty *'Hetzer'* tank destroyers)
      23. *SS-Freiwilligen-Panzergrenadier-Division 'Nederland'* (ten *'Hetzer'* tank destroyers)
      27. *SS-Freiwilligen-Grenadier-Division 'Langemarck'*
      *Führer-Begleit-Division* (twenty-three *Jagdpanzer IV/70(A)* tank destroyers, thirty *'Panther'* tanks, and fifteen *Panzer IV* tanks)
      *Divisionsgruppe Voigt*: contained at least three regiments (see Appendix III for a detailed order of battle under *Divisionsgruppe Ledebur*, ex-*Gruppe Voigt*)
   X. *SS-Armeekorps* (*Generalleutnant* Günther Krappe)
      *Führer-Grenadier-Division* (thirty-four *'Panther'* tanks, thirteen *Jagdpanzer IV/70(A)* tank destroyers, five *Panzer IV* tanks, and ten *Jagdpanther* tank destroyers)
      163. *Infanterie-Division:* The unit arrived in bits and pieces, but altogether, it had the strength of some 9,000 men.
      281. Infanterie-Division
      *Panzer-Jagd-Brigade 104* (existed from 26 January to 15 February 1945)

Initially, the German counterattack actually managed to reach the Arnswalde garrison and break the siege. This was achieved in spite of the fact that not all of the German divisions were ready on the fifteenth of January. Inside, the garrison of Arnswalde was made up of the following forces:

*Kampfgruppe Klossek*, with:
Hungarian Infantry Battalion 23/I
*Grenadier-Regiment 1604 (russische) der Grenadier-Brigade 499 der russische Volksbefreiungsarmee*[13]
*Volkssturm-Bataillon 'Seesen'*
*Führer-Anwärter-Bataillon 'Oder'* (Officer Candidate Battalion 'Oder')
*II. Bataillon, SS-Grenadier-Ersatz und Ausbildungs-Bataillon 103*

**Figure 73.** Positions of the short-lived *11. SS Panzerarmee* on 1 February 1945.

When the German relief forces reached Arnswalde, these six battalions eventually became *Divisionsgruppe Klossek,* and later, it was renamed as *Divisionsgruppe Voigt*. The counterattack eventually stalled after the Arnswalde garrison was relieved because (1) *11. SS Panzerarmee* encountered stiffer Soviet resistance, and (2) the SS army possessed only enough fuel and ammunition for up to three days of combat. At that point, the attacking divisions began to run into shortages of all kinds. While *III. (germanisches) SS-Panzerkorps* was able to achieve the first goal, its sister corps, *XXXIX. Panzerkorps,* met with stiff resistance from the Soviet 2nd Guards Tank Army. The offensive was effectively stopped on 18 February by a combination of Soviet resistance and lack of supplies.

## THE SIEGE OF KOLBERG

A week after the failure of the German offensive in western Pomerania, Marshal Konstantin Rokossovsky's 2nd Belarusian Front launched an offensive on 24 February between Danzig (Gdansk) and Bromberg (Bydgoszcz), which eventually cleared Pomerania of German forces. The climax of this offensive was the battle for the port city of Kolberg, fought between 4–18 March 1945.

In addition to employing some sailors in emergency infantry battalions and using the local *Volkssturm,* the German defenders at Kolberg included elements from the following formations:

 *163. Infanterie-Division*: 4,500 men (the survivors of the divisional defeat near Stargard)
 *Division Nr. 402 z.b.V.*: 4,000 men
 *15. Waffen-Grenadier-Division der SS (lettische Nr. 1)*: 5,000 men
 *33. Waffen-Grenadier-Division der SS 'Charlemagne' (französische Nr. 1)*: 6,000 men

In total, an estimate of around 20,000 troops took part in the defense of the city. Two days after the start of the Red Army attack on the city, the Soviet command handed over responsibility for besieging and capturing the city to the 1st Polish Army. The Polish divisions employed against the defenders were supported by Red Air Force bombers and attack aircraft, as well as several heavy tank regiments from the Red Army. Artillery fire was provided by several artillery divisions

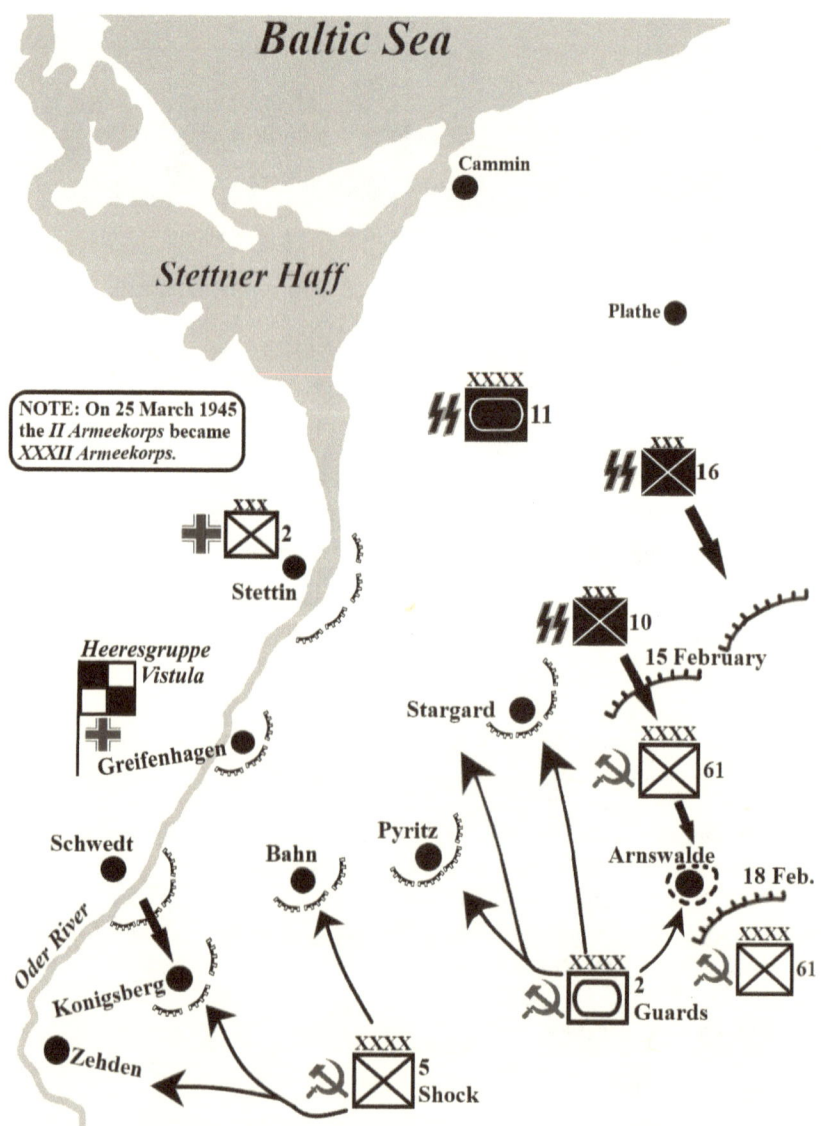

**Figure 74.** The military situation, 2–18 February 1945.

and four Katyusha rocket regiments. By 16 March, the German defenders were retreating toward the city's port, trying to evacuate as many civilians and soldiers as they could to Swinemünde. They left behind a small screening force that were ordered to delay the enemy advance. It was a suicide mission, but those chosen for this mission accepted their fate. Two days later, the last Germans withdrew by sea. In total, some 70,000 civilians and 40,000 troops were able to be evacuated to Swinemünde.

By the middle of February 1945, the Red Army had established itself well along the Oder River—the last natural barrier before the German capital. During February and March, several battles took place along the river, mostly for the defense or capture of key German towns and cities, in anticipation of the coming, final Soviet offensive. The German defenders braced themselves for the storm of steel that would come. Most German soldiers had no wish to die for a lost cause, but desertion was punishable by death through hanging. Literally hundreds of German *Feldjäger* units, Military Field Police, and SS flying squads were roaming the German rear areas—all looking for deserters or 'defeatists' to hang. At least in the front lines there was still a chance that one could survive the war, perhaps by surrendering. But leaving your post without proper documentation was a one-way ticket to a hanging.

**Figure 75.** A German soldier preparing to fire a *Panzerfaust*, somewhere along the Eastern Front during the winter of 1944–1945. The image of a haggard German landser, holding the *Panzerfaust*, the single-shot anti-tank weapon, is the very epitome of the German defense during the last year of the war. BUNDESARCHIV.

# Chapter 13

# BERLIN: THE LAST BATTLE

*DER ANFANG VOM ENDE ENTLANG DER ODER*

There were other German forces that had not taken part in the Arnswalde offensive. These were *5. Jäger-Division* and *Infanterie-Division Deneke*, plus other minor units. By 15 February, the *5. Jäger-Division* was committed under *X. SS-Armeekorps*. Another division, the *33. Waffen-Grenadier-Division der SS 'Charlemagne' (französische Nr. 1)*, was eventually sent to Army Group Vistula even before it completed its training. It first saw combat near Kolberg. By 25 March, it was located in Neustrelitz and still contained around 6,000 officers, NCOs, and men. From Neustrelitz, it then withdrew to Köslin in fierce rear-guard fighting. At Köslin, the division was encircled. Three *kampfgruppen* were formed. These took losses but were able to fight their way through to Kolberg, Schwerin, and Neustrelitz respectively. Later, a reinforced battalion under the command of the divisional commander *SS-Brigadeführer* Gustav Krukenberg reached Berlin, where it took part in the battle for that city in April 1945.

In the rear by Stettin was the *Wehrkreis II* (2nd Military District) headquarters, acting as a corps command. On 5 February 1945, it had under its control the *9. Fallschirmjäger-Division*. Also located in Stettin was the Armenian Legion with 474 volunteers and the *Turkistanische-Ersatz-Bataillon* (Turkestani Replacement Battalion) with 588 men. Foreign volunteers from the USSR were actually numerous all along the Oder front and took part in the final battle of the war, right alongside the Germans and western European volunteers. In Küstrin, the Turkestan Legion had 700 men. The Azerbaijani Legion also had 570 men in the city. In Frankfurt an der Oder, the remnants of the Georgian Legion held out with 367 men, along with the Volga Tartar Legion, which could count on 608 troops. Then there was the North Caucasian Legion with 608 men and the *Turkestanisches-Führerschule* (Turkestani Leadership School) with an additional 450 men.[1] Thus, Frankfurt an der Oder could count on 2,033 eastern troops.

There was also the *9. Fallschirmjäger-Division*, which was at the disposal of the army group. This parachute division contained three regiments of infantry, an anti-tank battalion, a flak battalion, an artillery regiment, an engineer battalion, a communications battalion, and a field reserve battalion. For 1945 German Army standards, the division was magnificently manned and equipped. In total, it had around 8,500 men. In February 1945, it was attached to *11. SS Panzerarmee* as a reserve. It remained in reserve in March but was now made a part of *3. Panzerarmee (Heeresgruppe Vistula)*. On 8 April, it was attached to *XI. SS-Panzerkorps*, and eleven days later, it was attached to *LVI. Panzerkorps*. In January 1945, *Division Nr. 471* was activated. It was led initially by *Generalleutnant* Erich Denecke, then in February, *Generalleutnant* Ernst Häckel assumed command. The division originated from *Division Nr. 471* but was referred to as *Infanterie-Division Deneke*. On 1 March 1945, the division was redesignated as *549. Volksgrenadier-Division* (commander: *Generalleutnant* Karl Jank).[2] The following units are known to have been added to the forming division in February and March 1945:

*Infanterie-Regiment 'Mensing'* (*Major* Georg Mensing)
*Artillerie-Abteilung 'Futtig'*
*Flak-Batterie der I./850* (37 mm)
*Flak-Batterie der I./335* (105 mm)
Added to the division on 2 February 1945:
*Polizei-Kompanie z.b.V.*
*Volkssturm-Bataillon 26/11*
*Volkssturm-Bataillon 26/29*
*Volkssturm-Bataillon 26/70*

*Kampfgruppe Bahn*
    *II. und III. Bataillone der Pommern-Regiment 4*
*Kampfgruppe Pyritz* (*Oberst* Otto Weiß)
    *Marine-Alarm-Bataillon*
    *Hitler-Jugend-Bataillon*
*Kampfgruppe 'Stargard'*
*III. Bataillon der SS-Panzergrenadier-Regiment 8* (until 7 February)
*Sperr Kompanie 918*
*II. Bataillon der Fallschirmjäger-Regiment 26* (added 15 February)

All of these various units were amalgamated and regrouped into a new division (See Appendix III for a detailed order of battle under *549. Volksgrenadier-Division*). On 29 January 1945, *Infanterie-Division Deneke* had to be evacuated from Friedberg. It moved through Landsberg, reaching Stargard on 31 January. On 2 February 1945, the division was ordered to take over the front line between the Oder River and Stargard. The division held this defense line until 6 February 1945. On 7 February, the positions were handed over to the *4. SS-Panzergrenadier-Division 'Polizei'*, and *Infanterie-Division Deneke* was shifted to the Greifenhagen bridgehead.

**Figure 76.** The west bank of the Oder River, March 1945. Here we see *Volkssturm* manning a machine gun. They are looking into the distance. By March 1945, the Red Army had established several bridgeheads over the Oder River. These would be used as the springboard for the final Soviet drive on the German capital. BUNDESARCHIV.

## FESTUNG KÜSTRIN

It was also in late January that the leading elements of 2nd Guards Tank Army and 5th Shock Army reached the Oder River by Neumark. Farther south, at Landsberg and Küstrin, the German defenders appeared to be making a stronger effort, so both armies simply bypassed these two towns and moved northward to Neumark. Early on 31 January, the Red Army was able to cross the Oder River and establish a bridgehead. The frozen river had allowed this to occur, but the Soviet heavy armor could not cross as the ice was not strong enough. Inside the city of Küstrin, the Germans were preparing to hold the city as a 'festung' (fortress). The first commander of the Küstrin garrison was *Generalmajor* Adolf Raegener (26 January to 2 February 1945). The last commander of the garrison was *SS-Gruppenführer und Generalleutnant der Polizei* Heinz Reinefarth. He held the post from 2 February to 30 March 1945. The garrison could count on 8,196 men, including 900 *Volkssturm* who were led by the *Burgermeister* (city mayor), Hermann Körner. The forces in the city included the following formations:

*Sturm-Bataillon I. AOK 9*[3]
*SS-Panzergrenadier-Ersatz und Ausbildungs-Bataillon 9*
*Panzerjäger-Kompanie-Allenstein*[4]
*Festungs-Infanterie-Bataillon 1450*
*Panzergrenadier-Ersatz-Bataillon 50*

*Maschinengewehr-Bataillon 1 z.b.V.*
*Maschinengewehr-Bataillon 2 z.b.V.*
*Maschinengewehr-Bataillon 3 z.b.V.*
*Pionier-Ersatz und Ausbildungs-Bataillon 68*
*Landesschützen-Pionier-Bataillon 513*
*IV. Festungs-Artillerie-Abteilung der Festungs-Stamm-Artillerie-Regiment 3132 (1.-2. Batterien) bewaffnet mit 152 mm Kanonenhaubitzen 433 (russiche)*

*Festungs-Artillerie-Abteilung I./3132* (four batteries)
*Artillerie Ersatz Abteilung 39*
*Festungs-Nachrichten-Kompanie 738*
4th Hungarian Infantry Battalion
*ein (1) turkestanisches Infanterie-Bataillon* (360 men)
*ein (1) nordkaukasisches Infanterie-Bataillon* (340 men)
*Aserbaidschanische Legion* (Azerbaijani Legion, with 570 men)
*Volkssturm-Bataillon 16/186*

The German military field police collected stragglers and soldiers who were in transit who were passing by the city and added them to the garrison. A convalescent company was created from soldiers who had been wounded and were

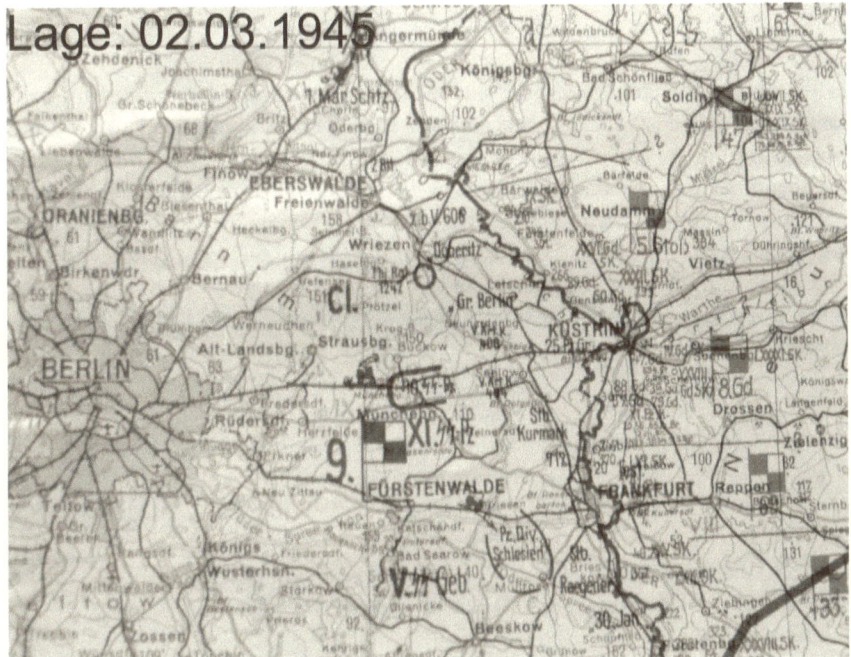

**Figure 77.** Position of 9. Armee forces, including Fortress Küstrin, on 2 March 1945.

recuperating in the city. There were also five immobile 'Panther' tank turrets with their 75 mm anti-tank gun. These tank turrets were placed at strategic locations around the city. The battle for the city lasted from 31 January, when the first Russian troops reached the outskirts of the city, until 30 March, when it was finally captured. An opportunity had been presented to the Russians when they noticed that one key division was being replaced. This was the *25. Panzergrenadier-Division*, which had been keeping a connection to the Küstrin defenders since 31 January, just west and northwest of the city around Genschmar, and was in the process of withdrawing.

To replace it, *20. Panzergrenadier-Division* was attempting to take its positions. This division had been withdrawn by rail from its positions along the Oder-Neisse River junction on 11 March. This was part of a German plan to launch a counterattack near Küstrin. In actuality, two attempts were made on 22 March and 27 March, but both were failures. As *25. Panzergrenadier-Division* was trying to extricate itself and *20. Panzergrenadier-Division* was trying to assume its positions, the Russians attacked on both flanks and cut off part of *20. Panzergrenadier-Division*. The Russians were thus able to obtain a bridgehead west of the city. The human toll during the battle for Küstrin was high on both sides. The Germans lost about 20,000 men (5,000 killed, 9,000 wounded, and 6,000 captured), while the Red Army lost about the same amount (5,000 killed and 15,000 wounded).

## *FESTUNG SCHWEDT*

At the end of January 1945, *Reichsführer-SS* Heinrich Himmler ordered his best commando officer, *SS-Obersturmbannführer* Otto Skorzeny, to head toward the lower region of the Oder River, by the town of Schwedt. He was to be under the command of *3. Panzerarmee*. His mission was to organize forces there and launch a flanking counterattack that Hitler had ordered, which (it was hoped) would throw the advancing Soviet forces back from the Oder River. The offensive never took place as there were insufficient and no proper forces available to attack with. Skorzeny had arrived at Schwedt with three SS commando and SS parachute battalions and a sharpshooter company:

*SS-Jagdverbände 'Mitte'*: *SS-Hauptsturmführer* Karl Fucker
*SS-Jagdverbände 'Nordwest'*: *SS-Hauptsturmführer* Hoyer (December 1944–March 1945) then:
  *SS-Hauptsturmführer* Willy Dethier (March–April 1945)
*SS-Fallschirmjäger-Bataillon 600*: *SS-Hauptsturmführer* Siegfried Milius
*SS-Scharfschützenkompanie*: *SS-Obersturmführer* Wiescher.

Although these SS formations were elite units, they were insufficient to even defend the town from a determined Soviet assault. Skorzeny began to scrape whatever forces he could find and gathered them together into what became known as *'Division Schwedt'*. Eventually his 'division' included the following units:

*Division Schwedt* (*SS-Obersturmbannführer* Otto Skorzeny)
Total strength of *Division Schwedt* on 15 March 1945: 154 officers, 1065 NCOs, and 4,754 enlisted men.[5]
*SS-Ersatzkommando 'Ungarn'*[6]
Hungarian Field Gendarmerie Company 10-H 'Schwedt'
*Panzergrenadier-Ersatz-Bataillon 3 'Aschenbach'* (486 officers, NCOs, enlisted men)
*Panzergrenadier-Ersatz-Bataillon 9 'Jakobs'* (863 officers, NCOs, enlisted men)
*Panzergrenadier-Ersatz-Bataillon 83 'Zapf'* (767 officers, NCOs, enlisted men)
*Volkssturm-Bataillon 'Hamburg'* (557 officers, NCOs, and enlisted men)
*Volkssturm-Bataillon 'Königsberg'* (262 officers, NCOs, and enlisted men)
*Volkssturm-Bataillon 'Strempel'* (501 officers, NCOs, and enlisted men)
*Pionier Bataillon (?)* (648 officers, NCOs, and enlisted men)
From *Fliegerregiment 53*:
    *Luftwaffe-Infanterie-Kompanie 'Steinke'* (121 officers, NCOs, and enlisted men)
    *Luftwaffe-Infanterie-Kompanie 'Galli'* (54 officers, NCOs, and enlisted men)
    *Luftwaffe-Infanterie-Kompanie 'Strassmann'* (133 officers, NCOs, and men)
*Luftwaffe-Gruppe 'Oder Süd'* (285 officers, NCOs, and enlisted men)
*Rumänisches Volksdeutsches Bataillon* (410 officers, NCOs, and enlisted men)
*Artillerie-Batterie 'Klassen'* (51 officers, NCOs, and enlisted men)
*Ausbildungs-Kompanie* (160 officers, NCOs, and enlisted men)
*Krankenwagen Werkstattzug* (95 officers, NCOs, and enlisted men)
*schwere Flak-Ersatz-Abteilung 12* (626 officers, NCOs, and enlisted men). Contained 105 mm flak guns in four flak batteries. It was renamed *schwere Flak-Abteilung 662 (v)* on 13 April 1944, but some kept referring to it by the old title.
*Auffangkommando Weiss* (167 officers, NCOs, and enlisted men)
*Versorgungs-Kompanie* (309 officers, NCOs, and enlisted men)
*Sanitätskompanie (*76 officers and enlisted men)

*SS-Kampfgruppe 'Solar'* (attached to Division Schwedt from February–March, then to *547. Volksgrenadier-Division* in April 1945). The initial commander was *SS-Sturmbannführer* Franz Solar, then *SS-Sturmbannführer* Siegfried Milius (on 27 April).
*SS Jagdverbände Mitte* (*SS-Hauptsturmführer* Karl Fucker)
*SS Fallschirmjäger-Bataillon 600* (*SS-Hauptsturmführer* Siegfried Milius)

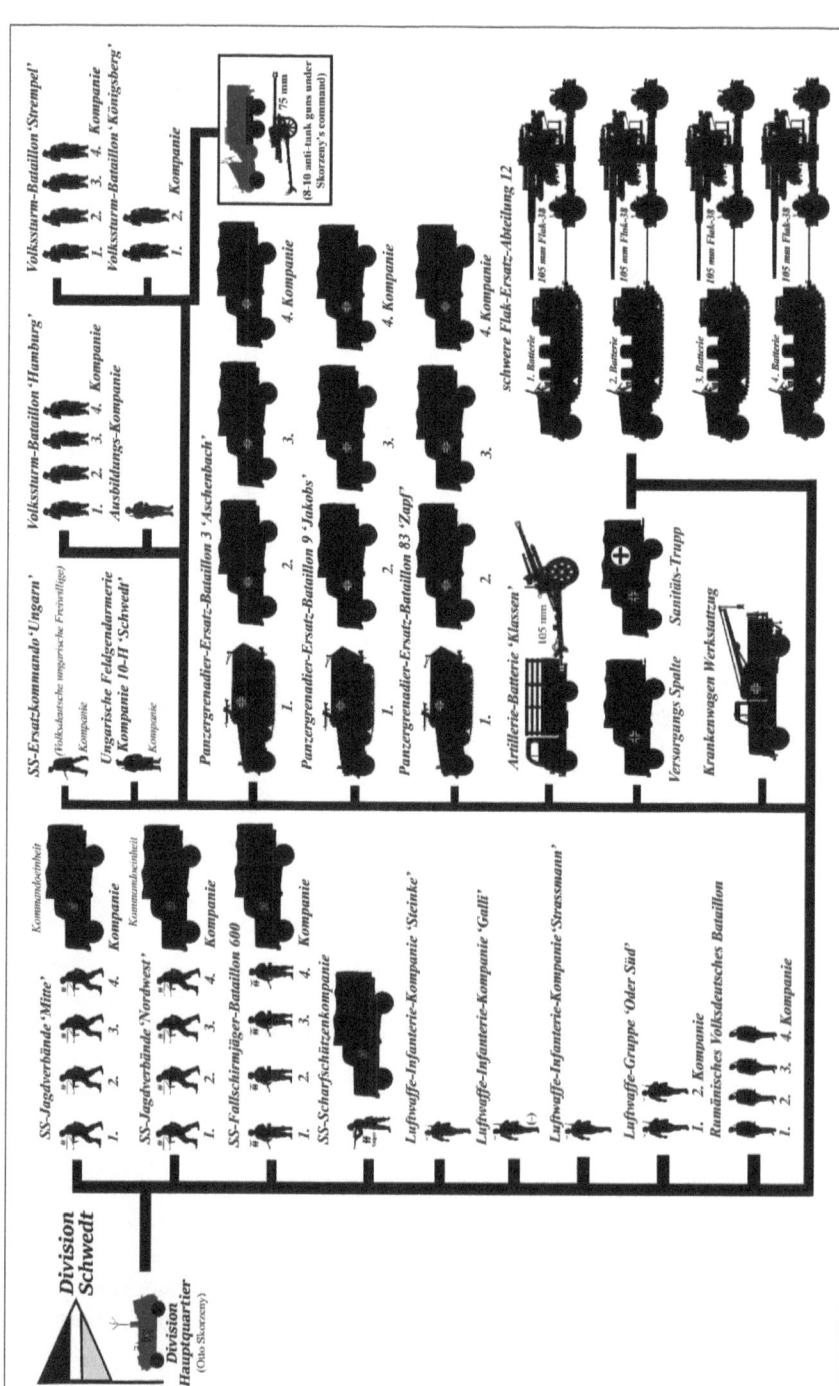

**Figure 78.** *Division Schwedt* in early March 1945.

Formations not listed in this Order of Battle but attributed to *Division Schwedt* were the following:

*Organization-Todt-Regiment 122*
*Volksgrenadier-Regiment 1091 (547. Volksgrenadier-Division)*
*III. Bataillon, Fallschirmjäger-Regiment 26 (9. Fallschirmjäger-Division)*
*Sturmgeschütz-Brigade 210 (Major* Dietrich Langel—beginning 7 February*)*
    *1. Batterie, 2. Batterie, 3. Batterie* (twelve *Sturmgeschütz IV* assault guns)

In addition, we know from German documents that in early February, Skorzeny could count on one German armored train *(Eisenbahn-Panzerzüge 77)*.[7] However, this armored train was listed as being destroyed on 26 February at Bublitz (Bobolice), so its employment in the Schwedt bridgehead was brief. Bublitz itself was captured by the Red Army on 3 March 1945, as part of the Soviet East Pomeranian offensive. The rest of *9. Fallschirmjäger-Division* was ordered to Schwedt on 15 February 1945. This command was given via a *'Fernschreiben'* issued by *SS-Gruppenführer und Generalleutnant der Waffen SS* Heinz Lammerding,

**Figure 79.** Schwedt an Oder, February 1945. Along the Oder River, the last natural barrier before Berlin, Hitler created Army Group Vistula with whatever scraps of rear area forces he could muster. Some units were actually composed of elite troops. Here we see Hitler's commando, *SS-Obersturmbannführer* Otto Skorzeny (left), conferring with other *Waffen-SS* officers in the town of Grabow, just east of Schwedt. Skorzeny arrived on the Oder River with two *Waffen-SS* commando battalions and a *Waffen-SS* parachute battalion. Using this force as the core, he established 'Division Schwedt' with whatever other forces he could scrape together. Bundesarchiv.

the Chief of the General Staff for Army Group Vistula.[8] From 2 February to 1 March, this motley crew of divergent German forces would hold a bridgehead across the Oder River, immediately east of the river town of Schwedt. Skorzeny's 'division' would hold up elements of three Soviet armies: 2nd Guards Tank Army, 49th Army, and 61st Army.

On 28 January, the leading elements of the Red Army were located just east of the town of Pyritz, a mere twelve miles away from Schwedt. The Soviet plan was to take Schwedt by storm and then establish a bridgehead there on the west bank of the Oder River. They would then be given orders to attack north, toward Stettin, Angermünde, to the west, and Oderberg and Eberswalde to the south. Though the Red Army managed to eliminate the German bridgehead east of Schwedt by 3 March, they could not take the town itself. Schwedt held out until 26 April, when the Germans withdrew, given that the entire Oder River line had by then been broken at numerous places and there was a threat of encirclement.

As the Red Army advanced westward into Germany in early 1945, the Oder River became the last major natural defensive line before Berlin. By early April, Soviet forces had reached the Oder, and General Georgy Zhukov's 1st Belarusian Front and Marshal Ivan Konev's 1st Ukrainian Front prepared for an assault to breach this line. The Germans had entrenched themselves on the Seelow Heights, a ridge that provided a natural vantage point and a formidable defensive position about sixty kilometers east of Berlin. Hoping to defend Berlin, Army Group Vistula had arrayed itself along the Oder River. In the north, *3. Panzerarmee* was located along the lower Oder River. Farther south were the divisions of *9. Armee* under General Theodor Busse. The *9. Armee* was directly in the main advance vector of the Red Army and Berlin. South of *9. Armee* was *4. Panzerarmee,* which took up defensive positions along the upper Oder River. Despite being understrength and composed of conscripts, *Volkssturm* and *Hitler Jugend,* whose ranks even included seventy-year-old men and fourteen-year-old boys, the German forces were entrenched in a series of defensive lines, giving the inexperienced troops a bit of cover.

## 16 APRIL 1945: THE ASSAULT BEGINS

On 16 April, at exactly 3:00 a.m., the Battle of the Seelow Heights commenced with an immense artillery barrage from the Red Army. This bombardment, involving thousands of artillery pieces, shook the German lines along the Oder River. Known as the 'god of war,' Soviet artillery unleashed a ferocious and relentless bombardment that was followed by the deployment of searchlights intended to blind the German defenders as Soviet troops advanced. This decision actually worked to inadvertently illuminate the advancing Red Army tanks and infantry, making it easier for the Germans to target them. Zhukov ordered a massive frontal assault on the German positions. However, the initial attack by

**Figure 80.** Three members of the *Volkssturm*, the 'People's Assault.' They are carrying the single-shot anti-tank weapon, the *'Panzerfaust'*. As the Red Army neared the borders of the Reich, the Nazi Party mobilized the male civilian population into the home guard. This also included the children of the Hitler Youth. The quality of these mostly overage and underage 'volunteers' was limited and dubious, at best. However, their employment showed the Nazi Party's total lack of regard for the welfare of the civilian population. BUNDESARCHIV.

Soviet infantry and armor faced significant difficulties. The first was the terrain. The Oder Valley was filled with marshes, and the approach to the Seelow Heights involved advancing across open, exposed ground, making Soviet armor vulnerable to German anti-tank weapons. The second were defensive obstacles. The German defenders had set up fortified positions with anti-tank ditches, minefields, and a series of interlocking defensive lines. This defensive setup, combined with the terrain, allowed the Germans to hold off the Soviet advance longer than expected.

## 17–18 APRIL 1945: THE BATTLE INTENSIFIES

As the battle progressed, Zhukov committed even more resources, including additional tanks and infantry units. The Soviets continued to suffer heavy casualties, especially as they encountered the German *Panzerfaust* and other close-range anti-tank weapons in urban-like fighting conditions. German forces, though outnumbered, were well dug in and determined to delay the Soviet advance. The 1st Ukrainian Front under Konev advanced from the south to flank the German lines, and by 18 April, the Soviet assault began to breach the German defenses along the Seelow Heights. However, Soviet casualties continued to mount as German troops conducted organized withdrawals, attempting to regroup and counterattack where possible.

## 19 APRIL 1945: GERMAN DEFENSIVE LINES BEGIN TO COLLAPSE

The Seelow Heights represented the last major defensive position before Berlin: elevated terrain that provided a natural defensive advantage. Despite this, the Germans, outnumbered and undersupplied, were up against overwhelming Soviet manpower, artillery, and air support. For three days, from 16–18 April, the Germans held off waves of Soviet attacks. However, the relentless Soviet assault, combined with high German casualties, eventually led to a breaking point. After days of brutal fighting and high casualties on both sides, the Soviet forces finally began to overwhelm the German defenses. Southeast of Berlin, major German divisions from *9. Armee* began to be surrounded. Soviet forces under Marshal Georgy Zhukov's 1st Belarusian Front finally breached the German defenses, forcing *9. Armee* to fall back toward Berlin. This occurred on 19 April, when the Red Army finally captured the Seelow Heights. The path to Berlin was now open, although remnants of the *9. Armee* and other German units fell back, fighting desperate rearguard actions. This retreat, marked by chaos and destruction, would set the stage for the final defensive battles around and within Berlin. The *LVI. Panzerkorps*, commanded by *General der Artillerie* Helmuth Weidling, withdrew into Berlin on 22 April 1945, as Soviet forces encircled the city. The corps, which had been part of the German defensive effort in the area east of Berlin, was pressed into the city's defense as the Soviet 1st Belarusian Front and the 1st Ukrainian Front slowly began to encircle the city.

## 20–23 APRIL 1945: SOVIET ADVANCE AND ENCIRCLEMENT OF BERLIN

Following the fall of the Seelow Heights, the Red Army quickly moved westward. Soviet forces crossed the Oder and encircled Berlin. Despite the collapse of the Oder defenses, the German High Command ordered a final, hopeless defense of the city itself. The Red Army now focused on isolating and encircling Berlin, meeting sporadic German counterattacks but advancing steadily. By 23 April, Berlin was fully encircled, and Soviet forces tightened their grip around the city, setting the stage for urban combat. During the retreat from the Seelow Heights, German units were forced to abandon heavy equipment, including artillery and armored vehicles, as they lacked fuel and faced mobility constraints in swampy, forested terrain. The rapidly advancing Soviet forces also captured significant amounts of German supplies, further diminishing the already depleted resources of *9. Armee*.

## 24–30 APRIL 1945: FINAL STRUGGLE AND THE COLLAPSE OF ODER RIVER DEFENSE

The remnants of *9. Armee*, cut off from Berlin and surrounded near the town of Halbe, fought a desperate battle to break out of Soviet encirclement and reach the Elbe River, where they hoped to surrender to American forces instead of the Soviets. This fighting was marked by severe casualties on both sides, with German soldiers, *Volkssturm*, and civilians suffering heavy losses as they attempted to escape. The Red Army, meanwhile, continued pressing toward Berlin. Encircled within the city, the remaining German forces, including members of the SS, *Volkssturm*, and remnants of the Berlin garrison, resisted in a final, increasingly fragmented defense.

### THE HALBE POCKET

The *9. Armee* was located in Brandenburg, just east and southeast of Berlin, and along the Oder River near the Seelow Heights. As Soviet forces broke through German defenses along the Oder, they drove *9. Armee* and parts of *4. Panzerarmee* into a precarious position, cutting off the *9. Armee* from other German forces in Berlin. By 24 April, *9. Armee* was encircled between the Soviet advance from the east and Soviet forces closing in from the south, forming a pocket that was gradually compressed around the forested area near Halbe. Once isolated, General Busse and his commanders faced a dire situation. Inside the Halbe Pocket were not only soldiers of *9. Armee* and parts of *4. Panzerarmee* but also members of the newly established *12. Armee*, which was led by *General der Panzertruppen* Walther Wenck. There were also a significant number of civilians in the pocket. Trapped between Soviet forces, they were heavily outnumbered, lacked adequate supplies, and had limited artillery and armor. On 16 April 1945, the *9. Armee* was organized as follows:

CI. *Armeekorps*
    303. *Infanterie-Division 'Doberitz'*
    309. *Infanterie-Division 'Berlin'*
    *Divisionsstab z.b.V. 606*

LVI *Panzerkorps*
    11. *SS-Freiwilligen-Panzergrenadier-Division 'Nordland'*
    18. *Panzergrenadier-Division*
    20. *Panzergrenadier-Division*
    712. *Infanterie-Division*

V *SS-Freiwilligen Gebirgsjäger Korps*
    32. *SS-Freiwilligen-Panzergrenadier-Division '30 Januar'*
    *Divisionsstab Raegener*[9]
    *Divisionsstab z.b.V. 391*

178   *The Bitter End*

The objective of *9. Armee* was now to attempt a breakout to the west, aiming to cross the Elbe River and surrender to the advancing American forces rather than to the Red Army, which many feared due to reports of Soviet reprisals. Busse ordered his forces to fight westward, hoping to link up with elements of Wenck's *12. Armee*, which had been ordered by Hitler to counterattack toward Berlin but instead attempted to provide a path for escape. The attempt to break out of the Halbe Pocket began on 24 April and continued until the end of the month, with intense fighting as the Germans made their way westward through the Spreewald Forest and swampy terrain near the village of Halbe. The Soviet 3rd and 4th Guards Tank Armies and the 28th Army encircled and continuously attacked the German columns, who had limited mobility and were constantly harried by Soviet artillery and air attacks. The fighting in the forests around Halbe was extremely brutal. The densely wooded area and marshes made tank maneuvering difficult, resulting in intense infantry combat.

The German forces, including *Volkssturm, Hitler Jugend,* and remnants of various units, fought desperately, often relying on ambush tactics and close-range

**Figure 81.** The Halbe Pocket and the encirclement of Berlin, 24 April 1945.

combat against Soviet forces. Alongside military personnel, tens of thousands of German civilians were caught in the pocket. As Soviet artillery and air raids targeted the retreating columns, casualties mounted, with significant losses among soldiers and civilians alike. The Soviet forces, often moving quickly and using overwhelming firepower, inflicted severe casualties. The Soviet command, aware that the breakout by *9. Armee* might disrupt their offensive on Berlin or allow thousands of German soldiers to escape, committed large forces to contain and crush the pocket. Soviet troops attacked the German forces continuously, showing little mercy in a push to annihilate the German resistance. The breakout attempt from the Halbe Pocket can be divided into three specific phases. These were as follows:

1. Initial Breakout Attempts (24–26 April): Early attempts to break through were met with heavy Soviet resistance. Soviet artillery barrages targeted German assembly points, disrupting their organization. Nonetheless, the *9. Armee* made some progress, using the cover of forests to move through Soviet lines.
2. The Halbe Massacre (27–28 April): As *9. Armee* attempted to cross major roads and open terrain, Soviet forces positioned artillery and tanks to block escape routes. The Germans suffered staggering losses, and the roadways became littered with destroyed vehicles and casualties. Soviet forces aimed to encircle smaller groups within the larger pocket, preventing them from reorganizing or effectively counterattacking.
3. Final Breakout Attempts and Link-up with *12. Armee* (29–30 April): By the end of April, remnants of *9. Armee* managed to reach the vicinity of the Elbe River, where they encountered elements of *12. Armee*. Some German soldiers and civilians managed to cross the Elbe and surrender to American forces, but the majority of *9. Armee* either perished during the battle or were captured by the Red Army.

The Halbe Pocket was effectively destroyed by April 30, with only a small fraction of the *9. Armee* escaping to the west. Estimates suggest that of the approximately 80,000 to 100,000 German soldiers trapped, fewer than 30,000 made it to the Elbe. Casualties were exceptionally high for both the Germans and the Soviets. German losses included tens of thousands killed or wounded, with Soviet forces also suffering significant casualties as they worked to seal off and dismantle the pocket. This encirclement and destruction of *9. Armee* removed one of the last organized German forces capable of reinforcing Berlin. By eliminating *9. Armee*, the Soviets ensured that Berlin was entirely isolated, leading to its capture on 2 May 1945, and bringing an end to the Battle of Berlin. The Halbe Pocket was one of the last major engagements on the Eastern Front and a testament to the chaos, desperation, and devastation of the war's final days.

## BERLIN: THE BATTLE

On 16 April 1945, Zhukov launched a massive assault on the Seelow Heights, the main defensive line protecting Berlin from the east. This battle, later known as the Battle of the Seelow Heights, saw brutal fighting as Soviet artillery and tanks smashed through German positions defended by the remnants of General Gotthard Heinrici's Army Group Vistula. While the German defenders managed to delay Zhukov's advance for several days, they suffered heavy casualties and were forced to retreat toward Berlin. By 20 April, Soviet forces had broken through the Seelow Heights and begun to encircle Berlin. On 23 April, Weidling's *LVI. Panzerkorps* found itself in the unenviable job of defending the German capital. In the doomed city were the remnants of the following German divisions:

- *18. Panzergrenadier-Division* (in reserve)
- *20. Panzergrenadier-Division*—Guarding western Berlin
- *9. Fallschirmjäger-Division*—Guarding northern Berlin
- *Panzer-Division Müncheberg*—Guarding northeastern Berlin
- *11. SS-Freiwilligen-Panzergrenadier-Division 'Nordland'*—Guarding southeastern Berlin

In addition, there were some 40,000 *Volkssturm* and *Hitler Jugend* in the city of questionable battle-worthiness. Other bits and pieces of destroyed formations were also in the capital. There was a battalion of Frenchmen from the *33. Waffen-Grenadier-Division der SS 'Charlemagne'*. In an ironic twist of fate, these French SS volunteers would help defend the *Reichstag* from the Red Army. In a similar situation, Gestapo headquarters, located at *Prinz-Albrecht-Strasse 8*, was guarded by a combination of German SD (*Sicherheitsdienst*) men, including fifteen Belarusian SD personnel from the now-defunct 30th (Belarusian) SD Battalion. A battalion of the Latvian *15. Waffen-Grenadier-Division der SS (lettische Nr. 1)* had also managed to get itself trapped inside Berlin. The Latvian SS soldiers were deployed primarily in and around the Tiergarten area, near the *Reichstag* and the Reich Chancellery. Their positions were part of the last line of defense for Nazi leadership, including Adolf Hitler's bunker, located under the Chancellery. An Arab company of trained paratroopers took part in defending Berlin while serving under *9. Fallschirmjäger-Division*.[10]

There was even a Spanish SS company known as *'Unidad Ezquerra'* ('Unit Ezquerra'), named after its commander, *Waffen-Hauptsturmführer der SS* Miguel Ezquerra-Sánchez. The official title of the unit was *Spanisch-Freiwilligen-Kompanie der SS 101*. In actuality, this Spanish SS 'company' had been whittled down to less than fifty men. In March 1945, the Spaniards had attached themselves to the *'Nordland'* SS division. Previously, they had served in the *28. SS-Freiwilligen-Grenadier-Division 'Wallonien'*. The Norwegian, Swedish, Swiss, Danish, and (a few) Dutch members of the *'Nordland'* SS division were positioned to defend three key areas in the center of the German capital. These were (1) the *Reichstag*, (2) the *Reichskanzlei* (Reich Chancellery and the *Führerbunker* below it), and (3) the area of Wilhelmstrasse and the Government District. Thus, for the last defense of the city center, a score of volunteers from all over Europe and the USSR now defended the heart of the Nazi capital. 'Truly ironic' are the two words that immediately come to mind when describing this end-of-the-war event in the heart of Nazi Germany. *SS-Brigadeführer und Generalmajor der Waffen-SS* Wilhelm Mohnke had also created a battle group from SS units stationed in the city. *SS-Kampfgruppe 'Mohnke'* controlled the following units: *Flak Kompanie 'Leibstandarte Adolf Hitler', SS Ausbildungs und Ersatz Batallion 1 'Leibstandarte Adolf Hitler', Begleit Bataillon Reichsführer-SS, Führer Begleit Kompanie,* and *SS Wach Bataillon 1 'Leibstandarte Adolf Hitler'*.

Finally, stationed in the city were roughly 15,000 policemen, from the *Gemeindepolizei, Ordnungspolizei, Schutzpolizei, Kriminalpolizei, Wasserschutzpolizei, Werkschutzpolizei, Feuerschutzpolizei, Verkehrspolizei,* and *Bahnschutzpolizei*. All told, Berlin could count on 60,000 soldiers (15,000 of them being policemen) and 40,000 *Volkssturm* and *Hitler Jugend*. The *Volkssturm* and the *Hitler Jugend* in Berlin were armed with handheld anti-tank weapons, some machine pistols, and a conglomeration of rifles from half a dozen European countries. Also trapped in

**Figure 82.** Berlin, April 1945. Red Army troops rush past the corpse of a *Reichsarbeitsdienst* (National Labor Service) member (see the arm patch on his left sleeve), who was part of the city defense. TASS.

**Figure 83.** Berlin, April 1945. Captured German 'soldiers.' The photograph says it all. Only one German veteran is seen, surrounded by old men and young boys. This was how the once-powerful *Ostheer* ended the war: with a child's whimper. TASS.

the city were approximately two million desperate German civilians. A few days before the Red Army closed the ring around Berlin, as the civilian tragedy in the city was beginning to unfold, those who wished to avoid being in the city when the attack began flocked to *Generalleutnant* Hellmuth Reymann's command post, in order to request a pass to leave the German capital. Reymann would be the garrison commander of Berlin from 6 March until 22 April 1945, when he was relieved by Hitler. Those who sought a pass from him in March and early April were mostly Nazi Party officials who also wished to avoid service in the *Volkssturm*. According to Reymann, he allowed most to leave, stating that he was actually glad to be rid of them.[11]

As the Soviet forces closed in on the German capital, Zhukov's 1st Belarusian Front advanced from the northeast, while Konev's 1st Ukrainian Front approached from the south. By 25 April, the two Soviet fronts had fully encircled Berlin, cutting off all remaining German forces within the city from potential reinforcements. Soviet units systematically pushed into Berlin's outskirts, encountering fierce resistance from German troops who were well-prepared for street fighting. The Soviet Army utilized extensive artillery bombardments to destroy German defenses, followed by coordinated infantry and tank assaults to seize strategic buildings, streets, and squares. This urban combat was brutal and highly destructive; entire neighborhoods were reduced to rubble. Soviet snipers, machine gunners, and grenadiers cleared buildings block by block, while German defenders fought tenaciously from barricades, buildings, and underground tunnels.

The battle intensified as Soviet troops advanced toward the city center. Key locations such as the *Reichstag,* the Brandenburg Gate, and the government district around the Reich Chancellery became focal points for both sides. The *Reichstag,* in particular, symbolized German power and thus became a symbolic target for the Soviets. On 30 April, Soviet troops reached the *Reichstag* after heavy fighting, but the building was fiercely defended by German troops, including foreign SS volunteers. Over the course of two days, Soviet soldiers fought room by room, often facing counterattacks from fanatical SS troops yelling *'Heil Hitler!'.* By 1 May, the Red Army finally raised the Soviet flag over the building, marking the symbolic fall of Nazi Germany. For all intents and purposes, the war in Europe was now over. All that was left was for the Germans to sign the articles of unconditional surrender.

## THE END IN THE *FÜHRERBUNKER*

In spite of numerous implorations by those still loyal to the Führer, Hitler refused to leave Berlin and remained in his bunker, unwilling to abandon the German capital. In a final attempt to direct the battle, between 19–22 April, Hitler engaged in what some historians have described as delusional plans for nonexistent divisions and phantom reinforcements. During this time period, the Führer, sensing the trap had closed around him, issued orders for *9. Armee,* which was now mostly surrounded south of Berlin, to attack northward and head toward the German capital. He also ordered that *General der Panzertruppe* Walther Wenck's *12. Armee* turn away from the Elbe River, where his small force was facing the Americans, and to head northeast to break the siege of Berlin from that direction. Finally, the German dictator directed *Armeegruppe Steiner-III. (germanisches) SS-Panzerkorps* to attack from the north.

It was a fantasy to believe that these three distinct military forces were in any shape and condition to launch such a relief attempt. Nevertheless, the generals that surrounded Hitler on a daily basis and shared his bunker never uttered a word about the futility and impossibility of such orders. That was because they knew that trying to reason with Adolf Hitler about the reality of the military situation would only bring a tirade of insults from the German dictator. When they received these impossible commands by telex, generals Buse, Wenck, and Steiner simply ignored these directives because they couldn't fulfill them anyway. In Steiner's case, his supposed army group did not exist. Only the headquarters of *III. (germanisches) SS-Panzerkorps* existed but with no troops.

The military situation of these three generals prevented them from following Hitler's order. They also saw these last-minute orders to relieve the city for what they were: a final, desperate attempt to escape justice by a man who was now cornered and about to face the consequences of his actions. The top generals in Hitler's inner circle, like *Generalfeldmarschall* Wilhelm Keitel and *Generaloberst* Alfred Jodl, refused to tell the Führer that no relief forces were coming to save

Berlin. It was, therefore, left up to *General der Artillerie* Helmuth Weidling, the new commander of the Berlin Defense Area, who got up the courage to finally inform Hitler on 22 April that no one could come to Berlin's aid. Upon hearing this news, the German dictator lashed out at his commanders. Needing someone to blame, he accused all of them of betrayal and cowardice. Those who were witness to this temper tantrum, which occurred during a military conference in the *Führerbunker,* actually claimed that at one point Hitler was foaming at the mouth. His frustration and despair became apparent as he began to realize that the situation was hopeless.

On 23 April, *Reichsmarshall* Hermann Göring, who was Hitler's designated successor, and who still held considerable influence as head of the *Luftwaffe* and President of the *Reichstag,* sent a telegram to Hitler in the *Führerbunker.* The message proposed that Göring would assume leadership of Germany if Hitler were incapacitated or otherwise unable to lead. As Soviet forces surrounded Berlin, Hitler was increasingly cut off and losing control of the situation. At the time, Göring was located in Berchtesgaden, in southern Germany. He likely saw an opportunity to assume the leadership of Germany and, possibly, negotiate with the Allies. It was probable that he believed he could potentially save Germany from complete destruction, or at the very least, save himself.

Göring argued that because he was officially Hitler's successor, according to a decree issued in 1941 by the Führer himself, he should take command if Hitler were unable to exercise his duties. The telegram ended by saying that if he did not hear from the Führer by a certain time period, he would assume that Hitler was incapacitated and Göring would then assume the office of Chancellor of Nazi Germany. That last sentence, which sounded a bit like an ultimatum, is what sealed his fate insofar as Hitler's desire to arrest him. The telegram had been handed to the Führer by Martin Bormann, Hitler's personal secretary and a man who despised Göring and was his political enemy.

With Bormann's egging, Hitler interpreted Göring's message as a power grab, indicating that Göring was attempting to usurp authority while Hitler was still alive. Enraged, the Führer ordered that Göring be stripped of all his positions and titles, even going so far as to expel him from the Nazi Party. Upon receiving Hitler's angry response to Göring's telegram on 23 April, Martin Bormann, Hitler's private secretary and known to many in Hitler's private circle as the 'Brown Eminence', coordinated with local SS personnel at Berchtesgaden to detain Hermann Göring.[12] Karl Freiherr von Eberstein, the SS and police leader in Bavaria and a longtime associate of both Hitler and Göring, played a key role in Göring's confinement. Under Bormann's directive, Eberstein and other SS officers stripped Göring of his titles and placed him under house arrest at the Berghof. Göring remained under close SS guard at his estate for the remainder of the war, though his 'arrest' was more of an enforced isolation than a strict imprisonment. This marked a definitive break between Göring and Hitler, showcasing the Führer's dwindling circle of trust and escalating paranoia in his final days.

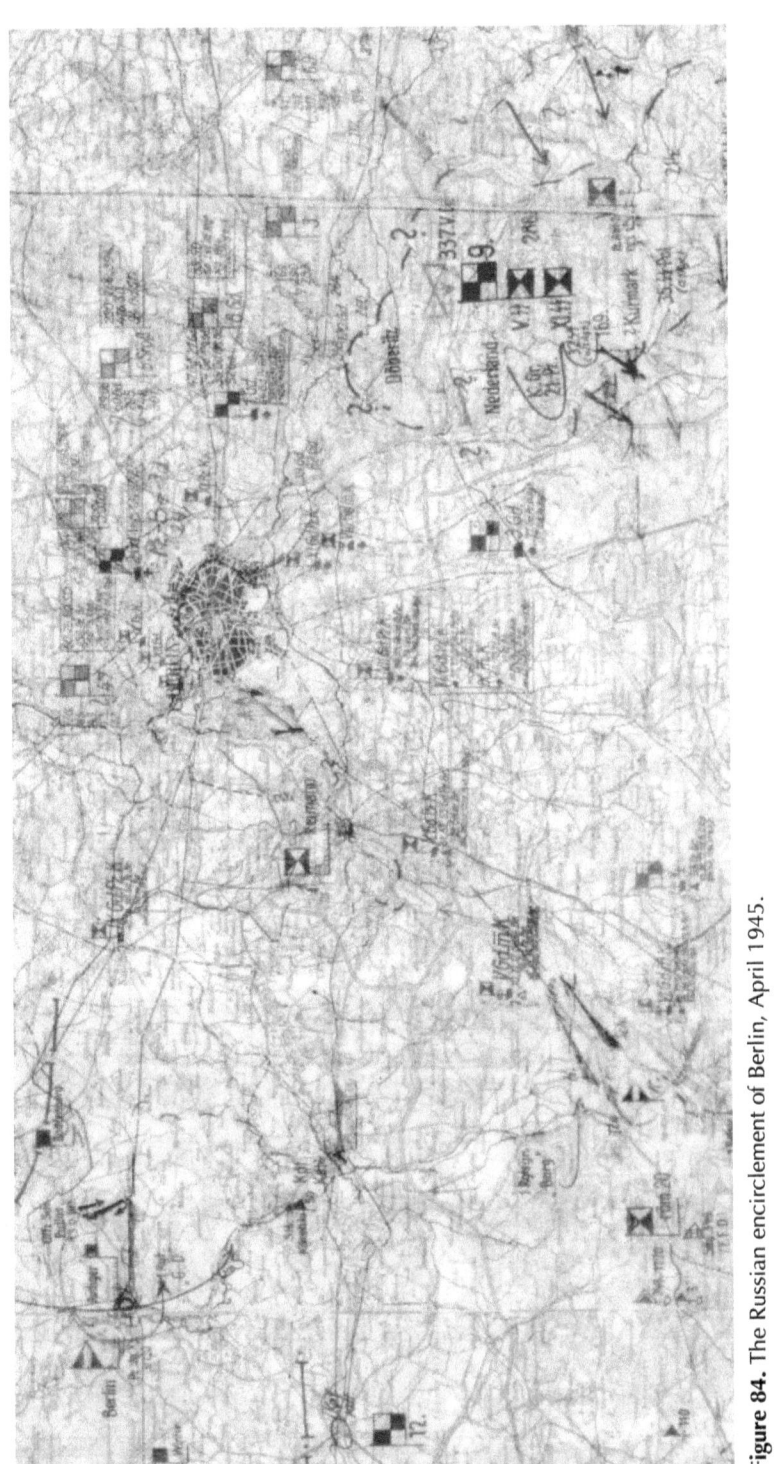

**Figure 84.** The Russian encirclement of Berlin, April 1945.

Then, to add insult to injury, five days later, on 28 April, Adolf Hitler found out that Heinrich Himmler had betrayed him. *Reichsminister* Albert Speer and Propaganda Minister Joseph Goebbels brought the news to the *Führerbunker*. They told Hitler that Himmler had secretly attempted to negotiate a surrender with the western Allies through the Swedish intermediary, Count Folke Bernadotte. This was verified by *SS-Brigadeführer und Generalmajor der Waffen-SS* Wilhelm Mohnke, through an intercepted British radio broadcast which verified that the *Reichsführer-SS* was attempting to negotiate, thus confirming the betrayal. The Führer reacted with shock and fury. Himmler's actions were a profound personal betrayal to Hitler, who had considered him one of his most loyal followers.

Until Mohnke brought proof, Hitler initially could not believe that *'Treuer Heinrich'* ('faithful Heinrich') had betrayed him. In response, he ordered Himmler's arrest and stripped him of all his titles and duties. As a further reaction, that same day, he ordered the arrest and execution of *SS-Gruppenführer und Generalleutnant der Waffen-SS* Hermann Fegelein, who was Himmler's liaison officer at the *Führerbunker*. He did this for two reasons. First, Hitler may have suspected that Fegelein was in on the betrayal. Secondly, Hitler couldn't get to Himmler because he wasn't in the German capital, but Fegelein was in Berlin. The Führer satiated his bloodlust by ordering the arrest and execution of Himmler's aide-de-camp in the *Führerbunker*. The hapless SS general was picked up in his apartment, where an SS security detachment found him, drunk and in bed with a woman who was not his wife. He was brought back to Hitler's bunker underneath the Chancellery, where he was quickly tried and sentenced to death. That same day, he was executed by a firing squad composed of members of the *Reichssicherheitsdienst* bodyguard detachment, led by SS General Johann Rattenhuber. The death of Fegelein was a blow to Eva Braun, Hitler's mistress, given that her sister had married the SS officer. But even being the future brother-in-law to the Führer was not enough to spare his life.

Hitler's realization that his armies could not (or would not) reach Berlin, and the betrayals by Göring and Himmler, led him to finally accept that the war was lost, culminating in his decision to commit suicide in the *Führerbunker* on 30 April 1945. Before he did so, he did two things. He wrote his last will and testament, and he married Eva Braun, who agreed to join him in death. His orders in those final days illustrate his refusal to accept the impending defeat and his profound disillusionment with his generals, the German people, and even some of his closest Nazi Party leaders. His last will and testament are basically a ranting manifesto of grievances and excuses for the actions of a man who caused the deaths of tens of millions of people. Along with his suicide came the suicide of hundreds of other Nazis who refused to live in a world without National Socialism. The *Tausendjähriges Reich,* which Hitler boasted would last a millennium, lasted only twelve years, three months, and eight days. During that time (1933–1945), forty million people

**Figure 85.** The very epitome of the Soviet victory over Nazi Germany: Red Army soldiers take time for a photograph atop a Joseph Stalin tank near the Brandenburg Gate in Berlin, May 1945. TASS.

(soldiers and civilians) perished in Europe on account of Hitler's war. Of that number, nineteen million were Soviet citizens: ten million soldiers and about nine million civilians. Around six million Polish civilians and soldiers also perished, of which three million were Polish Jews murdered by the Nazis.

## A NOTE ON GERMAN MILITARY LOSSES

Germany lost just over seven million people during the war: 4.3 million soldiers and three million civilians. From 22 June 1941 to January 1942, approximately 225,000 German soldiers were killed on the Eastern Front. During the same period, German casualties in the East (killed, wounded, taken prisoner, or missing) was said to have reached 930,000. This represents about 29 percent of the total force committed to the invasion in June 1941. German losses on the Eastern Front from February 1942 to February 1943 numbered 1,570,000 killed, wounded, taken prisoner, or missing. Of that number, around 750,000 were killed during this time period. From March–December 1943, approximately 550,000 men were killed in the East. From January–December 1944, about 900,000 soldiers were killed fighting on the Russian Front. Finally, from 1 January to 8 May 1945, around 590,000 German soldiers died. Altogether, 3,015,000 German soldiers died on the Russian Front from 22 June 1941 to 8 May 1945. If German military deaths during the war totaled 4.3 million men, then the 3,015,000 soldiers killed while serving in the

*Ostheer* represents a little over seventy percent of total German military deaths for the entire war. The other military theaters of war accounted for thirty percent of total German deaths in the war.[13] It is clear from the table below that the bloodiest period of the war for the *Ostheer* was the year 1944. The numbers support the hypothesis that the German Army in the East began to unravel in that year.[14]

**Table 3. German Military Losses on the Eastern Front from 22 June 1941 to 8 May 1945**

| Period of Time | Killed, Missing, Taken Prisoner, or Wounded | Total Killed |
| --- | --- | --- |
| June 1941–January 1942 | 930,000 | 225,000 |
| Feb. 1942–Feb. 1943 | 1,900,000 | 750,000 |
| March–December 1943 | 1,350,000 | 550,000 |
| 1 January–December 1944 | 3,500,000 | 900,000 |
| 1 January–8 May 1945 | 1,300,000 | 590,000 |
| Grand Total | 8,980,000 | 3,015,000 |

# APPENDIX I

## Major German and Soviet Armored Vehicles From 1943–1945

### German Armored Fighting Vehicles

**Figure 86.** *Panzerkampfwagen IV Ausf.* (abbreviation for '*Ausführung*', or 'version') F (*Sonderkraftfahrzeug 161*). This tank was the backbone of the German armored forces throughout most of World War II. It served in every theater of war, including North Africa. A total of 8,553 tanks (all versions: A, B, C, D, E, F, G, H, and J) were built from 1936–1945. The F version (shown here) carried the 75 mm KwK 40 L/48 anti-tank gun. Top speed for most versions was sixteen miles per hour.

**Figure 87.** *Panzerkampfwagen V Ausf. G 'Panther' (Sonderkraftfahrzeug 171)*. This German tank was probably the best medium tank in the world up until early 1950. Almost 6,000 Panther tanks (all versions: D, A, G, and Prototype F) were built from 1943–1945. It carried the effective 75 mm KwK 42 L/70 anti-tank gun. The Panther tank had been specifically designed to defeat the Russian T-34 tank. The vehicle, when manned by a veteran tank crew, was a formidable adversary. The one drawback was its complex electronics and mechanics, especially when it came to the electrical wiring and the intricate suspension system, with its overlapping wheels. As a result, the average repair time was longer than usual.

**Figure 88.** *Panzerkampfwagen VI Ausf. E. 'Tiger' (Sonderkraftfahrzeug 181)*. This German heavy tank is likely the most recognizable tank in all the world. Many people know that it belonged to the German Army of World War II and that it was a feared and daunting tank. Around 1,347 Tiger-I tanks were built (all versions: E and H) from 1942–1944. It carried the formidable 88 mm KwK 36 L/56 anti-tank gun. The first production model suffered teething problems. These tanks were only assigned to special heavy tank battalions.

**Figure 89.** *Panzerkampfwagen VI Tiger II Ausf. B (Sonderkraftfahrzeug 182)*. This AFV was nicknamed *Königstiger* ('King Tiger'). This was the final version of the German heavy tank production for the Third Reich era. Exactly 492 of these superheavy tanks were built from 1944–1945. There was only one version, the 'B' model, but two distinct production B versions, the original, which had many mechanical and electrical issues, and the 'refined' B version which corrected those weaknesses. In addition to having exceptional armor protection, the tank carried the deadly 88 mm KwK 43 L/71 anti-tank gun. Few Allied tanks could stand up to it. Only the American M-26 'Pershing' heavy tank, introduced in February 1945, and the Soviet Joseph Stalin 2 tank could go head-to-head with this German armored beast.

**Figure 90.** *Panzerjäger 'Jagdpanther' (Sonderkraftfahrzeug 173)*. This tank hunter was based on the Panther tank design, but like all tank destroyers, it was turretless. Only 413 were built during the war from 1943–1945 (two variants: G1 and G2). The G1 variant was the first version built and carried an 88 mm Pak 43/3 L-71 anti-tank gun. The G2 variant carried an 88 mm Pak 43/4 L-71 anti-tank gun. The vehicle had been designed to deal with the Soviet heavy KV tank line which German 75 mm anti-tank guns had trouble destroying. Like the Panther tank, the slick sloping armor design of this vehicle not only served to protect its crew but also made it a postwar favorite with military enthusiasts. Simply put, the vehicle is beautiful to look at.[1] So much so, that the image of a *Jagd-panther* was featured in several board games about World War II and was even the symbol of an American wargaming hobby magazine.[2]

**Figure 91.** *Panzerjäger Jagdpanzer IV L/70 (Sonderkraftfahrzeug 162)*. This tank hunter was based on the Panzer IV chassis. *Generaloberst* Heinz Guderian actually opposed production of this design. He claimed that the *Sturmgeschütz III*. assault gun was performing well enough for its intended role. Guderian instead wanted to streamline production by keeping the existing vehicles (but producing more of them) and limiting new designs. During the war, two versions of this tank hunter were built. The first version carried the 75 mm Pak 39 L/48 anti-tank gun. A total of 769 of these vehicles were built between January to November 1944. The second version carried the longer barrel 75 mm Pak 42 L/70 anti-tank gun. A total of 930 of these vehicles were produced between August 1944 and April 1945. Of the 930 built, 278 were produced between December 1944 and April 1945. In fact, during the Battle for Berlin, a factory located northeast of the German capital was delivering these vehicles (unpainted) as they were being produced from the factory to armored units belonging to Army Group Vistula. Its low silhouette made it a perfect tank hunter in broken terrain and areas with foliage. It was at a disadvantage in open ground, however, given its weak armor.

## SOVIET ARMORED FIGHTING VEHICLES

**Figure 92.** The SU-76 assault gun. Some 14,292 of these assault guns were built between December 1942 and October 1945 (two versions). The vehicle carried the 76.2 mm Zis-3 Model 1942 anti-tank gun. The second version, called the SU-76M, had an open armored casemate on top and partially from the rear. So many of these vehicles were built that a good number of the Red Army assault gun regiments in 1944 and 1945 were still armed with them, even though more powerful assault guns were employed beginning in 1943 and 1944. Many of these assault gun regiments equipped with the SU-76 AFV (armored fighting vehicle) took part in the Battle for Berlin.

**Figure 93.** The SU-85 assault gun. This AFV was based on the T-34/85 chassis and was produced from 1943–1944. A total of 2,650 were built during the war. This assault gun caried the 85 mm D5T anti-tank gun. Very soon after this vehicle was deployed to the assault gun regiments of the Red Army, it was discovered that, like the SU-76, a larger gun was needed to better tackle the new German armored vehicles being produced. This gave way to the introduction of the SU-100.

**Figure 94.** SU-100 assault gun. A total of 2,335 vehicles were produced from September 1944 to May 1945. However, after the war, an additional 2,641 vehicles were built before production ended. The vehicle carried the very effective 100 mm D-10S anti-tank gun, capable of penetrating thick armor, including the armor of the 'Panther' and 'Tiger' tanks at long range. The chassis provided reliable mobility, good cross-country performance, even in rough terrain, and ease of maintenance. Overall, it was an effective tank killer. Its drawbacks were its limited gun traverse and its cramped interior.

**Figure 95.** The SU-152 'Taran' assault gun. Although listed as an assault gun, it carried the 152 mm ML-20S gun-howitzer. The vehicle was designed specifically to tackle enemy fortifications, giving the Red Army infantry much-needed support. However, the assault gun regiments equipped with this AFV often had to deal with enemy armored units. At close range, it could destroy such vehicles as the 'Panther' tank, as well as the heavy 'Tiger I' tank and super-heavy 'Elefant' tank destroyer, with just one shot, if using high-explosive (HE) shells. It, therefore, earned its nickname, 'Beast Slayer'—Беаст Слаыер ('*Zveroboy*'), which reflected this capability. About 670 vehicles were produced from January to December 1943. Its drawbacks were (1) poor visibility, (2) no secondary weapon (no machine guns), and (3) slow, limited mobility because it used the heavy KV tank chassis.

**Figure 96.** The T-34/76 A tank. Introduced in the summer of 1941 to Russian tank units, it quickly became the mainstay of the Soviet armored forces during the war. It carried the 76 mm M 1940 F-34 anti-tank gun. Several versions were built (A, B, C, and D). Altogether around 35,120 T-34/76 tanks were produced from 1941–1943. This tank was eventually replaced by the T-34/85 tank, which carried a larger caliber anti-tank gun. It had great suspension and wide tracks, making it able to handle muddy terrain far better than German vehicles, especially the earlier German tank models which possessed narrow tracks. German tanks employed for Operation Barbarossa in 1941 were all far inferior in design, armament, and armored protection. No German tank up until the arrival of the Tiger I tank in late 1942 could deal effectively with this vehicle. The German 'Panther' tank was specifically developed as a response to the T-34/76 tank. The tank had three drawbacks. First, there was no radio. The tank commander could only communicate with other tanks using flags. This meant opening the top hatch of the turret and exposing himself to possible enemy fire. Secondly, the tank commander also had to aim and fire the cannon. This limited the situational awareness of the tank commander, which, therefore, reduced combat effectiveness. Three, the quarters inside this armored fighting vehicle were cramped.

**Figure 97.** The T-34/85 tank. During the war, a total of 23,741 T-34/85 tanks were produced from 1944–1945. However, another 25,209 tanks were produced after the war ended. The vehicle was meant to replace the T-34/76 tank, which, by mid-1943, was becoming inferior to newer German armored vehicles. The tank used an 85 mm ZiS-S-53 anti-tank gun modified from an 85 mm 52K model 39 antiaircraft gun. It had crew comfort compared to the T-34/76 tank, enhanced armor, good mobility, and ease of production on the tank assembly line. On the downside, the 85 mm gun still struggled to destroy late-war German armored vehicles. In addition to having inferior optical equipment as compared with the German vehicles, the side and rear armor remained relatively thin and were still vulnerable to flanking attacks and high-velocity anti-tank weapons like the *Panzerfaust* or *Panzerschreck*.

**Figure 98.** IS-1 heavy tank, also referred to as the JS-1 heavy tank. The JS-1 tank was produced between October 1943 and January 1944. It carried the same gun as the T34/85, and this is the very reason why it was soon replaced by the JS-2 heavy tank, which carried the heavier 122 mm D-25T anti-tank gun. That is why only 207 JS-1 heavy tanks were produced.

**Figure 99.** IS-2 heavy tank, also referred to as the JS-2 heavy tank. As stated above, it carried the heavier 122 mm D-25T anti-tank gun, which was able to penetrate the armor of even the Tiger-II ('King Tiger') heavy tank. A total of 3,854 JS-2 tanks were built from 1944–1945. Like all heavy tanks, it was employed in specialized (heavy) tank regiments. The JS-2 heavy tank, therefore, was far more numerous and more effective on the battlefield than the JS-1 tank.

# APPENDIX II

## *Estimate of Casualties Taken by the* Ostheer, *1941–1945*

**Table 4. Estimate of casualties incurred by the *Ostheer*, by year, army group, and type of losses.**[1]

| Year | Killed | Wounded | Captured | Total |
|---|---|---|---|---|
| | | Army Group North | | |
| 1941 | 50,000 | 60,000 | 15,000 | 125,000 |
| 1942 | 100,000 | 90,000 | 30,000 | 220,000 |
| 1943 | 70,000 | 90,000 | 40,000 | 200,000 |
| 1944 | 160,000 | 500,000 | 40,000 | 700,000 |
| 1945 | 40,000 | 80,000 | 200,000 | 320,000 |
| | | Army Group Center | | |
| 1941 | 100,000 | 380,000 | 35,000 | 515,000 |
| 1942 | 200,000 | 390,000 | 60,000 | 650,000 |
| 1943 | 220,000 | 230,000 | 150,000 | 600,000 |
| 1944 | 390,000 | 900,000 | 510,000 | 1,800,000 |
| 1945 | 300,000 | 200,000 | 30,000 | 530,000 |
| | | Army Group South | | |
| 1941 | 70,000 | 185,000 | 35,000 | 290,000 |
| 1942 | 450,000 | 350,000 | 230,000 | 1,030,000 |
| 1943 | 260,000 | 190,000 | 100,000 | 550,000 |
| 1944 | 350,000 | 100,000 | 50,000 | 1,000,000 |
| 1945 | 250,000 | 100,000 | 100,000 | 450,000 |
| | | | Grand Total: | 8,980,000 |

NOTE: These figures are approximate estimates of total German losses taken from 1941–1945.

The statistics that appear in Table 3. (German Military Losses on the Eastern Front from 22 June 1941 to 8 May 1945) support the total number of losses listed in this table (8,980,000). These figures, therefore, are the best estimate of German soldiers killed, wounded, or taken prisoner for the entire campaign in the East. For purposes of ease, I have added those soldiers listed as missing in action, with the confirmed dead. The table is very revealing. For example, if you compare the figures showing heavy losses, they coincide with a major battle or campaign launched in that particular region of the Russian Front, and in a specific year when it took place. Another tidbit of information that the table shows is that if you were a German *landser* serving in Army Group North, you were less likely to die than if serving in either Army Group Center or Army Group South.

# APPENDIX III

## Order of Battle for *11. SS Panzerarmee*, 10 February 1945

*11. SS Panzerarmee* (formed 10 February). The *11. SS Panzerarmee* was a part of Army Group Vistula in February 1945. On 1 March, it lost all its units. This army HQ was then transferred, without troops, to the Harz Mountains in March 1945.

*11. SS Panzerarmee* (*SS-Obergruppenführer* Felix Steiner)
Directly under *11. SS Panzerarmee* command:
*163. Infanterie-Division*

*Tettau Armeekorps:*
*Division Köslin* (Existed from 20 January–28 February 1945)
Renamed '*Grenadier Division Pommerland*' in late February. Destroyed on 12 March.
    *Regiment Krankewitz*
    *Regiment Jatzinhen*
    *SS Waffen Unterführerschule Lauenburg*
    *Baupionier Ersatz und Ausbildungs Bataillon 2*
*Division Bärwalde* (existed from February to March 1945)
    *Regiment 1 Division 'Bärwalde'*
    *Regiment 2 Division 'Bärwalde'*
    *Regiment 3 Division 'Bärwalde'*
    *Regiment 4 Division 'Bärwalde'*
    *Regiment 5 Division 'Bärwalde'*
    *Artillerie-Regiment Division 'Bärwalde'*
    *Pionier-Bataillon Division 'Bärwalde'*
    *Divisions-Nachrichten-Abteilung Division 'Bärwalde'*

*Korpsgruppe Munzel:*
    *Führer-Grenadier-Division*
    *Führer-Begleit-Division*

X. SS-Armeekorps:
5. Jäger-Division
Division Nr. 402 (renamed as Ausbildungs Division 402 in March 1945)

XVI. SS-Armeekorps:
15. Waffen-Grenadier-Division der SS (lettische Nr. 1)
Parts of SS Panzergrenadier-Regiment 49 'de Ruyter' (23. SS-Freiwilligen-Panzergrenadier-Division)
Kampfgruppe Joachim (formed from SS Grenadier Ausbildungs und Ersatz Bataillon 35)

III. (germanisches) SS-Panzerkorps:
Divisionsgruppe Voigt (renamed Divisionsgruppe Ledebur in March 1945)
281. Infanterie-Division
23. SS-Freiwilligen-Panzergrenadier-Division 'Nederland'
11. SS-Freiwilligen-Panzergrenadier-Division 'Nordland'
27. SS-Freiwilligen Grenadier Division 'Langemarck'

XXXIX Panzerkorps (February 1945 only. Transferred to 17. Armee in March 1945.)
4. SS Polizei Panzergrenadier-Division 'Polizei'
10. SS Panzer-Division 'Frundsberg'
28. SS-Freiwilligen Grenadier Division 'Wallonien'

Wehrkreis II (later redesignated II. Armeekorps)
9. Fallschirmjäger-Division
Divisionsgruppe Deneke (renamed 549. Volksgrenadier-Division on 1 March 1945)[1]
(Standort) Festungs-Division Swinemünde

Added to 3. Panzerarmee in late February 1945:
Divisionsgruppe Klossek (actually only the size of a regiment)
    1x *Volkssturm Bataillon V*
    1x *Landesschützen Bataillon*
    1x Hungarian Infantry Battalion

# APPENDIX IV

## Order of Battle for Army Group Vistula, 1 March 1945

*Heeresgruppe Vistula*:
Directly under army group command:
*Division Staff z.b.V. 610*
*Panzer-Division 'Schlesien'*

*9. Armee*:
Directly under army command:
*10. SS Panzer-Division 'Frundsberg'*

*V. SS-Freiwilligen-Gebirgs-Armeekorps:*
*Divisionsstab z.b.V. 391*
*32. SS-Freiwilligen Grenadier Division '30 Januar'*
*Festung Frankfurt*

*XI SS-Panzerkorps* (temporarily named a 'panzer' corps):
*712. Infanterie-Division*
*Panzergrenadier-Division Kurmark*
*25. Panzergrenadier-Division*
*Festung Küstrin*

*CI. Armeekorps:*
*309. Infanterie-Division 'Berlin'*
*303. Infanterie-Division 'Döberitz'*
*Division Stab z.b.V. 606*

*Oder Armeekorps:*
*1st Marine Division*
*Divisionsgruppe Klossek*

*Appendix IV*

*3. Panzerarmee*
Directly under army command:
*33. Waffen-Grenadier-Division der SS 'Charlemagne'*
*Panzer-Division 'Holstein'*

*II. Armeekorps:*
*9. Fallschirmjäger-Division*
*549. Volksgrenadier-Division* (renamed 1 March from: *'Divisionsgruppe Deneke'*)
 Temporarily attached to the division: *II. Bataillon/Fallschirmjäger-Regiment 26*

*III. (germanisches) SS-Panzerkorps:*
*261. Infanterie-Division*
*11. SS-Freiwilligen-Panzergrenadier-Division 'Nordland'*
*28. SS-Freiwilligen Grenadier Division 'Wallonien'*
*Divisionsgruppe Voigt*
*27. SS-Freiwilligen-Grenadier-Division 'Langemarck'*
*23. SS-Freiwilligen-Panzergrenadier-Division 'Nederland'*

*X. SS-Armeekorps:*
*5. Jäger-Division*
*Division Nr. 402 z.b.V.*
*163. Infanterie-Division*

*Tettau Armeekorps:*
*Ersatz und Ausbildungs-Division 'Bärwald'*
*Ersatz und Ausbildungs-Division 'Pommern'*
*15. Waffen-Grenadier-Division der SS (lettische Nr. 1)*

Table 5. 'Bayonet' Strength of 9. Armee on 17 March 1945

| Formation | Strength |
|---|---|
| **V. SS Freiwilligen-Gebirgs-Armeekorps** | **21,969** |
| 32. SS Freiwilligen-Grenadier-Division '30. Januar' | 2,846 |
| Panzer-Division 'Schlesien' | 3,200 |
| Divisionsgruppe Raegener | 3,266 |
| 391. Infanterie-Division | 3,618 |
| Festungs-Division Frankfurt an der Oder | 9,039 |
| **XI SS-Armeekorps** | **20,398** |
| Panzergrenadier-Division Kurmark | 2,375 |
| 25. Panzergrenadier-Division | 5,196 |
| Panzer-Division Müncheberg | 2,867 |
| 712. Infanterie-Division | 3,699 |
| 303. Infanterie-Division 'Doberitz' | 3,474 |
| Festung Küstrin (about 11,000 at its height) | 2,787 |
| **CI. Armeekorps** | **10,349** |
| 309. Infanterie-Division 'Berlin' | 5,889 |
| Infanterie-Division z.b.V. 606 | 4,460 |
| **9. Armee 'Bayonet' Strength on 17 March 1945:** | **52,716** |

# APPENDIX V

# Order of Battle for Army Group Vistula, 12 April 1945

*Heeresgruppe Vistula* (*Generaloberst* Gotthard Heinrici)
Being reformed under Army Group Vistula:[1]

18. Panzergrenadier-Division (*Generalmajor* Josef Rauch, 1 January–8 May 1945)[2]
    *Panzergrenadier-Regiment 30* (from *Panzergrenadier-Regiment 'Schlesien 1'*)
    *Panzergrenadier-Regiment 51* (from *Panzergrenadier-Regiment 'Schlesien 2'*)
    *gemischtes Panzer-Abteilung 118* (from *Panzer Abteilung 'Schlesien'*)
    *Artillerie-Regiment 18* (from *Panzer-Artillerie-Regiment 'Schlesien'*)
    *Pionier-Bataillon 18*
    *Feldersatz-Bataillon 18*
    *Panzerjäger-Abteilung 18*
    *Panzer-Aufklärungs-Abteilung 118*
    *Panzergrenadier-Divisions Nachrichten-Abteilung 18*
    *Versorgungseinheiten 18*

For special employment under the army group:
    *Kampfgruppe 1001 Nacht* (*Major* Gustav-Adolf Eugen Johannes Erich Blancbois)[3]
        *SS-Panzerjäger-Abteilung 560* (*SS-Sturmbannführer* Günther Wöst)
            *Bataillon Hauptquartier* (x2 *Hetzer* + 3x *Schwimmwagen* + 6 trucks)
                1. *Panzerjäger Kompanie* (x14 *Hetzer* tank destroyers)
                2. *Panzerjäger Kompanie* (x14 *Hetzer* tank destroyers)
                3. *Panzerjäger Kompanie* (x14 *Hetzer* tank destroyers)
                4. *Panzerjäger Kompanie* (x8 *Sturmgeschütz III.* assault guns)
    *Begleitbataillon Speer* (*Major* Hans-Joachim Heering) with:
    *Hauptquartier Kompanie* (2x *Sonderkraftfahrzeug 222* armored cars + 2x *Kübelwagen* + 4x trucks). Only two companies in the battalion:
    1. *Kettenkrad Kompanie* (ad hoc unit created specifically for A. Speer)
    (8x *Kettenkrad*, 2x *Kübelwagen*, and 2x *Schwimmwagen*)

206  *Appendix V*

    2. *Panzerspähwagen Aufklärungs Kompanie*
    (6x *Sd.Kfz. 222* and 6x *Sd.Kfz. 231*)

3. *Panzerarmee-* (*General der Panzertruppe* Hasso von Manteuffel)
Directly under *3. Panzerarmee* command on 12 April 1945:
    3. *Kompanie/Feldgendarmerie Abteilung 695*
    *Panzer-AOK 3 Sturm-Bataillon*[4]

The following tank destroyer brigade was attached to *III. SS-Panzerkorps* on 21 April 1945:
    *Panzerjagd-Verband Weichsel* (*Oberst* Wilhelm-Ernst Gedult von Jungenfeld)[5]
        *Panzer Jagd Brigade D*
            (*I., II., III. Bataillone*)
        *Panzer-Jagd-Brigade F*
            (*II. Bataillon*)
        *Panzer-Jagd-Brigade R*
            (*III. Bataillon*)
        *Panzer-Jagd-Brigade P*
            (*I., II., III. Bataillone*)

The following two SS divisions were attached to *III. SS-Panzerkorps* on 21 April 1945:
    27. *SS-Freiwilligen-Grenadier-Division 'Langemark'*
    (*SS-Oberführer* Thomas Müller)—regimental strength
    28. *SS-Freiwilligen-Grenadier-Division 'Wallonien'*
    (*SS-Obersturmbannführer der Reserve* Leon Degrelle)[6]—regimental strength

    (Standort) *Festungs-Division Swinemünde:*[7]
        *Festungs-Alarm-Regiment 1* (from air force personnel from the Wollin-Dievenow Air Base and the Air Signals School)
        *Festungs-Alarm-Regiment 2* (from men of Marine Flak School No. 3, plus men from Destroyer and Torpedo Boat School 'Osternothafen')
        *Festungs-Alarm-Regiment 3* (from men of various Marine flak schools)
        *Festungs-Alarm-Regiment 4* (from men of Marine Flak School No. 4)
        *Festungs-Alarm-Regiment 5* (from men of Marine Flak School No. 5)
            *I., II., III. Marine-Bataillone*
        3. *Marine-Flak-Regiment*
            *Marine-Flak-Abteilung 233*
            *Marine-Flak-Abteilung 711*
            *Marine-Flak-Abteilung 713*
        *Küsten-Artillerie-Lehr-Abteilung*

*Festungs Alarm Regiment 5* (listed above) was initially known as *Festungs Alarm Regiment Bahr*. It was led by *Fregattenkapitän* Klaus Bahr. It had three battalions:

Ausbildungs-Division 402 (*Generalmajor* Ernst von Bauer)[8]
   *Grenadier-Ausbildungs-Regiment 522*–Rostock
      *Fusilier-Ausbildungs-Bataillon 27/172*–Rostock
      *Grenadier-Ausbildungs-Bataillon 94*–Rostock
      *Grenadier-Ausbildungs-Bataillon 4/222*–Rostock
      *Grenadier-Ausbildungs-Bataillon 48/374*–Neubrandenburg,
      *Grenadier-Ausbildungs-Bataillon 89/368*–Schwerin
   85th Hungarian Infantry Regiment–Schwerin
   Hungarian Infantry Svhool *Varpalota*–Wismar
   *Flak-Ausbildungs-Bataillon 22*–Greifswald
   *Artillerie Ausbildungs Regiment 2*–Schwerin
      *Artillerie-Ausbildungs-Abteilung 257*–Rostock
      *Artillerie-Ausbildungs-Abteilung 12/32*–Rostock
      *Artillerie-Ausbildungs-Abteilung 38/2*–Schwerin
      *Kavallerie-Ausbildungs-Abteilung 100*–Ludwigslust

3. *Marine-Infanterie-Division* (*Oberst* Henning von Witzleben, 1 April–8 May 1945)
   *Marine-Grenadier-Regiment 8*
   *Marine-Grenadier-Regiment 9*
   *Marine-Grenadier-Regiment 10*
   *Marine-Füsilier-Bataillon 3*
   *Artillerie-Regiment 234*
   *Marine-Panzerjäger-Abteilung 3*
   *Marine-Pionier-Bataillon 3*
   *Marine-Nachrichten-Abteilung 3*
   *Marine-Feldersatz-Bataillon 3*

*XXXII. Armeekorps* (*General der Inf.* Friedrich-August Schack, 26 March–8 May 1945)

Directly under *XXXII. Armeekorps* command:
*Korps-Maschinengewehr-Bataillon 442*
   6. *Flak-Brigade* (*Oberst* August Sambach, 4 August 1944–8 May 1945)
      *Flak-Regiment 3*
      *Flak-Regiment 121*
      *Flak-Regiment 7*
      *Flak-Regiment 184*
      *Luftnachrichten-Abteilung 166*
*schwere Heeres-Artillerie-Abteilung 929 (mot.)* (*Oberst* Johann Wilhelm Kunz)–Listed as an artillery unit directly under the command of *XXXII. Armeekorps*.[9] Unfortunately, there was no numerical designation on the referenced documents for this artillery brigade led by *Oberst* Kunz.[10]

Divisionsgruppe Ledebur, ex-Gruppe Voigt[11] (Oberst Hans-Jürgen von Ledebur)[12]
   Kampfgruppe Voigt (Regiments Stab 293/Division Nr. 192)
     Regiment Kammler
     Volkssturm Bataillon von der Marwitz
     Grenzschutz Bataillon Beyer
   Kampfgruppe Paul
     1.-6. Alarm Bataillone
   Kampfgruppe Ledebur
     Pommern-Regiment 5 (1., II. Bataillone)
     Pommern-Regiment 6 (1., II. Bataillone)

549. Volksgrenadier-Division (Generalleutnant Karl Jank)[13]–6,500 men (16 April)
   Grenadier-Regiment 1097 (I.–II. Bataillone)
   Grenadier-Regiment 1098 (I.–II. Bataillone)
   Grenadier-Regiment 1099 (I.–II. Bataillone)
   Artillerie-Regiment 1549 (I.–IV. Bataillone)
   Füsilier-Bataillon 1549 (1.–4. Kompanien)
   Pionier-Bataillon 1549
   Divisions-Nachrichten-Abteilung 549

Note: The following units were not listed in the division from an order of battle for Army Group Vistula dated 17 April 1945. This may imply they were no longer in existence:

Panzerjäger-Abteilung 1549
   1. (Flak) Batterie
   2. Sturmgeschütz Batterie
   3. Sturmgeschütz Batterie
Feldersatz-Bataillon 1549 (1.–4. Kompanie)
Versorgungs-Regiment 549

281. Infanterie-Division (Generalleutnant Bruno Ortner, Sept. 1944–20 April 1945, then:
   Oberst Schmidt: 21 April–8 May 1945)[14]
     Grenadier-Regiment 322
     Grenadier-Regiment 368
     Grenadier-Regiment 418
     Artillerie Regiment 281
     Panzerjäger Kompanie 281
     Pionier-Bataillon 281
     Divisions Füsilier Kompanie 281
     Feldersatz-Bataillon 281
     Divisions-Versorgungs-Regiment 281

*Festungs-Division Stettin* (*Generalmajor* Rudolf Höfer, 22 March to 18 April; then-*Generalmajor* Ferdinand Brühl from 19 April to 8 May 1945)[15]
The city of Stettin was captured by the Red Army on 26 April 1945. Forces assigned to defend the city included the following units: [16]

*Festungs-Regiment 1*
   *1453. und 1454. Festungs Bataillone*
*Festungs-Regiment 2*
   *1455. und 1457 Festungs Bataillone*
*Festungs-Regiment 3*
   *Alarm-Bataillone 'Over' und 'Rog'*
*Festungs-Regiment 4*
   *Alarm-Bataillone 'Benner' und 'Laase'*
*Festungs-Regiment 5*
   *Marine Infanterie Bataillon*
   *Marine Polizei Kompanie*
   *Marine-Feldersatz-Bataillon 1*
*Festungs-Maschinengewehr-Bataillon 85*
*Festungs-Maschinengewehr-Bataillon 1 'Stettin'*
*Festungs-Artillerie-Regiment 3132*
   *II. Festungs-Artillerie-Bataillon*
   *76.2 mm Feldkanonen 288 (russische)*
   *III. Festungs-Artillerie-Bataillon*
   *150 mm schwere Feldhaubitze 461 (deutsche)*
   *Artillerie-Abteilung 3156*
   *Artillerie Abteilung 3158*
*Festungs-Pak-Verband VIII.* (twelve anti-tank companies)
   *(4., 7., 8., 10. Pak Kompanien) XXIV*
   *(1.–6., 8., 10. Pak Kompanien) XXVII*
*Polizei-Bataillon I*
*Polizei-Bataillon II*
*Bau-Pionier-Regiments-Stab 555*
   *Bau-Pionier-Bataillon 96*
   *Bau-Pionier-Bataillon 254*
   *Bau-Pionier-Bataillon 795*

*Korps Oder:* (February to 30 April 1945: *SS-Obergruppenführer und General der Polizei und Waffen-SS* Erich von dem Bach-Zelewski,[17] then *General der Infanterie* Walter Hörnlein)

Directly under army corps command:
*Artillerie-Brigade 418* (*Oberst* Robert von Below)
*Volksartilleriekorps 406 (motorisiert)* [brigade strength and only partially motorized]

*Division z.b.V. 610* (*Generalleutnant* Hubert Lendle, 28 January to 8 May 1945)
  SS *Panzergrenadier-Ersatz und Ausbildungs-Abteilung 9*
  SS *Polizei-Jäger-Brigade 1*
    SS *Polizei-Jägerregiment 8*
    SS *Polizei-Jägerregiment 50*
    *II. Bataillon, Feld-Ausbildungs-Regiment 'Oder'*

*Divisionsgruppe Klossek* (destroyed by 27 April 1945)
Not listed in an Order of Battle for 17 April 1945. When first activated, *Divisionsgruppe Klossek* contained the following units:
One (1) *Landesschützen Bataillon*
One (1) Hungarian infantry battalion[18]
*II. Bataillon, SS Grenadier-Ersatz und Ausbildungs-Bataillon 103*
One (1) *Bataillon der 9. Fallschirmjäger-Division*
*Führer-Anwärter-Bataillon 'Oder'*

Only these two battalions were listed in the Order of Battle for 17 April 1945:
*Volkssturm-Bataillon Hamburg*
*Volkssturm-Bataillon Brandenburg*

Listed in Order of Battle for 17 April 1945 but temporarily attached:
*Panzerjäger-Ausbildungs-Abteilung 5*
*Panzer-Ausbildungs-Verband 'Ostsee'* (as of 11 April 1945)[19]
(Commander: *Major* Reinhold Rehfeld)
  *Brigadestab* (from the former staff of *227. Infanterie-Division*)
    Regiment A:
      *Panzergrenadier-Ausbildungs-Bataillon 5*
      *Panzergrenadier-Ausbildungs-Bataillon 73*
    Regiment B:
      *Panzergrenadier-Ausbildungs-Bataillon 76*
      *Panzergrenadier-Ausbildungs-Bataillon 90*
    Regiment C:
      *Panzer-Ausbildungs-Abteilung 5*
      *Panzerjäger-Ausbildungs-Abteilung 2*
      *Panzerjäger-Ausbildungs-Abteilung 13*
      *Panzer-Aufklärungs-Ausbildungs-Abteilung 13*
      *Scharfschützen-Lehrgang Wehrkreis X*
      *4. Kompanie/Flak-Ausbildungs-Kompanie*
      *Panzer-Nachrichten-Ausbildungs-Kompanie 82*
      *Kraftfahr-Ersatz-Abteilung 4*
      *II. Bataillon/Grenadier-Regiment 1091* (*547. Volksgrenadier-Division*)
      *I. Bataillon/Feldausbildungs-Regiment 'Oder'*
      Listed under *Panzer-Ausbildungs-Verband 'Ostsee'*, but only temporarily:
      *Panzer-Pionier-Ausbildungs-Bataillon 218*

*XLVI. Panzerkorps:* (*General der Infanterie* Martin Gareis)

Directly under army corps command:
*Artillerie-Kommandeur 101* (*Oberst* Karl Fischer)
*Artillerie-Ersatz und Ausbildungs-Abteilung 75*

    547. *Volksgrenadier-Division* (beginning 1 April: *Generalmajor* Erich Fronhöfer)
    *I. Bataillon/Grenadier-Regiment 1091*
    *Grenadier-Regiment 1092 (I., II. Bataillone)*
    *Volkssturm Bataillon XXVI/82*
    *1. Kompanie / Feldersatz Bataillon 1547*
    *Pionier-Bataillon 1547*
    *Divisionseinheiten 1547*
    Listed as being temporarily attached on 17 April 1945:
    *II. Bataillon, Fallschirmjäger-Ersatz und Ausbildungs-Regiment 3*
    *III. Bataillon, Fallschirmjäger-Ersatz und Ausbildungs-Regiment 1*
    *V. Bataillon, SS Panzergrenadier-Division 'Nederland'*
    *II. Bataillon, SS Panzergrenadier-Regiment 49 'de Ruyter' ('Nederland')*
    *SS Panzerjäger-Abteilung 23/SS-Panzergrenadier-Division 'Nederland'*
Not listed in Order of Battle for 17 April 1945:
    *Grenadier-Regiment 1093*
    *Artillerie-Regiment 1547*
    *Füsilier-Kompanie 547*
    Temporarily attached:
    *Sturmgeschütz-Brigade 210* (*Oberleutnant* Althoff). The brigade was renamed *Heeres-Sturmartillerie-Brigade 210* on 4 April 1945. The brigade contained three batteries.[20]

1. *Marine-Infanterie-Division* (*Generalmajor* Wilhelm Bleckwenn, 1 March–4 May 1945)[21]
    *Marine-Infanterie-Regiment 1*
        *I., II. Bataillone*
    *Marine-Infanterie-Regiment 2*
        *I., II. Bataillone*
    *Marine-Infanterie-Regiment 4*
        *I., II. Bataillone*
    *Divisions Füsilier Kompanie 1* (April: *1.–4. Kompanien*)
    *Marine-Artillerie-Regiment 1.*
        *I. Artillerie Abteilung (1.–4. Batterie)*
    *Panzerjäger-Abteilung 1 der 1. Marine-Division (1.–4. Kompanie; 14 April: 5. Kompanie)*
    *Marine-Feldersatz-Bataillon 1 der 1. Marine Division (1.–6. Kompanien)*
    *Marine-Pionier-Bataillon 1* (from 15 April 1945)
    *Marine-Nachrichten-Abteilung 1* (from 15 April 1945)

212    *Appendix V*

Temporarily attached to *1. Marine Division* on 17 April 1945:
*SS-Kampfgruppe Solar* (*SS-Hauptsturmführer* Siegfried Milius)[22] with:
*SS-Fallschirmjäger-Bataillon 600* (*SS-Obersturmführer* Fritz Leifheit)
*SS-Jagdverbände Mitte* (*SS-Hauptsturmführer* Karl Fucker)
*SS Einheit Schwerdt* (company strength)
*SS-Jagdverbände-Nachrichten-Kompanie*
*SS-Jagdverbände schwer Infanterie-Geschütz*
*SS Scharfschützen-Zug*

For Special Employment:[23]
*III. (germanisches) SS-Panzerkorps:* (beginning 5 March, *SS-Brigadeführer* Joachim Ziegler)
As of 12 April, no units, headquarters only.

*9. Armee:* (*General der Infanterie* Theodor Busse)

Directly under *9. Armee* command:
*Volks-Artillerie-Korps 404* (*Oberst* Bartels)
*Volks-Artillerie-Korps 406* (*Oberstleutnant* Adams)
*Volks-Artillerie-Korps 408* (*Oberst* Vogt)
*Sturm-Bataillon AOK II*
*CI. Armeekorps:* (*General der Artillerie* Wilhelm Berlin: 9 February–18 April 1945, then: *Generalleutnant* Friedrich Sixt 18 April–8 May 1945)

309. *Infanterie-Division 'Berlin'* (*Generalmajor* Heinrich Voigtsberger)
    *Wach-Regiment 'Gross Deutschland'* (*I. und II. Bataillone*)
    *Grenadier-Regiment 652*
    *Grenadier-Regiment 653*
    *Füsilier-Bataillon 309*
    *Artillerie-Regiment 309* (*II. und III. Artillerie Bataillone der Luftwaffe*)
    *Panzerjäger-Abteilung 200* (from the *21. Panzer-Division*)
    *Divisionseinheiten 309*

606. *Infanterie-Division* (*Generalmajor* Rudolf Goltzsch)[24]
    *Alarm-Regiment 'Sator'*
        *Polizei-Bataillon 'Bremen'*
        *Alarm-Bataillone 'Potsdam'*
    *Alarm-Regiment 'Rohde'* (*Oberst* Hermann Rhode)
        *Alarm-Bataillone 'Spandau'*
        *Alarm-Bataillone 'Brandenburg'*
        *Alarm-Bataillon 'Neukölln'*
        *12. Kompanie*
        *14. Kompanie*

*Artillerie-Regiment 606*
  *III. Artillerie-Abteilung: 1. und 2. Batterie mit 105 mm FH 18*
  *IV. Artillerie-Abteilung: 1. und 2. Batterie mit 105 mm FH 18 und 3. Batterie mit 152 mm schwer F.H. 445 (russische)*
*Pionier-Bataillon 606*
*Panzerjäger-Kompanie 1606*
*Nachrichten-Kompanie 1606*
*Versorgungs-Regiment 1606*

*5 Jäger-Division* (*Generalleutnant* Friedrich Sixt: 15 Aug. 1944–18 April 1945, then 19 April–8 May 1945 *Generalleutnant* Edmund Blaurock)[25]
  *Jäger-Regiment 56 (I.–III. Bataillone)*
  *Jäger-Regiment 75 (I.–III. Bataillone)*
  *Artillerie-Regiment 5 (I.–IV. Artillerie Bataillone)*

*XI. SS-Panzerkorps:* (*SS-Obergruppenführer* Matthias Kleinheisterkamp)

Directly under *XI. SS-Panzerkorps* control:
*schwer SS-Panzer-Abteilung 502*
  23. *SS-Freiwilligen-Panzergrenadier-Division* 'Nederland'
  (*SS-Brigadeführer* Jürgen Wagner)—regimental strength
  712. *Infanterie-Division* (*Generalmajor* Joachim von Siegroth)
    *Grenadier-Regiment 732 (I.–II. Bataillone)*
    *Grenadier-Regiment 745 (I.–II. Bataillone)*
    *Grenadier-Regiment 764 (I.–II. Bataillone)*
    *Artillerie-Regiment 1712*[26]
      *II. Artillerie-Abteilung (4.–6. Batterien)*

303. *Infanterie-Division* 'Doberitz' (*Generalmajor* Walter Scheunenmann, 9 March–20 April 1945, then *Oberst* Albin Esch, 21 April–8 May)
  *Grenadier-Regiment 300 (I.–II. Bataillone)*
  *Grenadier-Regiment 301 (I.–II. Bataillone)*
  *Grenadier-Regiment 302 (I.–II. Bataillone)*
  *Artillerie-Regiment 303 (I.–IV. Artillerie-Abteilung)*
  *Füsilier-Bataillon 303*
  *Pionier-Bataillon 303 (1.–3. Kompanien)*
  *Panzer-Vernichtungs-Abteilung 303*[27] *(1.–3. Batterien)*
  *Divisions-Nachrichten-Abteilung 303 (1.–3. Kompanie)*
  *Feldersatz-Bataillon 303 (1.–4. Kompanien)*
  *Divisions-Versorgungs-Regiment 303*

169. *Infanterie-Division* (*Generalleutnant* Georg Radziej) [brigade strength]
  *Infanterie-Regiment 378*
    *(I.–III. Bataillone)*

*Infanterie-Regiment 379*
  *(I.–II. Bataillone)*—the *III. Bataillon* was dissolved in March 1945
*Infanterie Regiment 392*
  *(I.–III. Bataillone)*
*Artillerie-Regiment 230*
  *(I.–IV. Artillerie-Abteilung mit 12x Batterien)*
*Pionier-Bataillon 230*
*Jagdpanzer-Kompanie 1230* (14x *Jagdpanzer 38t* tank destroyers)
*Nachrichten-Abteilung 230*
*Nachschubführer 230*

20. Panzergrenadier-Division (*Generalmajor* Georg Scholze)[28]
  *Panzergrenadier-Regiment 76 (I.–III. Bataillone)*
  *Panzergrenadier-Regiment 90 (I.–III. Bataillone)*
  *Artillerie-Regiment 20 (I.–III. Artillerie Bataillone)*
  *Heeres-Flak-Artillerie-Abteilung 284*
  *Panzer-Abteilung 8 (1.–3. Kompanie)*
  *Panzer-Aufklärungs-Abteilung 120*
  *Nachrichten-Abteilung 20*
  *Panzerjäger-Abteilung 20 (1.–4. Kompanie)*
  *Panzergrenadier-Nachrichten-Abteilung 20*
  *Panzergrenadier-Nachschubtruppen 20*

9. Fallschirmjäger-Division (*General der Fallschirmtruppe* Bruno Bräuer, 2 March–18 April 1945, then: *Oberst* Harry Herrmann, 19 April–8 May 1945)[29]
  *Fallschirmjäger-Regiment 25 (I.–III. Bataillone)*
  *Fallschirmjäger-Regiment 26 (I.–II. Bataillone)*
  *Fallschirmjäger-Regiment 27 (I.–II. Bataillone)*
  *Fallschirmjäger-Artillerie-Regiment 9 (I.–III. Artillerie-Abteilung)*
  *Fallschirm-Granatwerfer-Bataillon 9 (1.–3. Kompanie)*
  *Fallschirm-Panzerjäger-Abteilung 9 (1.–3. Kompanie)*
  *Fallschirmjäger-Flak-Regiment 9 (I.–II. Flak Bataillone)*
  *Fallschirm-Pionier-Bataillon 9 (1.–3. Kompanie)*
  *Fallschirm-Nachrichten-Abteilung 9 (1.–2. Kompanie)*
  *Kommandeur der Fallschirm-Nachschubtruppen 9*

*Panzergrenadier-Division 'Kurmark'* (*Generalmajor* Willy Langkeit)
  *Panzer-Regiment 'Kurmark'*
    I. *Panzer-Bataillon (1.–4. Kompanie)*—all *Panzer IV* tanks
  *Panzergrenadier-Regiment Kurmark*
    I. *Panzergrenadier-Bataillon (1.–6. Kompanie)*
    II. *Panzergrenadier-Bataillon (7.–11. Kompanie)*
  *Panzer-Füsilier-Regiment 'Kurmark' (ex-Grenadier-Regiment 1235)*[30]
  *Panzer-Artillerie-Regiment 'Kurmark'*

I. *Artillerie-Abteilung*
    *1.–2. Schwer Artillerie Batterie (150 mm Feldhaubitze)*
    *3. Leicht Artillerie Batterie (105 mm Feldhaubitze)*
II. *Artillerie-Abteilung*
    *4.–6. Sturmgeschütz Batterie*
III. *Artillerie-Abteilung (from SS-Artillerie-Lehr-Regiment)*
    *7.–9. Artillerie Batterie*
*Pionier-Bataillon 'Kurmark' (1.–2. Kompanie)*
*Panzerjäger-Abteilung 151*
    1. *Panzerjäger-Kompanie* (only one anti-tank company)
*Panzer-Aufklärungs-Abteilung 151 (Major* Otto Christer von Albedyll)
    *Aufklärungs-Schwadron* (only a mixed recon company)
*Panzer-Nachrichten-Kompanie 151*
*Kommandeur der Nachschubtruppen 151*

LVI. *Panzerkorps: (General der Artillerie* Helmuth Weidling)

*11. SS-Freiwilligen-Panzergrenadier-Division 'Nordland'*
(*SS-Brigadeführer* Gustav Krukenberg)—brigade strength

*Panzer-Division 'Müncheberg' (Generalmajor der Reserve* Werner Mummert)
    *Panzergrenadier-Regiment 'Müncheberg 1'*
        I. *Bataillon (1–3 Kompanie)*
        II. *Bataillon (4–8 Kompanie)*
    *Panzergrenadier-Regiment 'Müncheberg 2'*
        I. *Bataillon (1–3 Kompanie)*
        II. *Bataillon (4–8 Kompanie)*
    *Panzer Bataillon Müncheberg*
        1. *Panzer-Kompanie* (11 *Panzer IV* tanks of varying models)
        2. *Panzer-Kompanie* (10 *Panther* tanks)
        3. *Panzer-Kompanie Kummersdorf* (15 April: 10 + 3 in repair)[31]
    *Aufklärungs-Kompanie 'Müncheberg'*
    *Panzerjäger-Kompanie 'Müncheberg'*
    *Pionier-Kompanie 'Müncheberg'*
    *Nachrichten-Kompanie 'Müncheberg'*

*286. Infanterie-Division (Generalleutnant* Friedrich-Georg Eberhardt)[32]
Remnants of this division had recently arrived from East Prussia in mid-April and was currently reforming. It absorbed *Division Raegener*.

*Kampfgruppe der 25. Panzergrenadier-Division (Generalleutnant* Arnold Burmeister)
    On 16 April 1945: the strength of a brigade, at best.

216   *Appendix V*

    *Panzergrenadier-Regiment 35*
        *I. Bataillon (1.–4. Kompanien)*
        *II. Bataillon (5.–8. Kompanien)*
        *III. Bataillon (9.–14. Kompanien)*
    *Panzergrenadier-Regiment 119*
        *I. Bataillon (1.–4. Kompanien)*
        *II. Bataillon (5.–8. Kompanien)*
        *III. Bataillon (9.–12. Kompanien)*
    *Panzer-Abteilung 5 (formerly: Panzer Abteilung 2107)*
        *(1.-4. Panzer Kompanien) 24x tanks (12 April 1945)*
        *(Versorgungs Kompanie + Werkstattzug)*
    *Panzer-Aufklärungs-Abteilung 125*
        1. *Panzer-Spähkompanie*
        2. *Aufklärungs-Kompanie*
        3. *Aufklärungs-Kompanie*
    *Artillerie-Regiment 25 (motorisiert)*
        *I. Artillerie-Abteilung (1.–3. Batterien)*
        *II. Artillerie-Abteilung (4.–6. Batterien)*
        *III. Artillerie-Abteilung (7.–10. Batterien)*
    *Heeres-Flakartillerie-Abteilung 292*
    *Pionier-Bataillon 25*
    *Panzerabwehr-Bataillon 25*
    *Nachrichten-Bataillon 25*
    *Feldersatz-Bataillon 25*
    *Nachschubführer 25*

*V. SS-Freiwilligen-Gebirgs-Armeekorps:* (*SS-Obergruppenführer* Friedrich Jeckeln)

*V. SS-Freiwilligen-Gebirgs-Armeekorps reserve:*
1. *Panzervernichtungsbrigade 'Hitlerjugend'* (*Oberbannführer* Otto Kern)[33]
    *I. Panzer-Vernichtungs-Bataillon*
    *II. Panzer-Vernichtungs-Bataillon*
    *III. Panzer-Vernichtungs-Bataillon*
    *IV. Panzer-Vernichtungs-Bataillon*

*Festungs-Division 'Frankfurt an der Oder'* (CO: *Generalleutnant* Hermann Meyer-Rabingen)
    Note: The Red Army captured this city on 16 April 1945.
        *Festungs-Grenadier-Regiment 1*
            *I. Bataillon*
            *II. Bataillon*
        *I. Festungs-Artillerie-Abteilung, Festungs-Artillerie-Regiment 3132*
            (1.-4. Batterien) using *Czech 150 mm hrubá houfnice vz. 25* howitzers

*Festungs-Grenadier-Regiment 2*
    *I. Bataillon*
    *II. Bataillon*
*Festungs-Grenadier-Regiment 3*
    *I. Bataillon*
    *II. Bataillon*
*Festungs-Grenadier-Regiment 4*
    *I. Bataillon*
    *II. Bataillon*
*Festungs-Infanterie-Bataillon 1449*
*Festungs-Maschinengewehr-Bataillon 84*
*Festungs-Maschinengewehr-Bataillon 829*
*Ersatz und Ausbildungs-Artillerie-Abteilung 59*
*Festungs-Artillerie-Abteilung 1325*
*Festungs-Artillerie-Abteilung 1326*
*Festungs-Artillerie-Abteilung 3157*
*Pionier-Sperr-Bataillon 952*
*Festungs-Panzerjäger-Abteilung XXVI*
*Festungs-Pak-Verband XXVI*
    *Festungs-Pak-Kompanien 1/XXVI–10/XXVI* (10x anti-tank companies)

Finally, a total of three *Volkssturm* battalions also served as part of the city garrison.

    *391. Infanterie-Division* (Generalleutnant Alex Göschen)
      *funf (5) Alarm Bataillone* (five 'Alarm' battalions of infantry)
      *ein Volkssturm Bataillon* (one Home Guard battalion)
      *Einsatz-Kompanie/SS-Panzergrenadier-Ersatz-Bataillon*
      *Reserve-Kompanie SS-Panzergrenadier-Ersatz-Bataillon*
      *Pionier-Brückenspreng-Kommando* (engineer bridge-blasting command)
      *1. Kompanie und 3. Kompanie/schwere Flak-Abteilung 656*
      *Pionier-Sperr-Bataillon z.b.V. 953* (constructing obstacles & fortifications)
      *Panzer-Zerstörer-Trupp/Polizei-Regiment 'Hartmann'*[34]
      *Brücken-Kommandant 'Fürstenberg'*
      *Arko—Artillerie-Kommandeur* (Oberstleutnant Rogge)

    *32. SS-Freiwilligen-Grenadier-Division '30 Januar'*
    (*Divisionskommandeur: SS-Standartenführer* Hans Kempin)
    *SS-Freiwilligen-Grenadier-Regiment 86 Schill*
      *I. Infanterie-Bataillon*
      *II. Infanterie-Bataillon*
    *SS-Freiwilligen-Grenadier-Regiment 87 Kurmark*
      *I. Infanterie-Bataillon*
      *II. Infanterie-Bataillon*

*SS-Freiwilligen-Artillerie-Regiment 32*
    *I. Artillerie-Abteilung*
    *II. Artillerie-Abteilung*
*SS-Panzerjäger-Abteilung 32*
*SS-Flak-Abteilung 32*
*SS-Fusilier-Bataillon 32*
*SS-Pionier-Bataillon 32*
*SS-Nachrichten-Bataillon 32*
*SS-Feldersatz-Bataillon 32*
*Divisions-Einheiten 32*

*Division 'Raegener'* (Generalleutnant Adolf Raegener)[35]
  *Grenadier-Regiment 'Becker' (ex-Polizei-Schützenregiment 34)*[36]
    I. Polizei-Bataillon, Schützenregiment-Regiment 34 (*Major der Schutzpolizei* Doerner)
    II. *Volkssturm Bataillon*
  *Grenadier-Regiment 'von Petersdorf'* (*Oberstleutnant* Manfred von Petersdorff)
    I. *Bataillon* (Hungarian noncommissioned officers' school)
    II. *Volkssturm Bataillon*
  *Fahnenjunker-Regiment 1237* (*Major* Fischer)
    *Bataillon 'Feldherrnhalle'* (*Hauptmann* Alfred Hille)
    *Volkssturm-Bataillon 'Main/Franken'*
    *Volkssturm-Bataillon 'Ober Donau'*
    *Volkssturm-Bataillon 'Dresden Thür'*
  *Füsilier-Kompanie* (forming)
  *Festungs-Pionier-Bataillon*
    1. *Pionier-Kompanie* (*Pionier-Sperr-Kompanie 939*)
    2. *Pionier-Kompanie* (*Pionier-Sperr-Kompanie 940*)
  *Nachrichten-Kompanie 511* (mixed)
  *Kraftfahr-Kompanie* (Motor vehicle company)
  *Fahr-Schwadron* (Driving squadron)
  *Verwaltungs-Kompanie* (Administration company)
  Attached to *Division Raegener*:
  *SS-Werfer-Abteilung 505* (*SS-Sturmbannführer* Dr. Hans des Courdes)[37]—
  24x 150 mm *Nebelwerfer* rocket launchers.

*z.b.V. (zur Besondere Verwendung)* ['for Special Employment']

*600. Infanterie-Division (russische Nr. 1)* [11,000 men]
  (CO: *Generalleutnant* Sergei Bunyachenko)
  *Grenadier-Regiment 1601 (I. und II. Infanterie Bataillone)*
  *Grenadier-Regiment 1602 (I. und II. Infanterie Bataillone)*
  *Grenadier-Regiment 1603 (I. und II. Infanterie Bataillone)*
  *Artillerie-Regiment 1600 (I. und IV. Artillerie Bataillone)*
  *Pionier-Bataillon 600 (1.–3. Kompanien)*
  *Divisions-Einheiten 1600*

# BIBLIOGRAPHY

### PRIMARY SOURCES

Bundesarchiv, Berlin-Lichterfelde (ex-'Berlin Document Center'): R-55/616.

Bundesarchiv, Koblenz: N-756/394, *Operationen und Kampfhandlungen mit Beteiligung von Einheiten der Waffen-SS vor allem in den Jahren 1944–1945, SS Obersturmbannführer Ottto Skorzeny und die Kampf um Schwedt.*

BA-MA (Bundesarchiv-Militärarchiv), Friedberg: RW-41, RW-58, RW-59, RW-60, RW-75, MS/332, MS-G1/976, MS-G2/1283, RH 19, RH 39/14, XV/19, K-46—*Kriegsgliederung Heeresgruppe Weichsel*; 2/348 bis RH 2/355; RH 2/356K und R 2/769—*Schematische Kriegsgliederungen 1939–1945*; RH 26-547—*Kriegstagebücher und sonstige Unterlagen*; N 756/328a–*Waffen-SS Jagdverbände und Kommando Einheiten.*

**National Archives, College Park, Maryland:**

T-311, Roll 171, T-175, Roll 140, Roll 174, Roll 225, RG 338, Box 1, RG 218, box 15, T-78, Roll 645, T-311, Roll 70, T-78, Roll 413, T-78, Roll 624, T-315, Rolls 1665, 1687, 2213, 2214, 2215, and 2216.

**German Armed Forces War Diaries:**

Mehner, Kurt. *Die Geheimen Tagesberichte der deutschen Wehrmachtführung im Zweiten Weltkrieg 1939–1945.* Osnabrück: Biblio Verlag, 12 vols., 1984–1989.

Schramm, Percy. *Kriegstagebuch Des Oberkommandos Der Wehrmacht 1939–1945*, 8 Vols. Herrsching: Manfred Pawlak, 1982.

**Publications Published During the War by the Third Reich:**

*Dienstalterliste der Schutzstafel der NSDAP (SS Obersturmbannführer und SS Sturmbannführer) Stand vom 1. Oktober 1944. Herausgegeben vom Personalhauptamt.* Berlin: Gedruckt in der Reichsdruckerei, 1944.

*Dienstalterliste der Schutzstafel der NSDAP (SS Obergruppenführer bis SS Standartenführer) Stand vom 1. Oktober 1944. Herausgegeben vom Personalhauptamt.* Berlin: Gedruckt in der Reichsdruckerei, 1944.

*Befehlsblatt des Chefs der Sicherheitspolizei und der SD, Nr. 14/44 Berlin, 1. April 1944. Herausgegeben vom Reichssicherheitshaupt-amt,* Berlin: Gedruckt in der Reichsdruckerei, 1944.

Dienstalterliste der Schutzstafel der NSDAP, stand vom 1 Juli 1944. Gedruckt in der Reichsdruckerei: Berlin, 1944.

## SECONDARY SOURCES

Adair, Paul. *Hitler's Greatest Defeat. The Collapse of Army Group Center*. New York: Sterling Publishing, 1994.
Anders, Wladyslaw. *Hitler's Defeat in Russia*. Chicago: Henry Regnery Company, 1953.
Anders, Wladyslaw. *Russian Volunteers in Hitler's Army, 1941–1945*. New York: Europa Books. 1997.
Alhfen, Hans von and Hermann Niehoff. *So kämpfte Breslau*. Munich: Graefe and Unzer Verlag, 1959.
Alhfen, Hans von. *Der Kampf um Schlesien*. Munich: Graefe and Unzer Verlag, 1961.
Andreyev, Catherine. *Vlasov and the Russian Liberation Movement. Soviet Reality and Émigré Theories*. Cambridge: Cambridge University Press, 1987.
Axworthy, Mark W. A. *Axis Slovakia: Hitler's Slavic Wedge, 1938–1945*. New York: Europa Books, 2002.
Bahm, Karl. *Berlin 1945: The Final Reckoning*. St. Paul, MN: Motorbooks International, 2001.
Ballentin, Günther. *Die Zerstörung der Stadt Schwedt/Oder 1945*. Rostock: Eigenverlag, 1990.
Baltuttis, Günter Emanuel. *Auf verlorenen Posten: Ostpreussen 1944/1945*. Leer: Rautenberg Verlag, 2015.
Banach, Jens. *Heydrichs Elite: Das Führerkorps der Sicherheitspolizei und des SD 1936–1945*. Paderborn: Ferdinand Schöningh, 1998.
Bauer, Eddy. *The History of World War II*. London: Galley Press, 1984.
Bayer, Hanns. *Die Kavallerie Der Waffen SS*. Heidelberg: Selbstverlag der Truppenkameradenschaft der SS Kavallerie-Divisionen, 1980.
Bayer, Hanns. *Kavallerie-Divisionen der Waffen-SS im Bild*. Osnabrück: Munin Verlag, 1982.
Beevor, Anthony. *The Fall of Berlin 1945*. New York: Penguin Books Inc., 2002.
Benz, Wolfgang and Angelika Schardt *Deutsche Kriegsgefangene im Zweiten Weltkrieg: Erinnerungen*. Frankfurt am Main: Fischer Taschenbuch. 1995.
Berthel, Hans Dieter. *Die Feldgendarmerie im Zweiten Weltkrieg und ihre Teilnahme an völkerrechtswidrigen Aktionen 1939–1945*. Norderstedt: Herstellung und Verlag, 2006.
Bethell, Nicholas. *The Last Secret: The Delivery to Stalin of Over Two Million Russians by Britain and the United States*. New York: Basic Books Inc., 1974.
Bonn, Keith E., Editor. *Slaughterhouse: The Handbook of the Eastern Front*. Bedford, PA: The Aberjona Press, 2005.
Bruns, Friedrich. *Die Brücke von Neuenburg: Eine Dokumentation über den Endkampf der 19 Armee in Elsaß 1945*. Celle: Self Published, 1990.
Buchner, Alex. *Ostfront: The German Defensive Battles on the Russian Front 1944*. West Chester, PA: Schiffer Military History, 1991.

Buttar, Prit. *Between Giants: The Battle for the Baltics in World War II*. London: Osprey Publishing, 2013.

Carell, Paul. *Scorched Earth: The Russo-German War 1943–1944*. Boston: Little, Brown, and Company, 1970.

Caroe, Olaf. *Soviet Empire: The Turks of Central Asia & Stalinism*. New York: Macmillan & Co., 1953.

Clark, Allan. *Barbarossa: The Russo-German Conflict, 1941-45*. New York: William Morrow and Company, 1965.

Costantini, Colonel Aimé. *L'Union Soviétique En Guerre (1941–1945)*. Paris: Imprimerie Nationale, 1968, three volumes.

Dallin, Alexander. *German Rule in Russia 1941–1945: A Study of Occupation Policies*. London: Macmillan and Co Ltd, 1957.

Dieckert, Ulrich and Horst Großmann. *Der Kampf um Ostpreußen: Der umfassende Dokumentarbericht über das Kriegsgeschehen in Ostpreußen*. Beltheim: Lindenbaum Verlag, 2010.

Duffy, Christopher. *Red Storm on the Reich. The Soviet March on Germany, 1945*. London: Routledge, 1991.

Dunnigan, James F., David C. Isby, E. C. McCarthy, Stephen Patrick, and Trevor N. Dupuy, Eds., *War in the East: The Russo-German Conflict, 1941-45*. New York: Simulations Publications Inc., 1977.

Erickson, John. *The Road to Berlin: Stalin's War with Germany*. London: Weidenfeld & Nicolson Ltd., 1983.

Ferrer, John, and Klaus G. Förg, editor. *Die Versprengten: Ostfront im Winter 1945*. Feldafing: Editions Förg, 2024.

Fischer, George. *Soviet Opposition to Stalin: A Case Study in World War II*. Cambridge: Harvard University Press, 1952.

Frieser, Karl-Heinz, et al., editors. *Die Ostfront 1943/44: Der Krieg im Osten und an den Nebenfronten. Das Deutsche Reich und der Zweite Weltkrieg*. Vol. 8. Munich: Deutsche Verlags-Anstalt, 2007.

Gellermann, Günther W. *Die Armee Wenck—Hitlers letzte Hoffnung*. Bonn: Bernard & Graefe Verlag, 1997.

Glantz, David M. and Harold S. Orenstein. *Belarusia 1944: The Soviet General Staff Study*. London: Frank Cass, 2001.

Gliesche, Erich. *Von Potsdam zum Polarkrei sund zurück: Der Weg der 163. Infanterie-Division, Band III., Rückzug und Untergang*. Berlin: Selbstverlag, 1995.

Gosztony, Petėr. *Der Kampf um Berlin 1945 in Augenzeugenberichten*. Munich: dtv Verlagsgesellschaft GmbH & Co. KG, 1985.

Großmann, Horst. *Der Kampf um Ostpreussen. Der umfassende Dokumentarbericht über das Kriegsgeschehen in Ostpreußen*, Stuttgart: Motorbuch Verlag, 1978.

Guillaume, General Augustin Léon. *The German Russia War 1941–1945*. London: The War Office, 1956.

Hartinger, Andreas. *Bis das Auge bricht: Als MG-Schütze im Feuersturm der Ostfront, 1943-45*. Selent: Pour le Mérite Verlag, 2000.

Haupt, Werner. *Das war Kurland: Die sechs Kurland-Schlachten aus der Sicht der Divisionen*. Eggolsheim: Dörfler Verlag GmbH, 2009.

Haupt, Werner. 1945. *Das Ende im Osten. Chronik vom Kampf in Ost- u. Mitteldeutschland. Der Untergang d. Divisionen in Ostpreussen, Danzig, Westpreussen, Mecklenburg, Pommern, Schlesien, Sachsen, Berlin.* Friedberg: Podzun Verlag, 1970.

Haupt, Werner. *Army Group Center: The Wehrmacht in Russia 1941–1945.* Atglen, PA: Schiffer Publishing, 1997.

Haupt, Werner. *Die 8. Panzer-Division im 2. Weltkrieg.* Friedberg: Podzun Pallas Verlag, 1987.

Haupt, Werner. *Die Schlachten Der Heeresgruppe Mitte 1941–1944.* Friedberg: Podzun Pallas Verlag, 1983.

Haupt, Werner. *Die Deutschen Infanterie-Divisionen.* Friedberg: Podzun Pallas Verlag, 1991. Three volumes.

Haupt, Werner. *Army Group North. The Wehrmacht in Russia 1941–1945.* Atglen, PA: Schiffer Publishers, 1997.

Haupt, Werner. *Die Schlachten Der Heeresgruppe Süd. Aus der Sicht der Divisionen.* Friedberg: Podzun Pallas Verlag, 1985.

Haupt, Werner. *Army Group South. The Wehrmacht in Russia 1941–1945.* Atglen, PA: Schiffer Publishers, 1997.

Haupt, Werner. *Leningrad: Die 900 Tage Schlacht 1941–1944.* Friedberg: Podzun Pallas Verlag, 1980.

Hausser, Paul. *Soldaten Wie Andere Auch. Der Weg der Waffen SS.* Osnabrück: Munin Verlag GmbH, 1966.

Heiber, Helmut. *Lagebesprechungen im Fuhrerhauptquartier: Protokollfragmente aus Hitlers Militarischen Konferenzen 1942–1945.* Munich: Deutscher Taschenbuch Verlag, 1963.

Herfarth, Heinrich H. *Festung Glogau 1945.* Hannover: Hrsg. vom Glogauer Heimatbund, 1982.

Hinze, Rolf. *Der Zusammenbruch Der Heeresgruppe Mitte Im Osten 1944.* Stuttgart: Motorbuch Verlag, 1980.

Hinze, Rolf. *Das Ostfront-Drama 1944.* Stuttgart: Motorbuch Verlag: 1988.

Hinze, Rolf. *East Front Drama 1944. The Withdrawal Battle of Army Group Center.* Winnipeg: J. J. Fedorowicz Publishing, 1996.

Hinze, Rolf. *Rückzugskämpfe in der Ukraine 1943/44.* Meerbusch: Verlag Dr. Rolf Hinze, 1991.

Hoffmann, Joachim. *Die Geschichte Der Wlassow-Armee.* Freiburg: Verlag Rombach, 1986.

Hoßbach, Friedrich. *Die Schlacht um Ostpreußen. Aus den Kämpfen der deutschen 4. Armee um Ostpreußen in der Zeit vom 19.7.1944–30.1.1945.* Koblenz: Generisch, 1951.

Hunt, Vincent. *Blood in the Forest: The End of the Second World War in the Courland Pocket.* Solihull: Helion & Co., 2017.

Isaev, Alexey. *Hitler's Fortresses in the East: The Sieges of Ternopol, Kovel, Poznan and Breslau, 1944–1945.* Barnsley: Pen and Sword Military, 2021.

Jurado, Carlos Caballero. *Breaking the Chains: 14. Waffen-Grenadier-Division der SS and Other Ukrainian Volunteer Formations, Eastern front, 1942–1945.* London: Shelf Books, 1998.

Jurado, Carlos Caballero. *Rompiendo Las Cadenas: La Division Ucraniana De Las Waffen-SS.* Granada: Garcia Hispan, 1992.

Karashuk, A., editor. *Russkiya Osvobodetelnya Armia 1939–1945* (Russian Liberation Army, 1939–1945). Moscow: Act Publishers, 1999.

Keilig, Wolf. *Rangliste Des Deutschen Heeres 1944/45*. Friedberg: Podzun Pallas Verlag, n.d.

Kempka, Erich. *Die letzten Tage mit Adolf Hitler*. Preussich-Oldendorf: Verlag K. W. Schütz KG 1975.

Kirchubel, Robert. *Hitler's Panzer Armies on the Eastern Front*. London: Pen and Sword, 2009.

Kleitmann, Dr. K. G. *Die Waffen SS: eine Dokumentation*. Osnabrück: Verlag "Der Freiwillige" GmbH, 1965.

Klemp, Stefan. *KZ-Arzt Aribert Heim. Die Geschichte einer Fahndung*, Berlin: Prospero Verlag, 2010.

Konev, Ivan Stepanovich. *Zapiski Komanduyushchego frontom* (Notes by the Commander of the Front). Moscow: Voenizdat Publishing, 1981.

Knopp, Guido. *Der Sturm. Kriegsende im Osten*. Berlin: Econ Verlag, 2004.

Kurowski, Franz. *Bridgehead Kurland. The Six Epic Battles of Heeresgruppe Kurland*. Winnipeg: J. J. Fedorowicz Publishing, Inc., 2002.

Lasch, Otto. *So fiel Königsberg*. Stuttgart: Motorbuch Verlag, 2002.

Le Tissier, Tony. *The Siege of Küstrin 1945: Gateway to Berlin*. Barnsley: Pen and Sword Military, 2009.

Le Tissier, Tony. *The Battle of Berlin 1945*. New York: St. Martin's Press, 1988.

Le Tissier, Tony. *Zhukov at the Oder: The Decisive Battle for Berlin*. Westport, CT: Praeger Publishing, 1996.

Logusz, Michael O. *Galicia Division: The Waffen SS 14th Grenadier Division 1943–1945*. Atglen, PA: Schiffer Publishing Ltd., 1997.

Lukes, Igor. *On the Edge of the Cold War: American Diplomats and Spies in Postwar Prague*. New York: Oxford University Press, 2012.

MacDonald, Jan, Callum and Kaplan. *Prague in the Shadow of the Swastika: A History of the German Occupation 1939–1945*. Prague: Melantrich Publishing, 1995.

Mehner, Kurt. *Die Waffen-SS und Polizei 1939–1945*. Norderstedt: Militair-Verlag Klaus D. Patzwall, 1995.

Michaelis, Rolf. *Die Russische Volksbefreiungsarmee 'RONA' 1941–1944*. Erlangen: Selbstpubliziert, 1992.

Michaelis, Rolf. *Ukrainer in der Waffen SS: Die 14. Waffen-Grenadier-Division der SS (ukrainische Nr. 1)*. Berlin: Michaelis Verlag, 2000.

Michaelis, Rolf. *Die Kavallerie-Divisionen der Waffen SS*. Erlangen: Selbstpubliziert, 1993.

Michaelis, Rolf. *The SS-Sonderkommando Dirlewanger: A Memoir*. Atglen, PA: Schiffer Publishing, 2013.

Michaelis, Rolf. *Der Weg zur 36. Waffen-Grenadier-Division der SS*. Rodgau: Verlag fuer Militaerhistorische Zeitgeschichte, 1991.

Michaelis, Rolf. *Russen in der Waffen SS*. Berlin: Michaelis Verlag, 2002.

Mitcham, Samuel W. *Crumbling Empire: The German Defeat in the East, 1944*. Westport, CT: Praeger Publishers, 2001.

Mitcham, Samuel W. *Hitler's Legions: The German Army Order of Battle, World War Two*. New York, Dorset Press, 1985.

Müller, Rolf-Dieter and Gerd R. Ueberschaer. *Hitler's War in the East 1941–1945: A Critical Assessment*. Providence, RI: Berghahn Books, 1997.

Müller-Hillebrand, Burkhart. *Das Heer 1933–1945: Entwicklung des organisatorischen Aufbaues*. Darmstadt: Mittler & Sohn, 1969. Three volumes.

Münch, Karl-Heinz. *StuG Abt./Brig. 210*. Łódź: Model Hobby, 2007.

Muñoz, Antonio. *Hitler's War Against the Partisans During Operation Barbarossa, June 1941 to the Spring of 1942*. Barnsley: Frontline Books, 2025.

Muñoz, Antonio. *Hitler's War Against the Partisans During the Stalingrad Offensive, Spring 1942 to Spring 1943*. Barnsley: Frontline Books, 2025.

Muñoz, Antonio. *Hitler's Luftwaffe Infantry. The German Air Force Field Divisions, 1942–1945*. Barnsley: Frontline Books, 2025.

Muñoz, Antonio. *The German Secret Field Police in Greece, 1941–1944*. Jefferson, NC: McFarland Publishers, 2018.

Muñoz, Antonio. *Göring's Grenadiers: The Luftwaffe Field Divisions 1942–1945*. New York: Europa Books, 2002.

Muñoz, Antonio. *The Last Levy: Waffen SS Officer Roster, March 1st 1945*. New York: Europa Books, 2000.

Muñoz, Antonio. *The Kaminski Brigade: A History, 1941–1945*. New York: Europa Books, 1996.

Muñoz, Antonio. *Forgotten Legions: Obscure Combat Formations of the Waffen SS, 1943–1945*. Boulder, CO: Paladin Press, 1991.

Murawski, Erich. *Die Eroberung Pommerns durch die Rote Armee*. Boppard am Rhein: Harald Boldt Verlag, 1969.

Neulen, Hans Werner. *An Deutscher Seite: Internationale Freiwillige von Wehrmacht und Waffen SS*. München: Universitas Verlag, 1985.

Newton, Steven H. *Retreat from Leningrad. Army Group North, 1944/1945*. Atglen, PA: Schiffer Publishing, 1995.

Niepold, Gerd. *Battle for White Russia: The Destruction of Army Group Centre June 1944*. New York: Brassey's Defense Publishers, 1987.

Overmans, Rüdiger. *Deutsche militärische Verluste im Zweiten Weltkrieg*. München: R. Oldenbourg Verlag, 1999.

Overy, Richard. *Russia's War: A History of the Soviet War Effort, 1941–1945*. New York: Penguin Putnam, Inc., 1998.

Pohl, Dieter, et al. *Der deutsche Krieg im Osten 1941–1944*, Munich: De Gruytyer, 2009.

Poirier, Robert G. and Albert Z. Conner. *The Red Army Order of Battle in the Great Patriotic War*. Novato, CA: Presidio Press, 1985.

Pottgeiser, Hans. *Die Reichsbahn in Ostfeldzug*. Neckargemünd: Kurt Vowinckel Verlag, 1960.

Präg, Werner and Wolfgang Jacobson. *Das Dienstagebuch des deutschen Generalgouverneurs in Polen 1939–1945*. Stuttgart: Deutsche Verlag Anstalt, 1975.

Rauchensteiner, Manfried. *Der Krieg in Österreich 1945*, Wien: Bundesverlag, Österreich, 1984.

Reinicke, Adolf. *Die 5. Jäger-Division 1939–1945*. Friedberg: Podzun Pallas Verlag GmbH, n.d.
Rürup, Dr. Reinhard and Dr. Peter Jahn, editors. *Der Krieg gegen die Sowjetunion 1941–1945*. Berlin: Berliner Festspiele GmbH, 1991.
Ryan, Cornelius. *The Last Battle*. New York: Simon & Schuster, 1966.
Schramm, Percy E. *Kriegstagebuch des Oberkommandos der Wehrmacht, Band V: 1. Januar 1944-9. Mai 1945*. Bonn: Bernard & Graefe Verlag, 1961.
Schrode, W. *25. Panzergrenadier-Division 1944–1945—Chronik*. Berlin: Eigenverlag, 1966.
Schröder, J. and Joachim Schultz-Naumann. *Geschichte der Pommeranische 32. Infanterie Division*. Bad Neuheim: Podzun Pallas Verlag, 1956.
Seaton, Albert. *The Russo-German War 1941–45*. New York: Praeger Publishers, 1970.
Seaton, Albert. *The Fall of Fortress Europe, 1943–1945*. New York: Holmes & Meier Publishers, Inc., 1981.
Seidler, Franz W. *Deutscher Volkssturm: Das letzte Aufgebot, 1944–1945*. München: F. A. Herbig Verlag, 1989.
Siegert, Richard. *Tygrys z Poznania*. Warsaw: Vesper, 2010.
Steenberg, Sven. *Vlasov*. New York: Alfred A. Knopf, 1970.
Stein, George H. *The Waffen SS: Hitler's Elite Guard at War 1939–1945*. Ithaca, NY: Cornell University Press, 1966.
Stöber, Hans. *Die 22. Panzer-Division; 25. Panzer-Division; 27. Panzer-Division; und die 233. Reserve Panzer-Division*. Friedberg: Podzun Pallas Verlag, 1985.
Stöber, Hans. *Die Flugabwehrverbände der Waffen SS*. Preussiche Oldendorf: Verlag K. W. Schütz KG, 1984.
Stoves, Rolf. *Die Gepanzerten und Motorisierten Deutschen Grossverbände 1935–1945*. Friedberg: Podzun Pallas Verlag, 1986.
Strik-Strikfeldt, Wilfried. *Against Stalin and Hitler. Memoir of the Russian Liberation Movement 1941–1945*. New York: The John Day Company, 1973.
Szczerepa, Maciej. *Festung Glogau 1945. Ku niemieckim liniom* ('Fortress Glogau. Towards German lines'). Staniszów: Archiwum-System, 2022.
Tessin, Georg. *Verbände und Truppen der Deutschen Wehrmacht und Waffen-SS im Zweiten Weltkrieg 1939–1945*. Bissendorf: Biblio Verlag, 1975–2002, 18 volumes.
Tessin, Georg, Norbert Kannapin, and Brün Meyer. *Waffen-SS und Ordnungspolizei im Kriegseinsatz 1939–1945*. Biblio Verlag: Osnabrück, 2000.
Tessin, Georg, with H. J. Neufeldt, and J. Huck. *Zur Geschichte der Ordnungspolizei, 1936–1945*. Koblenz: Bundesarchiv, 1956.
Thorwald, Jürgen. *The Illusion: Soviet Soldiers in Hitler's Army*. New York: Houghton Mifflin Harcourt, 1978.
Thorwald, Jürgen. *Die große Flucht. Es begann an der Weichsel. Das Ende an der Elbe*. Stuttgart: Steingrüben Verlag, 1965.
Tieke, Wilhelm. *Das Ende Zwischen Oder Und Elbe: Der Kampf Um Berlin 1945*. Stuttgart: Motorbuch Verlag, 1994.
Tolstoy, Nikolai. *The Secret Betrayal 1944–1947*. New York: Charles Scribner's Sons, 1977.

Ueberschär, Gerd R. and Rolf-Dieter Müller. *1945: Das Ende des Krieges*. Darmstadt: Primus Verlag, 2005.

Witte, Hans Joachim and Peter Offermann. *Die Boeselagerschen Reiter: Das Kavallerie-Regiment Mitte die aus ihm hervorgegangene 3. Kavallerie-Brigade/Division*. München: Schild Verlag, 1998.

Yelton, David K. *Hitler's Volkssturm: The Nazi Militia and the Fall of Germany, 1944–1945*. Lawrence: University Press of Kansas, 2002.

Zaloga, Steven. *Bagration 1944: The Destruction of Army Group Center*. Osprey Military: London, 1996

Zawodny, J. K. *Nothing But Honor: The Story of the Warsaw Uprising, 1944*. Stanford, CA: Hoover Institution Press, 1978.

Ziemke, Earl F. *Stalingrad to Berlin: The German Defeat in the East*. Washington, DC: Center of Military History, United States Army, 1986.

# NOTES

## CHAPTER 1

1. *Ostheer:* Eastern army—the German army fighting in the USSR.
2. OKW: *Oberkommando der Wehrmacht* (Armed Forces High Command).
3. *Wehrmacht:* the German Armed Forces.
4. Hosea, 8:7—'For they have sown the wind, and they shall reap the whirlwind.' This is taken from verse seven of the eighth chapter of the Book of Hosea in the *Tanakh* (the Hebrew Bible). It is also found as part of the Old Testament in the Christian bible.
5. STAVKA was the supreme decision-making command staff of the Soviet Union during the war. In June 1944 STAVKA was composed of the following individuals: Joseph Stalin, Semyon Timoshenko, Georgy Zhukov, Semyon Budyonny, Kliment Voroshilov, Boris Shaposhnikov, and Vyacheslav Molotov.
6. *Panzergrenadier-Division Feldherrnhalle* was simply a renaming of the *60. Infanterie-Division (motorisiert)*, which had been created mainly using former Nazi SA (storm-trooper) members. The redesignation occurred in southern France on 20 June 1943.
7. This tank destroyer was designated as *Sonderkraftfahrzeug 164* and was initially nicknamed the *Hornisse* (Hornet). The nickname for the vehicle was later changed to *Nashorn* (Rhinoceros). During Operation Bagration, the battalion was nearly wiped out. Only about one company survived to later be reformed into a new tank destroyer battalion. The new *schwere Panzerjäger-Abteilung 519* was established in August 1944 at Troop Training Ground Mielau. It would now contain seventeen *Jagdpanther* tank destroyers in its First Company. The Second and Third Company were both outfitted with the old *Sturmgeschütz III* assault gun.
8. The *4. Kavallerie-Brigade* had been created in March 1944. A year later, in March 1945, it was redesignated a division.
9. NARA RG 338, Box 1, Folder 2. *Korpsabteilung E* was composed of what remained of the *137. Infanterie-Division* and *251. Infanterie-Division*.

10. The *3. Kavallerie-Brigade* had been established in February 1944. On 3 March 1945, it was redesignated a cavalry division. In February 1945, it contained 11,333 officers, NCOs, and enlisted men.

11. *Landser* is the German equivalent of G.I.

12. NARA RG 338, Box 1, Folder 3. *Korpsabteilung D* was established on 2 November 1943 in the region of *Heeresgruppe Mitte* from the remnants of several shattered German divisions. These included *56. Infanterie-Division* and *262. Infanterie-Division*. These *Korpsabteilungen* were created by the *Ostheer* because the German Replacement Army lacked the necessary reserves to rebuild these smashed divisions. In addition, Hitler had refused to disband them; most likely because it gave him comfort to see more German divisional flags on his situation map. In order to offer them a better chance to survive the rigors of the Russian Front, these depleted formations were grouped into these corps' detachments. The *Korpsabteilungen* usually contained somewhere between two and four splintered divisions apiece. At best, these 'divisions' had the equivalent strength of a regiment each. In total, the Germans established eight *Korpsabteilungen* and labeled them 'A' through 'H'.

13. *Korpsabteilung D* was a headquarters command for several shattered German division that Adolf Hitler refused to disband. The divisions under this command were actually regiments in strength and divisions in name only. Several *Korpsabteilung* were created, employing capital letters as designations: 'A', 'B', 'C', etc.

14. Albert Seaton. *The Russo-German War 1941–1945*. Westport: Praeger Publishers, 1971, p. 438.

15. Paul Carell. *Scorched Earth: Hitler's War on Russia*. London: George G. Harrap & Co., Ltd, 1970, p. 501.

16. Alan Clark. *Barbarossa. The Russian-German Conflict, 1941–1945*. New York: William Morrow, 1965, p. 382.

17. Chester Wilmot. *The Struggle for Europe*. New York: Harper & Row, 1952, p. 386.

## CHAPTER 2

1. Seaton, op. cit., p. 446.

2. BA/MA RW-75, s. 13. According to German estimates, the 1st Guards Tank Army began the offensive with 346 tanks and assault guns.

3. The Red Army cavalry-mechanized groups varied in size and strength. On average, the size of a cavalry-mechanized group (CMG) could vary greatly depending on the operation and the units assigned. However, a typical CMG could range anywhere from 5,000 to 15,000 soldiers. A CMG might include several thousand cavalrymen, hundreds of tanks (often between 100 to 200), hundreds of motorized infantry and armored vehicles, and artillery support, including motorized multiple batteries of field artillery and rocket launchers. Some CMGs were larger, like 1st Cavalry Mechanized Group, which often contained two to four cavalry divisions and one to three tank brigades. Self-propelled artillery and multiple rocket support was provided by several artillery and rocket launcher regiments that would be attached. This structure allowed

the Red Army to conduct both fast-moving cavalry raids and more sustained mechanized operations. The Cavalry-Mechanized Group could be used in a variety of roles, including reconnaissance, shock attacks, and exploitation of breakthroughs in enemy lines.

4. *Generalfeldmarshall* Walther Model was the actual commander of *Heeresgruppe Nordukraine*; however, he had also recently been given control of *Heeresgruppe Mitte*. Thus, his adjutant for *Heeresgruppe Nordukraine* (Harper) assumed temporary command.

5. NARA T-315, Rolls 1665, various frames. The infantry divisions under *Heeresgruppe Nordukraine* had a combined total of around forty-three assault guns. Thus, the total tank / assault gun / tank destroyer strength for the army group was as follows: *schwere Panzerjäger-Abteilung 88* (thirty-five vehicles), *schwere Panzer Abteilung 506* (forty-four tanks), *1. Panzer-Division* (sixty-two tanks), *8. Panzer-Division* (fifty-seven tanks), *16. Panzer-Division* (seventy-five tanks), *17. Panzer-Division* (sixty-eight tanks), and 2nd Hungarian Armoured Division (thirty-six tanks). Counting the forty-three assault guns employed in the various infantry divisions serving with the army group, there was a grand total of 420 armored fighting vehicles available.

6. NARA T-78, Roll 413, Frames 0615-32. From 26 May to 25 July 1944, Lieutenant-General Károly Bereggfy was the commanding officer of 1st Hungarian Army. Then, from 25 July to 1 August 1944, Lieutenant-General Ferenc Farkas became the commander. From 1 August to 16 October 1944, it was Lieutenant-General Béla Miklós von Dalnoki. The final commander of the 1st Hungarian Army was Lieutenant-General Dezsö László, who led the army from 16 October 1944 to 11 May 1945.

7. This SS division was enroute to the command but had not yet arrived.

8. NARA T-78, Roll 413, Frame 0627. Five days later, the division contained the same number of Hungarian armored vehicles but had also received eleven *Panzerkampfwagen IV* tanks from the Germans.

9. Leo G. Niehorster. *The Royal Hungarian Army, 1920–1945*. New York: Europa Books, 1998, p. 201.

10. BA/MA MS-G2/1283, s. 24. In August 1944, this division would be serving under *XXVI Armeekorps* as part of *3. Panzerarmee*, Army Group Center.

11. Part of this division was in the process of being withdrawn.

12. *Korpsabteilung C* contained the remnants of *183. Infanterie-Division, 217. Infanterie-Division*, and *339. Infanterie-Division*.

13. I. S. Konev. *Zapiski Komanduyushchego frontom*. Moscow: Voenizdat Publishing, 1981, p. 224.

14. The numbers of Home Army troops per region on 1 July 1944 were as follows: Warsaw region: 42,900; Pomorze region: 6,300; Poznan region: 7,000; Bialystok region: 21,600; Novogrodek region: 3,400; Podole region: 4,700; Lublin: 40,600; Volhynia region: 5,000; Kielce region: 29,500; Lodz region: 35,400; Slask region: 46,000; Krakow and Rzeszow regions: 58,400; Lviv region: 14,400; Stanislav region: 4,900; and Tarnopol region: 16,000. In total (on paper), the Home Army had 336,100 men.

15. Richard N. Armstrong. *Soviet Operational Deception: The Red Cloak*. Fort Leavenworth: U.S. Army Combat Studies Institute, 1989, p. 42.

16. The Hlinka Guard (Slovak: Hlinkova Garda) was a paramilitary organization in Slovakia, closely associated with the country's pro-Nazi, fascist government, headed by

Josef Tiso, during the period of the Slovak Republic (1939–1945). This republic was a puppet state of Nazi Germany. Named after its founder, Andrej Hlinka, a Catholic priest and leader of the Slovak People's Party (*Hlinkova slovenská ľudová strana*), the Hlinka Guard played a significant role in enforcing the regime's anti-Jewish policies and the suppression of all opposition.

## CHAPTER 3

1. Patrick McTaggart. *The Battle of Narva, 1944.* Command Magazine: San Luis Obispo, CA, Issue 14, January–February 1992, p. 56.
2. David Glantz. *Soviet Military Deception in the Second World War.* London: Frank Cass, 1989, p. 299.
3. Newton, op. cit., p. 60.
4. Richard Landwehr. *Soldiers of Europe: The III SS-Panzerkorps (part 1).* Siegrunen Magazine: Glendale, AZ, July 1979. Vol. 3, Nr. 3, whole number 15, p. 9.
5. Werner Haupt. *Leningrad. 900 Tage Schlacht 1941–1944.* Friedberg: Podzun Pallas Verlag, n.d., p. 227.
6. Richard Landwehr and Holger Thor Nielsen. *Nordic Warriors. SS Panzergrenadier-Regiment 24 Danmark, Eastern Front, 1943-45.* Halifax: Shelf Books, 1999, p. 66.
7. Where *Feld-Division 1 (L)* was 'coincidentally' stationed.
8. Haupt, *Army Group North,* op. cit., p. 174.
9. Newton, op. cit., p. 59.
10. Ibid., p. 63.
11. Mehner, *Die Geheimen Tagesberichte,* op. cit., Vol. 9, p. 227.
12. Haupt. *Leningrad. 900 Tage Schlacht,* op. cit., p. 229.
13. Ibid., p. 230.
14. Haupt. *Die Deutschen Luftwaffen Feld-Divisionen,* op. cit., p. 54.
15. NARA Microfilm Roll T-311, Roll 70, Frames 349-350, '*Heeresgruppe Nord, Ia, 159/44, 17 January 1944.*'
16. Mitcham, *Hitler's Legions,* op. cit., p. 431.
17. Landwehr, *Soldiers of Europe,* op. cit., p. 12.
18. When the army had taken over the air force field divisions in November 1943, Hermann Göring had ordered that the flak battalion in every one of these field divisions were to be withdrawn and returned to the control of the *Luftwaffe*. This was done to prevent them coming under the command of the army. This selfish and mean-spirited decision by the *Reichsmarshall* further weakened these air force field divisions.
19. The *Grenadier-Regiment 503* and *II. Bataillon / 290. Artillerie Regiment* belonged to the *290. Infanterie-Division.*
20. NARA T-175, Roll 140, Frame 412. *Kampfgruppe Furguth* was what remained of *503. Grenadier-Regiment.*
21. Kurt Mehner. *Die Geheimen Tagesberichte der Deutschen Wehrmachtführung Im Zweiten Weltkrieg, 1939–1945.* Osnabrück: Biblio Verlag, 1988, 12 Vols., Vol. 8, p. 267.
22. Mehner, *Die Geheimen Tagesberichte,* op. cit., Vol. 9, p. 247.

23. Ibid., p. 251.
24. Haupt. *Leningrad die 900-Tage Schlacht,* op. cit., p. 235.
25. Mehner, *Die Geheimen Tagesberichte,* op. cit., Vol. 9, p. 255.
26. NARA Microfilm T-311, Roll 70, Frames 00567-8, *'Armeeoberkommando 18, Ia, 732/44 5 Februar 1944.'*
27. Newton, op. cit., p. 72.
28. Ibid., p. 120.
29. Ibid., p. 76.
30. Mehner, *Die Geheimen Tagesberichte,* op. cit., Vol. 9, p. 372.
31. Ibid., p. 331.
32. NARA T-175, Roll 225, Frame 0739.
33. Newton, op. cit., p. 343.
34. Ibid., p. 349.
35. Ibid., p. 76.
36. Mehner, *Die Geheimen Tagesberichte,* op. cit., Vol. 9, p. 372.
37. Newton, op. cit., p. 95.
38 Newton, op. cit., p. 105.
39. Haupt. *Die Deutschen Infanterie-Divisionen,* op. cit., Vol. 2, p. 97.
40. NARA T-78, Roll 645, Frame 0715.
41. Mueller-Hillebrand, op cit., p. 224.
42. Newton, op. cit., p. 109.
43. 'Division for Special Employment No. 300.'
44. Landwehr, et. al., *Nordic Warriors,* op. cit., p. 118.
45. Haupt. *Die Deutschen Luftwaffen Feld-Divisionen,* op. cit., p. 58.
46. Mitcham, *Crumbling Empire,* op. cit., p. 124.
47. NARA T-315, Roll 1687, Frame 0801. According to records, the other six divisions that were fully combat ready were the 11th, 21st, 30th, 58th, 61st, and 227th Infantry Division.
48. Haupt. *Die Deutschen Luftwaffen Feld-Divisionen,* op. cit., p. 58.
49. Haupt, *Army Group North,* op. cit., p. 240.
50. NARA T-175, Roll 225, Frame 0454. The battalion was formed with three rifle companies, a machine gun company, a staff company, a Jäger platoon, an anti-tank platoon, and an engineer platoon.
51. This regiment was composed of men who were listed as convalescent cases.
52. NARA RG 338, Box 1, Folder 2. This army detachment contained *XXXVIII. Armeekorps* with the following formations: *21 Feld-Division (L), 81. Infanterie-Division, 121. Infanterie-Division, 122. Infanterie-Division, 32. Infanterie-Division, 329. Infanterie-Division,* and *201. Sicherungs-Division.* The *52. Sicherungs-Division* was listed as available under special employment.
53. Haupt, *Leningrad,* op. cit., p. 261.
54. J. Schröder and Joachim Schultz-Naumann. *Geschichte der Pommeranische 32. Infanterie-Division.* Bad Neuheim: Podzun Pallas Verlag, 1956, p. 229.
55. Haupt, *Army Group North,* op. cit., p. 240.
56. *Segewald* is the German spelling for the Latvian town of Sigulda, in the Vidzeme Region. It lies about 53 kilometers northeast of the Latvian capital of Riga.

234   *Notes*

57. Albert Seaton. *The Fall of Fortress Europe 1943–1945*. New York: Holmes & Meier Publishers, Inc., 1981, pp. 135–36.


CHAPTER 4

1. BA/MA RW-60, s.12. *(Geb.) AOK 20, Ic, Nr. 1210/44, Tätigkeitsberichte der Abteilung Ic für die Zeit vom 1.1.-30.6.44. AOK 20 58631/1.*
2. Earl F. Ziemke. *The German Northern Theater of Operations 1940–1945*. Washington, DC: Department of the Army, 1959, p. 279.
3. The Ryti-Ribbentrop letter of agreement was a temporary pact between Finland's president and Adolf Hitler. In exchange for more weapons and German military assistance in order to help halt the Red Army summer offensive of 1944, Finland agreed to remain in the war on Germany's side. The agreement completely ignored the Finnish parliament, which should have ratified such a deal. However, when it became clear that the agreement would block Finland's ability to make a separate peace with the Soviet Union, it was abrogated by the Finns.
4. On 19 September, the Finnish High Command informed the Finnish parliament that the army could only resist for another three months. This knowledge pushed those members of parliament who were refusing to ratify the accord to agree to the Russian terms for peace.
5. Colonel-General Eduard Dietl had been the commander of *20. Gebirgsarmee* since 14 June 1942, but on 23 June 1944, he was killed in an airplane crash that occurred in Styria, Slovenia. Dietl had been on his way back from the Berghof, after meeting with Adolf Hitler. The subject of the meeting is known. Basically, Hitler wanted to know what suggestions Dietl (and others at the meeting) had on how the Eastern Front could be strengthened. When Dietl suggested abandoning Norway so that the 300,000 German troops garrisoning the country could be employed on the Russian front, Hitler flew into a rage and immediately dismissed him from the meeting. The plane crash occurred on Dietl's return flight from that meeting. He was flying in a Junkers Ju-52 transport plane. Rendulic replaced Dietl as commander of *20. Gebirgsarmee* on 25 June 1944.
6. The translation for *Division Stab z.b.V. 140* is 'Divisional Staff for Special Employment 140'. During World War II, the Germans often employed numerous divisional staff for special employment designations for divisions that were established with no integral units. Battalions, regiments and even brigades were added to these ad hoc divisional groups as the need and availability afforded it. It was a way of quickly establishing a German division-sized formation without the need to create integral units, which often took over a year to create.
7. The *16. Kompanie* and *17. Kompanie* were the machine gun and infantry gun companies in the regiment.
8. The amphibious transport battalions were created from American lend-lease equipment. They were employed in the landings that took place on the Srednii peninsula and, later still, in assisting the divisions of 14th Army in crossing the rivers of

the region. They proved particularly useful as the Germans destroyed every bridge during their retreat.

9. Both the LVT-4 and LVT(A)-4 would be employed by the United States Marine Corps during the Pacific campaign.

## CHAPTER 5

1. In the summer of 1944, the Romanian Air Force (Forţele Aeriene Regale ale României) fielded two basic types of fighters: (1) the IAR-80/81 (Romanian-designed and built), and (2) the German supplied *Messerschmitt Bf 109G*. The Romanian Air Force also had perhaps 100 to 150 bombers of various designs. These were (1) the Italian-built *SM.79 Sparviero*, (2) the *Heinkel He 111*, and the (3) *Junkers Ju 88* (the latter two of German manufacture). The 2,200 aircraft of the 17th Air Army were more or less evenly divided between fighters and bombers. The fighters included the Yakovlev Yak-1, Yak-3, and Yak-9 fighters, as well as the *Lavochkin La-5* and *La-7* fighters. The bombers included the *Ilyushin Il-2 Sturmovik* (considered a fighter-bomber), the Petlyakov Pe-2 (tactical bomber), the Tupolev Tu-2 (medium bomber), and the Ilyushin Il-4 (long-range bomber).

2. Seaton, op. cit., p. 470.

3. David M. Glantz. *Red Storm over the Balkans. The Failed Soviet Invasion of Romania, Spring 1944*. Leavenworth, KS: University Press of Kansas, 2006, p. 401.

4. The Focşani Gate is a topographical region of flat land between the Carpathian Mountains and Sereth River. In military terms, it is an area of vulnerability where the topography of the area is conducive for mobile warfare and particularly difficult to defend, given the relative flat terrain. It spans about fifty-three miles of open ground.

5. The TACAM T-60 tank destroyer was a Romanian marriage of a captured Russian T-60 tank chassis and the Soviet 76.2 mm M-1936 F-22 field gun. It was a moderately successful design in the tank destroyer role and represented the best that the Romanian armed forces could produce with captured Russian equipment.

6. The *Marder II* was a German tank destroyer based on the *Panzer II* chassis. There were two versions. The first version mounted a modified Soviet 7.62-cm gun firing German ammunition, while the second version carried the German 75-mm Pak-40 anti-tank gun.

7. BA/MA RW-41, s. 24-26. According to German records, this assault gun brigade withdrew from Romania into Hungary and then to Czechoslovakia. Its last deployment of significance was at the Szolnok Gran Bridgehead. This was followed by the retreat to Brno. Then it withdrew through the area of Wirschau, Kralitz and Mehren. Its last deployment was alongside *15. Infanterie-Division*.

## CHAPTER 6

1. Of the nearly 70,000 troops on Crete, 16,000 Germans and Italians remained until the end of the war. Rhodes had a garrison of 23,000, of which only 6,000 remained

to end the war. Thus, von Weich was able to withdraw around 71,000 German and Italian troops from both islands in the fall of 1944.

2. Seaton, *The Fall of Fortress Europe*, op cit., p. 151.

3. In April 1945, the Bulgarian First Army was located in eastern Austria.

4. The *Jäger-Ersatz und Ausbildungs-Regiment 1* was established on 1 June 1943, in Arys, *Wehrkreis I* (Military District I). The regiment was formed from the Hammerschmidt Task Force, which had been created on 12 April 1943 using two *Jäger* replacement battalions, named 'A' and 'B'. The regiment was initially subordinate to *Wehrkreis I* and provided replacement units for military districts I–XXI. On 9 August 1943, the regiment was divided into two formations: *Reserve Jäger-Regiment 1* (two battalions), initially stationed in Arys, and *Jäger-Ausbildungs-Regiment 1* (which initially had only five companies).

5. Institut für Zeitgeschichte-Archiv, Kommandierender General und Befehlshaber in Serbien, MA 512 / 1.

6. The *Serbisches Freiwilligen Korps* (Serbian Volunteer Corps) was a formation of approximately 15,000 Serbian fascists who served the Axis cause. The unit was split up into five infantry regiments, however, the *5. Regiment* only contained one infantry battalion. The unit withdrew with the Germans all the way into Austria. At the beginning of 1945 the SS assumed responsibility for the formation as far as supplies and other equipment. It was renamed the *Serbisches SS-Freiwilligen Korps*, although no SS uniforms were ever issued, and no SS officers assumed command of the formation. After the war those Serbians who survived and remained in Germany eventually applied for German pensions. Those who did were awarded German military pensions.

7. The *Russisches Gardekorps* (Russian Guard Corps) was a volunteer formation that eventually reached 12,000 men. It was composed of White Russian *émigrés* who had settled in Yugoslavia after they had lost the Russian Civil War. Most were elderly, while there were some younger men—the sons of many White Russians who had left Russia with their entire family, or the sons of Russian exiles who had married Serbian women. The formation actually operated fairly efficiently against the partisans, and when the Red Army entered Serbia in September 1944, the Russian Guard Corps was eager to engage them. The unit contained the following forces: *1. Kavallerie Regiment, 2. Infanterie Regiment, 3. Infanterie Regiment, 4. Infanterie Regiment,* and *5. Infanterie Regiment.* Fortunately for the Russian Guard Corps, almost all of them were saved from the clutches of Stalin's secret police because they were not citizens of the USSR prior to 1941. Only if you were a citizen of the USSR beginning 22 June 1941, were you subject to repatriation to the USSR, and the horrible fate that awaited you at the hands of Stalin's Secret Police. When they were released from captivity, many of these old Czarist volunteers sought to live out the rest of their lives outside shattered Europe. Many chose to immigrate to Canada, South America, Australia, and the United States, while some decided to remain in France, Germany, or Austria. Their hopes of seeing a renewal of the Romanov monarchy in Russia were now shattered.

8. NARA T-78, Roll 413, Frame 902.

9. Antonio Muñoz. *Hitler's Green Army, The German Order Police and Their European Auxiliaries, Volume II: Eastern Europe & the Balkans.* New York: Europa Books, 2006, p. 181.

## CHAPTER 7

1. The following divisions were assigned to this newly reformed *17. Armee*: *359. Infanterie-Division*, *544. Volksgrenadier-Division*, *545. Volksgrenadier-Division*, *371. Infanterie-Division*, and *14. Panzer-Division*. The *14. Panzer-Division* was only just arriving and was earmarked to be the army reserve.

2. Augustin Guillaume. *The German Russia War 1941–1945*. London: The War Office, 1956, p. 110.

3. In October 1944, the Royal Hungarian Army possessed three armored divisions. The 1st Hungarian Armored Division (1. páncéloshadosztály) had been created in 1942. There was also the 2nd Hungarian Armored Division (2. páncéloshadosztály). Formed in 1944, it was equipped with a variety of German tanks, including some captured Soviet models. This was the most well-equipped armored division of the Hungarian Army. Finally, there was the 3rd Hungarian Armored Division (3. páncéloshadosztály), which had also been formed in 1944. However, this final armored division was less developed and equipped than the 1st and 2nd. By October 1944, these armored divisions, such as they were, were involved in various fronts and battles, especially as the situation in Hungary became increasingly dire due to the advancing Soviet forces and the ongoing battles along the Eastern Front. The Royal Hungarian Army was under increasing pressure. These divisions were not as heavily equipped and proved less effective than their German counterparts.

4. The Turán I tank had a 40 mm gun, while the Turán II tank carried a better 75 mm anti-tank gun. There were a few *Panzer IV* tanks and *Sturmgeschütz III* assault guns in the divisions, but the mainstay of the division were the Turán tanks.

5. One Romanian division, the 4th, was actually surrounded during the battle and was forced to surrender.

## CHAPTER 8

1. This divisional group was composed of one regiment from *271. Volksgrenadier-Division*, two *Landesschützen* (regional defense) battalions, *Fusilier Bataillon 271*, and *Sicherungs Bataillon 455* (455th Security Battalion).

## CHAPTER 9

1. *Heeresgruppe Östmark* was created on 30 April to control what remained of the German *6. Armee*, *8. Armee*, and *6. Panzerarmee*. Its commander was an Austrian, *Generaloberst* Dr. Lothar Rendulic.

2. Karl-Heinz Frieser, et al. (eds.). *Die Ostfront 1943/44: Der Krieg im Osten und an den Nebenfronten. Das Deutsche Reich und der Zweite Weltkrieg*. Vol. 8. Munich: Deutsche Verlags-Anstalt, 2007, pp. 849–960.

3. The *Panzerfaust* was a disposable, single-shot anti-tank weapon that was invented by a German team of engineers at the company Hugo Schneider AG (HASAG) in

Leipzig. The weapon was developed under the leadership of Heinrich Langweiler. The *Panzerfaust* was first produced in 1943 and saw its initial use on the Eastern Front. It was designed as a simple, cost-effective weapon that could be operated by infantry with minimal training, giving German soldiers the ability to destroy armored tanks at close range, even the heavy tanks. There were several versions of the *Panzerfaust* developed during the war, with incremental improvements in range, penetration power, and ease of use. The first version, the *Panzerfaust 30,* was named for its effective range of 30 meters. Later versions, like the *Panzerfaust 60* and *Panzerfaust 100,* increased the range and penetration ability of the anti-tank round.

4. BA/MA R-55 / 616, s. 34. The Russian Liberation Army *(Russkaya osvoboditel'naya armiya),* or ROA, was a military force composed of Soviet POWs, volunteers, and anti-communist Russians who fought alongside Nazi Germany during World War II. It was led by General Andrey Vlasov, a former Soviet general who defected to the Germans after being captured on the Eastern Front. In the spring of 1942, Vlasov became disillusioned with Stalin's regime and agreed to collaborate with the Germans, proposing to form an army to fight against the Soviet Union.

5. What Bunyachenko didn't know, however, was that the western Allies had already discussed the issue of Russian collaborators with Stalin. The western Allies had agreed that all Russians taken by their forces were to be handed over to the Red Army. The only exception were those Russians who were not citizens of the USSR prior to 22 June 1941. Because of his high rank, Bunyachenko was sent to Moscow to stand trial. He was found guilty of treason and executed on 1 August 1946.

6. Jürgen Thorwald. *The Illusion: Soviet Soldiers in Hitler's Army.* New York: Houghton Mifflin Harcourt, 1978.

7. *Sanitäts Abteilung 'Wallenstein'* (*SS-Sturmbannführer* Dr. Hans Lucha) was created from *SS Sanitäts Schule Prag-Beneschau.* The name Lucha has also been spelled as 'Luchem'.

8. In the case of the French Army, there have been verified incidences where individual French officers and troops took it upon themselves to exact immediate retribution and vengeance on groups of captured German soldiers, ostensibly for the horrors which were perpetrated on French citizens by the Nazis during the German occupation. The most infamous case involved one of the highest-ranking officers in the French 1st Army, commanded by General Jean de Lattre de Tassigny. The episode involved General Philippe Leclerc. It occurred when French troops captured the town of Bad Reichenhall on 4 May 1945. There the men of the French 1st Army encountered several fellow Frenchmen who had volunteered to serve in the *33. Waffen-Grenadier-Division der SS 'Charlemagne',* an SS division composed of French citizens. When Leclerc inspected these French SS men, he stopped in front of one of them and asked 'Pourquoi portez-vous un uniforme allemand?' ('Why are you wearing a German uniform?'). The French SS private looked at General Leclerc and replied, 'Vous êtes très beau dans votre uniforme américain, mon general' ('You look very handsome in your American uniform, general'). Enraged, Leclerc ordered the immediate execution of all the prisoners.

9. Igor Lukes. *On the Edge of the Cold War: American Diplomats and Spies in Postwar Prague.* New York: Oxford University Press, 2012, p. 50.

## CHAPTER 10

1. In January 1945, Hitler ordered *19. Armee* to go on the offensive with *Unternehmen Nordwind*, an attack that lasted from 1–25 January 1945. The Germans aimed to strike along the Alsace-Lorraine border and push toward the Rhine River. The main thrust was directed toward the American and French positions in the Vosges Mountains and the Saar region, aiming to create a gap between the American and French forces. The attack basically failed for four principal reasons: (1) insufficient logistical support (not enough fuel, not enough munitions), (2) lack of strategic coherence, (3) exhaustion on the part of German forces, and (4) a stiffening Allied defense.

2. Helmut Heiber. *Lagebesprechungen im Fuhrerhauptquartier: Protokollfragmente aus Hitlers Militarischen Konferenzen 1942–1945.* Munich: Deutscher Taschenbuch Verlag, 1963, p. 679.

3. Ibid.

4. Franz Kurowski. *Bridgehead Kurland. The Six Epic Battles of Heeresgruppe Kurland.* Winnipeg: J. J. Fedorowicz Publishing, Inc., 2002, p. 82.

5. BA/MA RW-41, s. 15. In February 1945, *215. Infanterie-Division* was transported by ship to West Prussia. On 9 March 1945, the division had a combat strength of only 3,270 men. The division was then deployed to the Tuchloer Heide and eventually withdrew to Gotenhafen by April 1945.

6. Kurowski, op. cit., p. 136.

7. BA/MA RW-75, s. 11. In the winter of 1944/45 *Sturmgeschütz-Brigade 912* was renamed *Heeres Sturmartillerie Brigade 912*.

8. Prit Buttar. *Between Giants: The Battle for the Baltics in World War II.* London: Osprey Publishing, 2013, p. 357.

9. Kurowski, op. cit., p. 152.

10. Vincent Hunt. *Blood in the Forest: The End of the Second World War in the Courland Pocket.* Solihull, UK: Helion & Co., 2017, p. 99.

11. This assault gun brigade had featured prominently from 6–13 October 1944, when it took part in *Unternehmen Donner* (Operation Thunder), the disengagement of *18. Armee* from the Segewald positions, and its withdrawal behind *16. Armee* via Riga–Tukums–Courland. Its commander from 1 September to 17 December 1944 was *Hauptmann* (then *Major*) Johannes Karstens. The brigade had also seen heavy action in March 1944. By 11 March 1944, it had been reduced to twelve assault guns, of which only seven were operational and five were conditionally operational; that is, they needed repairs but could, if necessary, be employed.

12. The Vartaja River is a tributary of the Venta River.

13. Kurowski, op. cit., p. 153.

14. NARA T-78, Roll 624, various frames.

15. Created from *Panzerjäger-Abteilung 753*.

16. Ibid.

## CHAPTER 11

1. NARA T-78, Roll 413, Frame 0531. The units included: *Festungs Infanterie Bataillon 1445, Landesschützen Bataillon 1091, Pioneer Ersatz und Ausbildungs Bataillon 213, Pionier Kompanie 61 der Festungs Pioneer Stab 9, Festungs Artillerie Bataillon 61,* and members of a reserve officer candidate course.

2. Percy E. Schramm. *Kriegstagebuch des Oberkommandos der Wehrmacht (Wehrmachtführungsstab). Band V: 1. Januar 1944-9. Mai 1945.* Bonn: Bernard & Graefe Verlag, 1961, pp. 496–500.

3. The men of *269. Infanterie-Division* had been recruited from the north German regions of Hamburg, Bremen, and Schleswig-Holstein. The division itself was organized in Hamburg.

4. Antonio J. Muñoz. *Forgotten Legions. Obscure Combat Formations of the Waffen-SS.* Boulder, CO: Paladin Press, 1991, p. 151.

5. 'Army NCO School Striegau', 'Army Driver Training and Reserve Battalion No. 28', and 'Army Veterinary Training and Reserve Battalion No. 8', respectively.

6. Muñoz, *Forgotten Legions,* op. cit., p. 149.

7. T-311, Roll 70, Frame 0624-5. According to German records, in January 1945, *Flak Regiment 150* contained the following batteries: *Stab/109,* with *schwere Flak Batterie z.b.V. 10738, 10739, 10740, 10741, 10742, and 10743; Schwere Heimat Flak Batterie 265/VIII, 271/VIII, 272/VIII, 273/VIII, 275./VIII, leichte Heimat Flak Batterie 4/VIII, 23/VIII; Stab/570,* with *1.-4./s.570 (o), 3./leichte 838 (o), leichte Flak Batterie z.b.V. 6505; Schwere Heimat Flak Batterie 226/VIII, 258/VIII, 266/VIII, 267/VIII, 268/VIII, 269./VIII, 270/VIII, 274/VIII* and *leichte Heimat Flak Batterie 24, 25,* and *26./VIII; Stab/schwere 653 (o)* with *1., 2., 3.,* and *4./schwere 653 (o), 6./leichte 941 (o), schwere Heimat Flak Batterie 231/I; Stab/schwere 660 (o)* with *1.-2./schwere 660 (o), schwere Heimat Flak Batterie 209, 210, 211, 212, 213 /I, 216./I, 230/I, 234/I;* and *Stab/leichte 890 (o)* with *5./leichte 882 (b. motorisiert), 2./leichte 887 (o), leichte Heimat Flak Batterie 4./I, 12./I, 17./I,* and *23./I.*

8. Ibid., Frame 0626. *Flak Regiment 150* belonged to the *11. Flak Division,* which was formed on 8 September 1944, in Upper Silesia from the staff of the *15. Flak Brigade.* According to records, the division took command of the antiaircraft units in the area of *Luftgaukommando VIII,* which were mainly deployed in the Upper Silesian industrial area and in the city of Breslau for antiaircraft protection. The problem with some of the batteries was that they were stationary and therefore proved difficult or impossible to be employed against enemy ground forces.

9. Samuel W. Mitcham. *Hitler's Legions: The German Army Order of Battle, World War Two.* New York: Dorset Press, 1985, p. 306.

10. Reinkober was the former commander of a Russian POW camp.

11. Beßlein was promoted to *SS-Obersturmbannführer* on 1 March 1945.

12. Georg Tessin. *Verbände und Truppen der Deutschen Wehrmacht und Waffen-SS im Zweiten Weltkrieg 1939–1945.* Bissendorf: Biblio Verlag, *Vol. 14. Die Landstreitkräfte. Namensverbände. Die Luftstreitkräfte. Fliegende Verbände. Flakeinsatz im Reich 1943–1945,* 1980, pp. 24–25.

13. Richard Siegert. *Tygrys z Poznania.* Warsaw: Vesper, 2010, p. 45.

14. Wilhelm Lenzer was head of both *Amt C-V* and *Bauinspektionsbereich 'Reich Ost'*, the headquarters of which was located in Posen. He was wounded in the head and left thigh during the siege. He was taken prisoner at the end of the battle for the city. While marching east in a column of POWs, he was recognized and immediately removed from the line. He was not heard from ever again. It is likely that he was executed. According to some accounts during the battle, Lenzer, who had only worked in an administrative position, would actually take military advice from lower-ranking officers. He even took advice from some veteran NCOs who had recently been acting as teachers at a nearby SS training school. His regiment performed well enough to be considered a fire brigade for the fortress commander. However, toward the end of the siege, discipline in the unit began to break down.

15. Hans Schäufler. 1945 – *Panzer an der Weichsel. Soldaten der Letzten Stunde*. Stuttgart: Motorbuch Verlag, 1986, p. 79.

16. NARA T-311, Roll 70, Frame 218. On 9 October *551. Grenadier Division* was renamed *551. Volksgrenadier-Division*. The remnants of the division withdrew south under *IX. Armeekorps*.

## CHAPTER 12

1. After the breakthrough by the Red Army at the Baranov bridgehead on the Vistula River, *Heeresgruppe A (17. Armee, 9. Armee, 4. Panzerarmee,* and *Armeegruppe Heinrici)* withdrew, taking heavy losses, to the Oder River, beginning on 12 January 1945. On 25 January 1945, *Heeresgruppe A* was renamed *Heeresgruppe Mitte*.

2. Seaton, *The Fall of Fortress Europe*, op cit., p. 170.

3. The 9th Army would be taken over by *General der Infanterie* Theodor Busse on 21 January 1945.

4. BA/MA MS-G2/1283. At least one documented reference has called it *11. SS Armee*.

5. *11. SS Armee* was sent west and assigned to OB West on 2 April 1945. It then controlled *LXVII Armeekorps*. It became surrounded by US forces in the Harz Mountains. At that time, it controlled only one division and two smaller units: *26. Volksgrenadier-Division, Fallschirmjäger-Regiment 15,* and *Fallschirm Pionier-Bataillon 5*.

6. *Das Kriegstagebuch Der Heeresgruppe Weichsel*, Internet Archive, https://archive.org/details/das-kriegstagebuch-der-heeresgruppe-weichsel/page/25/mode/2up, p. 35.

7. Bundesarchiv, Gliederung *und Einsätze der Jagdverbände Mitte, Nordwest, Südwest und Süd*, Nr. 756 / 328a.

8. BA MA RH 26-402 *Division z.b.V. 402 / Division Nr. 402 / Ausbildungs-Division 402*.

9. The '*Wespe*' and '*Hummel*' were not assault guns or even tank destroyers. They were, in fact, mobile artillery pieces. The '*Wespe*' carried the 105 mm *leicht* (light) FH 18/2 L/28 howitzer, while the '*Hummel*' carried the 150 mm *schwer* (heavy) FH 18/1 L/30 howitzer.

10. *Generalkommando Tettau* had been created by employing the headquarters of *Division z.b.V. 604*, a divisional headquarters established in The Netherlands in

November 1944. Its commander was *General der Infanterie* Hans von Tettau. According to one source, during most of the war *General der Infanterie* Tettau had served as an inspector of troops and field fortifications. His only combat experience occurred during 'Operation Market Garden' (17–25 September 1944), where British, American and Polish paratrooper forces, in conjunction with British XXX Corps, attempted to cross the lower Rhine River at Arnhem. General Tettau and this divisional command were withdrawn from Holland in early 1945 and transferred to Belgard, in Pomerania. It is there that the divisional headquarters staff was elevated to a corps command *(Generalkommando Tettau)*. This occurred in February 1945. It was also in February that this headquarters was attached to *11. SS Panzerarmee*. However, in March it was detached and sent to serve under *3. Panzerarmee* along the Oder River.

11. Stefan Klemp. *KZ-Arzt Aribert Heim. Die Geschichte einer Fahndung*. Berlin: Prospero Verlag, 2010, p. 53.

12. In March and April 1945, the remnants of this panzer division were used reform *18. Panzergrenadier-Division*.

13. This was a unit from General Andrei Vlasov's German-sponsored Russian Army of Liberation (ROA).

## CHAPTER 13

1. BA/MA RH 58/46, *Walther Hansen, Als Ia bei der Inspektion 15 und stellvertretter Chef der Inspektion*, p. 7.

2. Erich Murawski. *Die Eroberung Pommerns durch die Rote Armee*. Boppard am Rhein: Harald Boldt, 1969, p. 143.

3. In 1945, *Sturm Bataillon AOK 9* was expanded to two battalion: *Sturm Bataillon I AOK 9* and *Sturm Bataillon II AOK 9*.

4. Tessin, op. cit., Vol. 16, Part I, p. 5. In January 1945 this company fought in the following towns: Danzig, Landsberg, Holstein region, Allenstein, Neidenburg, Rastenburg, Heilsberg, Preussisch Eylau, Schreitlacken, Schlossberg, and Putlos. It then ended up in the city of Küstrin in February 1945.

5. BA/MA N 756/328a, *Gesamtstärke, Division Schwedt*.

6. The *SS-Ersatzkommando* were established to recruit foreigners into the *Waffen-SS*. Each country in Europe had its own *SS-Ersatzkommando*. For example, for Croatia, it was *SS-Ersatzkommando Kroatien*. For the Baltic States, it was *SS-Ersatzkommando Ostland,* etc. These recruiting offices had the equivalent of a small company of men.

7. BA/MA N 756/394, *Operationen und Kampfhandlungen mit Beteiligung von Einheiten der Waffen-SS vor allem in den Jahren 1944–1945, SS Obersturmbannführer Ottto Skorzeny und die Kampf um Schwedt*.

8. Ibid.

9. *Division Raegener* had been created from German Army rear area forces and *Volkssturm* battalions. The composition of the division was as follows: *Grenadier-Regiment Fischer (I., II. und III. Bataillone), Grenadier-Regiment Becker (I. und II. Bataillone), Grenadier-Regiment Petersdorf (only the regimental HQ, Panzerjäger Kompanie, Füsilier Kompanie, Pionier Kompanie, Feldersatz Bataillon Raegener, Versorgungs Regiment Raegener*.

10. The Arab company was attached to *Fallschirmjäger-Regiment 25*, which was led by *Major* Schacht.

11. Anthony Beevor. *The Fall of Berlin 1945*. New York: Penguin Books Inc., 2002, p. 261.

12. Martin Bormann earned the nickname 'Brown Eminence' because of his powerful influence behind the scenes in the Nazi regime, operating as an almost invisible but highly effective manipulator. The term 'eminence' evokes the phrase *'éminence grise'* (literally 'gray eminence'), a title historically used to describe Cardinal Richelieu's adviser, Father Joseph, who exercised great power behind the throne. Bormann's influence was similarly covert and indirect, allowing him to control access to Hitler and shape major policy decisions without attracting much public attention. The 'brown' part of the nickname refers to the color of the Nazi Party uniform. Bormann, a fervent Nazi Party member, typically wore the brown party uniform and operated from within the party bureaucracy rather than the military. As head of the Nazi Party Chancellery and Hitler's private secretary, he became one of the most powerful men in Nazi Germany, leveraging his position to control Hitler's schedule, monitor communications, and isolate him from other officials. This control made Bormann an 'eminence' in his own right, as he influenced who could see Hitler and what information reached him, effectively making him one of the most feared figures within Hitler's inner circle.

13. During World War II, approximately seventeen million servicemen served in the ranks of the German Armed Forces, which included the *Wehrmacht* (the unified armed forces of Nazi Germany) and its branches: the *Heer* (Army), the *Kriegsmarine* (Navy), and the *Luftwaffe* (Air Force). This total includes soldiers, sailors, airmen, and other military personnel. These seventeen million men served in the following branches: *Heer:* thirteen million; *Luftwaffe:* three million; and *Kriegsmarine:* one million.

14. At the start of 1944, the *Ostheer* contained approximately 2,900,000 soldiers. Between 1 January and 31 December 1944, the German Army sent approximately 2,500,000 men as replacements and reinforcements to the Eastern Front. The loss of approximately 3,500,000 Germans killed, wounded, taken prisoner, or missing on the Russian Front during that same time period indicates that the year 1944 was the bloodiest for the *Ostheer*. It also implies that by the beginning of January 1945, the German Army in the East still possessed from 1,300,000 to 1,900,000 men. At the beginning of January 1945, the Red Army had approximately seven million soldiers actively engaged in combat against German forces on the Eastern Front. This figure represents the largest and most concentrated force of the war, reflecting the Soviet Union's strategic superiority at that stage. Therefore, as January 1945 began, the Red Army outnumbered the *Ostheer,* in terms of men, by a factor of more than three to one (best-case scenario), or five to one (worst-case scenario).

## APPENDIX I

1. I should place a disclaimer here about my choice of words. I am not in any way trying to paint the German Armed Forces of the Third Reich into a 'better' light, nor am I trying to glorify them in any way. But it is true that the Third Reich period is

replete with images and symbols that prove the Nazis knew how to garner attention. For example, has anyone ever wondered why the German uniforms of the period (both political and military) looked 'so cool'? Well, the answer is that the genius behind their style was none other than the famous fashion designer Hugo Boss!

2. *Jagdpanther Magazine* was first published in April 1973 by Stephen B. Cole, a Texas Tech University student in Amarillo, Texas. The magazine had been inspired by a tactical World War II game called *'Panzerblitz,'* published by the Avalon Hill Game Company (now defunct). The main box cover image of this game featured three *Jagdpanther* tank destroyers on the attack. *Jagdpanther Magazine* ran from 1973–1977. During that time, it won a wargaming magazine award for 'best amateur magazine' (Charles S. Roberts award).

## APPENDIX II

1. The figures come principally from the following works:

Rüdiger Overmans. *Deutsche militärische Verluste im Zweiten Weltkrieg*. München: R. Oldenbourg Verlag, 1999.

Burkhart Müller-Hillebrand. *Das Heer 1933–1945: Entwicklung des organisatorischen Aufbaues*. Darmstadt: Mittler & Sohn, 1969. Three volumes.

Wolfgang Benz and Angelika Schardt. *Deutsche Kriegsgefangene im Zweiten Weltkrieg: Erinnerungen*. Frankfurt am Main: Fisacher Taschenbuch. 1995.

## APPENDIX III

1. *Division No. 471* (*Generalleutnant* Erich Denecke, 28 September 1942–23 January 1945. In February *Generalleutnant* Ernst Häckel assumed command). *Divisionsgruppe Deneke* was created from *Division No. 471*.

## APPENDIX V

1. BA MA RH 39/14 H 31-0/14 *Panzer Abteilung 303*.

2. *18. Panzergrenadier-Division* was re-formed in April 1945 after being smashed in the Heiligenbeil Pocket in March 1945. It was re-formed using principally *Panzer-Division 'Schlesien'* and some elements from *Panzer-Division 'Holstein'*. Both of these panzer divisions had seen action under *Heeresgruppe Vistula* and had been smashed in March 1945. In early March 1945, *Panzer-Division 'Schlesien'* was organized as follows:

*Panzer-Division 'Schlesien'* (existed from 1 February–26 March 1945)

*Panzer-Division 'Schlesien'* (Oberst Ernst Wellmann, February–May 1945)

(*Panzer-Division 'Schlesien'* was originally supposed to be named *Panzer-Division Döberitz*, given that it was created at *Truppenübungsplatz Döberitz* in February 1945. However, the name 'Schlesien' was kept).

*Panzer Abteilung 'Schlesien'* (ex-Panzer Abteilung 303) 21x Panzer IV tanks then in March 1945: 10x more Panzer IV tanks and 10x Jagdpanzer IV L-70 tank destroyers.

*Panzergrenadier-Regiment 'Schlesien 1* (ex-Panzer Gren. Regt. 100)

*I. Bataillon (1.-4. Kompanien)*

(The *1.-3. Kompanien* were equipped with 52x *SdKfz. 251* halftracks and 6x Sd.Kfz.251/22 halftracks carrying the 75 mm Pak-40 L/46 anti-tank gun. The *4. Kompanie* was equipped with *Opel 'Blitz'* trucks.)

*II. Bataillon (5.-8. Kompanien)* Equipped with trucks.

*Panzergrenadier-Regiment 'Schlesien 2'*

*I. Bataillon (1.-5. Kompanien)* created 4 March 1945

*II. Bataillon (1.-3. Kompanien)* created 11 March ex-I. Bataillon,

*Panzergrenadier-Regiment 'Jüterbog 2'*

*Panzer-Artillerie-Regiment 'Schlesien'*

*I. Panzer Artillerie Abteilung 'Schlesien'* (established 20 February, ex-*Heeres Artillerie Abteilung I./106*—Hummel & Wespe vehicles).

*1. Artillerie Batterie*

*2. Artillerie Batterie*

*3. Artillerie Batterie*

*II. Artillerie Bataillon* (ex-*Luftwaffe schwer Flak-Abteilung 420*)

Assigned to the division by the *Luftwaffe* on 8 March 1945.

(1.–3. Artillerie-Batterien) - 1 light & 2 heavy batteries

*Panzer Aufklärungs Kompanie 'Schlesien'*

*Panzerjäger-Abteilung 'Schlesien'*

*1. Panzerjäger Kompanie* (10x *Jagdpanzer 38t 'Hetzer'* tank destroyers)

*2. Panzerjäger Kompanie* (forming)

*3. Panzerjäger Kompanie* (forming)

Supposedly, both the 2. and 3. *Panzerjäger* companies together had 21x *Jagdpanzer 38t 'Hetzer'* tank destroyers. Both companies were said to be forming in the rear.

*Panzer Pionier Abteilung 'Schlesien'* (may not have existed only on paper)

*Panzer Nachrichten Kompanie 'Schlesien'*

*Divisions Begleit Kompanie 'Schlesien'*

*Panzer Versorgungstruppen*

3. *Major* Blancbois was appointed to this command on 9 March 1945.

4. This battalion was lost in East Prussia in April 1945. Later that same month, another *Panzer AOK 3 Sturm Bataillon* was reorganized in Schwerin in Mecklenburg, in *Wehrkreis II*.

5. BA-MA RH 19 XV/19 K-46, *Kriegsgliederung Heeresgruppe Weichsel*.

6. Some sources say that on 20 April 1945 Degrelle was promoted to *SS-Standartenführer der Reserve*.

7. The city is now on Polish territory and is called Świnoujście.

8. Although *Division Nr. 402* was destroyed in Pomerania in March 1945, while serving under *X. SS-Armeekorps*, another *Division Nr. 402*, listed as a training division, was created in the second half of March 1045. This training division existed until the end of the war. The original *Division Nr. 402* (destroyed in Pomerania in March) was organized as follows: *Division Nr. 402* (**Generalleutnant** Siegmund Freiherr von Schle-

initz), *Grenadier-Ersatz-Regiment 258*, *Grenadier-Ersatz-Regiment 522*, *Artillerie-Ersatz und Ausbildungs-Regiment 2*, *Aufklärungs-Ersatz-Abteilung 5*, *Heeres-Flakartillerie-Ersatz und Ausbildungs-Abteilung 272*, *Kavallerie-Ausbildungs-Abteilung 100*, *Pionier-Ersatz und Ausbildungs-Bataillon 2*, *Pionier-Ersatz-Bataillon 12*, *Bau-Pionier-Ersatz und Ausbildungs-Bataillon 2*, *Fahr-Ersatz und Ausbildungs-Abteilung 2*, *Kraftfahr-Ersatz-Abteilung 2*. Only *Kavallerie-Ausbildungs-Abteilung 100* and *Grenadier-Ersatz-Regiment 522* survived the battles in Pomerania and were later incorporated into *Ausbildungs Division 402*.

9. BA MA, N 756/328a, p. 26.
10. Ibid.
11. *Divisionsgruppe Ledebur/Gruppe Voigt* was attached to the following higher commands between February and April 1945: 2 February—*II. Armeekorps/11. SS Panzerarmee*; 7–22 February—*III. SS-Panzerkorps/11. SS Panzerarmee*; 27 February–1 March *III. SS-Panzerkorps/3. Panzerarmee*; 28 March–3 April—directly under *3. Panzerarmee*; 9–12 April—*XXXII Armeekorps/3. Panzerarmee*.
12. Ibid.
13. Jank was promoted to *Generalmajor* in October 1944 and was promoted to *Generalleutnant* on 20 April 1945.
14. The *281. Infanterie-Division* had been established with the remnants of the *281. Sicherungs-Division* and some replacements reinforcements.
15. Tessin, op. cit., Vol. 14, p. 225.
16. BA MA, N 756/328a, - 'Heeresgruppe Weichsel' g. Kdo. Ia/Id Nr. 5420
17. *SS-Obergruppenführer und General der Polizei und Waffen-SS Erich von dem Bach-Zelewski* was commander of *X. SS-Armeekorps* in Pomerania from 26 January and 10 February 1945. By then the corps had all been wiped out. Afterward, he was reassigned as commander of *Korps Oder*.
18. Günther Ballentin. *Die Zerstörung der Stadt Schwedt/Oder 1945*. Eigenverlag, 1990, pp. 177-180.
19. *Panzer Ausbildungs Verband 'Ostsee'* was established on 28 March 1945 from various training and replacement units which were mobilized for frontline combat.
20. Karl-Heinz Münch. *StuG Abt./Brig. 210*. Łódź: Model Hobby, 2007, p. 301.
21. Bleckwenn, who prior to being appointed commander of the *1. Marine Infanterie-Division*, had been the commander of the *708. Volksgrenadier-Division*, was taken prisoner by the British on 4 May 1945.
22. The strength of this SS battle group was as follows (includes officers, NCOs and enlisted men): *SS-Fallschirmjäger-Bataillon 600* (689), *SS-Jagdverbände Mitte* (680), *SS-Einheit Schwedt* (208), *SS-Jagdverbände Nachrichten Kompanie* (164), *SS-Jagdverbände Scharfschützen Zug* (44), *SS-Jagdverbände schwer Granat Kompanie* (153). Total strength of *SS-Kampfgruppe Solar*: 1,938 officers, NCOs and enlisted men.
23. In March 1945 Adolf Hitler appointed *SS-Obergruppenführer und General der Waffen-SS* Felix Steiner, who had been commander of *III. (germanisches) SS-Panzerkorps*, to lead a soon-to-be-created army group, *Armeegruppe Steiner*. This command only existed in Hitler's mind, but nevertheless, Steiner stepped down from command of the *III. (germanisches) SS-Panzerkorps* and supposedly went about organizing this phantom army group. The headquarters command of *III. (germanisches) SS-Panzerkorps* was to be used to create this phantom army group, but nothing came of this. When

Hitler called on Steiner's imaginary army group to attack south from the Spree River and support Berlin, obviously no forces were available because this army group did not exist. On 27 April, Hitler relieved Steiner of this phantom command, for disobeying the order to relieve encircled Berlin.

24. This division was created on 11 April 1945 from the remnants of *Division z.b.V. 606* and the *541. Volksgrenadier-Division.*

25. Blaurock replaced *Generalleutnant* Friedrich Sixt, because Sixt was promoted to the post of commander of *CI Armeekorps.*

26. The *I. Artillerie Bataillon* of this regiment was disbanded on 25 March 1945. The *IV. Artillerie Bataillon* (containing the *7.* and *8. Artillerie Batterie*) were located in Bohemia (Czech). No *III. Artillerie Bataillon* existed.

27. This tank destroyer battalion was created using the *Sturmgeschütz III-G* assault guns that survived from what remained of *Sturmgeschütz Lehr Brigade 920.* This brigade was almost completely destroyed by the Russian January 1945 winter offensive just south of Warsaw.

28. About 8.000 men. Armored complement on 15 April 1945: 15x *Panzer IV* tanks +15x *Jagdpanzer IV L-70* tank destroyers.

29. *General der Fallschirmtruppe* Bruno Bräuer was the first commander of *9. Fallschirmjäger-Division.* His division began to fall apart beginning on 17 April, a day after the Red Army offensive against Berlin began. More and more reports kept coming in about more of his men deserting their posts. This apparently caused the paratrooper general to have a nervous breakdown and he eventually had to be relieved of his command. His 'Ia', *Oberst* Harry Herrmann, then assumed command of the division.

30. *Grenadier-Regiment 1235* was formed on 6 February 1945 in *Wehrkreis IV.* It was partly created from the *I Fahnenjunker-Schule I (Dresden)* (Officer Candidate School I in Dresden) for employment near Küstrin. Its strength was around 1,600 men and consisted of 25% officer candidates (400 men), 25% army replacements (400 men) and 50% *Volkssturm* (800 men). The regiment was eventually attached to Panzergrenadier-Division Kurmark.

31. The *3. Panzer Kompanie* was created from *Panzer-Bataillon-Kummersdorf*, which existed briefly. This tank battalion began on 25 February 1945 with the following AFVs: four Tiger-II tanks, one Tiger-I tank, and one Jagdtiger tank destroyer. Later, five additional Tiger-I tanks were added to the battalion from repair units. On 15 April, a day before the start of the Red Army offensive, ten out of the thirteen AFVs of *3. Kompanie* were ready, while three were being repaired.

32. This division was currently forming from the remnants of the old *286. Sicherungs-Division.*

33. This tank destroyer brigade was composed of 4,200 troops, mostly 14–17-year-old Hitler Youth members. The company and battalion commanders were either *Wehrmacht* or *Luftwaffe* officers, while the platoons were led by veteran *Wehrmacht* NCOs. By 12 April the brigade had been split up. About 2,000 of them remained under the *V. SS-Freiwilligen-Gebirgs-Armeekorps* rear area, around Beeskow, Storkow and Strausberg. Around 900 were transferred to Gotha to fight against the advancing U.S. Army, while 1,500 were placed under the control of the Berlin garrison commander. These 1,500 took part in the Battle for Berlin.

34. Tank Destroyer Troop of *Police Regiment Hartmann*. The company only contained three platoons of *Panzerschreck* (bazookas) with 18 *Panzerschrecks* per platoon. The company also had 18 Panzerschrecks as a reserve.

35. *Division Raegener* absorbed the remnants of *Division Nr. 463* and *Division Nr. 433*.

36. *Polizei Schützen Regiment 34* was disbanded on 5 February 1945. Its surviving police battalion, *I. Polizei Bataillon,* was sent to serve as the first battalion of *Grenadier-Regiment Becker* under *Divisionsgruppe Raegener*.

37. BA MA N-543/264, *Die letzte Schlacht der 9. Armee—Zur Gliederung der Artillerie des A.O.K. 9, 78/45 g.Kdos. Stand 24.2.1945, Ia Tgb.Nr. 2000/45 g.Kdos v. 25.2.1945.*

# UNIT INDEX

*Luftwaffe* (Air Force):
*Luftflotte 4*, 62
*Luftflotte 5*, 55
*Luftgaukommando VIII*, 240n8
*Fallschirm Panzerkorps Hermann Göring*, 157
*III. Luftwaffen-Feldkorps*, 29
*I. Flak-Korps*, 102
*Fallschirm-Panzergrenadier-Division 2 'Hermann Göring'*, 157
*6. Flak-Division*, 49
*11. Flak-Division*, 134, 240n8
*14. Flak-Division*, 134
*20. Flak-Division*, 71
*6. Flak Brigade*, 207
*15. Flak Brigade*, 240n8
*Flak Regiment 3*, 207
*Flak Regiment 121*, 207
*Flak Regiment 7*, 207
*Flak Regiment 184*, 207
*Flak-Regiment 150*, 134, 240n8
*Fliegerregiment 53*, 171
*Flak-Abteilung 420*, 245n2
*Luftnachrichten-Abteilung 166*, 207
*Flak-Ausbildungs-Bataillon 22*, 207
*schwere Flak-Abteilung 656*, 217

Special Army Commands:
*Oberbefehlshaber Südost*, 71
*Befehlshaber Serbien*, 71
*Befehlshaber Saloniki-Ägäis*, 71
*Befehlshaber Süd-Griechenland*, 71
*Befehlshaber Kroatien*, 71
*Kommandant der Festung Kreta*, 71

*Heer* (Army):
*Heeresgruppen* (Army Groups):
*Heeresgruppe A* (Army Group 'A'), 18, 59, 77, 141, 152, 154-155, 241n1
*Heeresgruppe B* (Army Group 'B'), 14
*Heeresgruppe 'E'* (Army Group 'B'), 69-70, 74, 92, 152
*Heeresgruppe 'F'* (Army Group 'F'), 68, 69F32, 99, 152
*Heeresgruppe Nord* (Army Group North), xi, 36-37, 41, 44, *45*F19, *48*F23, 49, 64, 106-108, *113*F51, 116, *117*F52, 128, 141, 144, 151-152, 197-198
*Heeresgruppe Kurland* (Army Group Courland), x, 112, *118*F53, 121, *122*F54, 123, *124*F55, 125, 128, 141, 152
*Heeresgruppe Mitte* (Army Group Center), 2-4, 6, 15, 44, 49, 63, 65, 81, 87, 141, 143, 152, 154-156, 197-198, 231n4, 231n10, 241n1
*Heeresgruppe Moldau* (Army Group Moldova), 59, 62

249

## Unit Index

*Heeresgruppe Östmark,* 99-100, 237n2
*Heeresgruppe Süd* (Army Group South), 18, 26, 86, *89*F38, *89*F39, 94, 96, 99, 111, 152, 197-198
*Heeresgruppe Nordukraine* (Army Group North Ukraine), 17-18, 22-23, 26, 77, 231n4
*Heeresgruppe Südukraine* (Army Group South Ukraine), 26, 59, *61*F28, *61*F29, 62, 64, 66
*Heeresgruppe Weichsel* (Army Group Vistula), 125, 139, 141, 155, 158, 160, 166-167, *173*F79, 174, 201, 205, 208, 242n2
*Armeegruppe Raus,* 18
*Armeegruppe Heinrici,* 18, 77, 241n1
*Armee-Abteilung Narwa* (Army Detachment Narva), *42*F18, 43-44, *113*F51
*Armee-Abteilung Grasser,* 44 (See: *Armee-Abteilung Narwa*)
*Gruppe Dumitrescu,* 59, 62, 65
*Gruppe Generalmajor Gothsche,* 45
*Gruppe Herzog* (see: *Gruppe Friessner*), 45

Rear Area Commands:
*Wehrkreis I* (1st Military District), 236n4
*Wehrkreis II* (4th Military District, See: *II. Armeekorps*), 161, 163, 200
*Wehrkreis IV* (4th Military District), 134, 247n30
*Kommandeur des Gebiets des Militärbefehlshabers in Serbien,* 71
*Wehrmachtbefehlshaber Mazedonien,* 71
*Wehrmacht Befehlshaber Weissruthenien,* 6
*Wehrkreis I* (Military District No. I), 13
*Korück 531 - Kommandant des rückwärtigen Armeegebiets 531* (Commander of Rear Army Area 531), 26
*Feldkommandantur 599,* 71
*Feldkommandantur 809,* 71

Armies:
1. *Panzerarmee,* 17-19, 23, 77, 80, 82, 84, 152
2. *Panzerarmee,* 70, 91-92, 152
2. *Armee,* 7, 14, *140*F61, 141, 152, *153*F69, 153, 156, 158
*Gruppe von Saucken* (See: 2. *Armee*), 14
3. *Panzerarmee,* 6, 12, 49, *103*F46, 107, *142*F62, 144, 152-153, *154*F70, 156, 158, 167, 170, 174, 200, 202, 206, 231n10, 242n10, 246n11
4. *Armee,* 2, 6, 12, 14, 111, 141, *142*F62, 143, 152-153, *154*F70, 156
4. *Panzerarmee,* 17-18, 22-23, 77, *101*F45, *103*F46, 141, *149*F65, 152, 174, 177, 241n1
6. *Armee,* 59, *60*F26, 64-66, *90*F40, 91, 99, 129, 152, 237n2
6. *Panzerarmee,* 91, 94, 99, 109, *110*F49, 111, 237n2
8. *Armee,* 18, 59, 64-66, 82-84, 95, *96*F43, 99, 152, 237n2
9. *Armee,* 6, 12, 14, 77, *103*F46, *149*F65, *151*F68, 152, 155, 158, *169*F67, 174, 176-179, 201, 203, 212, 241n1
12. *Armee,* 177-179
16. *Armee,* 37, *46*F20, 47, 49, 107, 126, 128, 151, 239n11
17. *Armee,* 59, 77, 84, 152-153, 200, 237n1, 241n1
18. *Armee,* 29-31, *30*n4, *38*f16, 39-41, 44, 49, 107, 120, 151, 239n11
19. *Armee,* 239n1
20. *Gebirgsarmee,* 50, 53-55, 58, 234n5
25. *Armee,* *113*F51

Corps:
*Oder Armeekorps,* 201, 209, 246n17
*Korps Gruppe Munzel,* 199
*Generalkommando Tettau* (See: *Tettau Armeekorps*), 158, 160, 202
*Tettau Armeekorps,* 199, 241n10, 242n10
*Korps Gruppe Kleffel* (See: *Armee-Abteilung Narwa*), *113*F51
*Panzerkorps 'Feldherrnhalle'* (See: *IV. Panzerkorps*), 95
*I. Kavallerie-Korps,* 91

Unit Index 251

I. Armeekorps, 36, 114
II. Armeekorps (See: Wehrkreis II), 120, 158, 200, 202, 246n11
III. Panzerkorps, 19, 24, 80, 87, 92
IV. Panzerkorps (See: Panzerkorps 'Feldherrnhalle'), 95
VI. Armeekorps, 6, 11, 141, 156
VII. Armeekorps, 66
VIII. Armeekorps, 7
IX. Armeekorps, 7, 10, 141
X. Armeekorps, 114-115
XI. Armeekorps, 18
XII. Armeekorps, 6, 12
XIII. Armeekorps, 19-22
XV. Gebirgs-Armeekorps, 70, 152
XVI. Armeekorps, 119
XVIII. Gebirgs-Armeekorps, 55
XIX. Gebirgs-Armeekorps, 53
XX. Armeekorps, 7, 156
XXI. Gebirgs-Armeekorps, 70, 152
XXII. Gebirgs-Armeekorps, 70, 92, 152
XXIII. Armeekorps, 7
XXIV. Panzerkorps, 19, 23, 26, 141, 148, 155
XXVI. Armeekorps, 43, 141, 231n10
XXVII. Armeekorps, 6
XXVIII. Armeekorps, 35-37, 39, 41, 108, 114, 144
XXXII. Armeekorps, 207, 246n11
XXIX. Armeekorps, 95
XXX. Armeekorps, 66
XXXIV. Armeekorps, 35, 152
XXXV Armeekorps, 6
XXXVI. Gebirgs-Armeekorps, 50, 54
XXXVIII. Armeekorps, 35-36, 45, 47-49, 115-116, 233n52
XXXIX. Panzerkorps, 6, 162-163, 200
XL Panzerkorps, 144
XLI. Panzerkorps, 156
XLIII. Armeekorps, 43-44
XLIV Armeekorps, 66
XLVI. Panzerkorps, 19, 211
XLVIII. Panzerkorps, 21, 45
XLI Panzerkorps, 6, 141
XLVIII. Panzerkorps, 19

L. Armeekorps, 31, 39
LII. Armeekorps, 66
LIII. Armeekorps, 7, 11
LV Armeekorps, 6
LVI. Panzerkorps, 167, 176-177, 180, 215
LVII. Panzerkorps, 65
LXVIII. Armeekorps, 70, 92, 152
LIX. Armeekorps, 19, 23-24, 70
LXVII Armeekorps, 241n5
LXXII. Armeekorps, 95
XCI. Armeekorps, 70, 92
CI. Armeekorps, 177, 201, 203, 212, 247n25
Korpsabteilung C, 19, 21-22, 231n12
Korpsabteilung D, 7, 10, 230n12, 230n13
Korpsabteilung E, 7, 229n9

Divisions:
Panzerjagd-Verband Weichsel, 206
Panzer-Division 'Döberitz', 242n2
Festungs-Division Swinemünde, 200, 206
Festungs-Division 'Breslau', 134
Festungs-Division Frankfurt an der Oder, 203, 216
Divisionsgruppe Deneke (See: 549. Volksgrenadier-Division), 200
Divisionsgruppe Klossek (See: Kampfgruppe Klossek), 163, 200-201, 210
Divisionsgruppe Kaiser, 95
Divisionsgruppe Ledebur, 208
Division Schwedt, 171, 172F78
Divisionsstab Raegener (See: Divisionsgruppe Raegener,), 177
Divisionsgruppe Raegener (See: Division Raegener), 203
Division Raegener, 215, 218, 242n9, 248n35, 248n36
Division Bärwalde (See: Ersatz und Ausbildungs Division 'Bärwald'), 199
Ersatz und Ausbildungs Division 'Bärwald', 202
Feldausbildungs-Division 'Kurland' (ex-Feldausbildungs-Division Nord), 126

## Unit Index

Infanterie-Division Köslin (See: Grenadier Division Pommerland), 160, 199
Grenadier Division Pommerland (See: Infanterie-Division Köslin), 199, 202
Ersatz und Ausbildungs Division 'Pommern', 202
Division Märkisch Friedland, 160
Divisionsgruppe Voigt (see Divisionsgruppe Ledebur), 162-163, 200, 202, 246n11
Divisionsgruppe Ledebur, 200, 246n11
Infanterie-Division Deneke, 166-167
Divisionsgruppe Kräutler (see: Divisions Stab z.b.V. 140), 54
Divisionsgruppe van der Hoop (see: Divisions Stab z.b.V. 613), 53-54, 57
Panzergrenadier-Division 'Großdeutschland', 137, 144, 157
Panzergrenadier-Division Feldherrnhalle (See: 60. Panzergrenadier-Division), 6, 43-44, 81, 229n6
Panzer-Division 'Feldherrnhalle 1' (See: Panzergrenadier-Division Feldherrnhalle), 98
Panzergrenadier-Division 'Gross Deutschland', 108, 144
Panzer-Division 'Holstein', 162, 202, 242n2
Panzer-Division Müncheberg, 180, 203, 215
Panzer-Division 'Schlesien', 201, 203, 242n2
Panzergrenadier-Division Kurmark, 201, 203, 214, 247n30
Führer-Grenadier-Division, 162, 199
Führer-Begleit-Division, 162, 199
1. Marine-Division, 201, 211-212, 246n21
1. Volksgrenadier-Division, 92
1. Infanterie-Division, 19
1. Luftwaffen-Feld-Division / 1. Feld-Division (L), 33, 34n15, 35, 232n7
1. Panzer-Division, 19, 21-22, 77, 80-81, 83, 92, 231n5
1. Gebirgs-Division, 71-72
2. Gebirgs-Division, 53, 58
3. Gebirgs-Division, 82-83
3. Panzer-Division, 24, 92
3. Kavallerie-Division, 91
3. Marine Division, 161, 207
4. Kavallerie-Division, 91
4. Luftwaffen-Feld-Division / 4. Feld-Division (L), 7
4. Panzer-Division, 14, 112, 115, 117-119, 125, 140
5. Panzer-Division, 14, 144
5. Jäger-Division, 7, 166, 200, 202, 213
6. Gebirgs-Division, 53-54
6. Infanterie-Division, 6
6. Luftwaffen-Feld-Division / 6. Feld-Division (L), 7
7. Gebirgs-Division, 54
7. Infanterie-Division, 7
7. Panzer-Division, 21f12, 108, 140, 144
8. Panzer-Division, 19, 21-22, 231n5
8. Jäger-Division, 39, 45, 95
9. Luftwaffen-Feld-Division / 9 Feld-Division (L), 28-31, 30n4, 32n13
9. Fallschirmjäger-Division, 166-167, 173, 180, 200, 202, 210, 214, 247n29
10. Panzergrenadier-Division, 64-65
10. Luftwaffen-Feld-Division / 10 Feld-Division (L), 28, 31, 30n4, 32
11. Infanterie-Division, 41, 43-44, 49, 117, 121-123
10. Luftwaffen-Feld-Division / 11. Feld-Division (L), 71, 92
11. Panzer-Division, 98
12. Infanterie-Division, 6
12. Panzer-Division, 14, 113-115, 117, 119-120, 122-123, 126
12. Luftwaffen-Feld-Division / 12. Feld-Division (L), 35-37, 39-41, 45, 119, 126
13. Luftwaffen-Feld-Division / 13. Feld-Division (L), 35-37, 40
13. Panzer-Division, 64-66, 85
14. Infanterie-Division (mot.), 6, 11, 143, 156
14. Panzer-Division, 115, 120-123, 126, 237n1

15. Infanterie-Division, 66, 83, 95
16. Panzer-Division, 20, 22-24, 98, 148, 231n5
17. Panzer-Division, 20, 148, 231n5
17. Flak-Division, 95
18. Panzergrenadier-Division, 6, 12-14, 140, 177, 180, 205, 242n12, 244n2
20. Infanterie-Division (motorisiert), 19, 22, 24
20. Panzergrenadier-Division, 170, 177, 180, 214
21. Panzer-Division, 212
21. Infanterie-Division, 35-36, 40-41, 143, 156
21. Luftwaffen-Feld-Division / 21. Feld-Division (L), 45, 47-49, 48n54, 113-114, 233n52
22. Luftlande-Infanterie-Division, 71
23. Infanterie-Division, 41, 131
23. Panzer-Division, 80-81, 83, 91
24. Infanterie-Division, 41, 114, 120-121, 123
24. Panzer Division, 81, 156
25. Panzergrenadier-Division, 6, 170, 201, 203, 215
26. Volksgrenadier-Division, 241n5
28. Jäger-Division, 14, 33, 35, 143, 156
29. Infanterie-Division, 123
30. Infanterie-Division, 41, 49, 115, 120, 123
31. Infanterie-Division, 6, 143
31. Volksgrenadier-Division, 126
32. Infanterie-Division, 40-41, 47-49, 115-116, 125, 140, 233n52
35. Infanterie-Division, 6
36. Infanterie-Division (motorisiert), 6
41. Festungs-Division, 70
44. Reichsgrenadier-Division 'Hoch und Deutschmeister', 91, 95
45. Infanterie-Division, 6
46. Volksgrenadier Division, 95
50. Infanterie-Division, 143, 157
52. Sicherungs-Division, 14, 233n52
56. Infanterie Division, 7, 157, 230n12
57. Infanterie-Division, 6

58. Infanterie-Division, 36, 43, 108, 144
60. Panzergrenadier-Division (See: Panzer-Division Feldhermhalle), 81, 229n6
61. Infanterie Division, 43-44, 112
61. Volksgrenadier-Division, 156
68. Infanterie-Division, 18, 26, 150
71. Infanterie-Division, 92
75. Infanterie-Division, 19, 77
76. Infanterie-Division, 81, 95
78. Sturm-Division, 6
81. Infanterie-Division, 41, 113, 123, 233n52
83. Infanterie-Division, 41, 47, 113, 140
87. Infanterie-Division, 41, 120-121
93. Infanterie-Division, 41, 114, 119, 126
95. Infanterie Division, 6, 11, 108, 144
96. Infanterie-Division, 19, 26, 91
101. Jäger-Division, 18, 95
102. Infanterie-Division, 6, 143, 156
104. Jäger-Division, 70, 92
106. Infanterie-Division, 66
110. Infanterie-Division, 6
117. Jäger-Division, 70
118. Jäger-Division, 70, 92
121. Infanterie-Division, 41, 48n54, 114, 120-121, 123, 233n52
122. Infanterie-Division, 53, 114, 122-123, 233n52
126. Infanterie-Division, 31-32, 32n13, 39, 41, 45, 120, 123
129. Infanterie-Division, 6
131. Infanterie-Division, 143, 156
132. Infanterie-Division, 41, 116-117, 121, 123
133. Festungs-Division, 71
134. Infanterie-Division, 6
137. Infanterie-Division, 229n9
Divisions Stab z.b.V. 140, 54, 234n6
153. Feldausbildungs-Division, 65
161. Infanterie-Division, 66
163. Infanterie-Division, 54, 57, 161-163, 199, 202
168. Infanterie-Division, 18, 22, 150
169. Infanterie-Division, 54, 213
170. Infanterie-Division, 14, 43, 143, 156

170. Volksgrenadier-Division, 143
181. Infanterie-Division, 70
183. Infanterie-Division, 21, 231n12
Division Nr. 192, 208
197. Infanterie-Division, 6
201. Sicherungs-Division, 6, 14, 233n52
203. Sicherungs-Division, 7
203. Infanterie-Division, 140
205. Infanterie-Division, 116, 119, 123
206. Infanterie Division, 7, 11
207. Sicherungs-Division, 47
208. Infanterie-Division, 19, 26
210. Infanterie-Division, 53
211. Infanterie-Division, 7
211. Volksgrenadier-Division, 95
212. Infanterie-Division, 39, 45
214. Infanterie-Division, 43
215. Infanterie-Division, 39, 41, 113, 116, 119-120, 125
217. Infanterie-Division, 21-22, 231n12
218. Infanterie-Division, 41, 122-123
221. Sicherungs-Division, 6
225. Infanterie Division, 41, 43, 49, 116-117, 121, 123
227. Infanterie-Division, 44, 49, 117, 126, 210
246. Infanterie-Division, 7
251. Infanterie-Division, 229n9
252. Infanterie Division, 7
254. Infanterie-Division, 19, 77
256. Infanterie-Division, 6
257. Infanterie-Division, 66
258. Infanterie-Division, 66
260. Infanterie-Division, 6
261. Infanterie-Division, 202
262. Infanterie-Division, 7, 230n12
263. Infanterie-Division, 41, 120, 123, 161
264. Infanterie-Division, 70
267. Infanterie-Division, 6
269. Infanterie-Division, 133-134, 240n3
271. Volksgrenadier-Division, 85, 95, 237n1
281. Sicherungs Division, 41, 119, 162, 208, 246n14
281. Infanterie-Division, 200, 246n14

282. Infanterie-Division, 66
285. Sicherungs-Division, 115
286. Sicherungs-Division, 6, 143
286. Infanterie-Division, 143, 215
290. Infanterie-Division, 41, 123, 125, 161, 232n19
292. Infanterie-Division, 6, 156
294. Infanterie-Division, 66
296. Infanterie-Division, 6
297. Infanterie-Division, 70, 92
299. Infanterie-Division, 6
Division z.b.V. 300, 40-41
302. Infanterie-Division, 66
303. Infanterie-Division 'Doberitz', 177, 201, 203, 213
306. Infanterie-Division, 66
309. Infanterie-Division 'Berlin', 177, 201, 212, 303
320. Infanterie-Division, 66
329. Infanterie-Division, 41, 113, 116-117, 233n52
335. Infanterie-Division, 66
337. Infanterie-Division, 6
339. Infanterie-Division, 21, 231n12
340. Infanterie-Division, 19
349. Infanterie-Division, 19, 21-22, 143
349. Volksgrenadier-Division, 156
356. Infanterie-Division, 92
357. Infanterie-Division, 76-77, 95
359. Infanterie-Division, 19, 237n1
361. Infanterie-Division, 19, 21
369. Infanterie-Division (kroatische Nr. 1), 70
370. Infanterie-Division, 66
371. Infanterie-Division, 19, 136, 237n1
373. Infanterie-Division (kroatische Nr. 2), 70
383. Infanterie-Division, 6
384. Infanterie-Division, 66
389. Infanterie-Division, 41, 114-115, 126
390. Feldausbildungs-Division, 6
391. Sicherungs-Division (see: Divisionsstab z.b.V. 391), 6
Divisionsstab z.b.V. 391 (see: 391. Infanterie-Division), 177, 200

*391. Infanterie-Division*, 203, 217
*392. Infanterie-Division (kroatische Nr. 3)*, 70
*Division-Stab 402* (see: *Division Nr. 402 z.b.V.*), 158-159, 163
*Division Nr. 402 z.b.V.*, 163, 200, 202, 241n8, 245n8
*Ausbildungs Division 402* (see: *Division Nr. 402*), 200, 207, 246n8
*454. Sicherungs-Division*, 19
*Division Nr. 471* (see: *Infanterie-Division Deneke*), 167, 244n2
*541. Volksgrenadier-Division*, 247n24
*542. Volksgrenadier-Division*, 140
*544. Volksgrenadier-Division*, 237n1
*545. Volksgrenadier-Division*, 237n1
*547. Volksgrenadier-Division*, 156, 173, 210-211
*548. Volksgrenadier-Division*, 144
*549. Volksgrenadier-Division* (see: *Divisionsgruppe Deneke*), 167, 200, 202, 208
*551. Volksgrenadier-Division*, 108, 144
*558. Volksgrenadier-Division*, 143
*561. Volksgrenadier-Division*, 143
*562. Volksgrenadier-Division*, 157
*563. Volksgrenadier-Division*, 123, 143, 161
*Division z.b.V. 604*, 241n10
*Divisionsstab z.b.V. 605*, 156
*Divisionsstab z.b.V. 606* (see: *606. Infanterie-Division*), 177, 201, 203
*606. Infanterie-Division*, 212, 247n24
*Division z.b.V. 609*, 134
*Division Staff z.b.V. 610*, 201, 210
*Divisions Stab z.b.V. 613* (see: *Divisionsgruppe van der Hoop*), 53
*707. Infanterie-Division*, 6
*708. Volksgrenadier-Division*, 246n21
*711. Infanterie-Division*, 91
*712. Infanterie-Division*, 177, 201, 203, 213

Brigades:
*Festungs-Pak-Verband XXVI*, 217

*1. Panzervernichtungsbrigade 'Hitlerjugend'*, 216
*Panzer Jagd Brigade D*, 206
*Panzer-Jagd-Brigade F*, 206
*Panzer-Jagd-Brigade R*, 206
*Panzer-Jagd-Brigade P*, 206
*Panzer-Jagd-Brigade 104*, 162
*Festungs-Pak-Verband VIII*, 209
*3. Kavallerie-Brigade*, 7, 230n10
*4. Kavallerie-Brigade*, 7, 229n8
*Gebirgs-Brigade 139*, 54
*Grenadier-Brigade 193* (ex-*Grenadier-Regiment 193*), 53
*Grenadier-Brigade 503*, 53
*Festungsbrigade 1017*, 70
*Festungs Brigade 968*, 70
*Festungsbrigade 966*, 70
*Brigade Stab z.b.V. 17*, 7
*Panzer-Brigade 105*, 13-14
*Panzer-Brigade 'Kurland'*, 121, 126, 127F56, 128
*Heeres-Sturmartillerie-Brigade 191*, 71
*Sturmgeschütz-Brigade 210* (see: *Heeres-Sturmartillerie-Brigade 210*), 173, 211
*Heeres Sturmartillerie Brigade 210*, 211
*Sturmgeschütz Brigade 228*, 64-65
*Sturmgeschütz Brigade 236*, 65
*Heeres-Sturmartillerie-Brigade 236*, 65
*Sturmgeschütz-Brigade 278*, 65
*Heeres-Sturmgeschütz-Brigade 286*, 65
*Sturmgeschütz-Brigade 303*, 53
*Sturmgeschütz-Brigade 912* (see: *Heeres-Sturmartillerie-Brigade 912*), 117, 120-121
*Heeres-Sturmartillerie-Brigade 912*, 121
*Sturmgeschütz Lehr Brigade 920*, 247n27
*Artillerie-Brigade 418*, 209
*Volksartilleriekorps 406 (motorisiert)*, 209
*404. Volks-Artillerie-Korps*, 212
*406. Volks-Artillerie-Korps*, 212
*408. Volks-Artillerie-Korps*, 212

Regiments:
Infantry Regiments (all types):
*Grenadier-Regiment 67*, 131

256  Unit Index

Grenadier-Regiment 193 (See: Grenadier-Brigade 193), 53
Grenadier Regiment 374, 41
Grenadier-Regiment 424, 32
Grenadier-Regiment 503, 33, 232n19
Grenadier-Regiment 652, 212
Grenadier-Regiment 653, 212
Grenadier-Regiment 732, 213
Grenadier-Regiment 745, 213
Grenadier-Regiment 764, 213
Grenadier-Regiment 1092, 211
Grenadier-Regiment 1097, 208
Grenadier-Regiment 1098, 208
Grenadier-Regiment 1099, 208
Grenadier-Regiment 1235, 247n30
Wach-Regiment 'Gross Deutschland', 212
3. Marine-Flak-Regiment, 206
Fallschirmjäger-Regiment 15, 241n5
Fallschirmjäger-Regiment 25, 214, 243n10
Fallschirmjäger-Regiment 26, 173, 214
Fallschirmjäger-Regiment 27, 214
Fallschirmjäger-Flak-Regiment 9, 214
Organization-Todt-Regiment 122, 173
Volksgrenadier-Regiment 1091, 173
Gnesen (Genesenden) Grenadier-Regiment, 43
Gneisenau-Regiment 1, 158–159
Fahnenjunker-Grenadier-Regiment 'Kurland', 126
Grenadier Regiment Fischer, 242n9
Regiment Kammler, 208
Marine Grenadier-Regiment 8, 207
Marine Grenadier-Regiment 9, 207
Marine Grenadier-Regiment 10, 207
Infanterie-Regiment 4, 115
Infanterie-Regiment 94, 116
Infanterie Regiment 96, 116
Infanterie-Regiment 378, 213
Infanterie-Regiment 379, 214
Infanterie Regiment 392, 214
Festungs-Alarm-Regiment 1, 206
Festungs-Alarm-Regiment 2, 206
Festungs-Alarm-Regiment 3, 206
Festungs-Alarm-Regiment 4, 206

Festungs-Alarm-Regiment 5 (see: Festungs Alarm Regiment Bahr), 206
Festungs Alarm Regiment Bahr (see: Festungs-Alarm-Regiment 5), 206
Festungs Regiment 1, 209
Festungs Regiment 2, 209
Festungs Regiment 3, 209
Festungs Regiment 4, 209
Festungs Regiment 5, 209
Festungs-Grenadier-Regiment 1, 216
Festungs-Grenadier-Regiment 2, 217
Festungs-Grenadier-Regiment 3, 217
Festungs-Grenadier-Regiment 4, 217
Bau-Pionier-Regiments-Stab 555, 209
Reserve-Jäger-Regiment 1, 70
1. Regiment Brandenburg (motorisiert), 70
2. Regiment Brandenburg (motorisiert), 70, 72
4. Regiment Brandenburg (motorisiert), 70–71
Jäger-Regiment 23 (L), 40
Jäger-Regiment 24 (L), 40
Jäger-Regiment 25 (L), 40
Jäger-Regiment 26 (L), 40
Jäger-Regiment 56, 213
Jäger-Regiment 75, 213
Pommern-Regiment 5, 208
Pommern-Regiment 6, 208
Festung Grenadier-Regiment Breslau, 134
Grenadier-Regiment 67, 131
Grenadier-Regiment 300, 213
Grenadier-Regiment 301, 213
Grenadier-Regiment 302, 213
Grenadier-Regiment 322, 208
Grenadier-Regiment 368, 208
Grenadier-Regiment 418, 208

Officer Candidate Regiments:
Fahnenjunker-Grenadier-Regiment 'Kurland', 126
Fahnenjunker-Grenadier-Regiment 'Kurland', 126
Fahnenjunker-Grenadier-Regiment 'Kurland', 126
Fahnenjunker-Regiment 1237, 218

Unit Index    257

Artillery Regiments:
Fallschirmjäger-Artillerie-Regiment 9, 214
Panzer-Artillerie-Regiment 'Kurmark', 214
Panzer-Artillerie-Regiment 'Schlesien', 245n2
Artillerie-Regiment Division 'Bärwalde', 199
Artillerie-Regiment Bärwalde, 160
Artillerie-Regiment 5, 213
Artillerie-Regiment 12 (L), 40
Artillerie-Regiment 15, 134
Artillerie Regiment 18 (from Panzer-Artillerie-Regiment 'Schlesien'), 205
Artillerie-Regiment 20
Artillerie-Regiment 230, 214
Artillerie Regiment 234, 207
Artillerie Regiment 281, 208
Artillerie-Regiment 303, 213
Artillerie-Regiment 309, 212
Artillerie-Regiment 606, 213
Artillerie-Regiments Stab z.b.V. 931, 54
Artillerie-Regiment 1547, 211
Artillerie Regiment 1549, 208
Artillerie-Regiment 1712, 213
Artillerie-Regiment 25 (motorisiert), 216
Festungs-Artillerie Regiment 3132, 209, 216

Alarm, Ad-hoc & Volkssturm Regiments:
Alarm-Regiment 'Sator', 212
Alarm-Regiment 'Rohde', 212
Regiment Kersten, 134
Regiment Schulz, 134
Regiment Seybold, 134
Regiment Krankewitz, 160
Regiment Jatzinhen, 160
Regiment Reinkober, 134
Regiment Frankenstein, 135
Infanterie-Regiment 'Mensing', 167
Regiment Karlowitz, 135
Regiment Krankewitz, 199
Regiment Jatzinhen, 199
Regiment R. V. Breslau: Genesenden Bataillon Fischer, Volkssturm Bataillon 55

Artillerie-Regiment Breslau, 135
Regiment-Bärwalde 1 (Regiment 1 Division 'Bärwalde'), 160, 199
Regiment-Bärwalde 2 (Regiment 2 Division 'Bärwalde'), 160, 199
Regiment-Bärwalde 3 (Regiment 3 Division 'Bärwalde'), 160, 199
Regiment-Bärwalde 4 (Regiment 4 Division 'Bärwalde'), 160, 199
Regiment-Bärwalde 5 (Regiment 5 Division 'Bärwalde'), 160, 199
Pommern-Regiment 4, 167
Grenadier-Regiment 'von Petersdorf', 218, 242n9
Grenadier-Regiment 'Mohr', 134
Regiment Breslau A: I. Bataillon, II. Bataillon, III. Bataillon, 135
Regiment Breslau J: Volkssturm Bataillon 25, Volkssturm Bataillon 27, Volkssturm Bataillon 28, 135
Volkssturm-Regiment 'Mentz', 159
Volkssturm-Regiment 'Bonin', 159
Volkssturm-Regiment 'Möring',159

Panzer & Panzergrenadier Regiments:
Panzer-Regiment 29, 126
Panzer-Regiment 'Kurmark', 214
Panzergrenadier-Regiment 'Schlesien 1, 205, 242n2
Panzergrenadier-Regiment 'Schlesien 2', 205, 245n2
Panzergrenadier-Regiment Kurmark, 214
Panzergrenadier-Regiment 'Jüterbog 2', 245n2
Panzergrenadier-Regiment 'Müncheberg 1', 215
Panzergrenadier-Regiment 'Müncheberg 2', 215
Panzergrenadier-Regiment 35, 216
Panzergrenadier-Regiment 119, 216
Grenadier Regiment 30 (mot.) [See: Panzergrenadier-Regiment 30], 14
Grenadier-Regiment 51 (mot.) [See: Panzergrenadier-Regiment 51], 14

*Panzergrenadier-Regiment 30* (See: *Panzergrenadier-Regiment 'Schlesien 1'*), 205
*Panzergrenadier-Regiment 51* (See: *Panzergrenadier-Regiment 'Schlesien 2'*), 205
*Panzergrenadier-Regiment 76*, 214
*Panzergrenadier-Regiment 90*, 214
*Grenadier-Regiment 92 (motorisiert)*, 71, 73

'Other' Types of Regiments:
*Kavallerie-Regiment Nord*, 33, 35
*Regiments Stab 293*, 208
*Nachrichten Regiment 530*, 99
*Divisions-Versorgungs-Regiment 281*, 208

Reserve & Replacement Regiments:
*Reserve Jäger-Regiment 1*, 70, 236n4
*Jäger-Ersatz und Ausbildungs-Regiment 1*, 236n4
*Festungs-Stamm-Artillerie-Regiment 3132*, 169
*Artillerie Ersatz und Ausbildungs Regiment 2*, 245n8
*Grenadier-Ersatz-Regiment 258*, 159, 245n8
*Grenadier-Ersatz-Regiment 522* (see: *Grenadier-Ausbildungs-Regiment 522*), 159, 245n8
*Grenadier-Ausbildungs-Regiment 522*, 207
*Regiment A, Panzer-Ausbildungs-Verband 'Ostsee'*, 210
*Regiment B, Panzer-Ausbildungs-Verband 'Ostsee'*, 210
*Regiment C, Panzer-Ausbildungs-Verband 'Ostsee'*, 210
*Feldausbildungs-Regiment 639*, 126
*Feldausbildungs-Regiment 640*, 126
*Jäger-Ausbildungs-Regiment 1*, 236n4

Battalions:
Reserve & Replacement Battalions:
*Fahr Ersatz und Ausbildungs Abteilung 2*, 246n8
*Kraftfahr Ersatz Abteilung 2*, 246n8
*Kavallerie Ausbildungs Abteilung 100*, 246n8
*Grenadier Ersatz Regiment 522*, 246n8
*Panzergrenadier-Ersatz-Bataillon 50*, 168
*Pionier-Ersatz und Ausbildungs-Bataillon 68*, 169
*Artillerie Ersatz Abteilung 39*, 169
*Heeres Flakartillerie Ersatz und Ausbildungs Abteilung 272*, 245n8
*Kavallerie Ausbildungs Abteilung 100*, 245n8
*Pionier Ersatz und Ausbildungs Bataillon 2*, 245n8
*Pionier Ersatz Bataillon 12*, 245n8
*Bau Pionier Ersatz und Ausbildungs Bataillon 2*, 245n8
*Artillerie-Ersatz und Ausbildungs-Regiment 2*, 159
*Grenadier-Ersatz-Bataillon 67*, 99
*Kavallerie-Ausbildungs-Abteilung 100*, 159, 207
*Panzergrenadier-Ausbildungs-Bataillon 5*, 210
*Panzergrenadier-Ausbildungs-Bataillon 73*, 210
*Panzergrenadier-Ausbildungs-Bataillon 76*, 210
*Panzergrenadier-Ausbildungs-Bataillon 90*, 210
*Sturmgeschütz-Ersatz und Ausbildungs-Abteilung 500*, 137
*Panzergrenadier-Ersatz-Bataillon 3 'Aschenbach'*, 171
*Panzergrenadier-Ersatz-Bataillon 9 'Jakobs'*, 171
*Panzergrenadier-Ersatz-Bataillon 83 'Zapf'*, 171
*Reserve-Jäger-Bataillon 'A'*, 236n4
*Reserve-Jäger-Bataillon 'B'*, 236n4
*Feldersatz Bataillon 1547*, 211
*Artillerie-Ausbildungs-Abteilung 257*, 207
*Artillerie-Ausbildungs-Abteilung 12/32*, 207
*Artillerie-Ausbildungs-Abteilung 38/2*, 207
*II. Bataillon, Fallschirmjäger-Ersatz und Ausbildungs-Regiment 3*, 211

# Unit Index 259

III. Bataillon, Fallschirmjäger-Ersatz und Ausbildungs-Regiment 1, 211
Marine Feldersatz Bataillon 3, 207
Marine-Feldersatz-Bataillon 1 der 1. Marine Division, 211
Bau-Pionier-Ersatz und Ausbildungs-Bataillon 2, 159
Pionier-Ersatz und Ausbildungs-Bataillon 2, 159
Pionier-Ersatz-Bataillon 12, 159
Panzer-Pionier-Ausbildungs-Bataillon 218, 210
Aufklärungs-Ersatz-Abteilung 5, 159
Fahr-Ersatz und Ausbildungs-Abteilung 2, 159
Kraftfahr-Ersatz-Abteilung 2, 159
Feldersatz-Bataillon 25, 216
Feldersatz Bataillon 18, 205
Feldersatz Bataillon 281, 208
Marine Feldersatz Bataillon 1, 209
Heer-Fahrausbildung und Ersatz-Bataillon 28, 134
Ersatz und Ausbildungs-Artillerie-Abteilung 59, 217
Heeres-Flakartillerie-Ersatz und Ausbildungs-Abteilung 272, 159
Baupionier-Ersatz und Ausbildungs-Bataillon 2, 160
I. Bataillon/Feldausbildungs-Regiment 'Oder', 210
Fusilier-Ausbildungs-Bataillon 27/172, 207
Kraftfahr-Ersatz-Abteilung 4, 210
Grenadier-Ausbildungs-Bataillon 94, 207
Grenadier-Ausbildungs-Bataillon 4/222, 207
Grenadier-Ausbildungs-Bataillon 48/374, 207
Grenadier-Ausbildungs-Bataillon 89/368, 207
Heer-Veterinär-Ausbildungs und Ersatz-Bataillon 8, 134
Panzerjäger-Ausbildungs-Abteilung 5, 210
Panzer-Ausbildungs-Verband 'Ostsee', 210
Panzer-Ausbildungs-Abteilung 5, 210
Panzerjäger-Ausbildungs-Abteilung 2, 210

Panzerjäger-Ausbildungs-Abteilung 13, 210
Panzer-Aufklärungs-Ausbildungs-Abteilung 13, 210
Panzer-Nachrichten-Ausbildungs-Kompanie 82, 210
Aufklärungs Ersatz Abteilung 5, 245n8

Infantry Battalions (all types):
Posen-Festungs-Infanterie-Bataillon 1442, 137
Posen-Festungs-Infanterie-Bataillon 1446, 137
I.-II. Bataillon, Festungs-Grenadier-Regiment 2, 217
I.-II. Bataillon, Festungs-Grenadier-Regiment 3, 217
I.-II. Bataillon, Festungs-Grenadier-Regiment 4, 217
Divisions-Füsilier-Bataillon 12 (formerly Panzer-Aufklärungs-Abteilung 12), 126
Divisions-Füsilier-Bataillon 14 (formerly Panzer-Aufklärungs-Abteilung 14), 126
Fusilier Bataillon 271, 237n1
Füsilier-Bataillon 309, 212
Fusilier-Bataillon 12 (L), 40-41
I. Bataillon/Grenadier-Regiment 1091, 211
Sicherungs Bataillon 455, 237n1
Festungs-Infanterie-Bataillon 1449, 217
Festungs Bataillon 1453, 209
Festungs Bataillon 1454, 209
Festungs Bataillon 1455, 209
Festungs Bataillon 1457, 209
Landesschützen-Bataillon 312, 137
Landesschützen-Bataillon 475, 137
Landesschützen-Bataillon 642, 137
Landesschützen-Bataillon 814, 137
Landesschützen-Bataillon 752, 43
Landesschützen-Bataillon 1091, 131
I. Bataillon/ Grenadier-Regiment 374, 40
Scharfschützen-Lehrgang Wehkreis X, 210
Skijäger-Bataillon, 54
13 Jäger-Bataillon 6, 54
Jäger-Bataillon 3, 54
I. Gebirgsjäger-Bataillon, 54
II. Gebirgsjäger-Bataillon, 54

260  Unit Index

III. Gebirgsjäger-Bataillon, 54
I.–III. Bataillone, Fallschirmjäger-Regiment 25, 214
I.–II. Bataillone, Fallschirmjäger-Regiment 26, 214
I.–II. Bataillone, Fallschirmjäger-Regiment 27, 214
II. Bataillon der Fallschirmjäger-Regiment 26, 167, 202
III. Bataillon/Fallschirmjäger-Regiment 26, 173
Festungs-Infanterie-Bataillon 1450, 168
I.-II. Bataillon, Festungs-Grenadier-Regiment 1, 216
I., II. Bataillone, Marine Infanterie Regiment 1, 211
I., II. Bataillone, Marine Infanterie Regiment 2, 211
I., II. Bataillone, Marine Infanterie Regiment 4, 211
Marine Füsilier Bataillon 3, 207
II. und III. Bataillone der Pommern-Regiment 4, 167
I. Bataillon, 2. Regiment Brandenburg, 72
Marine Infanterie Bataillon, 209
Marine-Bataillon Deutsch-Krone, 160
I. Bataillon, II. Bataillon, Grenadier-Regiment 732, 213
I. Bataillon, II. Bataillon, Grenadier-Regiment 745, 213
I. Bataillon, II. Bataillon, Grenadier-Regiment 764, 213
I. Festungs-Bataillon 'Beßlein', 134
II. Festungs-Bataillon 'Beßlein', 134
III. Festungs-Bataillon 'Beßlein', 134
IV. Festungs-Bataillon 'Beßlein', 134
II. Bataillon/Grenadier-Regiment 1091, 210
Führer-Anwärter-Bataillon 'Oder', 210
Jäger-Bataillon 8, 7
Jäger-Bataillon 13, 7
I. Jäger-Bataillon of Jäger-Regiment 25 (L), 40
II. Jäger-Bataillon of Jäger-Regiment 25 (L), 40

Grenzschutz Bataillon Beyer, 208
Bataillon 'Feldherrnhalle', 218
Festungs-Infanterie-Bataillon 1445, 131
Sturm-Battalion AOK 11, 212
Sturm Bataillon AOK 9, 242n3
Sturm Bataillon I AOK 9, 168, 242n3
Sturm Bataillon II AOK 9, 242n3
Panzer AOK 3 Sturm Bataillon, 245n4
Grenadier-Sturm-Bataillon 'Kurland' (formerly: Sturm-Bataillon AOK 16), 126
Fernmelde-Bataillon Bärwalde, 160
Führer-Anwärter-Bataillon 'Oder', 162
Infanterie-Bataillon 540 z.b.V., 43
Feldgendarmerie Abteilung 695, 206
Aufklärungs-Abteilung 'Stolp', 160
Rumänisches Volksdeutsches-Bataillon, 171

Artillery Battalions:
Fallschirm-Granatwerfer-Bataillon 9, 214
I. Panzer Artillerie Abteilung 'Schlesien', 245n2
IV. Festungs-Artillerie-Abteilung der Festungs-Stamm-Artillerie-Regiment 3132, 169
Festungs-Artillerie-Abteilung I./3132, 169
Festungs-Artillerie-Abteilung 61, 131
Festungs-Artillerie-Abteilung 1325, 217
Festungs-Artillerie-Abteilung 1326, 217
Festungs-Artillerie-Abteilung 3157, 217
II. Festungs-Artillerie-Bataillon, 209
III. Festungs Artillerie Bataillon, 209
I. Festungs-Artillerie-Abteilung, Festungs-Artillerie-Regiment 3132, 216
I., II., III. Artillerie-Abteilung, Panzer-Artillerie-Regiment 'Kurmark', 215
I., II., III. Artillerie-Abteilung, Artillerie-Regiment 25 (motorisiert), 216
Artillerie Abteilung 3156, 209
Artillerie Abteilung 3158, 209
I. Artillerie-Bataillon/Artillerie-Lehr-Regiment 5 'Groß-Born', 160
Artillerie-Ersatz und Ausbildungs-Abteilung 75, 211
Artillerie-Kommandeur 101, 211

Unit Index  261

*II. Bataillon / 290. Artillerie Regiment,* 232n19
*Küsten-Artillerie-Lehr-Abteilung,* 206
*III. Abteilung, Artillerie-Regiment 606,* 213
*IV. Abteilung, Artillerie-Regiment 606,* 213
*Heeres Artillerie Abteilung I./106,* 245n2
*Leichtgeschütz-Abteilung 424,* 54
*schwere Artillerie Abteilung 859,* 135
*II. Artillerie-Abteilung, Artillerie-Regiment 290,* 33
*II. Artillerie-Abteilung, Artillerie-Regiment 1712,* 213
*Artillerie-Abteilung 124,* 54
*Artillerie-Abteilung 'Futtig',* 167
*II. Artillerie-Abteilung des Artillerie-Regiments 82,* 54
*I.–III. Artillerie-Abteilung, Fallschirmjäger-Artillerie-Regiment 9,* 214
*Marine-Artillerie-Abteilung 530,* 31, 32n13

Engineer Battalions:
*Landesschützen-Pionier-Bataillon 513,* 169
*Pionier-Ersatz und Ausbildungs-Bataillon 213,* 131
*Pionier-Bataillon 25,* 216
*Pionier-Bataillon 1 'Kurland'* (from *Heeres-Pionier-Bataillon 44, motorisiert*), 128
*Pionier-Bataillon Bärwalde,* 160
*Pionier-Sperr-Bataillon 952,* 217
*Pionier-Bataillon 281,* 208
*Pionier-Bataillon 230,* 214
*Pionier-Bataillon 606,* 213
*Pionier-Sperr-Bataillon z.b.V. 953,* 217
*Bau-Pionier-Bataillon 96,* 209
*Bau-Pionier-Bataillon 254,* 209
*Bau-Pionier-Bataillon 795,* 209
*Heeres-Pionier-Bataillon 44,* 128
*Fallschirm Pionier-Bataillon 5,* 241n5
*Fallschirm-Pionier-Bataillon 9,* 214
*Pionier-Bataillon 'Kurmark',* 215
*Pionier-Bataillon der Divisionsgruppe Kräutler,* 54
*Pionier Bataillon 18,* 205
*Pionier-Bataillon 1547,* 211

*Pionier-Bataillon 1549,* 208
*Panzer Pionier Abteilung 'Schlesien',* 245n2
*Marine-Pionier-Bataillon 1,* 211
*Marine Pionier Bataillon 3,* 207
*Festungs-Pionier-Bataillon 66,* 137

Machine Gun Battalions:
*Korps-Maschinengewehr-Bataillon 442,* 207
*Maschinengewehr-Bataillon 1 z.b.V.,* 169
*Maschinengewehr-Bataillon 2 z.b.V.,* 169
*Maschinengewehr-Bataillon 3 z.b.V.,* 169
*Festungs Maschinengewehr Bataillon 1 'Stettin',* 209
*Festungs-Maschinengewehr-Bataillon 82,* 137
*Festungs-Maschinengewehr-Bataillon 83,* 137
*Festungs-Maschinengewehr-Bataillon 84,* 217
*Festungs Maschinengewehr Bataillon 85,* 209
*Festungs-Maschinengewehr-Bataillon 90,* 137
*Festungs-Maschinengewehr-Bataillon 829,* 217
*Festungs-Maschinengewehr-Bataillon Schneidemühl I,* 159
*Festungs-Maschinengewehr-Bataillon Schneidemühl II,* 159

Flak Battalions:
*schwere Flak-Ersatz-Abteilung 12,* 171
*Marine-Flak-Abteilung 233,* 206
*Flak-Abteilung 420,* 245n2
*Marine-Flak-Abteilung 711,* 206
*Marine-Flak-Abteilung 713,* 206
*Heeres-Flak-Artillerie-Abteilung 284,* 214
*I.–II. Flak Bataillone, Fallschirmjäger-Flak-Regiment 9,* 214
*Heeres-Flakartillerie-Abteilung 292,* 216

Panzer, Panzergrenadier, and Panzerjäger Battalions:
*schwere Panzer-Abteilung 501,* 24
*schwer Panzer-Abteilung 502,* 41, 44

## Unit Index

schwere Panzer-Abteilung 503, 81, 85
schwere Panzer-Abteilung 506, 18, 22, 231n5
schwere Panzer-Abteilung 508, 22
schwere Panzer-Abteilung 509, 24
schwere Panzer-Abteilung 510, 112F50, 115, 120, 126
Panzer Abteilung 'Schlesien', 242n2
Panzer-Bataillon 'Kurland', 126
Panzer-Bataillon-Kummersdorf, 247n31
Panzer-Abteilung 5, 216
Panzer-Abteilung 8, 214
gemischtes Panzer Abteilung 118 (from Panzer-Abteilung 'Schlesien'), 205
Panzer Abteilung 'Schlesien', 242n2
Panzer Bataillon Müncheberg, 215
Sturmgeschütz-Abteilung 184, 41
Sturmgeschütz-Abteilung 'Graf Dohna', 160
I. Bataillon und II. Bataillon, Panzergrenadier-Regiment 'Müncheberg 1', 215
I. Bataillon und II. Bataillon, Panzergrenadier-Regiment 'Müncheberg 2', 215
schwere Panzerjäger-Abteilung 88, 18, 231n5
Panzerjäger-Abteilung 151, 215
Fallschirm-Panzerjäger-Abteilung 9, 214
Panzerjäger-Abteilung 'Schlesien', 245n2
Panzerjäger-Abteilung 1 der 1. Marine Division, 211
Panzerjäger-Abteilung 1 'Kurland', 128
Panzerjäger-Abteilung 2 'Kurland', 128
Panzerjäger-Abteilung 18, 205
Panzerjäger-Abteilung 93, 64
Panzerjäger-Abteilung 200, 212
Festungs-Panzerjäger-Abteilung XXVI, 217
schwere Panzerjäger-Abteilung 519, 6, 10, 24, 229n7
Panzerjäger-Abteilung 1549, 208
Panzerjäger-Abteilung 20, 214
Marine Panzerjäger-Abteilung 3, 207
Panzerabwehr-Bataillon 25, 216
I.-IV. Panzer-Vernichtungs-Bataillone, 1. Panzervernichtungsbrigade 'Hitlerjugend', 216

I.-III. Bataillone, Panzergrenadier-Regiment 76, 214
I.-III. Bataillone, Panzergrenadier-Regiment 90, 214
I.-III., Panzergrenadier-Regiment 35, 216
I.-III., Panzergrenadier-Regiment 119, 216
Panzergrenadier-Bataillon 2105, 13
Panzer-Füsilier-Regiment 'Kurmark', 214
Panzer-Aufklärungs-Abteilung 125, 216
Panzer-Aufklärungs-Abteilung 118, 205
Panzer-Aufklärungs-Abteilung 120, 214
Panzer-Aufklärungs-Abteilung 151, 215

Signals / Communications Battalions:
Panzergrenadier-Nachrichten-Abteilung 20, 214
Nachrichten-Abteilung 20, 214
Nachrichten-Abteilung 230, 214
Divisions-Nachrichten-Abteilung 549, 208
Panzergrenadier-Divisions Nachrichten Abteilung 18, 205
Fallschirm-Nachrichten-Abteilung 9, 214
Marine Nachrichten Abteilung 3, 207, 211
Marine-Nachrichten-Abteilung 1, 211
Nachrichten-Bataillon 25, 216
Divisions-Nachrichten-Abteilung Division 'Bärwalde', 199

Alarm, Ad-hoc & Volkssturm Battalions:
Alarm Bataillon 'Over', 209
Alarm Bataillon 'Rog', 209
Alarm Bataillon 'Benner', 209
Alarm Bataillon 'Laase', 209
Alarm-Bataillone 'Potsdam', 212
Alarm-Bataillone 'Spandau', 212
Alarm-Bataillone 'Brandenburg', 212
Alarm-Bataillon 'Neukölln', 212
Bataillon 'Kolberg', 159
Bataillon 'Eutin', 159
Bataillon 'Treptow' 159
Bataillon 'Belgard', 159
Bataillon 'Anklam', 159
Bataillon 'Schneidemühl', 159
Bataillon 'Hannover', 159
Bataillon 'Feldhermhalle', 159

## Unit Index

*I. Bataillon, II. Bataillon, III. Bataillone der Regiment Kersten*, 134
*I. Bataillon, II. Bataillon, III. Bataillone der Regiment Reinkober*, 134
*I. Bataillon, II. Bataillon, III. Bataillone der Regiment Schulz*, 134
*I. Bataillon, II. Bataillon, III. Bataillone der Regiment Seybold*, 134
*Volkssturm Bataillon von der Marwitz*, 208
*Volkssturm-Bataillon 'Main/Franken'*, 218
*Volkssturm-Bataillon 'Ober Donau'*, 218
*Volkssturm-Bataillon 'Dresden Thür'*, 218
*Volkssturm-Bataillon 'Hamburg'*, 171
*Volkssturm-Bataillon 'Königsberg'*, 171
*Volkssturm-Bataillon 'Strempel'*, 171
*Volkssturm Bataillon Hamburg*, 210
*Volkssturm Bataillon Brandenburg*, 210
*Volkssturm-Bataillon 26/11*, 167
*Volkssturm-Bataillon 26/29*, 167
*Volkssturm-Bataillon 26/70*, 167
*Volkssturm-Bataillon 16/186*, 169
*Volkssturm Bataillon XXVI/82*, 211
*Volkssturm-Bataillon 'Seesen'*, 162

'Other' Battalions:
*Nachschubtruppen 818*, 54

Armored Trains:
*Eisenbahn-Panzerzüge 77*, 173
*Kampfgruppen* (Battlegroups):
*Kampfgruppe 1001 Nacht*, 205
*Kampfgruppe Bahn*, 167
*Kampfgruppe Bock*, 35-36
*SS-Kampfgruppe Demes*, 102
*Kampfgruppe Fischer*, 72
*Kampfgruppe Furguth*, 33
*Kampfgruppe Helling*, 32
*Kampfgruppe Hillebrandt*, 73
*Kampfgruppe Joachim*, 160, 200
*SS-Kampfgruppe Jörchel*, 102
*Kampfgruppe Junck*, 26
*SS-Kampfgruppe Klein*, 102
*Kampfgruppe Klossek*, 162
*Kampfgruppe Lenzer*, 137
*Kampfgruppe Major Volkmann*, 26
*Kampfgruppe Mathias*, 26
*SS-Kampfgruppe 'Mohnke'*, 181
*Kampfgruppe Ohlen*, 26
*Kampfgruppe Paul*, 208
*Kampfgruppe Pyritz*, 167
*Kampfgruppe Pohl*, 36
*Kampfgruppe Reimann*, 102
*Kampfgruppe Rintelen*, 26
*Kampfgruppe Schill*, 26
*Kampfgruppe Schuldt*, 35-36
*Kampfgruppe Schulz*, 45
*SS-Kampfgruppe 'Solar'*, 171, 212, 246n22
*Kampfgruppe Speth*, 33, 35-36
*Kampfgruppe Stargard*, 167
*Kampfgruppe Voigt*, 208
*SS-Kampfgruppe Wallenstein*, 102
*Panzer-Kampfgruppe Graf von Strachwitz*, 44
*Flak-Kampfgruppe 'Kurland'*, 128

*Waffen-SS, SS und Polizei* (Armed SS, SS & Police):
*Höhere-SS und Polizeiführer 'Warthe'*, 137
*Armeegruppe Steiner* (see: *III. [germanisches] SS-Panzerkorps*), 183, 246n23
*11. SS Panzerarmee*, 158, 160-163, *163*F73, 163, 167, 199, 242n10, 246n11
*11. SS Armee*, 241n5
*I. SS-Panzerkorps*, 91
*II. SS-Panzerkorps*, 91
*III. (germanisches) SS-Panzerkorps*, 29-30, 31n10, 32, 43-44, 114, 125, 128, 162-163, 183, 200, 202, 206, 212, 246n23
*IV. SS-Panzerkorps*, 87, 91, 94, 158
*V. SS-Freiwilligen-Gebirgs-Armeekorps*, 70, 152, 177, 201, 203, 247n33
*VI. SS-Freiwilligen-Armeekorps*, 45, 118-119
*IX. Waffen-Gebirgs-Armeekorps der SS*, 85
*X. SS-Armeekorps*, 158-159, 162, 200, 202, 245n8, 246n17
*XI. SS-Panzerkorps*, 167, 201, 203, 213
*XVI. SS-Armeekorps*, 158, 160-161, 200

1. SS-Panzer-Division 'Adolf Hitler', 21f12, 91
2. SS-Panzer-Division 'Das Reich', 91, 95-96, 105
3. SS-Panzer-Division 'Totenkopf', 87, 91, 95
4. SS-Panzergrenadier-Division 'Polizei', 35, 71, 81, 162, 167, 200
5. SS-Panzer-Division 'Wiking', 87, 91
6. SS-Gebirgsjäger Division 'Nord', 138
7. SS-Freiwilligen-Gebirgs-Division 'Prinz Eugen', 70
8. SS Kavallerie-Division 'Florian Geyer', 83
9. SS-Panzer-Division 'Hohenstaufen', 91
10. SS-Panzer-Division 'Frundsberg', 95, 162, 200-201
11. SS Panzergrenadier-Division 'Nordland', 32, 43, 115, 120, 125, 128, 162, 177, 180, 200, 202, 215
12. SS-Panzer-Division 'Hitler Jugend', 91
14. Waffen-Grenadier-Division der SS (Galizien Nr. 1), 19, 21-22
15. Waffen-Grenadier-Division der SS (lettische Nr. 1), 41, 113, 126, 160, 163, 180, 200, 202
16. SS-Panzergrenadier-Division 'Reichsführer-SS', 92
18. SS-Freiwilligen-Panzergrenadier-Division 'Horst Wessel', 26
19. Waffen-Grenadier-Division der SS (lettische Nr. 2), 18, 41, 113-114, 118-119, 121, 123, 138
20. Waffen-Grenadier-Division der-SS (estnische Nr. 1), 41, 43
21. Waffen-Gebirgs-Division der SS 'Skanderbeg', 70
22. SS-Freiwilligen-Kavallerie-Division 'Maria Theresia', 85
23. SS-Freiwilligen-Panzergrenadier Division 'Nederland' (See: 4. SS-Freiwilligen-Panzergrenadier-Brigade 'Nederland'), 125, 160, 162, 200, 202, 213
27. SS-Freiwilligen-Grenadier-Division 'Langemarck', 162, 200, 202, 206
28. SS-Freiwilligen-Panzergrenadier-Division 'Wallonien', 162, 180, 200, 202, 206
32. SS-Freiwilligen-Panzergrenadier-Division '30 Januar', 177, 201, 203, 217
33. Waffen-Grenadier-Division der SS 'Charlemagne' (französische Nr. 1), 163, 166, 180, 202, 238n9
44. SS Panzergrenadier-Division 'Wallenstein', 102, 104
4. SS-Freiwilligen-Panzergrenadier-Brigade 'Nederland', 28, 43, 114-115, 125, 128
Polizei-Jäger-Brigade 1, 210
SS-Regiment Leibstandarte 'Adolf Hitler', x
SS-Panzer-Grenadier-Regiment 'Nordland'
SS-Panzergrenadier-Regiment 49 'de Ruyter', 160, 200
SS-Grenadier-Regiment Nr. 1 'Wallenstein', 104
SS-Grenadier-Regiment Nr. 2 'Wallenstein', 104
Waffen-Grenadier-Regiment der SS (lettische Nr. 7), 113
SS-Freiwilligen Grenadier-Regiment 86 Schill, 217
SS-Freiwilligen Grenadier-Regiment 87 Kurmark, 217
SS-Freiwilligen-Artillerie-Regiment 32, 217
SS-Festungs-Regiment 1, 135
General-SS Regiment 109, 137-138
SS-Polizei-Regiment 1, 85
SS-Polizei-Regiment 5, 73
SS-Polizeiregiment 14, 70
SS-Polizei-Gebirgsjäger-Regiment 18, 70, 73
SS Polizei-Jägerregiment 8, 210
SS Polizei-Jägerregiment 50, 210
Police Regiment Schallert, 138
Polizei-Regiment 'Hartmann', 217, 247n34
SS-Pionier-Regiment 'Wallenstein', 104

## Unit Index

SS-Festungs-Regiment 1 (SS-Regiment 'Beßlein'), 133, 135
SS-Artillerie-Lehr-Regiment, 215
Freiwilligen-Artillerie-Regiment 32, 217
Grenadier-Regiment 'Becker' (ex-Polizei-Schützenregiment 34), 218, 242n9, 248n36
I.-II. Artillerie-Abteilung, Freiwilligen-Artillerie-Regiment 32, 217
SS-Ersatzkommando 'Ungarn', 171
SS-Ersatzkommando Kroatien, 242n6
SS-Ersatzkommando Ostland, 242n6
SS-Jagdverbände 'Mitte', 158, 171
SS-Jagdverbände 'Ost', 159
SS-Jagdverbände 'Mitte', 170, 212, 246n22
SS-Jagdverbände 'Nordwest', 170
SS-Fallschirmjäger-Bataillon 600, 170-171, 212, 246n22
SS Panzerjäger-Abteilung 560, 205
Begleitbataillon Speer, 205
I., II., III., IV. SS Festungs-Infanterie-Bataillone der SS-Festungs-Regiment 1, 135
V. Bataillon, SS Panzergrenadier-Division 'Nederland', 211
II. Bataillon, SS Panzergrenadier-Regiment 49 'de Ruyter' ('Nederland' SS Division), 211
SS Panzerjäger-Abteilung 23, 23. SS-Freiwilligen-Panzergrenadier Division 'Nederland', 211
III. Bataillon der SS-Panzergrenadier-Regiment 8, 167, 173
SS-Infanterie-Geschütz-Ausbildungs und Ersatz-Bataillon 1, 133
SS-Pionier-Bataillon 11, 30n4, 32
SS Ersatz- und Ausbildungs-Bataillon 13, 98
SS-Panzergrenadier-Ersatz und Ausbildungs-Bataillon 9, 168
SS Pionier-Schule 4, 102
SS-Junkerschule Prag, 102
SS Regiment 'Mahren', 102

SS-Aufklärung-Abteilung 'Wallenstein', 102
SS-Panzerjäger-Abteilung 'Wallenstein', 104
SS-Aufklärung-Abteilung 'Wallenstein', 104
SS-Fusilier-Bataillon 'Wallenstein', 104
SS-Sturmgeschütz-Abteilung 'Wallenstein', 104
SS-Nachrichten-Abteilung 'Wallenstein', 104
SS-Nachschub-Bataillon 'Wallenstein', 104
SS-Sanitäts-Abteilung 'Wallenstein', 104
SS-Panzergrenadier-Ausbildungs und Ersatz-Bataillon 1, 134
Sicherheitsdienst-Kompanie der Höhere-SS und Polizeiführer 'Warthe', 138
SS-Grenadier-Ausbildungs und Ersatz Bataillon 35, 160
SS-Grenadier-Ersatz und Ausbildungs-Bataillon 103, 162
SS Ausbildungs und Ersatz Battalion 1 'Leibstandarte Adolf Hitler', 181
II. Bataillon, SS Grenadier-Ersatz und Ausbildungs-Bataillon 103, 210
SS Panzergrenadier-Ersatz und Ausbildungs-Abteilung 9, 210 SS
schwer SS-Panzer-Abteilung 502, 213
SS-Panzerjäger-Abteilung 32, 218
SS-Werfer-Abteilung 505, 218
SS-Flak-Abteilung 32, 218
SS-Fusilier-Bataillon 32, 218
SS-Pionier-Bataillon 32, 218
SS-Nachrichten-Bataillon 32, 218
SS-Feldersatz-Bataillon 32, 218
Begleit Bataillon Reichsführer-SS, 181
SS Wach-Bataillon 1 'Leibstandarte Adolf Hitler', 181
Polizei-Bataillon I, 209
Polizei-Bataillon II, 209
Polizei-Bataillon 'Bremen', 212
Sicherheitsdienst Bataillon 30, 180
Spanisch-Freiwilligen-Kompanie der SS 101 (see: 'Unidad Ezquerra'), 180

266   Unit Index

Pro-Axis Balkan Forces:
*Serbisches-Freiwilligen-Korps*, 71, 236n6
5. *Regiment, Serbisches-Freiwilligen-Korps*, 236n6
*Russisches-Gardekorps*, 71, 236n7
1. *Kavallerie Regiment, Russisches-Gardekorps*, 236n7
2. *Infanterie Regiment, Russisches-Gardekorps*, 236n7
3. *Infanterie Regiment, Russisches-Gardekorps*, 236n7
4. *Infanterie Regiment, Russisches-Gardekorps*, 236n7
5. *Infanterie Regiment, Russisches-Gardekorps*, 236n7
*I. Reiter-Abteilung, 1. Kavallerie-Regiment, Russisches Gardekorps*, 72

Axis Allied Forces:
Eastern Troops:
1. *Kosaken-Kavallerie-Division*, 70, 92
600. *Infanterie Division (russische Nr. 1)*, 100, 105, 219
650. *Infanterie-Division (russische Nr. 2)*, 100, 105
*Grenadier-Brigade 499 der russische Volksbefreiungsarmee*, 162
*Grenadier-Regiment 1601(russische)*, 219
*Grenadier-Regiment 1602(russische)*, 219
*Grenadier-Regiment 1603(russische)*, 219
*Grenadier-Regiment 1604 (russische)*, 162
*Artillerie-Regiment 1600*, 219
*Pionier-Bataillon 600*, 219
*Turkistanische-Ersatz-Bataillon*, 166

Slovakia:
*Slowakisches Grenadier-Regiment Nr. 1 'Hlinka Garde'*, 102, 104

Romanian:
Romanian 1st Army, 67, 95
Romanian 3rd Army, 59, 129
Romanian 4th Army, 59, 67, 97, 129
Romanian 1st Armored Division, 64
Romanian 14th Infantry Division, 66

Hungarian:
1st Hungarian Army, 17-18, 77, 84, 231n6
3rd Hungarian Army, 80, 86, 92, 152
6th Hungarian Army Corps, 18
7th Hungarian Army Corps, 18
Szekler Border Guard Division, 80
1st Hungarian Armored Division, 80, 86, 237n3
2nd Hungarian Armored Division, 237n3
3rd Hungarian Armored Division, 237n3
1st Hungarian Cavalry Division, 7, 80, 86
2nd Hungarian Armoured Division, 17-18, 231n5
5th Hungarian Reserve Division, 7, 14
5th Hungarian Infanterie Division, 95
6th Hungarian Infanterie Division, 18, 80
7th Hungarian Infantry Division, 18
10th Hungarian Infantry Division, 86
12th Hungarian Reserve Division, 7, 86
16th Hungarian Reserve Division, 18
16th Hungarian Infantry Division, 77
18th Hungarian Reserve Division, 18
19th Hungarian Reserve Division, 18
20th Hungarian Infantry Division, 19, 77, 80
23rd Hungarian Reserve Division, 7
24th Hungarian Infantry Division, 18, 77, 95, 97
25th Hungarian Infantry Division, 18, 80, 92
27th Hungarian Light Division, 18
1st Hungarian Mountain Brigade, 18
2nd Hungarian Mountain Brigade, 18
6th Hungarian Infantry Regiment, 88
Hungarian Infantry Battalion 23/I, 162
4th Hungarian Infantry Battalion, 169
85th Hungarian Infantry Regiment, 207

Estonian:
*(estnische) Grenzschutz Regiment 1*, 47
*(estnische) Grenzschutz Regiment 3*, 43
*(estnische) Grenzschutz Regiment 4*, 47

## Unit Index

Finnish:
Finnish 3rd Army Corps, 50
Finnish 4th Army Corps, 50
Finnish Armored Division, 55
Finnish 3rd Infantry Division, 55
Finnish 11th Infantry Division, 55

Polish Forces:
1st Polish Army, 152, 161

Bulgarian Forces:
Bulgarian 1st Army, 236n1

Russian Air Army:
17th Air Army, 62, 235n1

Soviet Fronts:
Leningrad Front, 111
1st Baltic Front, 10, 111, 153-156
2nd Baltic Front, 111, 153, 155-156
3rd Baltic Front, 111, 153, 156
1st Belarusian Front, 2, 4, 10, 107, 147, 152, 174, 176, 182
2nd Belarusian Front, 4, 83, 107, 112-113, 118, 152, 163
3rd Belarusian Front, 4, 107, 141, 152
1st Ukrainian Front, 17, 20, 76-77, 79, 105-106, 141, 147, 152, 155, 174-176, 182
2nd Ukrainian Front, 59, 62, 71, 77, 79-81, 85, 97, 99, 105
3rd Ukrainian Front, 59, 62, 68, 74, 84-85, 87, 94
4th Ukrainian Front, 77, 82-84, 105

Soviet Armies:
1st Guards Army, 17
1st Guards Tank Army, 17, 230n2
2nd Guards Army, 141
2nd Guards Tank Army, 163, 168, 174
2nd Shock Army, 28-29, 32, 36, 42-43, 153
3rd Army, 153
3rd Guards Army, 17, 20, 24, 155

3rd Guards Tank Army, 17, 20-21, 42-43, 131, 155, 178
4th Guards Army, 85, 94-95
4th Shock Army, 49, 107
4th Tank Army, 20, 22, 153
4th Guards Tank Army, 17, 62, 178
5th Army, 11, 141
5th Shock Army, 62, 168
5th Guards Army, 17, 24, 131, 148, 153, 155
5th Guards Tank Army, 11, 49, 107, 108F48, 112, 115, 144, 157
6th Guards Army, 49, 119-121
6th Guards Tank Army, 79, 81-82, 85, 94-95
6th Tank Army, 10, 62-63
7th Guards Army, 62, 97
7th Guards Tank Army, 85, 97
8th Army, 43
8th Guards Army, 115
9th Guards Army, 94-95
10th Guards Army, 115, 120, 122
11th Guards Army, 11, 141
13th Army, 17, 19-20, 131, 155
14th Army, 54, 57, 234n8
18th Army, 17, 23
22nd Army, 49, 118
27th Army, 62, 82
28th Army, 141, 178
31st Army, 141
37th Army, 62
38th Army, 17, 20-21, 76-77, 79
39th Army, 11, 141
40th Army, 62, 97
42nd Army, 119, 121
43rd Army, 49, 141, 144
46th Army, 62, 80, 85, 95, 97
47th Army, 154
48th Army, 153, 157
49th Army, 153, 174
50th Army, 153
51st Army, 106-107, 120-121
52nd Army, 62, 153
53rd Army, 62, 79, 97-98
57th Army, 62, 72

## Unit Index

59th Army, 37, 43
60th Army, 17, 20, 153
61st Army, 154, 174
65th Army, 1, 153
70th Army, 153-154

Corps:
Baranów Mechanized Group, 17
Sokolov Mechanized Group, 17
Cavalry Mechanized Group Pliyev, 80-82
Cavalry Mechanized Group Gorshkov, 79, 81
Corps Group Pigarevich, 54
1st Cavalry Mechanized Group, 230n3
1st Guards Mechanized Corps, 95
1st Guards Cavalry Corps, 76-77
3rd Breakthrough Artillery Corps, 43
4th Guards Mechanized Corps, 73
5th Tank Corps, 119
5th Guards Tank Corps, 95
6th Guards Tank Army, 95
6th Rifle Corps, 39, 43
8th Estonian Rifle Corps, 43
9th Guards Mechanized Corps, 95
10th Tank Corps, 22
11th Guards Tank Corps, 24
12th Tank Corps, 114
14th Rifle Corps, 43
18th Rifle Corps, 1
19th Tank Corps, 119
30th Guards Rifle Corps, 43
31st Army Corps, 54
43rd Corps, 30, 43
49th Rifle Corps, 97
99th Army Corps, 54
109th Rifle Corps, 43
112th Rifle Corps, 43
117th Rifle Corps, 43
119th Rifle Corps, 39
122nd Rifle Corps, 30, 43
122nd Mechanized Corps, 114
124th Rifle Corps, 43
126th Army Corps, 54, 57
127th Army Corps, 54, 57

130th Infantry Corps, 118
131st Army Corps, 54
Divisions & Brigades:
1st Guards Cavalry Division, 77
2nd Cavalry Division, 77
3rd Cavalry Division, 77
11th Rifle Division, 30
18th Rifle Division, 39
43rd Rifle Division, 30
46th Rifle Division, 39
53rd, Rifle Division, 39
56th Rifle Division, 39
67th Guards Rifle Division, 77-78
86th, Rifle Division, 39
107th Rifle Division, 77-79
129th Rifle-Division, 77-78
131st Rifle Division, 30
140th Rifle Division, 78
152nd Tank Division, 30
153rd Rifle Division, 97
168th, Rifle Division, 30
183rd Rifle Division, 78-79
196th Rifle Division, 30
224th Rifle Division, 39
225th Rifle Division, 33
246th Rifle Division, 1
224th Rifle Division, 39
271st Rifle Division, 78-79
275th Rifle Division, 39
311th Rifle Division, 39
326th Rifle Division, 39
350th Rifle Division, 23
357th Rifle Division, 97
372nd Rifle Division, 33
29th Tank Brigade, 22
34th 44th Rifle Brigade, 33
44th Rifle Brigade, 33
50th Coastal Brigade, 30
58th Rifle Brigade, 33
91st Tank Brigade, 1
121st Tank Brigade, 1
46th Guards Heavy Tank Regiment, 148
55th Independent Tank Regiment, 148
56th Independent Tank Regiment, 148

## Unit Index

71st Independent Guards Heavy Tank Regiment, 148
1504th Self-Propelled Artillery Regiment, 148
1505th Self-Propelled Artillery Regiment, 148

Regiments & Battalions:
299th Rifle Regiment, 33
415th Sapper Battalion, 1-2
46th Guards Heavy Tank Regiment, 43
260th Guards Heavy Tank Regiment, 43
261st Guards Heavy Tank Regiment, 43
1902nd Self-propelled Artillery Regiment, 43

Russian Sponsored Czechoslovak Forces
1st Czechoslovak Corps, 77, 79, 83

1st Czechoslovak Infantry Division, 78
2nd Czechoslovak Parachute Brigade, 78
3rd Czechoslovak Infantry Brigade, 78
1st Czechoslovak Tank Brigade, 78

Yugoslav Partisan Forces:
Partisan 1st Army Corps, 74
Partisan 14th Army Corps, 72, 74

American Forces:
U.S. 3rd Army, 100

British Forces:
British XXX Corps, 242n10

French Forces:
French 1st Army, 238n9

# NAME INDEX

Adams, *Oberstleutnant,* 212
Ahlfen, Hans von, 134-136
Albedyll, Otto Christer von, 215
Algner, Kurt, 137
Allwörden, Klaus von, 104
Althoff, *Oberleutnant,* 211
de Angelis, Maximilian, 70
Antonescu, Ion, 67
Auleb, Helge, 70
Ax, Adolf, 161

Bach-Zelewski, Eric von dem 161, 209, 246n17
Bang, Gunther, 99
Bäume, Helmut, 104
Bartels, *Oberst,* 212
Bauer, Ernst von, 207
Below, Robert von, 209
Bercken, Werner von, 156
Beregffy, Károly, 231n6
Berlin, Wilhelm, 212
Bernadotte, Folke, 186
Beßlein, Georg-Robert, 133, 135, 240n11
Blancbois, Gustav-Adolf Eugen Johannes Erich, 205, 245n3
Blaurock, Edmund, 157, 213, 247n25
Bleckwenn, Wilhelm, 211, 246n21
Bonin, Bogislaw Oskar Adolf Fürchtegott von, 154-155
Bormann, Martin, 184, 243n12

Boss, Hugo, 244n1
Bräuer, Bruno, 214, 247n29
Braun, Eva, 186
Brühl, Ferdinand, 209
Budyonny, Semyon, 229n5
Bunyachenko, Sergei Kuzmich, 100, 238n6
Burmeister, Arnold, 215
Busch, Ernst, 36
Busse, Theodor, 174, 177-178, 212

Chernyakhovsky, Ivan, 156
Chuikov, Vasily, 139
Cole, Stephen B., 244n2
des Courdes, Hans, 218

Dalnoki, Béla Miklós von, 231n6
Decker, Karl, 162
Degrelle, Leon, 206
Denecke, Erich, 167, 244n2
Demelhuber, Karl-Maria, 161
Demes, Walter, 102, 104
Dethier, Willy, 170
Dietl, Eduard, 234n5
Dietrich, Sepp, 91-92
Doerner, *Major der Schutzpolizei,* 218
Dönitz, Karl, 124

Eberhardt, Friedrich-Georg, 215
Eberstein, Karl Freiherr von, 184

272    Name Index

Endre, László, 90
Erdmannsdorff, Werner von, 70
Ezquerra-Sánchez, Miguel, 180
Everoth, *Schütze,* 137
Eulenburg, Jonas Graf zu, 131-132

Farkas, Ferenc, 231n6
Fedyuninsky, Ivan, 29, 43
Fegelein, Hermann, 186
Fehn, Gustav, 70
Felber, Hans-Gustav, 71, 73
Felmy, Hellmuth, 70
Fischer, Gotthard, 31
Fischer, Karl, 211
Fischer, Major, 218
Frießner, Johannes, 64, 86
Fronhöfer, Erich, 211
Fucker, Karl, 170-171, 212

Gareis, Martin, 2211
Gause, Alfred, 161
Gehlen, Reinhard, 3
Gille, Herbert Otto, 87
Goebbels, Joseph, 186
Göring, Hermann, 184, 232n18
Göschen, Alex, 217
Götz, Heinrich, 156
Goltzsch, Rudolf, 212
Golz, Herbert 161
Glossner, Fritz, 137
Gonell, Ernst, 137-139
Gothsche, Reinhold, 45
Grasser, Anton, 43
Großmann, Horst, 156
Guderian, Heinz, 5
Gyldenfeldt, Heinz von, 99

Häckel, Ernst, 167, 244n2
Hanke, Karl, 132-133, 136
Harpe, Josef, 17, 23, 152
Haß, Siegfried, 156
Hauck, Leander, 104
Haus, Georg 157
Heckmann, Friedrich, 137
Heering, Hans-Joachim, 205

Heine, *Major der Polizei,* 138
Heinrici, Gotthard, 155, 158, 205
Herrmann, Harry, 247n29
Herzog, Kurt, 45
Hille, Alfred, 218
Himmler, Heinrich, 139, 158, 170, 186-187
Hitler, Adolf, xi, 3-5, 14, 86-87, 92, 96, 99, 109, 111-112, 128-130, 146, 150, 152, 155, *173*F79, 180, 182, 184, 186, *187*F85, 230n13, 234n3, 239n1, 243n12, 246n23
Hitter, Alfons, 11
Höfer, Rudolf, 209
Hohenzollern-Sigmaringen Michael (Mihai), 67
Horthy, Miklos, 63
Hoßbach, Friedrich, 143, 156
Hoyer, *SS-Hauptsturmführer,* 170
Hufenbach, Helmuth 157

Jank, Karl, 167, 208, 246n13
Jeckeln, Friedrich, 216
Jodl, Alfred, 105-106, 183
Jörchel, Wolfgang, 102, 104

Karstens, Johannes, 239n11
Katukov, Mikhail, 139
Keitel, Wilhelm, 183
Kempin, Hans, 156, 217
Kern, Otto, 216
Kirrmeie, *Schütze,* 137
Kleemann, Ulrich, 70
Kleinheisterkamp, Matthias, 213
Klein, Emil, 102, 108
Klöckner, Ludwig, 161
König, Arno, 104
Koetz, Karl, 156
Körner, Hermann, 168
Konev, Ivan S., 17, 79, 147, 155, 156, 174-175
Körner, Erhard, 104
König, Ernst, 256
Korovnikov, Ivan, 33, 43

*Name Index* 273

Kräutler, Mathias, 54
Krappe, Günther, 161-162
Krukenberg, Gustav, 166, 215
Kryuchenkin, Vasily, 139
Kunz, Johann Wilhelm, 207

Lammerding, Heinz, 173
Langkeit, Willy, 214
Langweiler, Heinrich, 237n4
Lanz, Hubert, 70
László, Dezsö, 231n6
de Lattre de Tassigny, Jean, 238n9
Leclerc, Philippe, 238n9
Ledebur, Hans-Jürgen von, 208
Lehmann, Curt, 160
Leifheit, Fritz, 212
Lendle, Hubert, 210
Lenzer, Wilhelm, 137-138, 241n14
Leyser, Ernst von, 70
Löhr, Alexander, 70
Lorenz, Karl, 157
Lucha, Hans, 238n8

Malinovsky, Rodion, 85
Manteuffel, Hasso von, 206
Mattern, Ernst, 137
Mayer, Johannes, 161
Meiners, Ernst, 156
Meretskov, Kirill, 57
Mensing, Georg, 167
Michael, Ernst Karl Paul, 31
Mihov, Nikola, 68
Mikhaylov, Captain, 1
Milius, Siegfried, 170-171, 212
Mironov, Vasili, 147-148
Model, Otto Moritz Walter, 14, 231n4
Mohnke, Wilhelm, 181, 186
Mohr, Otmar, 134
Molotov, Vyacheslav, 229n5
Moskalenko, Kirill, 79
Müller, Friedrich-Wilhelm, 71
Müller, Thomas, 206
Müller, Vincenz, 12
Mummert, Werner, 215

Neufeld, *Major der Polizei,* 138
Niehoff, Hermann, 136
Nobiz, *Oberst 156*
Nostitz-Wallwitz, Gustav Adolf von, 156

Ortner, Bruno, 208
Oven, Karl von, 43

Petersdorff, Manfred von, 218
Pfeffer-Wildenbruch, Karl, 85, 88
Phleps, Artur, 70
Popov, Lieutenant, 1-2

Quodbach, Joachim, 134

Rabingen, Hermann Meyer, 216
Radziej, Georg, 213
Raegener, Adolf, 168, 218
Rattenhuber, Johann, 186
Rehfeld, Reinhold, 210
Reichert, Karl-Heinz, 134
Reichert, Rudolf, 156
Reinefarth, Heinz, 168
Reimann, Richard, 102
Reinhardt, Georg-Hans, 152
Reinkober, Fritz, 134, 240n10
Rendulic, Lothar, 56, 99, 237n2
Reyman, Hellmuth, 182
Rhode, Hermann, 212
Ribbentrop, Joachim, 52, 234n3
Rittberg, Graf von, 126
Roberts, Charles S., 244n2
Rogge, *Oberstleutnant,* 217
Rokossovsky, Konstantin, 2, 163
Roman, Rudolf Freiherr von, 156
Ruff, Siegfried, 134
Rybalko, Pavel, 131
Ryti, Risto, 52, 234n3

Sambach, August, 207
Sander, Fritz, 137
Saucken, Dietrich von, 141
Saxe-Coburg-Gotha, Simeon Borisov, 68

274  Name Index

Schallert, Hermann, 138
Schenke, Erich, 32
Scheunenmann, Walter, 213
Scheurlen, Heinz, 71
Schlamelcher, Karl, 104
Schleinitz, Siegmund Freiherr von, 245n8
Schmalz, Wilhelm 157
Schön, Artur, 131
Schörner, Ferdinand, 59, 136, 151-152
Schneider, Erich, 156
Scholze, Georg, 214
Shaposhnikov, Boris, 229n5
Siegert, Richard, 137
Siegroth, Joachim von, 213
Sixt, Friedrich, 212-213, 247n25
Skorzeny, Otto, 170-171, *173*F79, 174
Solar, Franz, 171
Söth, *Oberst*, 157
Speer, Albert, 186
Speidel, Hans, 14
Sperl, Rudolf, 156
Stalin, Joseph, 2, 5, 10, 63, 74-75, 88, 229n5, 238n5, 238n6
Starikov, Filip, 43
Steiner, Felix, 43, 158, 162, 199, 246n23
Student, Kurt, 158
Sviklin, Teodor-Verner Andreevich, 33

Tettau, Hans von, 242n10
Thorwald, Jürgen, 102
Timoshenko, Semyon, 229n5
Tippelskirch, Kurt von, 12
Tiso, Josef, 232n16
Tito, Joseph Broz, 3, 63
Tolbukhin, Fyodor, 85
Toussaint, Rudolf, 106

Unrein, Martin, 162
Usedom, Horst von, 126

Vasilevsky, Aleksandr, 156
Varikhazi, Oskar, 88
Vlasov, Andrey, 238n5, 242n13

Vogt, *Oberst*, 212
Voigtsberger, Heinrich, 212
Volkov, Lieutenant, 1
Voroshilov, Kliment, 229n5

Wagner, Jürgen, 213
Weber, Gottfried, 35
Wegener, Wilhelm, 31
Weichs, Maximilian von, 68, 152, 236n1
Weidling, Helmuth, 156, 184, 215
Wellmann, Ernst, 242n2
Wenck, Walther, 177-178, 183
Wiescher, *SS-Obersturmführer*, 170
Witzleben, Henning von, 207
Wöhler, Otto, 59, 82, 87, 152
Wöst, Günther 205

Xavier, Boris Klemens (King Boris III), 68

Zhadov, Aleksei, 131
Zhukov, Georgy, 147, 174-176, 182, 229n5
Ziegler, Joachim, 212
Zutavern, Karl, 14

Codenames:
Operation Bagration, 2, 4, 229n7
*Unternehmen Birke* (Operation Birch), 53
*Unternehmen Casar,* 144
*Unternehmen Doppelkopf,* 144
*Unternehmen Donner* (Operation Thunder), 239n11
*Unternehmen Frühlingserwachen* (Operation Spring Awakening), 91
*Unternehmen Katzenkopf* (Operation Cat's Head), 76
*Unternehmen Konrad I,* 87
*Unternehmen Konrad II,* 87
*Unternehmen Konrad III,* 87
*Unternehmen Margarethe,* 73
*Unternehmen Nordwind,* 239n1
*Unternehmen Sonnenwende,* 161
*Unternehmen Sturm* (Operation Storm/Tempest), 22, 27

www.ingramcontent.com/pod-product-compliance
Lightning Source LLC
LaVergne TN
LVHW090055080526
838200LV00082B/8